The Unknown Sea

The

Unknown Sea

Navigating Death, Dying,
and Bereavement

Patricia L. Antoine

Chemeketa Press
Salem, Oregon

Chemeketa Press
Chemeketa Community College
4000 Lancaster Dr NE
Salem, Oregon 97305
collegepress@chemeketa.edu
chemeketapress.org

Cover design by Alexis Bravo Mota
Interior design by Ronald Cox IV

References to website URLs were accurate at the time of writing. Neither the author nor Chemeketa Press is responsible for URLs that have changed or expired since the manuscript was prepared.

Image credits are listed on page 298 and constitute an extension of the copyright page.

Printed in the United States of America.

Land Acknowledgment

Chemeketa Press is located on the land of the Kalapuya, who today are represented by the Confederated Tribes of the Grand Ronde and the Confederated Tribes of the Siletz Indians, whose relationship with this land continues to this day. We offer gratitude for the land itself, for those who have stewarded it for generations, and for the opportunity to study, learn, work, and be in community on this land. We acknowledge that our College's history, like many others, is fundamentally tied to the first colonial developments in the Willamette Valley in Oregon. Finally, we respectfully acknowledge and honor past, present, and future Indigenous students of Chemeketa Community College.

In loving memory of R. G., who taught me so much about living with dying, the honor of supporting a person as they leave this life, and the gift of memories

Contents

Death Comes Home

"Death, thy servant, is at my door. He has crossed the unknown sea and brought thy call to my home."
— "Gitanjali" (Song Offerings) of Rabindranath Tagore (1861–1941),
Collected Poems and Plays (1951)

Tagore's "unknown sea" describes the mysterious expanse between life and death. Writing a book is itself a kind of voyage through uncharted waters—one that demands persistence, reflection, and a willingness to confront uncertainty. The years I have spent working on this book have been marked by profound personal loss, social upheaval, and the global crisis of COVID-19. During these tumultuous years, the act of writing became *more* than an academic exercise; it was a way of channeling my grief.

This book is the embodiment of three decades of teaching as well as a response to the urgency of recent events that are reshaping the way we talk about mortality and the grieving process. In the classroom, I have worked with students new to the subject, as well as students who are seasoned professionals in the field of death and dying. These rich interactions with students and their collective personal and professional experiences and interests have helped shape my understanding and this book.

In my personal life, I witnessed firsthand the emotional, physical, and practical complexities of death during my father's final years. This intimate involvement broadened my understanding beyond the sterile presentation of these topics in textbooks. My family's experiences—most of us have or are currently working in emergency services and health care—also added insights and informed this work. My insights grew even more vivid when I lost my husband of forty-five years while writing this book. These personal encounters with death have infused this work with a layer of understanding that moves beyond academic theory into the realm of human experience.

Maybe you have lost a family member, colleague, close friend, or beloved pet. Perhaps you work in a profession where you confront death regularly. Or perhaps you feel your encounters with deep loss are nothing compared to what others have experienced. Whatever your background, I invite you to reflect on the experiences that have shaped your understanding of death. These personal reflections are invaluable to your study of this subject; they can deepen your connection to the material and offer insights beyond the academic content. Grief is universal, yet each of us experiences it uniquely—your losses may inform how you approach the concepts and stories in this book, adding another layer of meaning to your learning.

Needs Addressed by This Book

The topic of death and dying has gained attention, spurred by demographic changes such as an aging population. As interest in thanatology (the scientific study of death) continues to grow, so too does the need for comprehensive educational materials that cater to a wide array of disciplines—from emergency services to health care and chaplaincy.

Another need addressed by this book is the representation of diversity within death education, which has not kept pace with the changing demographic landscape. Too often, textbooks are skewed toward a middle-class White experience, neglecting the many cultural, ethnic, racial, and socioeconomic perspectives that shape the meaning of death. This book serves that need, offering a more inclusive lens that acknowledges and incorporates differing experiences.

Many death-related educational resources have a gap between theory and practical application. These resources often introduce academic concepts but do not show their impact on real-world situations. Moreover, the limited diversity in death education materials fails to represent the lived experiences of a significant portion of the population.

This textbook seeks to bridge those gaps by providing a grounded, sociological perspective that emphasizes both theory and practice while ensuring that a broader range of voices is included in the discussion. In each chapter, you will find the interweaving of current research, foundational studies, and personal examples and anecdotes. It connects academic knowledge to practical, real-world applications, allowing you to grasp how these concepts influence and shape your experience and career.

Purpose and Scope

The primary goal of *The Unknown Sea* is to provide an academically sound yet accessible exploration of death, dying, and bereavement from a sociological perspective. While sociology serves as the foundation, the interdisciplinary nature of the topic demands the inclusion of perspectives from other fields, such as psychology, anthropology, biology, and medicine. This blend of disciplines offers readers a comprehensive understanding of how different social, cultural, and biological factors shape experiences of death.

Each chapter is designed to provide both macro-level and micro-level analysis, giving readers the tools to examine death in broader social contexts and intimate, personal settings. The content will be particularly relevant to students and professionals in career fields where death is a significant factor, such as health care, human services, and emergency services. By employing a theory-to-practice approach, this book not only equips you with the academic knowledge you need but also illustrates how that knowledge can be applied in professional contexts.

Unique Features

The Unknown Sea is committed to inclusivity and real-world relevance. With an integration of both macro and micro perspectives, you will be encouraged to think critically about the broader social systems that influence death, as well as the individual experiences that shape personal encounters with dying and bereavement. This human element enriches the academic discourse, making the subject matter more approachable and relatable for students and practitioners alike.

To help you navigate this journey, each chapter is structured with features designed to deepen your understanding and engage you actively with the material. Every chapter begins with a vignette—a short personal story that connects directly to the topic at hand. These vignettes serve as windows into individual experiences, grounding the theoretical content in lived realities.

Learning objectives are provided to guide your focus on the key takeaways, ensuring you are aware of the most important concepts in each chapter. Key terms are bolded and defined within the text, and a complete glossary is provided at the end of the book for easy reference. Additionally, boxed features throughout the chapters highlight supplemental information and include questions to encourage critical thinking and engagement with the material.

Each chapter concludes with a summary and review questions designed to help you check your understanding and reflect on what you've learned. A comprehensive list of references is included at the back of the book for further exploration of the topics discussed.

Considerations for Readers

As you work through this book, you will inevitably encounter challenging and painful topics, including traumatic death, suicide, and other emotionally intense subjects. It's important to recognize that these discussions may stir up difficult memories or bring to the surface unresolved grief. To help you navigate this material while still fostering meaningful learning, I offer the following suggestions:

1. **Pace yourself**: Give yourself permission to take breaks as needed. Processing difficult topics requires time and emotional space. Step away from the material if it feels overwhelming, and return to it when you feel ready.

2. **Create a support system**: If the material brings up painful memories or emotions, consider discussing it with a trusted friend, family member, or counselor. Sharing your thoughts and feelings can be a valuable way to process difficult emotions while learning.

3. **Engage in reflection**: Use the questions provided throughout the book's boxed features as opportunities for self-exploration. Writing down your thoughts or keeping a journal as you read may help you process both the academic material and your reactions to it.

4. **Practice self-care**: When confronting emotionally charged topics, balance your mental and emotional health. Make time for activities that help you relax, whether that's exercise, mindfulness practices, or simply being in nature.

5. **Set boundaries**: Recognize your limits. It's okay to skip certain sections temporarily or to approach them at a different time. Not every reader will be in the right emotional place to fully engage with every topic, and that's perfectly acceptable.

6. **Seek professional support**: If any topic brings up particularly painful memories or trauma, consider seeking professional help. Counselors and grief professionals can offer guidance and support as you process your reactions to the material.

While this book will address difficult realities, remember that it is also an opportunity to better understand both death and the human experiences that surround it. By preparing yourself to engage thoughtfully with the material and take care of your emotional well-being, you can find meaning and growth in even the most challenging topics.

Conclusion

I invite you to approach the subjects of death, dying, and bereavement with both openness and empathy. Death is a universal experience, yet its meaning varies across cultures, societies, and individuals. Be mindful of the diversity of perspectives presented here, and consider how your own experiences and cultural backgrounds influence your understanding of death. Lastly, recognize that this is not just an academic study—it's a deeply human one. The concepts you'll encounter are not only meant to deepen your intellectual understanding, but also to resonate with your lived experiences and those of the people you will serve and work alongside in your professional life.

Death, as Rabindranath Tagore writes, is a servant who inevitably arrives at our door. The journey of understanding death—its meanings, rituals, and processes—is one that we all embark upon, whether personally or professionally. This book aims to serve as a guide for that journey, helping you navigate the complexities of death, dying, and bereavement from both academic and human perspectives.

The "unknown sea" of death represents not only the mystery of life's end but also the wide and varied experiences that surround it—cultural, religious, and personal. This text calls on you to reflect deeply on how death shapes our social structures and individual lives and, in turn, how our experiences with death shape our social institutions. As you engage with the material, you'll be invited to cross your own unknown seas, expanding your understanding of death's role in society while connecting these insights to the experiences of those around you.

Ultimately, this book seeks to demystify death, offering academic knowledge and pathways to real-world application and personal growth. By the time you finish this journey, I hope you'll find that the unknown sea is not so distant and mysterious after all, but rather a current that runs through our shared human experience.

Chapter 1

Understanding Death, Dying, and Bereavement

Vignette | **Watching Death Happen**

My husband had been living with a life-threatening disease for several years with manageable symptoms that only moderately impacted his day-to-day activities. However, as the disease progressed and his physical capabilities declined, he no longer had the energy and stamina to walk across the driveway to his woodshop. A nationally recognized woodworker, he was devastated and felt betrayed by his body. It got to the point that he could no longer help in the garden or enjoy the deck's panoramic view of the valley. Increasingly frustrated by his difficulty getting around the house without assistance, he often complained about how worthless he felt.

As his medical condition worsened and became more complex, some doctors and health care providers changed how they interacted with him. The shift was subtle but evident. In one situation, a cardiology physician's assistant stopped interacting with my husband during appointments. She started talking only to me, as if my husband could not understand what was going on and could not make decisions for himself. She became dismissive of our concerns about symptoms and possible treatments as if they no longer needed to be addressed since he was in end-stage heart disease. Another care provider avoided eye contact with my husband and minimized contact with both of us. Our appointments became briefer and more impersonal.

My husband was self-conscious about his physical appearance as the disease took a greater toll on his body. He avoided personal contact and shifted to phone visits with friends. Then, the phone calls became shorter. He would cut people off mid-sentence and end the call, declaring he had nothing else to say. It got to the point that he wouldn't answer the phone, and people eventually stopped calling. Our interactions became briefer and more utilitarian as he withdrew. I could see him pulling inward. He no longer looked out the window or showed interest in his favorite TV shows. At one point, he even started covering his head with a blanket to shut off interaction with the outside environment.

Looking back, it feels like we gradually lost him long before he died.

His Loving Wife, Patricia

Introduction

When does death happen? At first glance, the question may seem easy to answer—death occurs when the body stops working. In practice, many factors complicate how we determine when life ends and what that means.

Since the time of the ancient Greek philosophers, people have debated and proposed differing meanings of death and the dying process. Academics and scholars have pursued a deeper understanding of death. Much of the ongoing work in the study of death comes from biology, philosophy, psychology, sociology, and anthropology. Each discipline helps expand the understanding of death and dying by contributing subject-specific insights through the lens of its academic perspective.

While other disciplines may study death-related topics, the discipline of thanatology focuses on the study of death, dying, and bereavement (the experience of loss characterized by grief and mourning). This multidisciplinary approach to the study of death represents the work of scholars from varied academic backgrounds and those with professional experience and field expertise. The breadth of this academic work continues to add to the understanding of death.

The meaning of death is also shaped by our personal experiences, the circumstances surrounding death, and the cause of death. This chapter will explore definitions of death through clinical, legal, and social lenses and how various disciplines approach death and dying.

Learning Objectives

These learning objectives will help you identify what's most important in this chapter. By the end of this chapter, you should be able to do the following:

- » Discuss the challenges in defining death.
- » Describe academic approaches used to study and understand death.
- » Summarize the development of thanatology and death studies.
- » Explain how social and personal factors impact the understanding of death and dying.

Defining Death

Determining when death occurs has never been straightforward or obvious. Historical accounts tell of people who were declared dead when, in fact, they were very much alive. For example, in 1867, a young woman died from suspected cholera. Her burial took place within six hours of her presumed death, but as attendants shoveled dirt onto her coffin, they heard a knock on the lid from the inside. They quickly raised the coffin and, upon opening it, found the young woman alive (Bondeson, 2002). Although uncommon, mistaken death declarations were often a result of shallow breathing or faint heartbeats that went undetected.

The fear of being buried alive was nevertheless real and prominent, especially during the nineteenth century. People formed societies to draw attention to the perceived problem of premature burial. These societies advocated for an improved death certification process and promoted the development of "security coffins." These coffins included breathing tubes and bells in case a person was mistakenly buried (Bondeson, 2002). Figure 1.1 shows illustrations for a coffin "to be used in cases of doubtful death." The image shows a vent for breathing and a series of levers to open the coffin lid from the inside.

Figure 1.1. The "coffin to be used in cases of doubtful death" was patented by Christian H. Eisenbrandt in 1843.

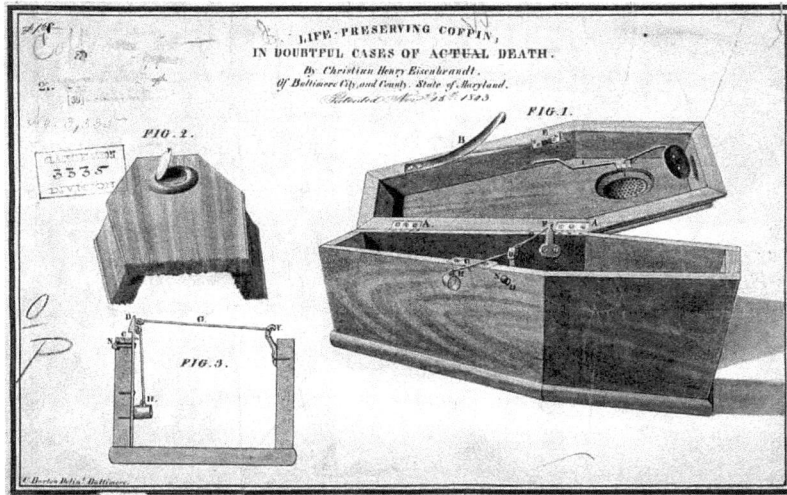

Advancements in medical technology have given us more precise methods to determine when a person's breathing or heart has stopped, referred to as cessation. At the same time, technological advancements have introduced new challenges in determining when death occurs. Modern medicine's ability to keep people alive as their bodies fail raises new and challenging questions about the moment of death. This chapter discusses the need to clearly define death, delineate the criteria used to establish that death has occurred, and develop a process to legally certify and socially recognize a death.

Clinical Death

The customary method of determining death has centered on the cessation of basic vital signs of life, or **clinical death**, defined as the absence of breathing and a heartbeat. However, technological advancements have raised issues and challenges in using these conventional methods for establishing death. Advanced life support systems, such as ventilators, respirators, and cardio-pulmonary support, can artificially support life for long periods. A person can be kept "alive" through mechanical means for days, months, and sometimes years.

The ability to keep a person breathing and the heart beating through artificial means for long periods has required the medical community to define the concept of **brain death**. Based on the work of the Harvard Medical School Ad Hoc Committee in 1968, brain death, or what became known as the whole-brain definition of death, is defined by the following criteria:

- » absence of spontaneous muscle movement, including breathing
- » lack of brain stem reflexes
- » absence of brain activity
- » lack of response to external stimuli (American Medical Association, 1968)

These criteria for brain death augment the customary use of vital signs, such as body temperature, pulse rate, and respiration rate, to determine death.

Many high-profile cases where medical intervention kept a person's body functioning for long periods have raised medical, legal, social, and ethical issues that have been litigated in the courts (Fine, 2005; Hook & Mueller, 2005). For example, Karen Ann Quinlan fell into a coma in 1975 but lived in a persistent vegetative state, aided by a ventilator until 1976 and then a feeding tube until she died in 1985. Terri Schiavo spent fifteen years on life support systems after suffering cardiac arrest. She died in 2005 after a protracted legal battle between her husband, parents, and the state of Florida. In situations like these, is the person alive, or has death already occurred?

Legal Death

A person's death triggers government laws that regulate how their body is handled and options for the final disposal of their corpse. A government-issued death certificate with verified information like the date, place, and, in some cases, the cause of death is needed to execute wills and inheritances, file necessary taxes, determine any civil and criminal responsibilities, and manage other government-regulated legal issues.

The growing acceptance of the medical criteria for death by health care professions led to legislative talks toward a standardized, legal definition for death. In 1981, the Uniform Determination of Death Act (UDDA) was drafted by a U.S. presidential commission and approved by the American Medical Association and the American Bar Association. This model legislation focused on revising and updating the legal criteria of death to align with clinical death definitions. All states adopted this legislation, most using the exact language, although several states have added additional regulations.

The UDDA focused on establishing a standard for **legal death**, defined as irreversible circulatory and respiratory cessation and whole-brain death, widely accepted by the medical community and the public. This standard also addresses the complexities of organ donation at the time of death. Efforts to revise the UDDA were suspended in 2023, leaving the uniform model law unchanged. For the foreseeable future, no changes to this standard are expected (Nair-Collins, 2024).

Social Death

Death is more than a biological process or a legal status. It is also a social experience. Death and the dying process obviously affect the person dying. It also affects others, and in turn, others affect the death experience. Death occurs in an interactive social context—we are social beings living and interacting with others. Through interaction, relationships, and the use of symbols, we create meaning and shared patterns of behavior. Death interrupts and alters these social interactions, requiring a shift in social expectations and relationships.

Social death involves the loss of social identity in relation to others and increasing social disconnectedness (Králová, 2015). This change can be marked by a specific event, such as biological death. However, social death can also involve a series of changes during the end-of-life and the dying process, impacting daily activities, social relationships, or one's social identity. A social death changes a person's place in society, what sociologists call their **social status**. The shift in someone's social status denotes a separation from society. For example, as Marie's mobility decreased due to Parkinson's disease, she got fewer lunch invitations from former colleagues. After Dan's diagnosis of terminal cancer, he started being excluded from long-term projects at work. Social death can also change social role expectations. A parent may no longer be able to care for their children, or adult children may become the primary care provider for an aging parent.

Sociocultural beliefs, values, and norms of dominant culture generally determine the meaning of social death. Dominant culture refers to the cultural group with the most economic, political, and social power over time. For example, in the United States, the dominant cultural perspective of social death is linked to the absence of medical or biological indicators like breathing, heartbeat, and brain-based reflexes. A social death then leads to funerary rituals that mark a person's transition from the world of the living to the spiritual realm or the world of ancestors, depending on their culture's traditions. Chapter 3 explores the complexities and challenges of looking at death and dying from the perspective of U.S. dominant culture.

In some cultural belief systems, biological death is just one aspect of determining social death. For example, the Toraja people of Indonesia do not recognize social death until the body leaves the home. Though biologically deceased, a person's body may remain in the home as a social member of the family and community for weeks, months, or even years. During this time, the person is perceived as being sick or in a prolonged sleep. They are fed and bathed, and their clothes are periodically changed (figure 1.2). They are talked to, hugged, caressed, and moved to various settings to ensure they are included in family and community activities. Removing the body from the home and completing funerary rituals denote the change in social status and social determination of death (Baan et al., 2022).

Figure 1.2. The ritual of the Toraja people goes beyond cleaning and dressing the deceased; it symbolizes the enduring importance of family bonds.

Academic Approaches and Perspectives

Much of what we know about death and dying comes from the natural sciences and the social sciences. However, no single academic discipline can fully explore the complexities of this subject. Combining the strengths of multiple areas of study provides a more holistic understanding of death and the dying process. In this section, we'll explore several academic approaches to the study and understanding of death and dying, as shown in box 1.1.

Box 1.1: Academic Approaches to Death and Dying

This partial inventory of academic approaches accentuates some of the key scholarly viewpoints and their interplay with the subject of death and dying. Although this book centers on the socio-logical perspective, these diverse frameworks expose this subject's multifaceted and intricate nature.

As you read through the various academic perspectives, consider their overlapping and intersecting concerns. How might these disciplines contribute to a better understanding of holistic, patient-centered care?

Academic Perspective	Application to Death and Dying
anthropological approach	examines social, cultural, and biological factors to gain a holistic understanding of humanity's response to death events
biological approach	examines the structure, function, growth, evolution, interactions, and biological conditions of organisms
medical approach	relies on biological sciences and the scientific approach to understand the nature and condition of human life
philosophical approach	examines the existential questions that surface when someone is dying or has experienced the death of a loved one
psychological approach	examines human behavior and mental processes with a core focus on the individual and their emotions
sociological approach	examines how aspects of society and social processes impact death and the dying process

---

The theoretical foundation for this book rests heavily on a sociological perspective, which emphasizes the role of social systems, social processes, and social interaction in understanding the meaning and experience of death. However, the interdisciplinary perspective woven throughout this chapter and the entire book is essential to the holistic understanding of death, dying, and bereavement. For instance, an anthropological approach may be used to explore the impact of cultural beliefs, practices, and rituals. In contrast, the biological and medical approaches are useful in examining issues related to the human body and treatment concerns. The research, information, and insights from multiple disciplines yield a richer understanding of death, dying, and bereavement.

Biological Approach

Biological concerns often dominate day-to-day activities during the terminal phase of life. A biological approach, focusing on the science of life and living organisms, explores death by examining organisms' structure, function, growth, evolution, and their interactions with each other and the environment. The biological sciences and their application to the human body form the foundation of Western health care systems. **Western medicine** is a system that treats diseases and ailments as they arise using evidence-based medicine and scientifically proven methods. For example, anatomy and physiology help scientists understand the human body through the study of the body's structure, parts, physiology, and the functions and activities of living matter, such as organs, tissues, or cells.

Research from biology gives scientists a baseline for what is considered normal in terms of the human body. Therefore, biology also determines what is perceived as abnormal or problematic. This research informs and sets the standards for medical pathology, the branch of medicine that deals with the nature of disease, changes in body tissue and organs associated with disease, and the manifestations of disease. For instance, Monica goes in for monthly blood tests to monitor the effects of her cancer treatment. The results showed a concerning change in her red cell count when compared to the range of expected readings. Based on this biological change, it was recommended that she make an appointment with her doctor to discuss this change and possible treatment adjustments.

Medical Approach

The medical approach to death and dying in the United States is steeped in the biological sciences and a scientific approach to understanding the nature and condition of human life. Historically, the interplay between biology and Western health care systems has shaped the field of medicine and its institutional processes and ideology. Most medical professionals are grounded in biology and scientific methodology as part of their educational foundation. These professionals then enter the medical field, where this ideology is reaffirmed through organizational processes, procedures, and professional expectations.

Western medicine applies biological science and scientific methods to establish diagnoses, prognoses, treatments, and strategies for disease prevention. Therefore, medical professionals must interpret evidence, data, and research findings in response to existing health conditions and issues. The practitioner's academic education, professional training, and the involved health care system influence their decisions and actions.

The medical approach raises important questions and issues when looking at death and dying in Western medicine and health care. For example, scientific evidence may establish that a particular biological condition exists, but medical professionals must determine if it is a problem. If a biological condition is considered a problem, when is medical intervention needed, and what is a desirable outcome? The answers to these questions are subject to interpretation and can vary from practitioner to practitioner.

Consider the example of blood pressure or blood sugar levels. How high do these levels need to be before they are considered a problem? In both cases, the general medical recommendations have changed over time, and even the accepted standard may vary depending on a patient's situation. Or, in the case of determining when death occurs, how does the medical interpretation of biological conditions impact the definition of death?

As you've learned, the definition of clinical death has evolved and continues to evolve as science and medical technologies improve. The answers to questions like "Does death occur when the heart stops or when brain activity stops?" change depending on the understanding of medical professionals. Although biological factors may establish the foundation of the condition, the social institution of medicine—with its requisite structure, processes, norms, and values—also clearly influences the outcome.

Psychological Approach

Death is the ultimate individual and personal event. A psychological approach focuses on how people feel, act, and think about death. As a broad field of study, psychology explores how consciousness, cognition, and social interaction impact human behavior. As a behavioral science, psychology also bridges the social and biological sciences in its study of the relationship between physiological and neurological processes, mental functioning, and human behavior. Psychologists are interested in understanding how perception and cognition affect human behavior. They examine personality characteristics, emotions, and interpersonal relationships in the context of behavior.

The psychological approach provides a framework for studying death and dying across various death-related topics. This includes the study of death fears and death anxiety, denial reactions, defense mechanisms, issues surrounding mortality, fears of growing old, and emotions associated with death and dying. Chapter 2 will discuss death fears in more depth. Other research explores the impact of cognitive development, age, and maturation by looking at death through children's perspectives, life stage position, and responses and understanding based on age. Chapter 11 will explore grief across the life course.

A psychological perspective expands our understanding of grief, mourning, and bereavement issues. Research examines aspects of the grieving process, the conceptualization of abnormal, disenfranchised, and prolonged or complicated grief. Psychology also examines the emotions associated with death and dying, including the emotions experienced before and after death by the dying person and those coping with their death.

Anthropological Approach

Anthropology takes a broad approach to understanding different aspects of the human experience, including culturally shared rituals and practices. An anthropological approach examines social, cultural, and biological factors in end-of-life and death events to understand the human condition more fully. As a social science, anthropology employs scientific research methods and uses empirical evidence to study human language, culture, societies, and biological and material remains. Anthropology considers the past as it explores the distinctiveness of humans as a species and the forms of social existence across time and geographic space.

The discipline of anthropology includes several areas of study. The subfield of cultural anthropology examines human societies and the elements of culture. Cultural anthropologists look at how cultures are organized and influenced by their physical and social environments. They also study how a culture's beliefs and values affect and interact with the physical environment. Linguistic anthropologists study how language shapes and influences social life. A culture's language is a symbolic representation of what people think and why they behave as they do. Studying the history of language and how it changes and is influenced by other languages provides important insights into cultural beliefs and behaviors.

Archaeology, as a branch of anthropology, looks back in time to understand people and cultures of the past. Analyzing the physical structures, pottery, human bones, and other artifacts that cultures leave behind reveals who they were, what they believed, how they lived, and how their practices connect to present-day cultures. The examination of archaeological dig sites reveals the nature of the rituals, beliefs, and practices of people from the past. The material remains of ancient people are used to investigate their lives and tell their stories. The study of burial sites—where the sites are located, how bodies were prepared, which artifacts are placed with the bodies, and what memorials are present—can shed light on crucial aspects of a culture.

Burial practices provide a window into the beliefs, norms, and values of ancient cultures. For example, the discovery of a burial site during the excavation for a new building in Germany offers valuable perspectives into the burial practices of the Globular Amphora culture of Central Europe (ca. 3400–2800 BCE). Archaeological researchers found the grave of a man buried along with a pair of cattle that had been sacrificed. Cattle were the foundation of the Globular Amphora people's subsistence and were the most highly valued type of livestock. As the guarantors of life and survival, cattle were their most precious possession, making them a fitting offering to the gods (Schroeder et al., 2019; Georgiou, 2024).

Rituals, practices, and beliefs surrounding death and dying reflect a culture's values. As the final rite of passage, death practices highlight fundamental social and cultural beliefs. What a culture emphasizes at the end of life indicates what is most valued in life. For example, Hmong family burial practices often reflect their cultural beliefs about death and the afterlife. The Hmong are an ethnic minority from the mountainous region of Southeast Asia, many of whom immigrated to the United States after the U.S.-Vietnam War. Traditional Hmong culture includes ancestor worship and the belief that the spirit world, including ancestor spirits, coexists with the physical world. These ancestor spirits can influence the health, safety, and prosperity of the family. Hmong families that maintain these traditional beliefs place great care in the proper burial of their loved ones to show respect for the deceased and ensure the well-being of their family members (Bliatout, 1993).

An anthropological perspective allows us to compare past and present practices, but it can also help us understand contemporary cross-cultural variations in death practices. Examining various cultural practices reveals a wide range of approaches—no single emotional response is inherently right or wrong, no disposal method is universally correct, and no single set of post-mortem practices applies to all.

Philosophical Approach

As a discipline, philosophy uses reason, logic, critical thinking, and logical analysis to explore fundamental questions about knowledge, life, mortality, and human nature. A philosophical approach is useful in exploring questions surrounding the meaning of life, death, and human existence that often surface when someone is dying or has experienced the loss of a loved one.

Philosophers have long pondered the meaning of death and debated questions about life, mortality, and the afterlife. Basic questions focus on the search for the meaning of our existence, the nature of human thought, the essence of the universe, and the connections between them. The philosophical approach challenges humans to examine their own beliefs and the validity of those beliefs. As questions emerge during this process, philosophy encourages people to explore and evaluate possible answers by developing reasoned arguments.

The study of philosophy often involves two approaches to death and dying: the existential and phenomenological perspectives. The existential perspective emphasizes the importance of the individual and their experience. It highlights humans' unique freedom to determine their actions, focusing on personal choice and autonomy concerning death and dying. The phenomenological perspective focuses on the phenomenon of death itself. This approach involves the structures of consciousness related to death and the sensory qualities of seeing, hearing, feeling, perception, desire, and bodily awareness. Existentialism and phenomenology provide different approaches to engaging with important philosophical questions and the meaning of life and death.

A philosophical perspective is not about discovering all the answers—it's a strategic way to ask and answer questions. For instance, questions about the relationship between medical ethics and life and death are rooted in core beliefs and moral values. This philosophical question came up during the COVID-19 pandemic when the health care system was confronted with massive infections and overwhelming numbers of critical patients that far outstripped the available hospital resources. Decisions had to be made about which patients would be admitted to the hospital, who would be placed in the intensive care unit with increased nursing care, or who would be placed on the limited number of ventilators that increased a patient's possible survival. Whether to give priority to the sickest first, to patients with the greatest chances of long-term survival, or to those based on their social worth and contributions (e.g., medical providers) was rooted in core beliefs and values (Cage, 2020; Emanual et al., 2020).

Belief systems impact hospital triage protocols and policies that determine who is treated first in an emergency. Whether priority is given to the patient with the best chance of survival or to the patient with the most serious, urgent condition will be based on core moral values and beliefs. Neither policy is necessarily better, and each has challenges, problems, and obvious concerns. However, a philosophically grounded approach, which involves applying rational thinking, developing logical arguments for both positions, and seeing from someone else's perspective, offers a useful tool for sorting through these moral dilemmas.

Sociological Approach

Because all human behavior is social, death and the dying process are impacted by the social environment in which they occur. The death experience, expected behaviors, and factors impacting the death event are all shaped by social forces and processes. As an academic discipline, sociology studies society, social structures, social processes, and social interactions. A sociological approach focuses on how aspects of society and social processes impact death and the dying process.

Sociologists examine how society is organized, how society affects human behavior patterns, and, in turn, how humans shape society. Sociology examines macro-level (or large-scale) phenomena, such as the nature of social change, social problems, and patterns of collective behavior. It also explores the impact of social structures and processes, including how social institutions like families, education, government, and the economy are organized and what purposes they serve. The discipline also examines the dynamics of micro-level (or small-scale) aspects of society inherent in the day-to-day social interactions of life. This systematic study of society and social interactions underscores how external social factors affect people's beliefs and behaviors.

Sociologists use scientific research methods to study society, social institutions, and social interaction. Sociological research allows our understanding of society to move from anecdotes based on an individual's experiences to an empirically based understanding of social phenomena. This research-based approach helps identify common human behavior patterns, how various factors influence these patterns, why people adopt certain patterns, and—equally important—why some people do not.

Sociologists address the diversity of subject matter at the macro and micro levels using various theoretical approaches. The three primary approaches sociologists use are structural functionalism, social conflict theory, and symbolic interaction. Each of these approaches that we'll examine in the next section shows different aspects of society, including its organization and patterns of social interaction (figure 1.3).

Figure 1.3. This table provides an overview of the three primary sociological perspectives with examples.

Sociological Approach	Level of Analysis and Focus	Example
Structural-Functional	Macro; Examines how social structures maintain stability and order in society.	Funerary practices provide a sense of closure and reinforce social norms around mourning.
Social Conflict	Macro; Identifies and explores power dynamics and inequalities that create tension and possible change.	Access to quality end-of-life care varies based on socioeconomic status, highlighting healthcare disparities.
Symbolic Interaction	Micro; Focuses on everyday interactions and how people construct shared meaning through symbols.	A grieving parent finds comfort in wearing their child's favorite necklace as a symbolic connection.

Structural-Functional Approach

The **structural-functional approach** is a macro-level theoretical perspective that focuses on the structure of society and how social institutions are designed and organized to meet its needs. Structural functionalists see society as a set of interrelated parts or social institutions, each with a function or role contributing to society's well-being. It's helpful to think about a functioning society like a human body. The body is made up of specific parts like the heart, lungs, kidneys, and digestive system. Each part has its role and is connected to the other parts. The overall body is balanced and healthy if each part fulfills its role.

Structural functionalists apply this same approach to understanding society and social phenomena. Society is viewed as being made up of social institutions like families, schools, the economy, government, health, and medicine. Each institution has its functions and roles in society, and each is connected to the other social institutions. If each institution fulfills its intended purpose, you have a healthy society. Structural functionalists believe that if a problem exists in society, it is because one or more parts aren't fulfilling their role or there have been changes in the functioning of the parts. For example, in the case of rising crime rates, a structural functionalist might examine the impact of increased unemployment (changes in the economy) or high school dropout rates (failure of education to fulfill its function).

When examining death and dying, the structural-functional approach could explore the inability of many rural residents to access end-of-life medical services as a failure of the social institution of health and medicine to meet its intended function. A structural functionalist approach could also focus on how governmental regulations, as a function of a social institution, define how human remains can be legally handled.

Social Conflict Approach

The **social conflict approach** is a macro-level theoretical perspective that examines how issues surrounding power and competition for resources impact social order, social structure, and social processes. This approach believes that society's power structures and the struggle for resources between unequal social groups provide a foundation for understanding social phenomena. From a social conflict perspective, the elite control resources and impose social structures and social order to maintain their power and wealth.

Conflict theorists focus on how the unequal distribution of valued resources affects which members of society have power and control. Valued resources differ from society to society, but common examples may include money, gold, land, water, jobs, and health care. Possession and control of these resources translate into power, including gaining access to others in power, influencing major economic, political, and governmental decisions, and, ultimately, shaping society. When valued resources are unequally distributed, conflict and competition are inevitable.

The social conflict perspective is often used to examine the division between the "haves" (people who are wealthy and socially powerful) and the "have-nots" (people who are not wealthy and have little, if any, social power). For example, a conflict theorist might examine how income and wealth distribution relate to who has access to education, living-wage jobs, or health care. In the context of death and dying, a social conflict perspective is useful in understanding the unequal distribution of end-of-life health care and support resources. This theoretical lens highlights the connection between a person's social class, geographic location, the existence of "health care deserts" with limited resources, and how these factors impact their end-of-life experience.

Symbolic Interaction Approach

The **symbolic interaction approach** is a micro-level theoretical perspective that examines social interaction and studies how people communicate and interact with others. Specifically, this perspective focuses on socially shared symbols, language, and social constructs and how they shape patterns of socially expected interaction. Sociologists use this approach to analyze how patterns of interactions build social structure and provide social order.

The symbolic interaction perspective explores how communication patterns and human interactions are developed, shared, and maintained. This approach also examines how social structure and social order are affected when agreed-upon behavior patterns break down. For example, think about how socially expected behaviors shape the interaction between teachers and students within a classroom. Each knows how they are expected to behave and their expectations of each other. If each participant behaves accordingly, learning can take place. When these expectations aren't mutually agreed upon or when participants don't fulfill them, structure and social order break down, resulting in a more chaotic classroom where learning is more challenging.

In the case of death and dying, a person may need simultaneous care from several medical specialists as they approach the end of life. Effective coordination of medical services relies upon the shared expectation and understanding of each doctor's responsibility and actions to meet the patient's overall health care needs. For example, during the last few months of his life, R. G. received health care from several different medical specialists, each attending to specific medical conditions. It was important for these care providers to have a shared meaning of what constituted needed medical care that aligned with his wishes. This shared understanding enabled coordinated care and guided medical decisions about when and whether to prescribe curative medication to maximize life expectancy or focus on palliative support care and quality of life.

Thanatology and Death Studies

Thanatology is the scientific study of death, dying, and bereavement. This multidimensional field includes the study of death, the practices associated with the dying process, the needs of the terminally ill and those who are socially connected to the dying person, and the experience of loss and grief. American academic Robert J. Kastenbaum (1993) asserted that thanatology might be defined more precisely as "the study of life with death left in." He also noted the importance of understanding that the study of death reflects social and cultural death concepts, norms, and values. We'll explore more of Kastenbaum's and his colleagues' work in chapter 2 when we examine different views on the state of death.

The study of death necessitates using a wide lens that examines the whole person and their social surroundings. For a dying person, multiple dimensions shape the death experience, including physical, psychological, spiritual, and social aspects (Corr, 1992). The physical aspects involve physiological conditions associated with the dying process, like changes in the body, pain, and physical functioning. Psychological aspects focus on cognition and learning, including thoughts, behaviors, understanding, and perceptions. The spiritual aspects of death and dying are related to the psychological dimension but represent a distinctive system of beliefs and practices related to the supernatural, an existence beyond mortal life, and beliefs of the afterlife. Spirituality can be a personal belief system or come from a more formalized religious system. Finally, the social aspects involve interpreting, understanding, and assigning meaning surrounding death and are influenced by aspects of our social environment.

As a field of study, thanatology recognizes the necessity and value of an interdisciplinary approach to the topic of death and dying. Specific disciplines contribute critical information and insights to develop a more holistic understanding of death and death-related experiences. As a result, thanatologists come from various backgrounds, experiences, academic disciplines, and professional training. They recognize that contributions from differing perspectives push the understanding of death-related experiences forward.

Historical and Cultural Roots of Thanatology

Social and cultural perspectives of death are woven through the works of early philosophers, poets, musicians, and artists. Each expression reveals beliefs, practices, and questions of their historical time. Death themes have long been a significant part of culture, folklore, rituals, and practices. For instance, in Greek mythology, Thanatos was the son of Nyx, the Goddess of night, and Chronos, the personification of time and the twin brother of Hypnos, the embodiment of sleep. In figure 1.4, Thanatos and Hypnos are depicted carrying off the body of Sarpedon, a Trojan War hero. The ancient Greeks began to use *thanatos* as a generic word for death, incorporating the concepts of night, sleep, and time within their understanding of death (DeSpelder & Strickland, 2007; Narayanan, 2021). The Greek word *thanatos* provided the historical root for thanatology, the study of death.

Throughout recorded history, questions about the meaning of life, the understanding of death, and the nature of the afterlife were often left to religion and systems of spirituality. Clergy and spiritual leaders helped people answer

Figure 1.4. This ancient Greek vase shows Hypnos, or Sleep (on the left), and Thanatos, or Death (on the right). They are carrying the body of a Trojan soldier while Hermes, a Greek god, watches.

these questions with what was known then, the beliefs of the time, and current religious doctrine. Shared beliefs and death practices came from their answers and understandings, which were then integrated into culture and daily life. For example, during the fourteenth century, when the Bubonic Plague (known as the Black Death) killed over one-third of Europe, people turned to clergy and spiritual leaders for guidance and answers. Physicians and healers relied on superstitious practices such as bloodletting and lancing boils to rid the body of excess blood, believing the cause of illness was too much blood in the body. As the plague spread and the number of deaths rose, people turned to religion for answers. Believing the origin of the disease was based on sin and God's will, clergy often asserted the plague was God's punishment for the sinfulness of humankind. Therefore, people felt the need to demonstrate their repentance and faith through prayer, acts of flagellation (self-punishment), and pilgrimages to holy sites (Hajar, 2012). Hence, death understandings reflect social institutions and the social environment—in this instance, religion, culture, and the historical period (Noppe, 2007).

The nineteenth and early twentieth centuries saw many advancements in the biological sciences and medicine, adding another dimension to the understanding of death. Medical practices aimed at extending life and postponing death were developed from increased knowledge of human biology, illness, and disease. The use of science to extend life marked a shift away from accepting death as a part of everyday life. These advancements fostered an interest in understanding the aging process and the nature of death within the scientific community.

Élie Metchnikoff, a Russian microbiologist, was an early advocate for establishing a field devoted to studying death. In 1903, he argued for creating two fields of scientific study: thanatology and gerontology, which is the study of old age, the aging process, and the problems people face as they age. He argued that dying people had few resources to address the experience of dying and that research and academic study would provide more information and understanding of the phenomenon and reduce fear. Despite the growing interest in the scientific community, the field of thanatology did not take hold for decades (Kastenbaum, 1993).

Rise of the Contemporary Death Movement

The late nineteenth and early twentieth centuries were marked by a pervasive reluctance to think or talk about death. Motivated mainly by industrialization, this period saw a significant shift in population distribution across the United States. As more people moved to urban areas following the growing number of jobs created by mechanized production, the proportion of the population in rural America declined. By the 1920s, for the first time, more Americans lived in cities than in rural areas. Urban residents were removed from the natural cycle of life and the day-to-day exposure to death associated with farm life, like raising and butchering animals.

The Victorian era (1837–1901) ushered in a focus on self-control, social control, and human control over nature and the environment. Advances in science and technology led to a greater ability to dominate and manipulate the natural world in farming, mining, and logging. People also tried to control and distance themselves from the unpleasant aspects of life whenever possible and to minimize the negative impact of any unavoidable unpleasantness. For example, rituals and social expectations offered a means to take control over the unavoidability of death. If people couldn't control whether death happened, they could have autonomy over how they responded to it. When a loved one died, it was customary for a family to place a wreath with a large black bow or sash on the home's front door to let others know a death had occurred. They would turn family pictures face down, cover mirrors as a sign of mourning, dress in black mourning attire, and display the body in the home for visitors to view and pay their respects to the family. These rituals offered some sense of control when families were confronted with the death of a loved one.

In the early 1900s, distance and aesthetics guided the beliefs and practices associated with death. Cemeteries were relegated to the outskirts of town and landscaped to be peaceful and visually pleasing. Body preparation and burial were handed off to professional undertakers to soften the aesthetics of death, and funeral rituals were entrusted to clergy or spiritual leaders. Subsequently, social institutions outside the family started addressing death and the needs of dying people. This transferal of responsibility enabled people to further distance themselves from death or the need to think about death.

The 1950s and '60s marked a shift in the social response to death. Society had witnessed the devastating human impact of World War II and was living with a renewed awareness of the realities of violent death and the inevitability of loss and grief. Confronting the massive casualties from the war, the atrocities of genocide, and the devastation of nuclear weapons made the reality of death unavoidable. At the same time, improvements in the health care system, medicine and vaccines, trauma care, and medical technology were extending life expectancy. People who previously would have died quickly from many diseases, infections, and trauma were now living longer.

Also during this period, medical advancements and new medications, like antibiotics, helped increase life expectancy. However, treatments for other conditions—such as cancer, heart disease, and chronic illness—made less progress. As people lived longer, new health issues began to appear. Researchers and health care practitioners began exploring questions about physical, mental, and emotional quality of life, pain management, and social isolation during the dying process. The unintended consequences of rapid medical advancements spawned broad discussions about what to do, what not to do, and under what circumstances to do something (Kemp, 2014).

Death Studies as an Academic Field

After World War II, societal changes led to the publication of several critical works on death-related topics. American psychologist and thanatologist Herman Feifel was an early pioneer in the study of death who advocated for open discussions of death and dying. In World War II, Feifel had been stationed in the Pacific when nuclear bombs were dropped on Hiroshima and Nagasaki, Japan. His wartime experience was believed to have inspired his interest in studying death. While working for the Veterans Administration as a practicing psychologist after the war, Feifel edited *The Meaning of Death*, a 1959 volume of essays on death by prominent psychologists, philosophers, and theologians. This anthology and his research on the value of honest discussions concerning death and dying between physicians, family, and dying people began to encourage more open dialogue. Feifel's work created a foundation for further scholarly study of death issues (Ansell, 1997; Strack, 2003).

On Death and Dying, written by Elisabeth Kübler-Ross in 1969, remains one of the most notable publications in death studies. A Swiss-born psychiatrist who emigrated to the United States, Kübler-Ross worked with terminally ill people and taught seminars for medical students on the importance of listening empathetically to dying patients to improve the quality of end-of-life care. Kübler-Ross's theory of the five stages of grief provided a model for understanding how people adjust to the dying process, and her work encouraged doctors, nurses, and medical staff to treat dying people with dignity. Contemporary responses to her developmental model are discussed in chapter 11.

Scholars point to the work of pioneers like Feifel and Kübler-Ross as initiating the contemporary death movement. Their efforts in exploring death and dying and the mounting interest in related topics spurred a flurry of research and new publications. Throughout the 1960s and '70s, academics from multiple disciplines and professionals in death-related fields conducted research, generated information, searched out new bodies of knowledge, and made connections with others doing similar work.

In the late 1960s and early '70s, research centers opened at universities, and academic and professional organizations formed to facilitate and promote the study of death. One of the earliest thanatological professional organizations was the Forum for Death Education and Counseling. Founded in 1976 by educators, clinicians, and practitioners, it allowed members to connect with others doing similar work, share research, and explore best practices grounded in a theory-to-practice paradigm. As the association grew and evolved, it became the Association of Death Education and Counseling (ADEC).

Today, ADEC remains a renowned organization in the field of thanatology whose members come from various academic fields—such as education, medicine and health care, counseling, social services, and emergency services—and professional backgrounds, including clergy, students, and volunteers. ADEC's mission states that the organization is "dedicated to promoting excellence and recognizing diversity in death education, care of the dying, grief counseling, and research in thanatology. Based on quality research, theory, and practice, the association provides information, support, and resources to its international, multicultural, multidisciplinary membership and to the public."

Death Goes Mainstream

After World War II, interest in death studies expanded among academics and practitioners and drew attention from outside academia. As U.S. society adjusted to a postwar reality, the public's interest in death and dying spilled into popular culture. *The High Cost of Dying* by Ruth Mulvey Harmer and *The American Way of Death* by Jessica Mitford, both published in 1963, criticized the funeral industry, piqued public interest in death, and gained widespread popularity. Mitford described the funeral industry's unsettling and manipulative practices. She revealed ways the funeral industry had commercialized grief by convincing bereaved families to pay more than necessary for funerals and related services. For example, she pointed to how funeral workers pressured families to purchase luxury satin-lined caskets, use roses in funeral wreaths, print expensive funeral cards, and provide multiple limousines for the extended family during the cemetery processional. Public reaction to her book resulted in a congressional hearing on funeral practices in 1964. In 1969, Elisabeth

Kübler-Ross was profiled in *Life* magazine, bringing the topic of death, dying, and bereavement into living rooms across America.

Public curiosity about death-related topics continued to grow through the end of the twentieth century and accelerated in the first quarter of the twenty-first century. The pursuit of accessible information and open discussion of death and dying has, in part, been spurred by ongoing advancements in science, medicine, and technology. Developments in research, diagnosis, and treatments have helped people live longer. But at the same time, the ability to keep people alive well into their 80s and 90s opens new ethical questions surrounding the quality of life. Should life be extended simply because science can? At what point should death be allowed to progress? If life is extended, what costs are incurred, not just in monetary terms, but in physical and psychological pain? These increasingly complex medical questions and decisions require more open and direct discussions of death and dying.

Mass media's rapid growth has drastically changed how information is sent and received, including content about death and dying. With the widespread use of smartphones, tablets, and computers and the growing number of content sources, death and death-related topics stream into people's lives unimpeded. The hundreds of television channels, numerous streaming services, and nonstop scroll of social media posts allow death to enter our lives daily and on a far broader scale. This social reconnection to death as a part of the life cycle brings it to the forefront, generating more open dialogue, interest, and questions.

Death Education

Death education encompasses a variety of educational activities and experiences focused on understanding death, the dying process, bereavement, and care for people affected by death. The philosophy underlying death education is grounded in the belief that an expanded understanding of death, dying, and bereavement will better prepare individuals, social institutions, and communities to deal with death and death-related practices (Wass, 2003). Its goals focus on developing a deeper understanding of death and dying, improving the quality of end-of-life care, and enhancing support for those impacted by death across the dying process and through bereavement. However, the intended goals of death education can also vary depending on the participants and the specific context. Often, the outcomes focus on developing more effective communication among those experiencing or connected to death, clarifying values for oneself and others, and acquiring skills for practitioners.

Generally, death education occurs in both formal and informal formats. A formal design uses a structured curriculum, identified outcomes, and specified assessments. Courses are grounded in research and can involve a theory-to-practice approach. Common in universities and colleges, death and dying courses may reside in specific academic programs, such as sociology, psychology, or anthropology; be rooted in an interdisciplinary approach; or be focused on a specific career field, such as medicine, nursing, or social work. Although less commonly found at the K-12 level, death education is more likely to be offered in private or religious-based schools. A formal design structure is also employed in professional development seminars and practitioner training.

Informal death education takes place in the context of specific situations. When something happens, "teachable moments" emerge, questions arise, and conversation about death ensues. Regardless of the specific situation, a death event provides the opportunity for questions to be asked and answered and experiences to be shared. In any context, whether it involves a public incident such as the school shooting in Uvalde, Texas, or a more private loss when a person's beloved cat dies, a death event offers the opportunity to engage in meaningful conversation about death and grief. However, the knowledge and background of those involved affect the accuracy and validity of the information imparted.

Instructional pedagogy in death education may take either a didactic or experiential approach or a combination of both, as shown in figure 1.5. A didactic method imparts knowledge using lecture and audio-visual resources to convey information that focuses on cognitive learning. This approach often includes the instructor engaging students through probing questions to encourage deeper understanding and critical thinking about the content. An experiential approach, in contrast, emphasizes active learning through shared personal and professional experiences with death, role-playing, simulations, and hands-on or field-based activities. These activities evoke feelings, encourage empathy, and promote understanding of death and dying. Experiential learning is intended to change students' attitudes toward death and provide an opportunity to engage in the theory-to-practice application of death studies.

Figure 1.5. These two illustrations show (a) The Kolb model of experiential learning and (b) the didactic model.

Experiential Model (A)

Concrete Experience
(*feeling*)

Reflective Observation
(*watching*)

Active Experimentation
(*doing*)

Abstract Conceptualization
(*thinking*)

Didactic Model (B)

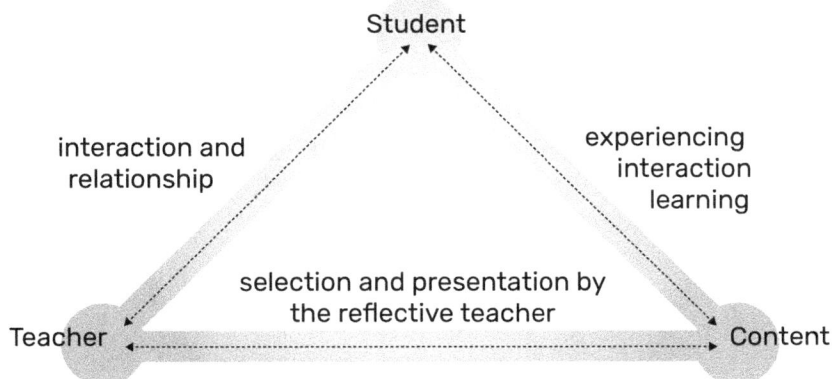

Student

interaction and
relationship

experiencing
interaction
learning

selection and presentation by
the reflective teacher

Teacher

Content

Death education is expanding through diverse avenues, catering to both public interest and professional development. Adult education and personal enrichment courses focusing on a broad range of death-related topics are becoming more common (Corr & Corr, 2003). Many of these courses and seminars are open to the public. In contrast, other death education courses support ongoing professional development for practitioners in the field, like medical staff, care providers, social workers, hospice, clergy, and funeral staff. These continuing education courses may be hosted or sponsored by colleges and universities, the health care industry, religious organizations, professional associations, or local community groups. They can occur in a face-to-face format, webinars, recorded videos, or self-directed resources.

Death education includes content focusing on experiences and activities associated with death, helping people cope with the dying process, dealing with dying, and managing grief and loss. This content incorporates objective and subjective concerns, personal and professional interests, and skill-based training. Although thanatology is grounded in a multidisciplinary approach, the content of courses offered within a specific academic discipline, such as psychology, sociology, or philosophy, or as part of a professional program, will often be viewed through that discipline's framework. The specific framework may impact the content, topics, or issues highlighted and how they are understood. See box 1.2 for a discussion on how the transformative model in death education takes an inclusive approach to death-related content.

Box 1.2: Transformative Models in Death Education

Ongoing efforts in death education are shifting away from a model that simply adds examples from different cultures, groups, and religions to an existing curriculum. Instead, some educators are adopting a transformative model that involves critically examining underlying assumptions in the field, ensuring that diverse experiences and understandings are integrated throughout the content and are reflected in teaching practices (Morey & Kitano, 1997).

By incorporating diverse perspectives and experiences, death education aims to create a comprehensive understanding of death, dying, and bereavement that acknowledges the impact of different identities and experiences. The goal of this inclusive approach is to promote social justice, equitable access to resources and care, and openness to multiple interpretations of death, dying, grief as well as a focus on healing and resilience.

As you read about how death has been shaped by historical context and cultural influences, reflect on the following questions:

» How has your own perspective on death been shaped by your cultural background and experiences?

» How might inclusivity in death education contribute to more equitable access to resources and care?

» What steps can educators, caregivers, and communities take to incorporate diverse perspectives into death education effectively?

Historical Context and Cultural Influences

Social and personal factors shape how we process the experiences of death, dying, grief, and bereavement. Social factors, such as culture, not only influence values, beliefs, and norms but also provide a path to navigating death, dying, and bereavement. Culture is a complex system of shared meanings and behaviors that sets social expectations of what will be done and how it will be completed. Culturally held beliefs and practices provide guidance during the uncertainties of death and dying, lend meaning to life and death, and offer support in processing loss and grief.

In addition to cultural influences, the sociohistorical context affects the interpretation of death and death-related issues. Social factors and trends—political, economic, environmental, or scientific—influence values, beliefs, and behaviors. Historical events, such as World War II, the 9/11 terrorist attacks, and the COVID-19 pandemic, touch every aspect of life, including the meaning of death. Media coverage, social institutions' responses, and public reactions define the situation, influence our collective understanding, and delineate accepted and expected behaviors. For instance, the social response to the massive loss of life among 9/11 emergency personnel reaffirmed the value placed on the work of first responders and military forces, the need to honor the loss of life, and the importance of supporting the friends and loved ones of those who died (figure 1.6). The events of 9/11 and their aftermath continue to impact the understanding of death in firefighting, paramedics, law enforcement, and the military.

Within shared societal and cultural patterns of values, beliefs, and behaviors, a person's social position and role may change how death is understood. A person's **social location**, which includes age, race, gender, marital status, education, or social class, confers a set of social role expectations that affect how one sees, understands, and experiences the world. Age, for example, can be a significant factor in how a child understands the death of a parent. A young child is in a significantly different situation from a middle-aged adult child whose parent dies. The understanding and meaning of death, the nature of grieving, and the need for support vary based on socially and culturally constructed age expectations. Similarly, social class can affect the meaning of death and dying by impacting a person's ability to access end-of-life care, home health care, or hospice.

Figure 1.6. The 9/11 Memorial at the site of the former Twin Towers commemorates the attacks of September 11, 2001, and the World Trade Center bombing of 1993.

Personal Experiences

Disruptions or shifts in daily activities affect how people experience their world. Sociologists use the concept of life events to describe changes that are likely to impact future beliefs, understandings, and actions. Life events can be positive, such as a graduation, marriage, or birth of a child, or negative, as in the case of a divorce, death of a family member, or traumatic accident. Life events may be major or minor stressors. When a negative situation is ongoing, such as overwhelming personal or professional responsibilities, heavy work schedules, financial struggles, or chronic health issues, otherwise minor stressors can accumulate into major events.

Regardless of the cause, life events influence people's identities, beliefs, and behaviors. These events can be assimilated into an individual's identity or accommodated by changing one's identity to fit the life event (Whitbourne, 1987; Toller, 2008). For example, the death of a child can impact a parent's social identity and their requisite social expectations as a parent. Through self-reflection and internalization, the individual may assimilate the life events into a new parental identity: "I am a parent of a child who died." Or they may accommodate the life event into their pre-existing parental identity: "I am a parent, and my child died" (I was a parent and even though my child died, being a parent will always be who I am). In either case, major life events impact people's understanding of their social identities, social role expectations, and social interactions. Death and dying as life events can impact the social construct of self-identity. In other words, when someone experiences a death event or faces the prospect of dying, it can affect how they are seen by others and how they see themselves.

Causes and Circumstances of Death

The causes and circumstances surrounding a death affect its meaning, including how people understand and respond to the death event. If death comes quickly, as with acute disease, natural disasters, accidents, or suicides, the dying person and their loved ones have little or no warning. They are often unprepared to address the realities of death and are less likely to have support systems in place. In contrast, an elongated dying process allows people to prepare, begin grieving, and plan for the eventuality of death. However, time and awareness can pose new challenges with the need for pain management, the loss of physical and cognitive functioning, and the processing of anticipatory grief.

Death meanings are often influenced by how members of a society view the cause of death. Specific causes or issues contributing to death can further complicate how people respond. Socially or culturally held beliefs about drug or alcohol-related deaths, murder, suicide, or the choice to access death-with-dignity options can impact the availability of social support, result in a hesitancy to seek support during the dying or grieving process, and prevent others from offering support.

Bereaved family members can feel isolated in their grief when socially unacceptable behaviors or decisions are factors in the death of a loved one. Nevaha's family experienced this when she died in a car crash while on her way home from a party. Under the influence of alcohol, Nevaha swerved into oncoming traffic and crashed into another car, killing two of its occupants. While her family was mourning their loss, they were confronted with local news reports detailing the role of their loved one in the tragic death of the other vehicle's occupants. They received hurtful and, at times, threatening messages on social media. Nevaha's family hesitated to reach out for grief support, fearing the responses they would receive. Many friends and community members hesitated to reach out to the family, not knowing what to say or how to support them. Others focused more on the responsibility the intoxicated driver played in the death of others and were more attentive to the needs of the other family and their grief.

Conclusion

While the social determination of death may not always align with medical and legal criteria, it represents a substantive change in an individual's social roles and interactions. As you saw in the vignette that opened this chapter, death centers on social relationships and the loss of social connections and social identity. As my husband neared the end of life, he became more socially invisible to others, withdrew into his own world, and retreated from social interactions while others distanced themselves from him.

Likewise, our understanding of death is affected by our social environment and our specific personal experiences. Consider if, as an adult, you had a grandparent die due to age-related causes as opposed to the death of a grandparent in a car crash caused by a drunk driver. In both cases, you would grieve the loss of your grandparent, but the meaning of the death and the bereavement process may be very different for each experience. A person's understanding of death is also shaped by societal events such as natural disasters, mass shootings, or the COVID-19 pandemic. These types of situations can change our exposure to death and illuminate the consequences of loss and grief.

Taking an interdisciplinary approach and considering the perspectives offered by various academic disciplines allows us to see and explore the complexity of the end-of-life and the death experience. Readers working in death-related professions may find it challenging to make connections between academic research on the topic and their daily work. However, academic research and insights are often used in the development of professional training, current techniques, accepted protocols, and field practices. As you think about the disciplines highlighted in this chapter, look for aspects of your work that are grounded in each of the academic areas.

Summary

» The presence or absence of respiration and a detectable heartbeat were once the only factors for determining death.

» Advances in medical technology that can artificially support breathing and heart function have made determining death more complex.

» Legal definitions of death regulate societal aspects of death, such as the disposal of the body and distribution of the deceased's assets.

» Social definitions of death affect the nature of social relationships and social identity.

» Much of what has been learned about death comes from biology, medicine, philosophy, psychology, sociology, and anthropology.

» Three sociological theories examining death and dying include structural functionalism, social conflict theory, and symbolic interactionism.
» The interdisciplinary field of thanatology focuses on studying death, dying, and bereavement.
» World events and the rise of the contemporary death movement opened a broader public dialogue about death and dying.
» Sociohistorical events, personal experiences, and specific causes and circumstances surrounding death impact the meaning of death, dying, and bereavement.

Review Questions

1. What are the difficulties in determining what constitutes death?
2. What methods have scholars employed to examine and comprehend death?
3. How has the field of thanatology and death studies evolved?
4. How do societal and individual considerations shape our perception of death and the dying process?
5. What are examples of how personal and social factors affect your understanding of death?

Key Terms

Review these key terms from the chapter. You can find their definitions in the glossary at the end of the book.

» brain death
» clinical death
» legal death
» social conflict approach
» social death
» social location
» social status
» structural-functional approach
» symbolic interaction approach
» thanatology
» Western medicine

Chapter 2

Learning About Death

| Vignette | ## How I Learned About Death |

At seventeen years old, I had never really known someone who died. Then, in a single year, one friend died from an asthma attack, one in a car crash, and another drowned. It's not that I didn't understand what death meant. Growing up during the Vietnam War, I saw graphic images of death enter our living room every night. This was the first "televised war" where video captured the brutality and carnage of the battlefield, and within hours, families across America were seeing the realities of war on the nightly news. Reports routinely included images of wounded soldiers, battlefield deaths, and grieving families, but somehow, those deaths felt different. Television created a barrier between the reality of death and my day-to-day life. I could turn it off and walk away when it became too much.

But losing my friends was personal—I could not distance myself. We hung out together, went to football games, and saw each other daily in class. As teenagers, we felt invincible. Death was the farthest thing from our minds—only older adults were supposed to die. Suddenly, I was faced with the fact that people die every day, at all ages, and in unforeseen circumstances.

With the death of each of my classmates, school officials would call us together to make the announcement. I watched as the news sank in. Many students started crying and hugging each other, while some sat quietly, stunned. Others walked away to be alone. These patterns of behavior were repeated at the funerals held for each student. The death of my friends shattered my world. I was devastated. Since my family rarely showed outward emotion and never talked about death or grief, I was unsure what to say, what to do, or whom to speak with about their deaths and my feelings. I didn't know if what I felt was normal or what to do about my overwhelming sadness. Through my teenage eyes, it seemed everyone else knew what to say and how to react. I certainly didn't want my peers to think I didn't, so I pulled back, faded into the background, and did my best.

A year after graduation, my grandmother died. At the funeral, I saw a tear roll down my grandfather's cheek—I had never seen him cry. At the same time, he hugged and comforted his grandchildren. I was moved by his ability to grieve the loss of his wife of over fifty years while reaching out to others who were sharing the loss of this beloved woman. Years later, I marveled at the grace and strength of my niece, who spoke at the funeral of her young son. She shared her grief and loss while holding on to the joy of her son's life. Her openness and authenticity helped us come together to support one another during a time of immense grief.

I have thought about these situations and all my other exposures to death, remembering the people and experiences that helped me navigate the loss of friends and family. What I have learned about death, such as how loss can be processed and the importance of connecting with others, has been invaluable to me as I work through my husband's recent death. As I delivered his eulogy, I looked around at all our family and friends and thought about how they were experiencing his death. By sharing in this moment of grief, we added to each other's understanding of what it means to lose a loved one.

Patricia

Introduction

As you read in chapter 1, death is subjective and shaped through social interactions. Our understanding of death is influenced by what and how we learn about death. Family is often the first to teach us about death. However, across the life course—a sociological term that refers to the span of a person's life from birth to death—our understanding continues to evolve as we receive information and social messages about what it means to die. Exposure to media, the arts, or social events such as war or natural disasters continues to shape death's social and personal meaning.

Global events like the COVID-19 pandemic affect our understanding of death. In 2020, we followed the daily death count in our cities and communities, and we saw the images of refrigerated trucks used to store bodies when there was no longer any room in local morgues (figure 2.1). Similarly, as in the case of the televised body counts during the Vietnam War described in the opening vignette, the number of infections and the death counts of the pandemic forced us to confront the fact that our family members, our neighbors, and our friends could die at any time. As we will see in this chapter, the lessons learned across the life course from experiences and exposure to events such as a global health crisis shape our orientation toward death and influence death attitudes and the content of our death fears.

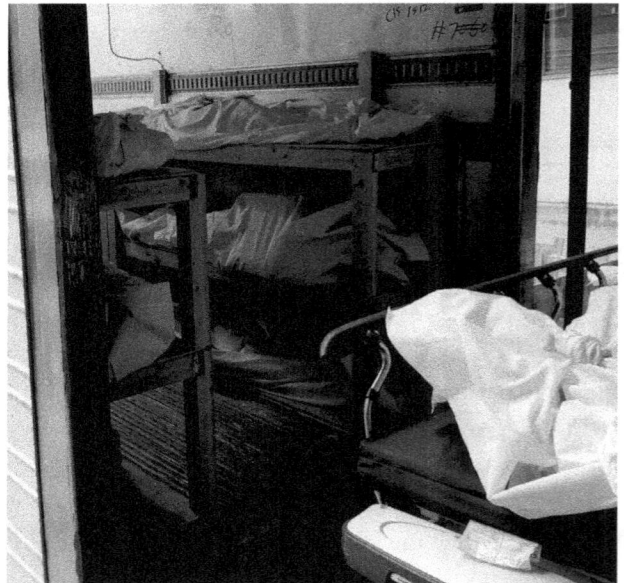

Figure 2.1. A mobile morgue parks outside a hospital in Hackensack, New Jersey, on April 27, 2020.

Learning Objectives

These learning objectives will help you identify what's most important in this chapter. By the end of this chapter, you should be able to do the following:

» Understand death as a social construct and identify commonly held views of death.
» Analyze how sociohistorical influences, artistic representation, cultural beliefs, and personal experiences influence the meaning of death.
» Discuss how social institutions shape the understanding of death.
» Examine the factors that influence death attitudes and the content of death fears.

Understanding Death

Death is a scientific, biological fact, but the understanding of death is socially constructed. In other words, what it means to be dead and what we think about death is a social construct, a concept we learn by interacting with others. The **social construction of reality** is the process whereby people create a shared understanding of their world through observations, actions, and social interaction. This shared social experience then becomes viewed as fact. Subjective interpretations of the natural and social environment are shaped, learned, and confirmed through social interaction with groups, creating our objective reality (Berger & Luckmann, 1966). For example, in the context of death and dying, the notion that there needs to be a specific ritual to mark a person's death is a social construction of reality. Although personal, familial, or social rituals can help process grief, there are many other ways to mourn that can be equally effective. Figure 2.2 illustrates the interconnectedness of values, behaviors, norms, institutions, and perceptions that are reinforced through social interaction.

Figure 2.2. Our understanding of reality is constructed through social interaction.

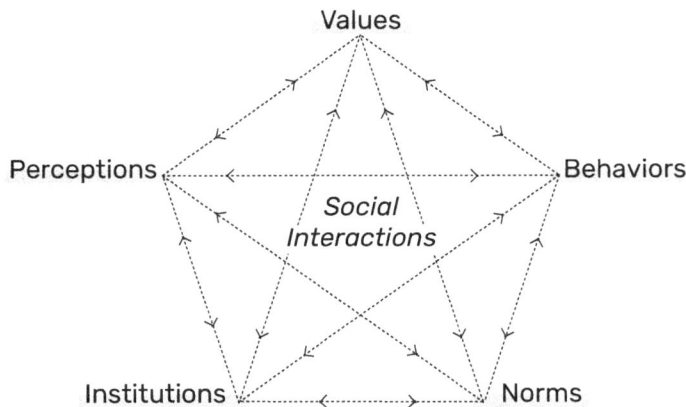

The social groups we interact with often have specific views of life and death. These groups teach us what death is and what it does or does not mean. These socially shaped ideas and assumptions about death are learned through interaction with others. The social groups we are connected to influence what we think, how we understand a situation, and the ideas we develop about a situation or topic. The resulting notion of what we believe is real then determines what we expect and consider socially appropriate beliefs and responses.

American sociologist W. I. Thomas and his research assistant and wife Dorothy Swaine Thomas developed what has become known as the Thomas Theorem: if people define situations as real, they become real in their consequences (Thomas & Thomas, 1928). For instance, what people believe about COVID-19 becomes their reality. The social groups we interact with can affect what information we deem valid and factual. How we perceive the reality of the COVID-19 virus—its origin, transmission, health risk, vaccinations, and treatments—influences how we understand the emerging scientific information and the gravity of the pandemic, which in turn shapes subsequent beliefs and behaviors. Through this same social construction process, people learn from others about death and dying. What they learn becomes their reality, leading to specific actions and behaviors.

Diverse Meanings of Death

Though sociologists study commonly held views on death, the meanings we bring to death are not universal. Because human experiences and social environments vary, the understanding of death has diverse meanings. American academic and expert on aging and death Robert J. Kastenbaum (2012) identifies the following commonly held views on the state of death:

» death as a continuation of life
» death as a state of perpetual development
» death as waiting and transition
» death as nothingness

The following sections will explore each of these views in more detail.

Death as a Continuation of Life

Across both traditional and contemporary societies, death is often viewed not as an end but as a continuation of life. Traditional societies often regard death as another stage of the human experience, projecting familiar life experiences into the realm of death. For some Indigenous communities, the deceased person may embark on a journey to the eventual final state of being, while in other traditions, a person who dies may directly enter the realm of the dead. During the journey or upon reaching the final destination, those who have died continue with the same routines, challenges, joys, and tribulations. Many contemporary Indigenous families and communities have maintained these beliefs and incorporate them into current practices.

Death as a State of Perpetual Development

Death can be understood as a part of ongoing human development. From this perspective, death is considered in the context of cosmic interconnectedness. This metaphysical perspective assumes that the universe is in a state of perpetual development, and death is a part of this process. Individuals are at various stages of development, each moving to a different state of being based on their actions, experiences, and growth. A person's state of death is based on the spiritual growth achieved up to the time of death, but death also represents the opportunity for continued spiritual growth.

For example, within the Hindu religion, teachings about death include the belief in reincarnation, where the essence of the self gives up one body to be reborn into another. In this transformation process, the thoughts and actions of the past determine the present state of being, and the present offers the opportunity for ongoing spiritual advancement. Death and rebirth provide the pathway to spiritual liberation, thus freeing a person from this ongoing cycle.

Death as Waiting and Transition

The period immediately after death can be seen as a transition between earthly life and death as a new state of being. Some see this time as a long rest to prepare for the transition, while for others, this is a turbulent and unsettled time to endure. After a certain waiting period, a higher power judges or evaluates a person's life, which can be a time of uncertainty or anxiety. Actions and deeds are evaluated, and an outcome is determined. A person might face consequences or need to make amends for wrongdoings before being forgiven or given a second chance.

The belief in a transitional period can be observed in the burial practices of the Dena'ina Athabascan people. This Native Alaskan community in southwest Alaska traditionally cremated their dead, leaving the ashes on birch bark in the belief that the spirit would make its final journey in its own time. Missionaries from the Russian Orthodox Church who arrived in Alaska in the mid-1800s converted the Athabascan people to Christianity, altering their burial practices to conform to church doctrine. Russian Orthodox beliefs include a forty-day period after death, during which the spirit of the deceased person can linger in the physical world. Some spirits may be anticipating everlasting joy and peace, while others may fear eternal torment after the final judgment. To accommodate these blended beliefs, small spirit houses (about the size of a large doll house) were built over the graves, as shown in figure 2.3, to provide shelter for traveling spirits and encourage them not to bother the living until they make their journey (Flintoff, 2012). Today, Dena'ina burial practices vary, reflecting both their ancestral traditions and the enduring influence of the Russian Orthodox Church.

Figure 2.3. Spirit houses combine traditional Dena'ina Athabascan funeral practices with those of the Russian Orthodox Church.

Death as Nothingness

Dying happens; it is an actual physiological event. However, some people do not view death as a change to an alternative state of being. Instead, they see death as the end of being—an end of life—nothingness, nonexistence. The notion of death as eternal oblivion is associated with religious skepticism and atheism. This view also aligns with a neuroscientific perspective that frames death as the end of brain activity, the complete lack of awareness, and the cessation of consciousness.

Death, as the end of everything, challenges human thinking. Describing the final state as a void, nonexistence, or nothingness provides a label and a way to talk about this concept, but it is difficult to grasp "nothing." Death as nothingness also opens a debate about whether there can really be a "death experience." If death is a state of nonexistence, can death be experienced?

Socialization and Death

The meaning of death and death-related behaviors are learned from social interaction and our social environment. **Socialization** is the process by which people learn the characteristics, beliefs, and behaviors of the groups to which they belong. Social interaction, observation, and direct instruction teach what is socially accepted and expected. For example, when a person attends their first funeral, they may not be aware of or familiar with social expectations. Family and friends who have previously attended funeral services may describe and explain common elements. While at the funeral, they may take cues from others. With more funeral experiences, they internalize expectations and behaviors as part of an ongoing socialization process. Through social reinforcement, customs and beliefs become cultural scripts that are internalized so that they are no longer questioned and are simply accepted.

The socialization process continues across the life course as social expectations are passed from generation to generation. Changes in the social environment can result in changes in social expectations, beliefs, and practices, including those about death. For example, there is a growing social acceptance and expanded use of virtual funerary services. Advances in technology and its pervasiveness in our lives are changing social expectations of funerals and celebration of life services. Virtual funerals and celebrations of life address the challenges of work schedules and travel involved in gathering friends and family who are far away. Virtual services may now include attendees' use of emojis during the service to communicate their feelings of loss and their support for one another. Virtual obituaries often replace printed newspaper obituaries, and funeral programs and funeral cards might be posted online. Although this shift was amplified by the requirement for social distancing during the COVID-19 pandemic, these practices continue to be used and are gaining popularity and social acceptance.

The understanding of death can shift with exposure to alternative beliefs and practices, new knowledge and information, or specific situations involving crisis, trauma, or personal experiences. However, death meanings rooted in core religious values or cultural traditions tend to be more resistant to change. These values give meaning to our mortality and help people cope with dying. They provide a sense of comfort, help mitigate death fears, and offer a process for closure (Pentaris & Tripathi, 2022). When a person grows up in a culture, they internalize traditions, which become a foundational aspect of self-identity. To change aspects of one's cultural beliefs is to change the essence of one's self. Beliefs rooted in religious or spiritual ideology represent the sacred and have eternal implications. As a result, the meaning and understanding of death, grounded in culture or religious beliefs, tend to be less malleable.

Societal Influences on the Meaning of Death

Society and social forces can impact beliefs and patterns of human behavior, including those associated with death and dying. **Society** refers to a group of people involved with each other through persistent interactions or to a large social group sharing the same geographical or social territory. In today's globalized world, mass media allows an event to impact beliefs and behaviors far beyond the society in which it occurs. News, information, and images can now spread around the world in a matter of minutes, potentially affecting the socialization of more people than ever before. In this section, we'll discuss how sociohistorical events, the arts, cultural values and beliefs, and personal experiences influence our lives and affect how we understand and respond to death.

Sociohistorical Events and Death Meanings

Sociohistorical events such as wars, terrorist attacks, or disasters have a far-reaching influence on the meaning of death. **Sociohistorical context** combines "social" and "historical" to refer to how historical events and societal practices influence each other. This contextual framework involves understanding how social structures, relationships, and cultural practices are shaped by historical events and vice versa. In essence, the sociohistorical context examines the interplay between society and history, recognizing that social norms, values, and behaviors are often deeply influenced by historical circumstances and events. These social events are broadly shared and capture the attention of a wide swath of the population. Whether experienced directly or indirectly, deaths due to these events or situations become contextualized in the historical period's shared social and political environment.

Sociohistorical events influence the beliefs and practices surrounding the deaths that follow them. For example, governments build war memorials to honor those who died while serving their country. Terrorist attacks, such as those that took place on 9/11, influence national security policies. Disasters that lead to loss of life motivate others to contribute money and supplies to relief organizations. Shared social meanings surrounding sociohistorical events can help explain or provide answers about death, define rituals and customs, or help console and support the survivors.

War

Historically, a soldier's death has been understood as a special kind of death. In cultures that engage in war, dead warriors often gain the admiration and gratitude of others for giving their lives to protect others, preserve values, and maintain or establish a desired way of life. The loss of one's life in service to a nation, culture, ideology, or religious belief is seen by many as one of the purest sacrifices that can be made for others (Pajari, 2015). Soldiers are honored and mourned in specific cultural ways. U.S. service members' deaths are honored with rituals like the tying of yellow ribbons, military escorts and honors at the burial service, and the presentation of a folded flag to Gold Star families (those who have had an immediate family member die while serving).

Recognizing the war-related deaths of noncombat individuals or civilians can be more challenging because their roles in conflict are often ambiguous, making it harder to define the meaning or context of their loss. There may be political motivations to avoid or minimize the topic of noncombatant casualties. People acknowledge civilian deaths during the war but increasingly discuss them in a rationalized, distant manner as an unfortunate cost of war (Nate, 2013). Over the last several decades, the government has employed the phrase "unintended collateral damage" to reduce the emotional impact associated with noncombatant deaths during war. This terminology provides a psychological distance from death, allowing for a shift in what might be considered an acceptable military target. The use of "collateral damage" is an attempt to describe the incidental and unintended deaths of civilians as an objective and necessary outcome of war (Crawford, 2013).

Terrorism

The use of violence by extremist groups as a strategy for political advancement has led to numerous deaths around the world. Defining terrorism can be subjective due to the political component of the act. However, organizations that monitor terrorist activity generally agree that terrorism involves the unlawful use of violence or the threat of violence in pursuit of political, religious, or cultural goals. Terrorist attacks can involve criminal acts such as murder, kidnapping, bombings, arson, the taking of hostages, cyberattacks, or the disruption of essential services, the economy, or the government. Terrorism intends to damage social and political structures and spread fear and intimidation among the population. Terrorist groups can be domestic, foreign, or externally inspired and supported.

For many years, the United States experienced fewer incidents of terrorism compared to other regions, fostering a sense of relative safety. Most Americans only experienced terrorism secondhand through reports from other countries. Over the last few decades, however, terrorist attacks in the United States have resulted in significant destruction and loss of life. These attacks have greatly impacted Americans' perception of safety and their understanding of death (Hartig & Doherty, 2021). Devastating events such as the bombing of the Alfred P. Murrah Federal Building in Oklahoma City in 1995, the 9/11 terrorist attacks in New York, Washington, DC, and Pennsylvania in 2001, and the Boston Marathon bombing in 2013 forced Americans to confront death due to terrorist acts.

Deaths caused by terrorist acts are especially traumatic for friends, families, and communities. The inability to psychologically or logistically prepare for an unexpected death causes trauma and often triggers a flood of overwhelming emotions: shock, panic, anxiety, fear, and anger. Cognitive effects may include confusion, indecision, or flashbacks. Common physical symptoms are fatigue, nausea, or changes in sleep or eating patterns. Social withdrawal, distrust, and heightened sensitivity can also accompany or follow emotional responses.

When acts of terrorism involve mass casualties and massive destruction, the rescue and body recovery process may take hours, days, or even weeks, as it did after the 9/11 attacks. Family, friends, and colleagues endure long periods of stress and anxiety, waiting to find out if a loved one is among those who are injured or deceased. Once their death is accepted, survivors enter a prolonged grieving and recovery process. The ability to conduct a burial service, complete the final interment, and memorialize the loss can be delayed by the need to process a massive crime scene and complete the recovery of any human remains (Anstett, 2022). Sometimes, no body or remains can be recovered.

Disasters

Disasters are sudden events that cause massive damage and loss of life. For example, at the time of publication, the greater Houston, Texas, region had experienced twenty-six federally declared disasters since 1980, including hurricanes, tropical storms, fires, floods, severe winter storms, and others that have caused power and water outages, damaged property, and loss of life (Natural Disaster Risks in Houston, n.d.). These calamitous events disrupt the functioning of the community or affected area and cause significant human, economic, or environmental losses. A catastrophic situation makes it difficult for the affected area to cope with the disaster and provide necessary goods and essential services without assistance from outside sources.

Disasters fall into two groupings:

» natural disasters: earthquakes, floods, hurricanes, tornadoes, blizzards, and wildfires caused by forces of nature that often involve significant damage to property and infrastructure, overwhelm public services, and result in significant injuries and loss of life

» human-caused disasters: cataclysmic events that result from people's actions, contribute to higher losses of property and lives, and may have been avoidable

Human-caused disasters like bridge failure, building collapse, or airplane crashes can sometimes be traced to engineering errors, defective construction, or design flaws. In other situations, faulty decision-making, human error, negligence, carelessness, or indifference trigger tragic events or intensify damage, destruction, and loss of life.

Industrial disasters and nuclear accidents can often be traced to human error, neglected maintenance, or corporate indifference to safety issues, resulting in significant property damage, injuries, and loss of life. For example, in 2010, a coal dust explosion at a mine in Raleigh County, West Virginia, killed twenty-nine miners. After the investigation of the incident, the mining company was issued multiple safety violations (West Virginia Office of Miners' Health, Safety, and Training, 2010).

Sometimes, individuals are responsible, as in the case of a California wildfire started by a serial arsonist. In August 2020, an individual was charged with setting a wildfire to cover up a murder he had committed. He is currently facing trial for arson and three charges of murder because two other people were killed by the fire. The Markley Fire spread and joined other surrounding wildfires to form the LNU Lightning Complex fires, which grew to nearly 320,000 acres and destroyed 1,400 structures (Chan & Williams, 2021; Solano County Office of Emergency Services, n.d.).

Disasters often change people's lives. Common immediate reactions include shock, panic, anxiety, emotional overwhelm, anger, and grief. There may also be cognitive effects, physical symptoms, and interpersonal responses like those seen in survivors of terrorist attacks. Survivors may develop anger at loved ones for dying and leaving them alone or at others if the disaster was human-caused or could have been prevented. In the wake of these stressful situations, resolving losses and rebuilding lives usually takes much longer than people imagine (Substance Abuse and Mental Health Administration, 2017).

People not directly affected by disasters often feel overwhelming sympathy and a compassionate drive to help, intensified by the twenty-four-hour news cycle, unfiltered social media posts, and easy access to graphic details of the damage, injuries, and deaths. Although not directly experiencing the disaster, people at a distance may feel a sense of collective loss and experience some of the same emotional, physical, and cognitive reactions as victims.

Artistic Representations of Death

Society and the arts are reciprocal, interacting with and influencing each other. Works of art are a symbolic reflection and interpretation of society and, simultaneously, can impact and influence society. Art acts as a representation of life and an expression of the beliefs, behaviors, and ideas of the time. Art can portray what brings people joy, their hopes and fears, as well as sources of grief and sorrow. It can represent routine activities, challenges people face in life, and social issues. Artistic creations can be statements about or provide insights into the nature of the human condition, including the understanding of death and dying.

Visual Arts

Death and dying have long been a source of inspiration in the visual arts, creative works designed to be experienced visually. These art objects can include paintings, drawings, sculptures, crafts, prints, and ceramics. As technology has advanced, the field of visual arts has expanded to encompass photography, video, film, and computer-generated examples of virtual reality. Artistic works provide a visual representation and expression of emotions and feelings that may be difficult to articulate verbally.

From the earliest periods of recorded history, artists have created objects to represent the beliefs and practices of their time. Much of what we know about early peoples comes from recovered art objects and artifacts. These works of art serve as symbolic translators of human thought and experiences. Artistic images and representations change to reflect shifts in society's ideas, beliefs, and practices (Bertman, 2003).

For instance, *memento mori* (Latin for "remember you must die") were popular art objects in Europe during the sixteenth century. These small, hand-sized ivory carvings featuring skulls, human heads, and death scenes were collected by the elite (figure 2.4).

As living conditions improved in Europe and the privileged expanded their wealth, memento mori served as a reminder to consider one's mortality and concentrate on what was important: living a righteous spiritual life and not focusing on social position, possessions, and matters of the physical world (Meier, 2017; Duncan, 2023).

Art objects and images can capture the emotional complexity and range of experiences associated with death and dying. For example, California high school student Lauren Cheng's graphic design titled "646" was awarded first place in the 2024 Congressional Art Competition for California's 15th

Figure 2.4. This memento mori prayer bead from the sixteenth century served as a reminder of the inescapability of death.

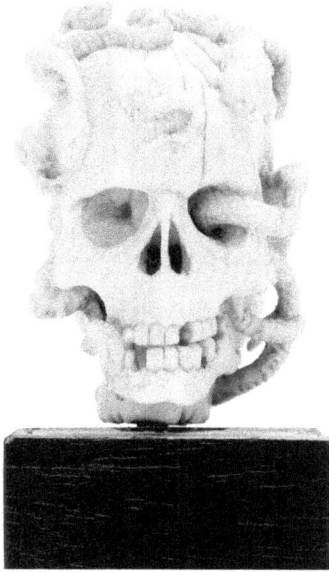

Congressional District. Her work included the placement of 646 dots around the words "Please. No more dots." The dots represented mass shootings in the United States in 2022, as recorded by the Gun Violence Archive. This work of art expressed her feelings and thoughts as a young person growing up in the era of mass shootings. The symbolic message is a reminder of the seriousness of this social issue. Highlighting the ongoing loss of life, Cheng's art is a plea to address the gun violence epidemic in the United States (Nesbitt, 2024). Symbolic representations provide a window into the beliefs and customs surrounding death and give a broader understanding of death across time and cultures.

Some grief therapies and interventions use artistic expression to explore responses to death and loss. Research shows that making art can help people work through grief (Weiskittle & Gramling, 2018). The loss of a loved one triggers an array of intense thoughts and emotions. These responses to death can impact us so deeply that words are insufficient. The creative process gives individuals a way to make their feelings concrete. Artistic expression provides an opportunity to portray their grief experience symbolically while memorializing the loss in a visible form.

Literature

Artistic representations can also encompass written forms of expression. Literature includes a variety of forms and styles, such as prose, poetry, and creative essays. Forms of literature focused on death, dying, and grief include the eulogy, epitaph, and elegy.

A eulogy is written to honor and pay tribute to a person who has died. After it is written, a eulogy is typically delivered in a speech format at a funeral or celebration of life. Written excerpts may be used as part of an obituary published in local newspapers, online memorial sites, or social media. The text may include poems, essays, or literary quotes, but the focus of a eulogy is to capture and share the essence of the person's life. A eulogy frequently provides a brief overview of the person's life, highlighting their accomplishments and defining characteristics. It may include personal anecdotes about what made them special, how they impacted others, and what loved ones will miss the most about them.

Epitaphs are often written on plaques or tombstones to memorialize the deceased and may be accompanied by visual symbols, such as flowers, angels, or religious representations. These commemorative statements are often brief poems, short phrases, or just a few words containing expressions of love or respect. They may also denote the deceased's family role ("Beloved Mother"), their career or special interests ("Accomplished Woodworker"), or perhaps include sentiments about mortality and the fleeting nature of life ("Live Every Day to the Fullest").

Elegies are a type of poem usually written as a lament for someone who has died. Eulogies and epitaphs focus on the person who died, but an elegy addresses survivors' grief. Although elegies and epitaphs both revolve around commemorating or memorializing the deceased, and excerpts from elegies may be used as epitaphs, an elegy focuses specifically on the grieving process. An elegy is an expression of grief that turns feelings into metaphors to describe the experiences of loss while moving from grief to acceptance. Box 2.1 provides an excerpt of a famous elegy written by the poet Walt Whitman for President Abraham Lincoln.

Box 2.1: The Poetry of Grief

Walt Whitman wrote a long poem, "When Lilacs Last in the Dooryard Bloom'd," as an elegy for President Abraham Lincoln, who was assassinated on April 15, 1865. Lincoln's death took place in spring, the season when the lilacs mentioned in the title were in full bloom.

As you read a short passage from this poem, consider that Lincoln's assassination took place just days after Confederate General Robert E. Lee surrendered, effectively bringing about the end of the Civil War. In his elegy, Whitman, a supporter of Lincoln, mourns the loss of the president and expresses grief, both personal and communal, for a leader whose death was felt throughout the country. Figure 2.5 shows a memorial card of Abraham Lincoln being embraced by George Washington as he enters heaven. Whitman displayed a copy of this image in his home.

Figure 2.5. After death, many people displayed memorial cards like this one, showing Lincoln and Washington in heaven.

Excerpt from Walt Whitman's "When Lilacs Last in the Dooryard Bloom'd"

O how shall I warble myself for the dead one there I loved?
And how shall I deck my song for the large sweet soul that has gone?
And what shall my perfume be for the grave of him I love?

Sea-winds blown from east and west,
Blown from the Eastern sea and blown from the Western sea, till there on the prairies meeting,
These and with these and the breath of my chant,
I'll perfume the grave of him I love.

Elegies have no set form, but they typically include three thematic components: a lament, where the author expresses sadness, grief, and the depth of the loss; praise that celebrates the qualities of the person who died; and solace, where the writer tries to find comfort and a way to carry on. An elegy offers the reader an opportunity to consider different ways to process and reframe the death of a loved one. Written works can explore endless topics, pose unbounded possibilities, and stretch the imagination. At the same time, these works are impacted by the sociohistorical context and the values and beliefs of the times.

Death themes have played a significant role in literature across time and culture. Literature uses imagination and creativity to consider the meaning of death in varied situations. Specific writings may be reflective of shared experiences in working through grief and the loss of a loved one. Literature can present incomprehensible scenarios or explore extreme examples of death and dying. For example, *The Crying Tree*, a book by Naseem Rakha (2009), explores the impact of death by murder, the complexities of carrying out the death penalty, and the impact on those connected to this murder. These types of works can expand the understanding of death experiences.

Since death is only fully understood by those who have died, literature allows the living to explore the possibilities of death through a diverse range of settings and situations. Common genres focus on war and related atrocities, mass death, and traumatic loss of life, often viewed through the lens of law, police, emergency services, and medicine. For example, the book *Letters from Vietnam* by Bill Alder (2007) contains a collection of letters written by military and medical personnel, humanitarian volunteers, and the allies of South Vietnam. These first-person accounts span the entire U.S. engagement in the Vietnam War (1965–1973), detailing the realities of war through the eyes of those who were there. The letters describe the destruction and despair of war, the experiences of firefights, bombings, ambushes, snipers, and booby traps, and personal reflections on the purposes and progress of a war that divided the United States.

Literary works frequently incorporate beliefs and images of the afterlife, various death scenes, themes of love, loss, grief, and sorrow, and modes of recovery. These written expressions of death can give insight into the universality of loss and grief and, therefore, be consoling and reassuring.

Culture, Belief, and the Meaning of Death

Everyone is born into a cultural context that is learned and reinforced through daily social interaction. Culture, including language, beliefs, values, and behaviors, affects almost every aspect of self-identity and sets expectations of how one should act. These collectively shared beliefs and practices shape the interpretation and understanding of the world. They provide a framework for understanding what is socially expected and accepted regarding who does what, when, and how. Through socialization, cultural customs and beliefs are learned and internalized, and we are often unaware of culture's pervasive influence. Collective ways of life can be taken for granted and come to feel like simply who we are and how things are done—for example, greeting people with a smile and a handshake in U.S. dominant culture.

Cultural beliefs and practices set social expectations surrounding the dying process. Cultural values frame a shared sense of who is responsible for caring for a dying person and what is expected of the person dying and those around them. For example, in many Hispanic cultures, there is a communal understanding that families should care for and support family members at the end of life.

Cultural beliefs also shape the collective understanding of death. Cultural frameworks lead to a shared understanding of death meanings, appropriate rituals and practices concerning the disposition of the body, and the grieving process. We will explore cultural frameworks for death in more detail in chapter 4.

Personal Experience and Death Meanings

Socialization is a lifelong, ongoing process. How people see and understand social identity, relationships, and social expectations is a product of their socialization up to that point in their lives. Although people are shaped by their accumulated social experiences, not all experiences and interactions have an equal impact. Some experiences leave an indelible impression, influencing lifelong beliefs and behaviors, while others are temporal and have a minimal impact. In addition, the effect of previous experiences can be overridden or modified by new, more powerful experiences.

Alongside the cultural context, critical factors like the attributes and characteristics of the deceased person, those surviving the loss, and the factors surrounding the death can contribute to understanding death and dying. The deceased person's social indicators, such as age at death, assigned social roles, occupation, or perceived contributions to society, can impact the understanding of death. Sayings like "only the good die young" or "at least she lived a full life" are attempts to make meaning of a death based on the individual's age. Sometimes, remembrances center on the context of the deceased person's occupational contributions and the loss to the community, as in the case of the death of a valued teacher, public servant, or emergency responder.

The cause of death can also significantly impact the understanding of death and dying. The ability to make meaning of death is very different if it is due to trauma, chronic or acute disease, or suicide. Additionally, we understand death differently depending on whether it was expected or unexpected, or if the dying process was quick or drawn out. All these personal factors contribute to the socialized understanding of death and dying.

In the same way, when someone witnesses the dying process and death, their attributes and experiences add another dimension to the understanding of death. The meaning of death is affected by an individual's characteristics, such as age, cognitive development, and personality traits. How we navigate, understand, and internalize death depends on our capacity and existing psychological frameworks to process death events and respond to grief and loss.

We each understand death through experiences and exposure to death and dying. The number of exposures someone has to death, the nature of the death experiences, and the closeness or type of relationship to the deceased person all have an impact. These death events also provide an opportunity to observe and internalize the responses of others. The responses and behaviors of family, friends, and the broader social community give people cues for how to make sense of death. Through the interaction of these experiences, death meanings are created and internalized.

Social Institutions and the Understanding of Death

A **social institution** is an organized system of social behavior with a recognized purpose. Each institution establishes how things should be done and compels as many people as possible to follow that behavior pattern. These broad social systems provide a structure to meet a society's needs. Social systems include institutions for education, religion, government, family, mass media, medicine, science, the military, and more. Each fulfills a specific need for the overall functioning of society.

Social institutions and significant individuals and groups are known as **agents of socialization** because they influence our beliefs and behaviors and help us function in society. As members of society interact with social institutions, these agents of socialization impart and reaffirm expected beliefs and behaviors. Social messages are communicated, and behaviors are modeled directly and indirectly. For instance, education as a social institution is designed to help people learn the knowledge and skills needed to live in society. While learning math, science, and language arts, students also develop socially appropriate behaviors such as respect for teachers and other authority figures, social interaction skills with other students, and work skills like personal responsibility and follow-through.

How a social institution handles a significant event, such as a death, can tell us a lot about how society as a whole views that event. For example, within the educational system, the lack of a formal death studies curriculum in K-12 schools and many teachers' hesitation to talk about death with students sends the message that discussing death is difficult, awkward, and best avoided (Schonfeld & Kappleman, 1992).

Family as a Socializing Agent

For most people, family is the first source of socialization and is a conduit for transmitting cultural and societal expectations, including those surrounding death. As an institutional system, the family includes a broad range of forms and structures that depend on the specific culture or society. Although a family is often defined as those related through ancestry, marriage, or adoption, the functions of a family may include any group that comes together to care for the young and each other. Families form a cooperative emotional and economic unit, have a shared identity, are intimately attached to the group, and are committed to the group over time. The closeness and continuity of family relationships make it easier to pass on beliefs and practices. The opening vignette illustrates this socialization process, recounting how family experiences shaped the understanding of death and grief.

A child's first experience with death usually occurs within the family context. It may be the death of a grandparent, a member of the family, a friend, or a beloved pet. Through these early exposures, children grapple with the feelings of loss and the disruptions associated with death. Children seek to grasp the meaning of death by asking questions and observing the responses of those around them. Adults' responses—if they respond at all—communicate their fears and feelings about death, which children internalize. In some situations, what adults don't say or the behaviors they try to hide can send a powerful message to children. As they watch how family members respond to death, children absorb social and cultural expectations concerning how to discuss death, honor and memorialize the deceased person, and process grief and loss. These expectations are also affected by past experiences, the child's developmental age, and birth order (Stanford Medicine Children's Health, n.d.).

Mass Media and Socialization

Many scholars agree that portrayals of death and discussions of death-related topics have recently gained more public attention due to mass media. Public consumption of death-related images and information through mass media acts as an agent of socialization. Actions and beliefs embedded in mass media images, videos, audio, and text affect the understanding and perception of death. Internalizing these understandings shapes people's behaviors and how organizations and social institutions respond to death (Sumiala & Hakola, 2013).

Although death has always been a common topic in mass media, the amount of media we consume and the technology used to share it have changed. Screen time has steadily increased with the proliferation of electronic devices and internet access. According to market research groups, adults consume over eleven hours of screen time daily, teens nine hours (not including schoolwork), and children (eight to twelve years) six hours (Brooks, 2023; American Academy of Child and Adolescent Psychiatry, 2020). Electronic devices are becoming the primary mode to access information and interact with others. Due to mass media, we can be exposed to death events, regardless of who or where, instantly and often unfiltered.

One recent and poignant example was the death of George Floyd in 2020, a Black man who died while being detained and pinned to the ground by White Minneapolis police officers. Numerous bystanders recorded the police officer's actions as Floyd lost consciousness, stopped breathing, and was eventually found to have no pulse. Within hours, the unedited video images of his death were broadcast by news media and went viral on social media. These images prompted a national grief response that took the form of anger, frustration, protests, and reflection on the influence of race on police responses. The spread of death experiences and images from varied perspectives brings embedded social messages that can shift or modify death's meaning and the expected social behaviors surrounding it.

Mass media also provides easy access to information concerning topics that may be uncomfortable to discuss face-to-face. The internet, particularly social media platforms, is commonly used to ask questions, seek meaning, and observe social expectations concerning death. Although the internet offers a broad array of perspectives and practices related to death and dying, algorithms used by technology companies can limit the information you see. For example, if you visit a website that discusses death from a philosophical viewpoint, your browser may suggest more websites with similar philosophical perspectives on death. Over time, this repeated exposure may lead you to think that the philosophical view of death is the most accepted framework instead of one of many frameworks for understanding death. On a more personal note, when I was looking for a headstone for my dad, advertisements for headstones followed me everywhere. They showed up in my email accounts, in social media feeds, and on random websites I visited. I know this is how algorithms work, but it was still haunting.

Socialization in the Workplace

As a major part of the economy, our jobs contribute to the process of socialization. Adults spend much of their time interacting with others within the work environment. Most people have friends at work, and more than half of Americans have met a close friend through their workplace or their spouse's workplace. Over two-thirds of employees also share personal issues with their coworkers, and most report feeling supported by coworkers (Orrell et al., 2022).

Social interaction with coworkers and supervisors, whether face-to-face or working remotely, as well as the expectations of business processes, create pressure to conform to socially accepted behaviors. Workers learn valued skills needed in the workplace, but they also internalize cultural norms that guide appropriate professional behavior, foster effective work relationships, and delineate workplace expectations.

Social expectations govern acceptable displays of emotions in the workplace. Depending on the type of work and the worker's role, there are standards for appropriate demonstrations of emotion and how to manage emotional distress stemming from personal or professional situations. These expectations may be included in training, workplace standards, or the evaluation process.

Subtle yet direct messages are also sent through work policies or employee contracts. For instance, if the employer grants bereavement leave, clearly identified parameters usually guide when it can be used. Policies may list the relationships between the employee and the deceased person that qualify (often limited to immediate family), specify the length of leave offered (generally 1–3 days), and whether the leave will be paid or unpaid. These guidelines indirectly convey social and cultural messages about death and grieving. Workplace bereavement policies transmit the social and cultural beliefs that your relationship with the person determines the impact of death, identify a specific amount of time needed to grieve and get back to regular routines, and demonstrate the social value placed on the importance of the grieving process.

Death Attitudes

Most research surrounding death attitudes centers on death anxiety and fear, the denial of death, and the acceptance of death. Other attitudes exist concerning death, such as sorrow, but these three elements are more widely discussed and studied due to their significant impact on people's death experiences. Anxiety, manifested as worry, unease, and nervousness about death, can trigger fears. Death's uncertainties then heighten these fears—Will it be painful? How will it affect my loved ones? Is there an afterlife, and if so, what will it be like?

Denying death is one of the more common strategies used to avoid death anxiety and fear. To alleviate the pain, stress, and fear of death, some people seek relief by consuming alcohol, taking drugs, engaging in intense physical activity, or fleeing the situation through physical, psychological, or emotional distancing. Denial involves rejecting or negating specific aspects or features of reality. For example, Aaron, a terminal patient diagnosed with stage IV metastatic liver cancer, was prescribed radiation treatments to control the pain as the cancer spread. When he talked with his family later, he told them, "I'm getting radiation treatments to help me beat this cancer." Denial of his diagnosis provided psychological and emotional distance from his imminent death. While we usually think of denial as a negative approach to understanding a situation, in studying death attitudes, denial is also understood as another way to respond to the fear and anxiety associated with death.

Alternatively, accepting the end of life can also relieve death anxiety and fear. We are often encouraged to accept what we cannot control or avoid, but it is not always clear what that means in terms of death. Accepting death is subjective and personal and involves different beliefs and behaviors based on the individual and circumstance. For Hiroko, who was diagnosed with terminal cancer, acceptance of death involved focusing on tending her roses and spending time with her grandchildren for as long as she could manage. In contrast, Jonathan, also terminal, traveled across the country to a private clinic to take part in experimental treatments the doctors said might extend his life by six months. Regarding the death of others, acceptance can involve coming to terms with the end of life, the implications of the loss, and decisions about how to move forward.

U.S. Society: Death Denying or Death Accepting?

By examining the death messages woven into social interaction and social systems, you will see that some cultures tend to deny death, while others tend to accept or affirm death. Societies dominated by a **death-denying perspective** avoid or mask the realities of death, while a **death-accepting perspective** incorporates death-related beliefs and behaviors into social systems and everyday social interactions.

Death Denying

Many argue that the United States is a death-denying society. Those who take that position note that while Americans acknowledge death, they often avoid or gloss over it using phrases that obscure the actuality of death, like "passed away," "met their maker," "kicked the bucket," "was laid to rest," "is pushing up daisies," "is no longer with us," "croaked," "bit the dust," "went to be with the Lord," or "met the Grim Reaper." When a person's death does come up in conversation, there is an acknowledgment of the death and loss. But the subject makes people uncomfortable. We struggle to find the right words to use, and we worry about not knowing what to say.

The heavy reliance on technologically advanced medical treatments and medications to delay death also points to the United States being a death-denying society. We are often encouraged and socially pressured to use all available treatments, medications, and technical options to extend life, regardless of individual preferences. Over two-thirds of the deaths in the United States occur in medical and health care facilities such as hospitals and nursing care facilities (Centers for Disease Control and Prevention, 2020). Death is considered a failure in the U.S. health care system, where saving lives and extending the life span are seen as successful outcomes. This focus on the role of technological advances in extending life has also led to other extreme and untested fringe ideas, such as the use of cryonics. Cryonics involves freezing someone at the time of death to reduce damage to the body and brain until advances in science can bring them back to life and cure them.

The funeral industry represents another aspect of a death-denying society in that it primarily provides funerary services and burial logistics rather than the family or community. When a person dies, the funeral industry steps in. The funeral staff picks up the deceased person from the health care facility or home, prepares the body for final disposition, and provides any requested death rituals such as a funeral service, celebration of life, or religious service. This distance allows family and loved ones to avoid the bodily realities of death.

In addition, aesthetic choices for the deceased person and death rituals attempt to distance death. In some funeral services involving a burial, the casket is lined with soft, luxurious fabric, and a pillow is placed under the head of the dead person, making them look as if they are napping. The deceased person is dressed up, and make-up is used to conceal the metabolic changes, such as skin discoloration, that accompany death. Due to muscle deterioration and the loss of fluid pressure after death, sutures and wires are used to reposition the jaw, eye caps are placed under the eyelids to maintain their curvature, and sutures are used to close the lips to preserve a normal facial appearance. After the burial service, the casket is often not lowered into the ground and covered with soil until the attendees leave, further distancing the mourners from the finality of death.

Death Accepting

For each example that the United States is a death-denying society, counterexamples show that it is a death-accepting society. For instance, when we say that someone has "passed away," do we deny death, or are we being sensitive and compassionate toward the grieving person by avoiding the harshness of words like "death" and "died"? Is taking advantage of all available treatments more about living life to its fullest for as long as possible while recognizing death is at some point inevitable? Health care providers routinely ask patients if they have an advance directive on record that identifies how they want medical end-of-life decisions made in case they are incapacitated. The use of funeral staff to care for deceased individuals might reflect the influence of a consumer-focused, capitalistic economy. These alternative interpretations of the evidence suggest a death-accepting society.

In support of the United States being more death-accepting, people point to the prevalence of death and death images in the media. The public acceptance and demand for death themes in movies, television programs, and video games drive the entertainment industry. The consumption of death-related news events, both online and in television programming, remains high, with daily reports of shooting deaths, natural disasters, and mass deaths during the COVID-19 pandemic. The permeation of these death images across all media platforms makes it difficult to ignore the reality of death.

Further evidence that the United States is becoming more death-accepting can be seen in the increased use of hospice care services. Hospice programs provide compassionate care and prioritize quality of life for people in the advanced stages of terminal medical conditions. Recent data indicate that about half of the people who died while on Medicare were enrolled in hospice services at the time of their death, and 98% of hospice patients received this care and support in their own homes (National Hospice and Palliative Care Organization, 2020). The rise in hospice enrollments indicates a broader acceptance of death and a return to the historical tradition of dying at home.

In the United States, the **death-positive movement** is gaining popularity and support. This movement includes social activities that promote awareness of death through open discussion. For example, death cafes are gatherings where people discuss death and share refreshments in an informal setting. They are a global phenomenon with a significant presence in the United States. Nonprofits host these get-togethers and facilitate group-directed discussions of death with no agenda or specific objectives.

Evidence of the death-positive movement can also be seen in the proliferation of social media content dedicated to death education. Caitlin Doughty hosts *Ask a Mortician*, a YouTube channel with over two million followers. Doughty is an American mortician, blogger, YouTube personality, and advocate of death acceptance who discusses death and dying, preparing the body, and options for final disposition. Another example of death-related content creators is Julie McFadden (a.k.a. Hospice Nurse Julie), whose material can be found on many social media platforms. McFadden focuses on educating people about how we die and demystifying the dying process to help people understand the end-of-life experience.

Death Fears

The nature of death fears depends on what a person has learned about death. Because the meaning of death is subjective, the presence and intensity of death fears are shaped by social influences and personal experiences. What do we know about the presence of death fears and the content of those fears in U.S. society? Research shows that only 11% of Americans stated that they were "very afraid" of death. But if you include respondents who indicated they were "somewhat afraid" and those who were "not very afraid," 69% of respondents reported they had some level of death fear (Statista Research Department, 2024).

Most Americans do not consider themselves very fearful of death, but people may not be forthright about their feelings, especially if those fears are more intense. Noting these concerns and questions, much of the research about death fears is based on self-reported survey data, often using a questionnaire format. This research gathers information from large groups of people from various backgrounds and ages. The data provide a snapshot of what people are feeling at that moment. Therefore, respondents may answer differently at another point, as personal experiences and social events can shift people's feelings.

Death Anxiety Data

Generally speaking, research data reveal consistent findings as to the impact of gender, age, spiritual belief, and situational experiences on death anxiety and death fears. Women frequently report they are more fearful or anxious about death than men (Eshbaugh & Henninger, 2013). However, questions remain as to whether women have higher rates of death fears or whether they are more open in reporting their anxiety.

In terms of age, death anxiety tends to decline as one ages, but higher rates often appear in older youth and middle-aged adults. As teenagers' exposure to death increases through media and personal experiences, they begin to understand that death can happen to anyone and that they could die before having a chance to experience life and achieve their goals. During middle age, people are more likely to experience the death of friends and family or face the challenges of living with a life-threatening disease just as they approach retirement and look forward to what they have waited so long to do. In both cases, the heightened awareness of death may impact death anxiety and fears.

Death anxiety is also affected by spiritual beliefs and religiosity (the strength of a person's religious feelings and beliefs). People who self-identify as being religious tend to show lower death anxiety than their counterparts. Those who believe in a spiritual or religious ideology often anticipate a better after-life and have a prescribed perception of what happens after death. This belief and certainty help alleviate death anxiety and death fears. However, a person's level of religious commitment may be a better indicator of death fears. Although people with higher levels of religiosity have lower levels of death fear than those with lower levels of religiosity, those with moderate religious commitment reported the highest levels of fear. People with a moderate level of commitment may not have followed specified religious beliefs or fulfilled requisite religious practices and rituals, which introduces the uncertainty of receiving the benefits associated with religious beliefs (Bassett & Bussard, 2021).

Content of Death Fears

Death fears are complex and multidimensional. People often talk about the fear of death as a singular, universal feeling. However, the meaning of death is complex and varies from person to person, as does the content embedded in death fears. To begin, let's focus on what people fear most often. Conceptually, death fears can be organized into four general concerns: the death of self, the death of others, the dying process, and the state of being dead.

While these categories are useful in understanding death fears, specific fears can be examined in greater detail within each area. For instance, the following fears can be understood in the context of the death of self and the death of others:

» dependency (having to rely on others for care) and loss of independence
» pain and indignity associated with the dying process
» social isolation and separation as part of the dying process
» leaving loved ones
» concerns about the afterlife
» the finality of death and the impact on others
» the fate of the body (Leming, 1980)

Death fears vary based on an individual's perspective and are influenced by a person's social position and social roles. Their age, whether they have younger children or dependent elders, are the financial supporters for a household, or hold a key position in a business or community may affect which death fears are most prominent. However, despite these variables, studies consistently show high death fear scores surrounding the dying process, like fear of dependency and fear of pain during the dying process, with lower scores surrounding the afterlife and the fate of the body (Leming & Dickinson, 2020).

Conclusion

The understanding of death is socially constructed and shaped by social interaction and our personal experiences. It is not a static concept, nor is it the same for every person. Our understanding of death evolves across the life course as we participate in social institutions and engage with others. We may all receive social messages about death from social institutions, but a person's life experiences with death can also influence their understanding. The opening vignette demonstrates how personal experiences can have an impact on our responses to death. The experiences of losing classmates, a grandmother, and a nephew, and the interaction with others who shared these losses, added to the understanding of death. These types of social interaction help shape, and at times alter, what we know, how we think, and how we respond to death. They become the basis for our attitudes and beliefs and influence any death fears we may acquire.

Summary

» The meaning of death is learned through social interaction with others and is influenced by the social messages embedded in social institutions such as the family, the media, and the work environment.
» We learn about death and its meaning from the social world, including our family, the media, and art.
» Cultural scripts surrounding death and our personal experiences and exposure to death become our guide for understanding death.
» The United States can be described as both a death-denying and a death-accepting society.
» People's fears about death are shaped by many factors, such as age, gender, beliefs, and life experiences.
» Research shows that most people worry more about the pain and loss of independence while dying than about what happens after death.

Review Questions

1. How is death considered a social construct, and what are the most widely accepted views of death?
2. How do factors such as historical and cultural influences, artistic representation, and personal experiences shape the meaning of death?
3. How do social institutions play a role in shaping people's understanding of death?
4. What factors impact people's attitudes toward death and their fear of death?
5. In what ways do sociohistorical and cultural beliefs shape the meaning of death?

Key Terms

Review these key terms from the chapter. You can find their definitions in the glossary at the end of the book.

» agents of socialization
» death-accepting perspective
» death-denying perspective

» death-positive movement
» social construction of reality
» social historical context

» social institution
» socialization
» society

Chapter 3

Death and the U.S. Experience

Vignette | **The Fallout of Fear**

In Woodburn, Oregon, in 1962, I was seven years old. The adults in my life were tense and worried; something was definitely wrong. I saw nightly news reports of nuclear bombs based in Cuba that could reach the United States. Maps flashed across the TV screen with arcs showing how far the bombs could travel. Oregon, my home, was at risk. Neighbors organized meetings to share information about preparing to survive a nuclear attack. My parents got plans from the Civil Defense Department to build an underground bomb shelter in our backyard. They began to stock food, water, and first aid supplies needed to survive a nuclear attack.

My school held duck-and-cover drills every week. When the local fire department sounded a World War II-era air raid siren, the teacher would yell "flash!" to represent the flash of bright light that would come from an actual nuclear explosion. We crawled under our desks, tucked into a ball, covered the back of our heads with our hands, and remained in that position until the all-clear siren sounded.

My parents pointed out all the neighborhood houses with basements in case a nuclear attack happened while I was outside playing or on my way home from school. I had seen pictures of the destruction and loss of life from the nuclear bombs dropped on Hiroshima and Nagasaki at the end of World War II. I understood what nuclear bombs could do, and it was terrifying to know that we could die at any time. I was afraid to leave home. What if there were a nuclear attack and I couldn't get home? What would I do if my parents died?

The looming fear of a nuclear attack and the possibility of death lingered long after the Cuban Missile Crisis of 1962 had passed. As an adult, my childhood fears and memories came back during the nuclear arms race of the 1980s. To this day, hearing one of those old sirens triggers a visceral response that transports me right back to the scared child hunkered under my classroom desk who was afraid my family and I could die at any time.

Patricia

Introduction

Throughout U.S. history, the tides of time have shaped our perspectives on death. Significant events, societal changes, scientific advances, and technological discoveries have made indelible marks on our collective experiences. In past wars, the large number of young, healthy adults who died shifted how we understood and experienced death. Similarly, advances in medicine, such as the development of cancer-fighting drugs and organ transplants, have affected how we view the course of life and the role of death. Navigating these changes, we can embark on a journey to better understand death and dying.

In this chapter, we'll look at how the sociohistorical context affects our understanding of death, exploring major social events and changes that have influenced the U.S. experience with death. We'll examine distinct historical patterns of death beliefs and practices and how they were shaped by social influences. Finally, we'll consider the relationship between social factors and the development of shared cultural attitudes and practices surrounding death.

Learning Objectives

These learning objectives will help you identify what's most important in this chapter. By the end of this chapter, you should be able to do the following:

» Understand the influence of the sociohistorical context in shaping the understanding of death.

» Identify major social events and changes in the social environment that shaped the U.S. experience with death.

» Differentiate between distinct historical patterns of U.S. death beliefs and practices based on social influences.

» Explain the relationship between social factors and the development of commonly shared patterns of death beliefs and practices.

Complexities of Death in the U.S.

As discussed in chapter 2, death is a learned social construct. In other words, people in a society create a shared understanding of death through their observations, actions, and social interactions. The meaning of death is not innate. People learn what death means, what to think about it, and how to feel about it. My seven-year-old self learned about death by watching my parents, listening to news reports, and participating in drills at school. What I learned at that early point in my life continues to influence my understanding of death. Experiences across the life course shape our beliefs and values about death and dying, which are passed from person to person and generation to generation through socialization.

Social influences help determine whether we accept death as a natural part of life or deny death by fighting against it. Elements of death beliefs are also learned within the context of sociohistorical events, such as the threat of nuclear war, and societal trends, such as the unprecedented rise of social media. The consequences of living during times of war, benefiting from incredible advances in medicine, or struggling through the effects of a pandemic all affect how death is understood and experienced.

In examining the U.S. experience with death, this chapter avoids using the term "America" to refer to the United States. First, using the term "America" to describe the United States is imprecise. Although we commonly use America as a shorthand for the United States of America, the term technically describes the entire continent and includes both North and South America. Conflating the name of the country with the name of the continent reflects the uneven power position the United States has over the rest of North America. It negates the shared experiences of people in the other nations of the American continents (Mergen, 1999).

Second, the United States is a multidimensional, multicultural society. Since the migration of humans into North America, there have always been diverse cultural and religious practices surrounding death and dying. In addition to the varied beliefs and practices of Indigenous peoples, the arrival of European colonists and centuries of ongoing immigration from around the world broadened the diversity of beliefs and practices in the United States, as shown in the chart in figure 3.1. Factors shaping these differing experiences about death and dying, such as age, gender, culture, and religion, will be further explored in subsequent chapters.

Figure 3.1. This chart shows the four top regions for immigration to the U.S. over time. Immigration from the Americas includes North, Central, and South America. Source: U.S. Department of Homeland Security, Yearbook of Immigration Statistics 2022.

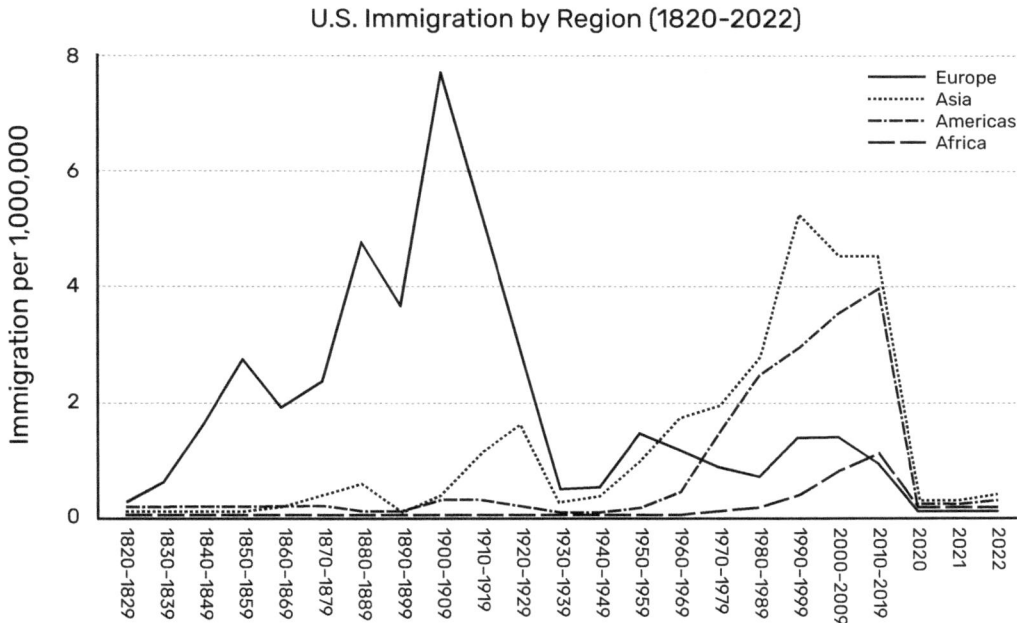

U.S. Dominant Culture

Within the multicultural society of the United States, there is a distinctive **dominant culture**. A dominant culture is one that possesses the most economic, political, and social power, making it distinct from other subcultures. A **subculture** is a distinct group within a dominant culture that maintains its own separate beliefs and practices. Subcultural groups can be based on ethnicity, interests, or activities (Scot, 2022). Social institutions, such as health care, education, family, and legal and political systems, reinforce and perpetuate the dominant culture's beliefs and practices because they are more widespread and influential than those of other subcultures. As a result, the dominant culture sets a common standard of expectations.

U.S. dominant culture is grounded in Northern and Western European Christian traditions but has been influenced and modified by cultures from around the world. It has evolved into a distinctive set of beliefs and practices, including those about death and dying. The power of the dominant culture and its influence to shape social processes is important to examine when discussing a shared experience with death.

Sometimes people question the presence of common cultural patterns and point out individual differences in beliefs and practices about death and dying. These questions may be especially prevalent in the United States, where individuality is considered a cultural value. Individual variations do indeed exist within U.S. dominant culture. But what may at first glance appear to be a practice or belief unique to one specific person may be broadly held by many. Therefore, that practice is part of a larger pattern that exists across society.

Because the dominant culture sets the standards, its values and practices get woven into social systems such as schools, government, and the work environment, perpetuating these expectations and imposing them on society. Even though the dominant culture has the power to shape expectations and social processes, these standards are not the only way, nor the right way—they simply offer one way. Because the dominant culture's beliefs and practices often act as the standard, groups that are not part of the dominant culture may be marginalized. This means they have less political or social power, are pushed to the periphery of society, and are excluded from mainstream participation.

Multicultural Society

A **multicultural society** is one that includes a diverse array of ethnic and cultural groups. The concept of U.S. dominant culture and the idea that the United States is a multicultural society may seem contradictory at first, but these two ideas coexist and interact in complex ways. As mentioned previously, U.S. dominant culture refers to the set of values, traditions, and practices that set the standard for what is broadly accepted and expected across society. For example, the majority of the U.S. population speaks English, with 78% speaking English as their only language, according to the 2020 U.S. Census.

While the population of the United States is becoming increasingly diverse over time, 2020 census data show that White Americans still represent the majority (60%) of the population. According to a 2022 Pew Research Center study, 64% of Americans identified as Christian, down from 90% in the early 1990s. However, regardless of shifting demographics, the ongoing social and political power of

U.S. dominant culture means its beliefs, values, and norms continue to be perpetuated and amplified through laws, the educational system, and the media.

At the same time, the United States is also a multicultural society, and many of the country's foundational documents lay the groundwork for a diverse and inclusive society. For example, the First Amendment (1791) granted the freedom of religion, ensuring that people of different religious backgrounds could worship freely. The Thirteenth Amendment (1865) abolished slavery, and the Fourteenth Amendment (1868) provided for equal protection of all people under the law. The Fifteenth Amendment (1870) granted Black men the right to vote, and the Nineteenth Amendment (1920) granted women the right to vote. Although not fully realized at the time, the revolutionary idea that a country could be built on "Life, liberty, and the pursuit of happiness" is embedded in the U.S. Declaration of Independence. These values serve as a cornerstone for movements advocating for the rights of various cultural and ethnic groups.

The United States has more immigrants than any other country in the world, and being a "nation of immigrants" is part of the uniquely American story. When we look at the United States as a multicultural society, we acknowledge the contributions of these diverse cultural groups. While the country clearly has a dominant culture, its multicultural nature influences and reshapes it. Throughout the country's history, these interactions continually redefine the U.S. perspective on all topics that touch our lives, including how we experience the dying process, death itself, and how we mourn for those we've lost.

Living with Death: 1600–1850

The period from 1600 to 1850 was formative in shaping the United States' evolving death practices, laying a foundation that reflects the interplay of diverse cultural, religious, and historical influences. During this time, mortality was a visible and inescapable part of daily life, shaped by high rates of disease, limited medical knowledge, and the hardships of frontier existence. Death was not abstract or distant; it was experienced within families, communities, and public spaces, influencing cultural norms and collective attitudes.

This era was marked by a blending of Indigenous and European perspectives on mortality. Indigenous populations had well-established death rituals emphasizing continuity, community, and the spiritual relationship with the natural world. European colonists brought diverse Christian traditions, focusing on the soul's preparation for an afterlife, reflected in burial customs, sermons, and memorial art. The enslaved African population also introduced rich death practices, merging African traditions with Christian influences and further diversifying the cultural landscape. These varied practices created a patchwork of meanings and responses to death, emphasizing its communal and spiritual dimensions.

The sociohistorical conditions of this time—colonization, westward expansion, and the rise of Enlightenment thinking—also shaped how Americans approached mortality. Cemeteries became not only places of rest but also public spaces for reflection and social interaction. Death records, sermons, and epitaphs reveal a shift from collective fear of damnation to an emerging focus on individual legacy and memory. Together, these developments reflect how the period laid the groundwork for uniquely American attitudes toward death, blending reverence for tradition with adaptability to changing cultural and social realities.

Indigenous Populations in the Americas

For Indigenous peoples in the Americas, the arrival of European colonists and the first settlements in the 1600s led to catastrophic death rates. Although determining exact population counts is challenging, research generally indicates that North American Indigenous populations dropped by 85–90% during this period. The introduction of both European and African diseases decimated Indigenous societies, with the deadliest being smallpox, typhus, and measles. Throughout the next two centuries, the westward expansion of European immigrants resulted in massive deaths of Indigenous peoples because of wars, enslavement, and the government-sanctioned genocide of Native Americans. The seizing of Native lands, the stress of forced relocation and removal, and the disruption in tribal subsistence patterns also contributed to the increase in deaths among Indigenous tribal populations (Thornton, 1990).

From the colonial period to today, Indigenous burial sites in the United States have been subject to theft and desecration, severely disrupting cultural traditions and ancestral practices. The removal of human remains, sacred objects, and funerary items from these sites not only disrespects the dead but also erases vital connections to Indigenous histories, spirituality, and identity. Because of the sacredness of these sites and their vulnerability to theft, many Native Americans do not share information about traditional burial practices with members outside their tribe. The Native American Graves Protection and Repatriation Act (NAGPRA), passed in 1990, sought to protect Indigenous cultural heritage by requiring federal agencies and institutions to return human remains and cultural items to their rightful tribes. Despite its implementation, enforcement challenges persist, and the preservation of sacred sites remains an ongoing concern for many Native communities.

Tribal cultures continue to thrive, with vibrant efforts to reclaim and revitalize traditions, languages, and spiritual practices despite centuries of displacement, erasure, and exploitation. As of 2025, there are 574 federally recognized Native American tribes in the United States. This broad array of cultural groups with different perspectives and practices surrounding death and dying means that no single funeral practice can represent the totality of Native American culture. Though affected by European colonization, these distinctive Indigenous tribal traditions have been carried forward and are reflected in many contemporary tribal death beliefs and practices.

Colonialism and European Influences

A more broadly shared pattern of death meanings and practices began to develop with the arrival of early European colonists. They came from varied ethnic backgrounds, but most were Christian and shared a common set of fundamental religious precepts. Christianity is monotheistic (one God as the supreme being) and its followers have a shared set of fundamental beliefs such as the acceptance of Jesus as the son of God, the trinity (Father, Son, and Spirit), the resurrection of Jesus Christ, and the Bible as the word of God (The Boisi Center for Religion & American Public Life., n.d.). According to Christian beliefs, a final judgment will permanently separate the wicked from the righteous, and the righteous will spend eternity in the presence of God (Ayodeji, 2013).

Despite differences in church doctrine, the common belief that death was a time of judgment by God guided every aspect of life. Therefore, how early European colonists lived and the choices they made would influence where they spent eternity. This religious ideology, coupled with the harsh realities of colonial life, necessitated an ever-present need to accept and prepare for death.

Death was a grim reality in colonial America, striking people of all ages. The high rates of infant mortality and the risks of death from childhood accidents and illnesses meant that 40% of children failed to reach adulthood in seventeenth-century America. Infections and contaminated food and water threatened the health of colonists of all ages. The hazards of farming accidents and hunting for food, frequent epidemics such as diphtheria, measles, scarlet fever, and smallpox, along with the spread of intestinal parasites, pneumonia, and influenza, made death a regular part of life (Vinovskis, 1976).

As the number of European colonists grew, they moved further west. Spreading their beliefs and practices through evangelical efforts, coercion, or force, European colonists asserted dominance, relegating Native cultures to subcultural status. The blending of Northern and Western European cultures with Christian beliefs established the foundations of U.S. dominant culture. Within this new dominant cultural framework, death-related practices and beliefs set the standard for what was accepted and expected.

Figure 3.2. Patterns in the design elements of headstones are often symbolic representations of commonly held norms and values of the time. This stone grave marker emphasizes human mortality (death's head image), the importance of remembering those who have died, and the significance of social position (son).

During the early colonial period, Protestant funerary practices included the traditions the colonists brought with them from their homelands. When a death occurred, the tolling of the town's church bells spread the word across the community. After a death, family members washed the body and held a wake in the home. The wake was a communal gathering with food, drink, and companionship for those mourning. The funeral took place quickly after the death. The service tended to be somber, austere, and relatively silent. Funerals typically included few words, with no eulogy or sermon, though brief remarks might be shared before burial. The cemetery was usually some distance away, so sets of pallbearers were needed to carry the coffin. The pallbearers would take turns carrying the coffin to help alleviate the burden.

By the eighteenth century, this stark view of death began to fade, and people began to engage in more overt remembrance. Headstones made of more permanent material began to replace the earlier practice of using wooden markers that decayed over time. Inscriptions on the headstones often noted the social roles the person played and included a reminder for living to honor and remember those who had died (figure 3.2).

Death shifted to a more communal and social event during this period. When a person died, people in the community stopped working, and many came to the home to help with daily tasks and preparation for the burial. Burials became more elaborate, and public displays of mourning also became more common. Funerals were more likely to include sermons and eulogies. It was customary for written verses and poems to be attached to the coffin and bier (the movable frame on which a coffin is placed before burial). Funeral attendees were given small gifts and trinkets as tokens of remembrance. Wealthy families often sent a pair of gloves to those invited to the funeral. Gloves were an expensive item and an important necessity; thus, they were seen as a sign of affluence.

Death and Resilience Among Enslaved Africans

Slavery in what is now the United States began in 1619, when a Dutch ship brought 20–30 enslaved Africans to the English colony of Virginia at Point Comfort (modern-day Hampton, Virginia). These individuals were traded for supplies and became the first documented Africans in the colonies. Initially, their status was unclear—they were treated as indentured servants in some cases—but over the following decades, laws were enacted that codified lifelong, race-based slavery.

Slavery expanded as the colonies grew, with enslaved labor becoming integral to the agricultural economy, especially in the Southern colonies. By the late seventeenth and early eighteenth centuries, the transatlantic slave trade had firmly established slavery as a racialized and hereditary institution in the colonies. Death in enslaved African communities was shaped by the harsh realities of slavery, yet it also reflected the resilience and spiritual depth of those who endured this system. Mortality rates were high due to the brutal conditions of enslavement, including poor nutrition, lack of medical care, overwork, and exposure to diseases. Despite this, enslaved Africans created and maintained distinct death practices that blended their cultural traditions with influences from Christianity and U.S. dominant culture (figure 3.3).

For many enslaved Africans, death was not seen as an end but as a transition, a return to Africa or the ancestors. Historically, African American funerals were communal events, providing a rare space for expressing grief and solidarity. Rituals often included singing, drumming, and oral storytelling, symbolizing continuity between the living and the dead. Over time, these practices came to be colloquially known as homegoing services. Homegoing, in the context of funerals and death rituals,

Figure 3.3. This painting, *The African American Burial Ground* by Charles Lilly, was created for the National Parks Service's interpretive literature for the African Burial Ground National Monument in New York.

emphasizes a spiritual perspective on death as a journey of the soul returning to its heavenly home. This belief, rooted in African traditions and Christian theology, celebrates death not solely as a loss but as a transition to eternal rest and unity with ancestors or God.

Separating Death from Daily Life: 1850–1915

Wave after wave of rapid changes flooded the Western world from 1850 to 1915. Death practices in the United States were strongly influenced by the Victorian era, the post-Civil War period of industrialization, and the increased prominence of science and technology.

Across the American continent, settlers encroached on Native lands, extending urban areas and taking vast tracts of what they perceived to be wilderness. The introduction of new technologies, discoveries in science, and growing access to education all led to significant changes in how people lived. Rational thought with a focus on systematic efficiency became a guiding principle used to structure social institutions. European settlers strived to organize and control their environment as much as possible. During the Industrial Revolution of the eighteenth and nineteenth centuries, ideas of human dominance shaped views on life and death. Death, once seen as inevitable, became an event people attempted to control and compartmentalize.

Obsession and Control

The Victorian era (1837–1901) was characterized by an obsession with death. People were surrounded by death, but they could do little about it. Epidemics of typhoid fever, cholera, and scarlet fever were exacerbated by rapidly growing urban areas, lack of sanitation systems, and contaminated drinking water. Further emphasizing this obsession, one of the most powerful monarchs of the time, England's Queen Victoria, became fixated on death after her beloved Prince Albert died at an early age. The Queen went to extreme efforts to surround herself with his symbolic presence. She had casts of the prince's face and hands made to keep on her bedside table and continued to dress in black for forty years as an expression of her ongoing grief. The Queen regularly commissioned new statues, busts, and paintings of the prince, many of which were placed throughout the royal residence. His room was maintained as if he were still alive: servants set out his clothes every morning, brought hot water for his shaving cup, and cleaned his chamber pot every morning (Reynolds & Matthew, 2007; Rappaport, 2003).

Queen Victoria's global influence fueled a widespread obsession with death and elaborate death rituals. This morbid fascination with death and dying was so widespread that historians often refer to this preoccupation as the "cult of death" era and note its influence in defining this period. The topic of dying was an open and ongoing conversation, and even young people planned for their eventual death. It was common to make death shrouds and to design one's own coffin as part of a wedding dowry. People made elaborate plans describing every aspect of their funeral and burial (Taylor, 1983). When death did occur, these detailed plans left little doubt as to what a deceased person wanted and what they expected from their family.

While Victorians understood death as a fundamental reality of life, they also saw it as an eventuality to plan for in a structured and disciplined manner. One needed to prepare for death, experience it, and then return to daily activities in an orderly process. Social pressures emphasized formalizing and standardizing death practices and social expectations. Prescribed social rules of etiquette defined the mourning period, which could last up to two years. A complex set of expectations outlined specific phases of mourning, for whom one should mourn, and what should be done and worn during each phase. The length of the mourning period depended on one's relationship to the deceased. Commonly, social guidelines specified a mourning period of two years for the death of a spouse, one year for parents or one's child, six months for a grandparent or sibling, and three months for more distant relatives or a close friend (Celiberti, 2021).

The mourning process was also broken down into types of mourning, each accompanied by social standards regarding appropriate attire to be worn. For example, the deepest mourning was typically reserved for widows grieving the loss of their husbands. During the first year of her grieving period, a widow wore only the deepest black with no shiny fabrics and no trimmings. In the second year, the clothing restrictions gradually lessened. First mourning, which included the grief for the death of other relatives, still required black clothing but was styled with less fabric and trim restrictions. In the case of the death of immediate relatives, regarded as secondary mourning, the expected black attire could include white cuffs and collars (Celiberti, 2021). Violating these social expectations was interpreted as being disrespectful of the deceased person, even if compliance resulted in financial hardship (Brean, 2019).

During the Victorian era, people attempted to keep the harsh realities of urbanization and the work world separate from the sanctuary of their homes and families. When separation wasn't possible, they attempted to soften the effects of the situation. For death and dying, this meant having others take care of people who had died and their burial. A growing middle class could afford to hire others for undesirable death-related work. The emerging funeral industry would prepare the body for burial and provide services associated with the funeral and interment. The funeral industry expanded by offering amenities like ornate coffins, an elaborate funeral carriage, music, and mourning decor.

The Importance of Aesthetics

Throughout time, mourners have attempted to ritualize and beautify death to temper the pain and sadness of loss. Victorians, with their inclination toward excessive ornamentation, took the rituals of death to the next level. They believed that if a situation could not be prevented or controlled, focusing on the **aesthetics**, the visual, sensory, and symbolic elements of the funeral tradition, could change the experience. Many Victorian rituals and practices reflected the era's emphasis on displays of wealth and the rich trying to look richer. But people from the middle and lower classes also attempted to emulate many of these practices as best they could within their limited resources.

Most funerals took place at home, and the home had to be appropriately prepared. Mourners hung black wreaths on their front doors and draped black crepe fabric (a distinctive textured fabric with a bumpy, crinkled appearance) on doorknobs and over mirrors in the house. The body was embalmed to preserve its appearance. Family members dressed their loved ones in their finest clothes and laid them out in ornately decorated coffins. Flowers and music were incorporated into the funeral service, and the coffin was loaded onto an elaborately adorned carriage for the funeral procession to the cemetery (figure 3.4). The burial often

Figure 3.4. This carriage was designed for funeral processions by James Cunningham & Co, Factory Rochester, NY.

took place in a cemetery designed to emphasize the beauty of nature. These park-like settings included intentional landscaping, decorative fencing, benches, and statuary (National Park Service, 2011). Chapter 10 explores the social and cultural aspects of American cemeteries in more detail.

Significant effort was put into memorializing the deceased individual and denoting the mourning period. Memorial cards acted as funeral invitations, and postmortem cards were sent to those who couldn't attend. These cards contained information about the deceased person, including their name, date of birth, date of death, and the date, time, and location of the funeral. A photo appeared on one side, and a tribute to their life, selected scripture, or poem was on the other side. These cards were kept as a remembrance and often placed in family photo albums.

Pictures of the deceased person lying in the coffin at the funeral were taken to commemorate the event. People grieving the loss of a loved one were also photographed in mourning attire and wearing memorial jewelry that often included a photo of the deceased person and a lock of their hair. The cards and photographs were intended to mark the death event and provide a more enduring memorial (National Park Service, 2011).

Confronting Death in Wartime: 1915–1989

Major sociohistorical events in the twentieth century altered how Americans viewed and understood death. The influenza epidemic of 1918–1919 was the first modern-day pandemic to dramatically impact the United States. Influenza spread quickly across the country. With little that could be done at the time to escape infection and possible death, Americans were forced to confront death daily.

Multiple wars also impacted Americans' death experience in ways not seen before. The United States' involvement in a series of wars—World War I, World War II, the Korean War, and the Vietnam War—resulted in the deaths of hundreds of thousands of predominantly young adults. Families lost parents, spouses, sons and daughters, and brothers and sisters, while communities mourned the death of friends and neighbors.

Overlapping the war experience was the development of nuclear weapons and the widespread images of their ability to obliterate property and human life. As described in the vignette at the beginning of the chapter, this experience was followed by the ongoing nuclear arms race among global powers and the increased possibility of mutually assured destruction resulting from a nuclear war. These broadly experienced events contributed to a heightened awareness of the fragility of life in an increasingly uncertain world.

Influenza Pandemic

The 1918–1919 influenza epidemic was one of the most significant pandemics in modern history. The rapid spread of influenza affected people in nations throughout the world. In the United States, it is estimated that over 675,000 people died due to influenza during the pandemic, while globally, an estimated fifty million people died. While death due to influenza was not a new phenomenon, the massive death rates across multiple age groups within a short time marked this event as significantly different from previous experiences. Influenza infected people of all age groups, but children under the age of five, young adults ages twenty to forty, and those over the age of sixty-five suffered the highest mortality rates. Of particular concern was the high mortality rate in otherwise healthy adults, which was a unique feature of this influenza epidemic (Centers for Disease Control and Prevention, 2018).

Figure 3.5. Two nurses demonstrate safety precautions at the Red Cross Emergency Ambulance Station in Washington, D.C., during the influenza pandemic of 1918.

With no available vaccines or antibiotics to treat secondary bacterial infections, public health efforts to curb the spread of influenza focused on encouraging good public hygiene and using masks and disinfectants (figure 3.5). People were encouraged to self-isolate when infected, quarantine when exposed, and limit social and public gatherings. These efforts to control the spread of infection received varied support across communities, and adherence was inconsistent.

Urban areas with densely populated neighborhoods, close living quarters, and crowded workplaces facilitated the spread of influenza.

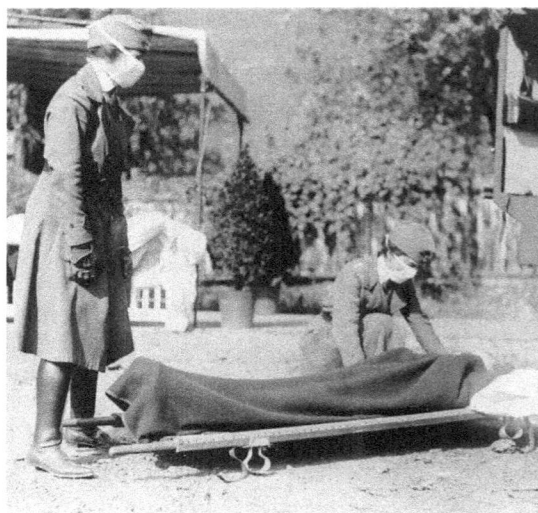

Despite public health interventions to quickly educate the public about the use of masks and social distancing, city conditions made it difficult to stem the spread of infection. Working-class urban areas that were already challenged by overcrowded housing conditions, poor sanitation systems, and unsafe drinking water were even more vulnerable to infection. Cities struggled to care for the overwhelming numbers of influenza patients. The stress on the health care system was exacerbated by the large number of doctors, nurses, and medical staff who had been called up for military duty during World War I, leaving U.S. hospitals and communities understaffed (Roberts & Tehari, 2020).

Smaller communities were not spared from the epidemic and, in many cases, experienced higher infection and mortality rates than larger cities. Geographic isolation did not protect against infection. Based on their sparse population and distance from urban areas, many smaller communities developed a false sense of security and took few precautions. Once influenza cases broke out in rural communities, they spread quickly, contributing to a higher mortality rate than in urban areas. As the highly contagious virus spread through rural America, multiple members of a family often became infected, and in some cases, the entire family died together. Those who recovered from the virus were faced with the reality that family members and friends, many of whom had been in the prime of life, had died (Watkins, 2015).

War

War has long been an aspect of the human experience, but the twentieth century marked a significant change in the scope and nature of war. World Wars I and II were the first truly global conflicts, and they killed tens of millions of people. In addition, regional wars affected countries worldwide. For the United States, involvement in World War I, World War II, the Korean War, the Vietnam War, and Desert Storm played a significant role in shaping the nation's understanding of death. U.S. military deaths during wartime from 1917 to 1995 numbered over 668,000, with World War II alone (1942–1945) accounting for more than 400,000 deaths (U.S. Department of Veterans Affairs, n.d.). The loss of so many young lives touched families and communities across the nation.

Alongside the scale of war in the twentieth century, the development of new weaponry and strategic battlefield changes led to mass military casualties. Rifles, machine guns, and artillery became more efficient and powerful. Aircraft became increasingly important in warfare, with planes, helicopters, and jet aircraft, along with the bombs and other munitions they carried, causing more damage. The use of rockets and satellites, the introduction of biological and chemical weapons, and the development of nuclear weapons made the scope of devastation much broader and the death rates higher.

During World War II, civilians played a crucial role in the war effort. Many people who couldn't serve in the military worked in factories and industries supplying materials, ammunition, and machinery to the war. This blurred the line between those who were part of the fighting forces and those who weren't, leading to cities and industrial areas becoming direct targets to disrupt the supply chain for weapons and ammunition. As a result, civilian casualties increased significantly. In the Vietnam War, much of the fighting took place in the tropical jungles and small villages of the Vietnamese countryside, where civilians were often directly and indirectly involved. The frequent use of guerrilla warfare tactics, combined with the involvement of civilians, contributed to high civilian fatalities (Kearl, 2003).

Media

In the twentieth century, news accounts, including photographs, radio, and film, increased public awareness of the brutality and destruction of war. During World Wars I and II, newspapers, newsreels shown at movie theaters, and radio reports were the primary sources of news about the war. The media reports were heavily censored and used to promote the war and boost public spirits. Images often focused on the power of U.S. weaponry, heroic efforts by military troops, and smiling soldiers doing their work. However, along with these news accounts came a steady stream of graphic images of battle scenes and the destruction. Reports from the front lines brought daily information to homes nationwide. Civilians could not escape the realities of war. Amid this media coverage, families received military notifications of the deaths of their loved ones, and communities mourned friends and neighbors.

The Vietnam War, often called the first television war, changed the way people understood life and death in combat. Between 1950 and 1960, television ownership increased from 9% to 90% (Library of Congress, n.d.). For the first time, people saw war in real time. The style of news coverage also changed as competition for television viewers increased. News networks clamored for the best reporters and most dramatic stories. Figure 3.6 shows reporter Walter Cronkite conducting a televised interview in Vietnam in 1968. Technology and embedded reporters in military units made reporting directly from the battlefield possible, resulting in more realistic, graphic, and uncensored news reports.

Figure 3.6. Walter Cronkite of CBS interviews Professor Mai of the University of Hue in Vietnam in 1968.

This approach to news reporting provided a more realistic glimpse into soldiers' lives and war experiences (Kratz, 2018). Advancements in media technology reduced the distance between those in combat and the public at home. While watching these stories on TV, Americans had to process the deaths of more than 90,000 military troops and civilian support personnel (U.S. Department of Veterans Affairs, n.d.).

Nuclear Weapons

The use of the atomic bomb at the end of World War II ushered in a new era in weapons development. As images emerged from the U.S. atomic bombing of Hiroshima and Nagasaki, Japan (1945), people were able to see and understand the power of nuclear weapons. The ability to inflict unprecedented destruction and the devastating loss of life stunned the American public. While the United States was the first to develop nuclear weapons, other nations, most notably the Soviet Union, were concerned about one nation holding a monopoly over such powerful weapons and technology. Within a few years, the Soviet Union had developed its atomic bomb, followed by several other nations that joined the nuclear-armed ranks.

A growing conflict between the United States and the Soviet Union developed after World War II. The United States had emerged as a dominant global power after the war, and the Soviet Union was trying to broaden its scope of global influence. The Cold War was the political and economic rivalry between U.S.-led Western nations and Soviet-bloc countries that escalated during the second half of the twentieth century. It was fueled by posturing, threats, and propaganda that led to public fear of a military conflict. Each country believed that the other was willing to use nuclear weapons. This threat led to a nuclear arms race, with each country building more destructive weapons and a more extensive arsenal, always trying to one-up the other. Some strategists said that peace could be maintained only through mutually assured destruction (MAD), where each side knew that if they launched an initial nuclear attack, the other would launch a counterattack, ensuring that neither would survive. However, the development of strategic intercontinental missiles that could deliver a nuclear warhead anywhere on the globe within minutes only heightened public fears of possible nuclear destruction and death (Kearl, 2003).

The development of nuclear weapons affected the psyche of society. In the wake of the atomic bombing of Japan, Congress authorized funds to build a nationwide system of bomb shelters in case of a nuclear attack. As the nuclear arms race intensified, the government tried to lessen fears of a nuclear attack among Americans. The Office of Civil Defense produced public service videos, distributed family guides, and supported community efforts to instruct the public on preparing for and responding to a nuclear attack.

People were urged to build underground shelters. Plans for backyard bomb shelters were published, along with lists of survival equipment and supplies (U.S. Federal Civil Defense Administration, 1953). Schools like the one described in the opening vignette conducted duck-and-cover drills. Students practiced how to quickly crawl under their desks and cover their heads with their hands to protect themselves in case of a nuclear bomb attack (Eisenhower Foundation, 2020). Local communities and neighborhoods held regular preparedness meetings. The looming possibility of nuclear destruction throughout the Cold War kept topics of life and death at the forefront of life in the United States.

Observing Death from a Distance: 1990–Present

In contemporary America, ongoing advancements in technology, science, and medicine continue to shape society. These rapid and extraordinary changes significantly impact how people understand and experience death. Technology and media platforms now rapidly spread information and images of deaths and tragic events. People are bombarded with a constant flow of news about death from social media, the internet, and 24-hour news cycles, which cover events like mass shootings, accidents, disasters, and the COVID-19 pandemic. The sheer amount of information and frequent exposure to graphic images make it hard for people to process. Deaths that used to be shocking may now seem commonplace, with many people becoming less sensitive to the emotional and psychological impact of such events (Mrug et al., 2015; Bushman & Anderson, 2009).

Discoveries and innovations in technology and science have simultaneously facilitated advances in health and medicine. From 1970 to 2020, the average life expectancy has increased by eight-and-a-half years due to medical research in genetics, physiological processes, and chronic diseases, along with advancements in medications and treatments (O'Neill, 2024). The increased understanding of disease has led to improvements in prevention strategies, early diagnosis, and more effective treatments. Survival rates for many diseases and medical conditions have increased to the point that they are now considered to be chronic, manageable conditions. A diagnosis of cancer or heart disease is no longer an automatic indicator of imminent death.

Media and Technology

Today, mass media affect nearly everything we do. People are rarely away from their computers, tablets, and cell phones. News alerts on phones are interspersed within people's social media feeds. News apps, government-based alert systems, and community social media sites send notifications concerning national and local events. People at the scene of an event often post eyewitness accounts, along with photos and videos, which can go viral within minutes. Information from around the world, across the country, and within our communities is shared in real time. This rapid dissemination and the steady stream of news reports have impacted all aspects of life, including social perceptions of death and dying.

News coverage is often dominated by reports of tragic events involving injuries and loss of life: mass shootings in the United States, floods in India, earthquakes in Haiti, a tsunami in Indonesia. Although this daily exposure makes people more aware of death, it also has the effect of creating more distance from the realities of death. Knowledge can provide the opportunity to make personal connections to the experience of death. But the detached method of presentation and the perceived distance offered by the mass media format can lead people to a false perception that death only happens to others (San Filippo, 2006). This ongoing bombardment of media reports can desensitize people to the realities of death. Therefore, as people become accustomed to what was once seen as tragic or shocking, death becomes a repetitive, everyday event that happens in someone else's life.

The COVID-19 Pandemic and Mass Death

Throughout recorded history, events involving mass death have been a global reality. Whether a result of natural forces such as hurricanes and earthquakes or human-initiated situations, as in the case of terrorist activities and mass shootings, people are frequently confronted with incidents involving large-scale loss of life. These events tend to be time-bound, thus giving people a chance to process the effects of the event, grieve and recover, and resume routines. People can end wars and deter terrorist threats; weather and natural events are periodic. But how does it affect people when the massive deaths are continuous and the result of an ongoing threat that is resistant to human intervention?

When mass death is ongoing and caused by a persistent, uncontrollable threat, it can create widespread uncertainty, fear, and societal disruption. The first cases of SARS-CoV-2 (COVID-19) infections among the general population were identified in late 2019 in Wuhan, China. As a novel virus (new to the human species), little was known about the virus and the implications of these infections. By

March 2020, the rapid spread and alarming fatality rate of the infections prompted the World Health Organization (WHO) to officially declare COVID-19 a global pandemic. Early scientific and medical efforts to address the pandemic focused on understanding the nature of the virus and developing treatment regimens and an effective vaccine. Public health and government agencies encouraged people to follow basic infectious disease precautions to minimize the spread of the virus: promoting personal hygiene, wearing a mask to cover the mouth and nose, and social distancing (AJMC staff, 2021).

Within a year of the initial identification of the virus, advances in scientific research led to the development of several vaccines (Centers for Disease Control and Prevention, n.d.-a). These vaccines were effective in reducing hospitalizations and deaths, offering a path to recovery from the pandemic. But despite vaccine availability, the United States continued to see regional surges in the number of COVID-19 infections and deaths. The ongoing spread of inaccurate information and the politicization of the COVID-19 pandemic fueled a backlash against government guidelines and public health mandates. This resistance led to a decline in vaccination rates and challenges to mask-wearing and social distancing, which threatened to stall the progress made against the spread of the virus.

Illnesses, such as the COVID-19 pandemic, continue to pose a threat to the United States and the world. Vaccination hesitancy and inequalities in global access to vaccines increase the threat that new variants will surface, some of which may challenge vaccine effectiveness. Regional surges in infections continue to stress health care services. Reports of shortages in health care staff, medical equipment and supplies, and hospital beds continue. The surge in COVID-19 cases has been so severe that some states have had to ration access to health care (Boone, 2021).

For several years, information about COVID-19 outbreaks, hospitalizations, and deaths permeated the 24-hour news cycle. Schools and workplaces opened, only to close again due to a COVID-19 outbreak. Events were scheduled and then canceled. Vaccination breakthrough infections occurred, reminding people of the looming threat. In an environment of continuous uncertainty and pending risk, people became desensitized to the loss of life. This response is one way people cope with ongoing tragedy. The brain can engage in a protective process that shields a person from becoming emotionally or neurologically overwhelmed, explains Dr. Bruce Harry, an associate professor of clinical psychiatry and forensic psychiatry at the University of Missouri School of Medicine (as cited in Ducharme, 2018). Over time, we become numb to fear-inducing health news and information and have a blunted emotional response to the ongoing tragedy, despite a rising death toll (Stevens et al., 2021).

Through May 2, 2023, the spread of COVID-19 was responsible for over 1.1 million deaths in the United States and an estimated 6.9 million deaths globally (Elflein, 2024). On May 5, 2023, the World Health Organization declared an end to the public health emergency for COVID-19, followed by an end to the U.S. federal declaration on May 11, 2023. Though the public health emergency has ended, COVID-19 infections continue to result in hospitalizations and deaths. Most epidemiologists agree that the virus has shifted from its disruptive and devastating pandemic phase to an endemic phase, where the virus is a constant yet contained presence.

The sheer number of deaths from COVID-19 is difficult for people to comprehend. It is easier to identify and empathize with the death of one person. People can connect to the experience of sadness and grief based on their experiences, but still experience numbness when dealing with prolonged events or situations that involve overwhelming losses. As the number of deaths increases, it becomes more difficult to fully grasp the reality of death (Concannon, 2020). While psychological distancing from death facilitates the ability to adapt and persevere in the face of massive loss of life, it also reinforces the notion that these deaths are a remote event.

Science and Medicine

Advancements in science and medicine have made huge strides in improving overall human health, unlocking the complexities of illness and disease, and extending life expectancy. Before World War I, Americans commonly died from infectious conditions such as influenza, pneumonia, diarrhea or enteritis, tuberculosis, and diphtheria. But by the 1950s, the introduction of sulfa drugs, followed by the development of antibiotics, helped save lives and removed these conditions from the top five leading causes of death (Centers for Disease Control and Prevention, n.d.-b). Building on these successes, science then turned its attention to chronic and degenerative conditions such as heart disease, cancer, strokes, and diabetes that topped the list of leading causes of death by the end of the twentieth century.

Decades of success in extending life expectancy led to a concerted effort by some of the best scientific and medical minds to focus on research that could further extend the human lifespan (Samuel, 2013). Life expectancy in the United States had risen by over ten years between 1950 and 2010 (U.S. Census Bureau, 2017), leading many researchers to believe that advances in science and medicine could extend life expectancy to well over one hundred years of age. They believed that if degenerative and chronic disorders, especially those correlated with the aging process, could be tackled and mitigated as had been the case for many other diseases and conditions, life expectancy could be further elongated.

Progress in the screening, diagnosis, and treatment of chronic diseases such as heart disease, cancer, kidney disease, and diabetes continues to increase the survival rates for these disorders. For instance, in the mid-twentieth century, a cancer diagnosis was frequently perceived as a death sentence. However, survival rates have changed significantly over the last four decades. The five-year survival rate for all cancers increased from 49% during the mid-1970s to 69% during 2013–2019. As survival rates continue to improve, many types of cancer are now more commonly understood as manageable chronic diseases. For example, survival rates are high for cancers of the thyroid (99%), prostate (97%), testis (95%), and melanoma (94%) (Siegel et al., 2024; National Cancer Institute, 2020).

As chronic diseases become increasingly manageable, modern medicine becomes more successful in delaying death. Although people are likely to live longer, many face the ongoing challenges associated with disease symptoms, medication side effects, and needed medical procedures. These scientific and medical advances have elongated and slowed the trajectory toward death. Today, dying is more often a prolonged process, and death "has become more of a phase of our life, instead of being just an instantaneous sort of flash event" (Warraich, 2018). These scientific and medical advances allow people to be aware of the inevitability of death yet still keep it at a distance.

Conclusion

The meaning of death and its relationship to daily life are contextualized within a given historical framework. Major social events, such as living under the constant threat of nuclear attack or navigating the daily challenges of the COVID-19 pandemic, shape a commonly held understanding of death. In the opening vignette, you read about a child living through the height of the nuclear war era. The social messages during that period affected how many came to understand their connection to death and dying. Similarly, living through the COVID-19 pandemic will impact how people understand death and dying for generations to come. In addition to major social events, any significant change in a society can impact how death is understood and experienced. Notably, the ability to quickly transmit death-related information and images to a broad audience will also affect how people understand death. Thus, in addition to the impact of diverse cultural backgrounds, varied religions, and personal experiences, sociohistorical events and social changes in society can contribute to a broadly shared experience of death.

Summary

»   The concept of an "American" experience with death describes the effects of the collectively shared exposure to societal forces that shape the understanding of death.
»   Cultural and religious factors, as well as individual experiences, can act to modify or alter these generalized experiences.
»   Broadly experienced changes in the social environment and sociohistorical events, such as war or pandemics, exert influence on the shaping of beliefs and practices surrounding death and dying.
»   Indigenous peoples of North America include numerous nations and tribal groups that are culturally diverse in their beliefs and practices concerning death and dying.
»   Death was a grim reality of daily life in colonial America. With the arrival of European colonists, a more broadly shared pattern of death beliefs and practices, grounded in commonly held Christian beliefs, began to develop and spread.
»   By the mid-nineteenth century, the American understanding of death was strongly influenced by Victorian-era beliefs and practices and the rapid industrialization of society. Death was still a part of daily life, but the focus shifted to beautifying and memorializing aspects surrounding death and the grieving process.
»   In the twentieth century, high mortality rates associated with the global influenza pandemic, war and military actions, and advancements in weapon lethality brought death in unprecedented numbers to families and communities across the country.
»   A flood of images and information about death can create a psychological and emotional desensitization to death.
»   Advancements in science and medicine have also delayed death by extending life spans and forestalling the inevitability of death.

Review Questions

1. How does the sociohistorical context shape our understanding of death?
2. Can you identify significant social events or changes that have impacted the U.S. experience with death?
3. What are the differences in historical patterns of U.S. death beliefs and practices based on social influences?
4. Discuss the relationship between social factors and the development of death beliefs and practices in the United States.

Key Terms

Review these key terms from the chapter. You can find their definitions in the glossary at the end of the book.

- » aesthetics
- » dominant culture
- » multicultural society
- » subculture

Chapter 4

Cultural and Religious Perspectives on Death

Día de los Muertos

It hits you without warning. That feeling of deep sadness and wanting to cry without knowing why, and then you remember: you lost a mother, a father, a brother, a child, or your life partner.

In my Mexican culture, Día de los Muertos is one of the ways we remember and honor our loved ones who are no longer with us in this world. On Día de los Muertos, we believe their souls visit us, so we prepare a big fiesta for them. We make their favorite food and get their favorite drinks. We make a beautiful altar in our home with their pictures, scented candles, and the traditional flower cempasuchil (marigolds).

Our family looks forward to this tradition every year, but this is not the only time of year we remember. We keep them close to us every day by keeping the altar permanently in our home. On birthdays, Mother's Day, Father's Day, and other special days, we light candles to honor and celebrate them, and their pictures remain on the altar all year long. It is comforting to feel them there with us.

In our culture, men and women deal with the loss of a loved one in different ways. My husband usually does not cry, but he tells me he cries from the inside of his heart. Over the last five years, he has had many losses: a younger brother, his mother, and, most recently, his father and older brother. Last Sunday, we went to a nephew's birthday party. Suddenly, I could see tears in my husband's eyes, and then he began to cry uncontrollably. It only lasted a couple of minutes, but I felt his sorrow. Later, he told me that this nephew's party last year was the final family party his father had attended before he died. He said, "I looked around and said to myself, someone is missing." Then he remembered it was his father.

We will ask the Father at our Catholic Church to dedicate a Mass for my father-in-law. This is what we do for all our loved ones. Afterward, we will go to the cemetery and take flowers to his grave. In the midafternoon, our family will gather at my sister-in-law's home to share stories. We will laugh, and we will cry. This is how our healing happens.

Linda H.

Introduction

This chapter will examine how cultural and religious beliefs provide guidance and structure to support people in their journey through the death experience. Describing world cultures and religious groups is riddled with challenges. How does one choose which groups to include and which to exclude? If a few examples are highlighted, how do you describe a culture or religion in its entirety? Although information about commonly shared cultural and religious practices can be a valuable resource for understanding and supporting people, it is less useful as a predictor of the beliefs and behaviors of any one specific individual.

The diversity within a culture and the complexity of people's experiences often make generalized assumptions, such as "Nigerians do X as part of their death rituals," difficult, if not impossible. To say, "Adrian is Nigerian; therefore, she will want to do X for her deceased father," could be potentially inaccurate or insensitive. Nevertheless, developing a greater understanding of differing cultural beliefs and practices surrounding death does provide an essential foundation from which to continue seeking a deeper, more specific understanding of a person's experience with death. This chapter aims to provide concrete examples of cultural and religious beliefs about death and dying from societies around the globe. Ultimately, you need to approach individuals as individuals and seek to understand how their particular social location, culture, and religious beliefs inform their understanding of death and dying.

Regardless of our cultural identity, each of us will experience and confront, alongside someone we love, these three phases of the death experience: the end of life, the time after death, and the grief that follows. During these phases, our cultural and religious beliefs, customs, and rituals guide us, help us process and express grief, and provide ways for the community to support the bereaved and reestablish a new rhythm of life. A fundamental understanding of how cultural and religious practices fulfill these needs acts as a base from which we can listen, ask how we can help, and offer support mindfully and compassionately. This chapter will explore the complexity of our cultural and religious beliefs and their impact on the common tasks across the death experience. We'll also discuss effective strategies to assist others during this challenging time.

Learning Objectives

These learning objectives will help you identify what's most important in this chapter. By the end of this chapter, you should be able to do the following:

» Describe how cultural and religious frameworks influence individuals and groups, resulting in diverse beliefs and practices about the death experience.

» Explain how cultural and religious traditions evolve through the interplay of enduring practices, individual variation, and the reciprocal influences of religion and culture.

» Identify how cultural and religious beliefs and practices shape the shared human experience of the three phases of death.

» Apply culturally responsive strategies for working with diverse groups of people within the context of the death experience.

Diverse Beliefs and Practices Surrounding Death

When you get up each day, you likely don't think about why you do what you do. Your behaviors are grounded in what you have learned in your culture and, perhaps, your religion. For example, Mila, a practicing Muslim, starts her day with Salat or daily prayers, considered one of the Five Pillars of Islam (figure 4.1). Ian may go for a morning walk as his family had always done in their native England, and Isabella's grandmother insists she finishes her chilaquiles, a Mexican breakfast dish, before she goes off to school. Both culture and religion guide people's lives, routines, conduct, and social interactions. These beliefs and practices shape all aspects of life, from what we eat for breakfast to how we greet the day and interact with others. These expectations are learned and passed down from generation to generation and from person to person.

It's challenging to discuss systems of belief and practice because they are so interwoven. **Culture** is a complex system of norms, language, symbols, beliefs, values, and specific rituals and practices that express these elements. **Religion** is a social institution or community whose members share beliefs and practices about a power greater than themselves. Often, we don't recognize our specific beliefs and practices until we're confronted by someone who does things differently. Culture is "just the way you live," and if you're surrounded by people of similar beliefs, there's nothing to call your attention to culture's importance. The experience of death is one of those moments that disrupt routines and responsibilities, making the systems of belief and practice more noticeable.

Figure 4.1. Salat is the Islamic practice of performing five daily prayers at prescribed times as an act of devotion, discipline, and connection to God.

Cultural and religious beliefs shape how people respond to death. These beliefs can reveal the purpose of life, explain the meaning of death, and describe what happens after death. They help unravel the mysteries of death and provide guidance to cope with the unknown. For example, Christians who believe in God's gift of eternal life may fear death less because they believe that after death they will go to heaven. Other cultures believe the spirits of those who die leave the body but remain nearby. From the invisible spirit world, they care for their family, alert them to dangers, and protect them from harm. Many traditional African cultures where ancestor worship is practiced believe that the souls of the dead can directly influence the living. These family members may find some solace and reassurance in knowing that loved ones who have died are watching over them.

Shared cultural and religious belief systems provide a meaningful way for people to navigate loss. While the experience of death is universal, the way that death is experienced and expressed is shaped by an individual's cultural and religious frameworks. In this section, we'll look at how these frameworks provide guidance and stability during uncertain times surrounding the death experience.

Cultural Frameworks and Rites of Passage

A person's **cultural framework** is the underlying structure or system that organizes and shapes one's beliefs and practices. This framework guides our daily activities. It influences how we perceive and understand the world. For example, respect for elders might be a cultural value, but the specific way that respect for elders is shown, such as bowing or using terms of honor, represents one's cultural framework. In the face of significant life events, such as the birth of a child or a family hardship, or when social conflicts or community needs arise, one's cultural framework offers solutions and appropriate responses. These shared patterns of beliefs and behaviors produce predictable social processes, social order, and support from others when needed.

Cultures designate **rites of passage** to mark a change in a person's social status and social role expectations. Rites of passage often align with a specific chronological or biological point in life that takes on a particular social meaning. For instance, getting married or becoming a parent represents a shift in social position, associated responsibilities, and public expectations. Specific rituals often accompany rites of passage and serve as a public acknowledgment of the person's new social position. This shared understanding alerts others to what to expect from the person and how to interact with them socially. Cultures often delineate key life stages, such as when a person achieves legal adulthood, becomes eligible to drive, celebrates turning a certain age ("Sweet 16" or Quinceañeras), or reaches retirement age (figure 4.2). With these changes in social status, culture helps people reorient to new types of social interaction, power, responsibility, and authority structures.

Death represents the ultimate change in social status. As the end of life nears, culture can guide people through this uncertain time. Cultural frameworks can provide predictable role expectations, a community support network, and beliefs and practices that comfort the dying person and their loved ones. For example, Teresa and her cousins grew up in a traditional Mexican family that stressed respect for their elders and the importance of familial responsibility. As their grandmother approached the end of her life, they took turns staying with her to ensure she had the twenty-four-hour care she needed. This example illustrates how cultural values and practices can offer structure, support, and meaning during life's final transition.

Figure 4.2. A quinceañera is a traditional Latin American celebration marking a girl's transition to womanhood on her fifteenth birthday.

Religious Frameworks and Rituals

French sociologist Émile Durkheim, who helped establish sociology as a discipline, focused much of his research on the functions of religion. Durkheim described religion as a system of beliefs and practices focused on the **sacred**, elements set apart and deserving of great respect and admiration. According to Durkheim, the opposite of the sacred was the **profane**, the everyday concerns of the individual. A belief in the sacred unites believers into one moral community. On the other hand, the profane is everything else—the routine, commonplace aspects of life that lack the special reverence associated with the sacred. Durkheim's work identified three fundamental aspects of religion: 1) a shared understanding of the sacred and sacred objects that are kept separate and distant from the everyday, "profane" world; 2) a set of beliefs and practices surrounding the sacred; and 3) a moral community of followers (Durkheim, 1915/1947).

Religious frameworks provide meaning, purpose, and a sense of connection to a higher presence. Religion can provide answers to existential questions about the purpose of life and our role in the universe, questions that otherwise intrigue us but remain beyond our comprehension. Scripture and faith-based religious teachings provide explanations for the origins of the universe, the Earth, and life. Creation stories often describe how people, animals, and plants emerged from nothingness as the will of God or Gods, deities, supernatural forces, or the natural forces of the physical world. Religious beliefs such as these provide a foundation for moral beliefs and behaviors. They also form a shared sense of community and connection to tradition through the continuity of rituals and practices.

Religion seeks to make sense of life's profound mysteries, particularly those surrounding death and what lies beyond. It offers answers where science cannot. Religious traditions often describe death as a transition to another life or state of being, rebirth and renewal in an endless life cycle, or a passage from mortality to immortality. In the afterlife or the next life, you might be reunited with loved ones and others who have died. For example, in The Church of Jesus Christ of Latter-day Saints, members in good standing may participate in a temple marriage, where their union is sealed for eternity. In contrast to the belief that marriages only last "until death do us part," temple sealings are a covenant or promise that the relationship will continue after this life and that nothing, not even death, can separate them.

Religion guides believers through the death experience and gives structure to the loss and grief after death. Most religions have specific traditions and rituals related to death and mourning, including practices for the final disposition of the body, that guide and comfort the bereaved. Generally, a designated ceremony honors the person who has died and supports the bereaved. Through these ceremonial practices, participants often find solace and comfort, allowing them to come to terms with the loss of their loved one.

Religion also provides a community from which strength and support can be drawn during grief and loss. A faith community with shared beliefs and practices stands by the bereaved and assists with daily tasks, such as food preparation, childcare, or household chores. The community can also be a source of encouragement and spiritual guidance by praying, reading scripture, engaging in rites and rituals, or giving moral and emotional support during grieving.

Similar to cultures based on religious and ethnic frameworks, occupational cultures also form around shared beliefs, norms, and values. Box 4.1 takes a closer look at how occupational groups, such as first responders, develop a subgroup within a culture.

Box 4.1: First Responder Culture

First responders, as a category of professionals, have their own occupational culture that has developed around their specific job responsibilities and work environment. These occupational groups generally include law enforcement, firefighters, emergency medical services (EMS), public safety (911) telecommunicators, rescue personnel, and the military, particularly the National Guard. Employed by government agencies and private companies, they provide immediate assistance and response to emergencies regarding the safety and security of people and property. Many people are attracted to this profession by a desire to help people and a shared value of the importance of public service.

First responders generally work physically and mentally demanding shifts where every call is a potential life-or-death situation. They develop a hyper-vigilant awareness as every detail may matter in preparing for the unpredictability of each call for service. The work necessitates an astute observation of people and the environment, pragmatic and rational thinking, and complex problem-solving skills. Intensive ongoing training and adherence to procedures are critical in ensuring the safety of the public and the first responders. These characteristics are often so internalized that they become an integral part of how they perceive and understand their world, both on and off duty.

The nature of this work fosters a strong in-group connection among first responders, reinforced by their shared work experience. Tragedy, suffering, and death are not just a part of their job. It is the very core of their daily work. First responders frequently have contact with people experiencing their worst day and take care of situations other people don't want to or couldn't deal with. They witness horrendous scenes and tragic situations so disturbing that others don't want to hear about them. Some situations are confidential and can't be discussed outside of work or should not be shared to protect the privacy of those involved. This requirement makes it difficult for first responders to discuss their day or even respond to innocuous conversation starters from family and friends such as "How was your day?" or "Anything interesting happen at work?"

Despite occupational commonalities, not all first responders are the same, nor do they share the same beliefs, behaviors, and values. **Microcultures** are subgroups within a culture. They exist within first responder culture as variations based on job categories and their requisite responsibilities and experiences: police officers differ from firefighters, who differ from EMS personnel, who differ from 911 telecommunicators, such as dispatchers and call takers. Although each microculture has variations in first responder characteristics, members still share sufficient attributes of first responder culture to be socially recognized and to self-identify as part of this overarching occupational culture. Mixed into these microcultures are individuals' personal beliefs and identities. However, despite all these variations, fundamental shared beliefs, behaviors, and values bond first responders within their professional culture.

Variation Between and Within Groups

Evidence shows that some form of religion has been practiced in every culture throughout human history. Global estimates as of 2020 show that 31.1% of the population identifies as Christian, 24.9% as Muslim, 15.2% as Hindu, and 6.6% as Buddhist (Pew Research Center, 2022). Figure 4.3 shows the worldwide percentage of major religious groups, including the approximately 16% of the population that is unaffiliated with a religion. Compare these numbers with the religious affiliation in the United States, as shown in figure 4.4. In the United States, 68% of the population identifies as Christian, with 33% identifying as Protestant, 22% as Catholic, and 13% as belonging to other denominations.

Although three in four Americans report a preference for a specific faith, there has been a notable shift away from religious affiliation in recent years. The number of people who report no religious affiliation has steadily increased from 3% in 1970 to 22% in 2023. There also appears to be a change in the influence of religion in people's lives. Attendance at churches, mosques, and temples has declined from 44% in 2000 to 32% in 2023 (reported as attendance in the last seven days), and when asked how important religion is in their lives, the number who stated it was "very important" has dropped from 61% in 1998 to 45% in 2023 (Gallup, 2024). Despite declining church attendance, religion remains deeply significant to many people, offering a sense of purpose, community, and a connection to something greater than themselves.

Figure 4.3. This chart shows the worldwide percentage of religious affiliation. Not shown on this chart: Other greater than 1%. Source: Pew Research Center, 2022.

Figure 4.4. This chart shows the percentage of religious affiliation in the U.S. Source: Gallup, 2024.

Global Religious Affiliation

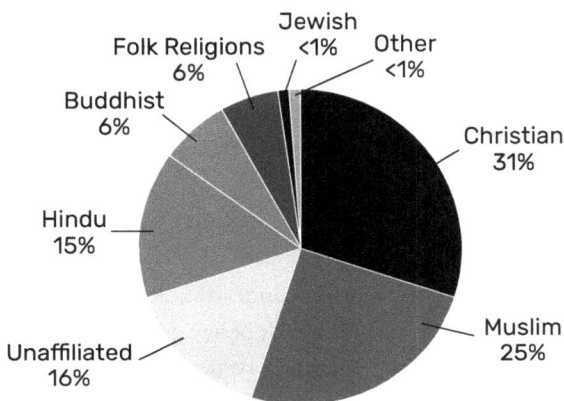

U.S. Religious Affiliation

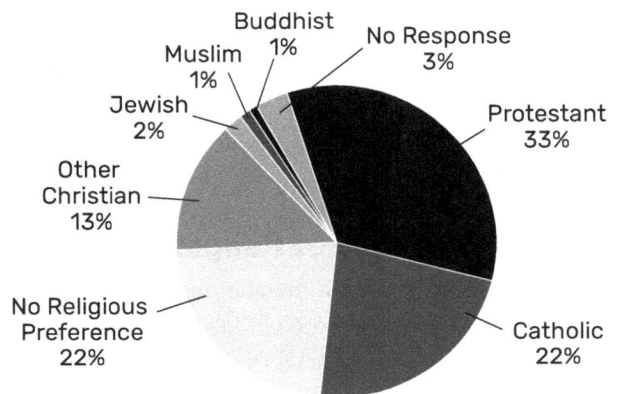

Cultural and religious groups share common beliefs and practices, but not all members think or act the same. Differences among individuals within a specific group are partly a result of ongoing changes in the group itself and differences in the social influences on individual members. Cultural and religious traditions are both static and dynamic. Some aspects of a culture endure and are passed from generation to generation and person to person, while other elements are discarded and new ones are added.

How Variation Happens

Most people are or have been members of several different cultures and subcultures, each contributing to a person's potential pool of cultural attributes. Perhaps you are part of a multicultural family or have immigrated and become part of another cultural community. Globalization has broadened the population diversity in the United States, increasing exposure to and interaction with people from around the world. Each of us is a part of numerous subcultural groups centered on professional, social, and leisure activities. For example, you could be a first responder, belong to a volunteer civic group, and be an avid hunter. Each of these subcultures has a set of shared behaviors, values, symbols, and beliefs that become a part of our overarching cultural framework.

Group variation occurs in many ways, but two specific ways variation happens are assimilation and amalgamation. **Assimilation** is when members of a subordinate group adopt aspects of a dominant group. For example, an African immigrant to Australia who learns English as a second language and adopts the typical dress and habits of other Australians is assimilating into the dominant cultural group. **Amalgamation** is when members of a dominant group combine with members of a subordinate group to form a new group. For example, Mexican culture is an amalgamation of Indigenous, European, and African cultures that resulted over many generations.

Differing combinations of subcultural interactions can influence the beliefs and behaviors of each member. These variations are even more complex as individuals make intentional decisions to incorporate or discard specific cultural elements based on personal preference. Changes in culture also occur over time, often hastened by technological advances. For example, smartphones and the internet have significantly impacted cultural ways of communication as people shift from face-to-face interaction to texting, instant messaging, and email. Even the language used to communicate has changed with the adoption and increasing acceptance of text speak and emojis.

Reciprocity of Religion and Culture

Religion is often a foundational element of our cultural frame, shaping our understanding of the meaning and purpose of life—both our mortal life and our eternal existence. For believers, religious beliefs and teachings form the core of their value system, determining what is considered right and wrong. Therefore, religion and culture have a reciprocal interaction as these beliefs, norms, and values co-exist in society. Cultural and religious beliefs interact and influence each other, and changes in one often cause a reaction or change in the other. The juxtaposition of these belief systems can be a source of tension or cohesion. One must examine the relationship and interconnectedness between religion and culture to understand the impact of religious beliefs on a person's cultural frame (Beyers, 2017).

The influence of religion on a culture is further complicated by the diversity of religious organizations within a cultural community. Religious groups often hold significantly different beliefs about the nature of the sacred and their relationship to a higher power, resulting in variations in their beliefs, practices, and rituals. Each major world religion has distinct branches, denominations, or sects with their own interpretation of religious doctrine and accompanying beliefs and practices.

For example, if you identify as a Christian, you share fundamental beliefs with other Christians. But you may also interpret and apply those principles differently depending on the teachings of your denomination or church. In the case of Easter, a high holy day for Christians, rituals and expectations vary depending on whether you are Baptist, Pentecostal, Latter-day Saint, Lutheran, or Catholic. These variations also occur in other major world religions. You can find differences within Islam between the two major branches, Sunni and Shia, the subsects within each branch, and the teachings of various Imams. Buddhism has several distinct branches, including Theravada, Mahayana, and Vajrayana, which share common tenets.

Even at the community level, local religious groups are not homogenous, as individual members or families may not adopt or adhere to all beliefs and practices. For example, a family may adhere to the fundamental tenets of their faith, regularly attend church services, and observe holy day rituals, but not follow church teachings regarding fasting or dietary and alcohol restrictions. While significant variations in beliefs and practices exist across and within cultural and religious groups, common experiences related to death can be found.

Common Tasks of the Death Experience

Since cultural and religious frameworks shape the meaning of death, they also structure how people respond to common challenges, tasks, and needs. Cultural and religious beliefs and practices can guide us through this complex experience, providing comfort, solace, and support. They can help foster a sense of order and predictability through familiar practices and rituals. In the following sections, we'll explore how cultural and religious traditions guide people through the tasks common to the three phases of the death experience: the end-of-life phase, the actively dying phase, and the grieving loss phase. While we have categorized tasks into three distinct phases, some activities span the phases.

Care Tasks Before Death

A person nearing the end of life is confronted by their mortality. Once-fleeting questions about the meaning of death become urgent and immediate. As they approach the end of life, they can't avoid the reality of death and its impact. Disruptions to the rhythm of life force them to react and tend to end-of-life needs. Social roles change, and medical appointments dominate routines. They may need to make difficult decisions about treatment and increasingly complex medical and personal demands. Medical care, individual needs, and quality of life become their primary focus and that of the family and friends who support them.

A person's response to the end of life is also influenced by their expectations of life and their understanding of the life cycle. Yak, a Buddhist from Thailand, was raised to believe that only nature knows when it is your time to die. For him, life has a natural rhythm, and things happen as nature intended. Yak's belief orientation differs dramatically from Anna's, who grew up in a culture that emphasizes individual agency and control. For Anna, life and death are to be controlled as much as possible through technology and medical interventions. These contrasting cultural frames can lead to differing responses to life-threatening diagnoses, medical treatment decisions, and preferences for end-of-life care.

Medical Decision-Making

Medical issues and overall physical, psychological, and emotional needs often consume more time and energy at the end of life, with numerous doctor appointments and ongoing medical decisions. Minimizing pain, managing troubling symptoms, and staying as comfortable as possible become the priority. As these needs intensify, people nearing the end of life rely more on others for help with daily activities and responsibilities like household chores, finances, and personal grooming.

Making medical decisions is one of the most time-sensitive and time-consuming end-of-life tasks. A steady stream of decisions must be made as medical conditions, patient preferences, and comfort issues emerge, including which procedures or medications are needed or preferred. At some point, a decision may have to be made concerning the efficacy of treatments and whether treatment should be suspended, especially when side effects and quality of life are counter-considerations. Chapter 6 will discuss end-of-life treatment decisions in more detail.

Cultural perspectives and beliefs may provide guidelines for determining who receives the patient's medical information and who makes treatment decisions on the patient's behalf. For instance, in many Asian cultures, such as traditional Chinese or Pakistani communities, family members actively shield terminally ill patients from any information about their condition to protect them from unnecessary distress (Kaufert & Putsch, 1997). However, U.S. dominant culture believes patients should receive medical information directly and make their own medical decisions whenever possible.

Some traditional Japanese communities have a more collectivist perspective, meaning these communities value group decisions, with the family taking the lead in making medical and treatment decisions. For example, when Himari's mother was diagnosed with stage IV cancer, her family gathered to make treatment and care decisions for her (Matsumura, 2002). Within some cultural communities, consulting with elders, cultural healers, or spiritual leaders may be customary before making a final treatment decision. For instance, after receiving a diagnosis from a Western doctor, a Native American might choose to consult with their Tribal medicine man or healer to discuss the medical results and seek counsel before making a treatment decision (Esposito & Kahn-John, 2020).

Cultural beliefs can include a preference for traditional medicines instead of or to augment Western medicines. This preference can affect end-of-life decisions and who will make those decisions. For instance, many African cultures avoid talking about or contemplating death or the death of others. In turn, this cultural tendency can determine whether people are open to discussing end-of-life directives like "Do Not Resuscitate" (DNR) or "Portable Orders for Life-Sustaining Treatment" (POLST) (Ekore & Lanre-Abass, 2016).

Whole-Person Care

Predicting the precise time that a person will die can be difficult. As individuals with unique physical and psychological characteristics, our bodies will shut down and cease functioning in their own way and at their own time. However, as a person gets close to death, common physical and psychological changes happen, such as irregular or shallow breathing, skin discoloration, hallucinations, and social withdrawal. These indicators generally appear during the last few days or hours before death. A person is in the **active dying phase** when they enter this final stage of the death experience (Hui et al., 2014). During the active dying phase, family and loved ones often observe these changes and can sense that death is near. See chapter 7 for more information about the active dying phase.

With heightened awareness of imminent death, caregivers prioritize making the dying person comfortable, providing support to their loved ones, and preparing for the end. As a person approaches death, the best possible quality of life involves recognizing the needs of the whole person in a respectful way that protects their dignity. Meeting the psychological, emotional, and social needs often involves providing a nurturing environment with loving relationships and opportunities for social interaction, all within the cultural or religious framework of the dying person (Staudt, 2013).

End-of-life care is a personal and emotional issue. As the dying person and their loved ones face this life transition, cultural and religious beliefs and customs offer a path and a system of support. One's cultural frame prescribes who cares for the dying person and where they should spend the end of their life. In some cultures, the family is expected to provide care for their dying loved one rather than home health care, nursing homes, or other medical staff. Marisol described what an honor it was for her family to care for their dying grandmother. She explained, "Growing up, she shared her love and wisdom with me. In my Mexican family, it was not only my responsibility to help but also was a way to show my love and respect for her."

Cultures may also identify specific family members who should provide the care: parents, children, immediate family, extended family, or honorary family members. As an example, Vietnamese customs of family-centered care include the specific expectation that the eldest son will take on this responsibility, with much of the hands-on care falling heavily on the daughter-in-law (Donovan & Williams, 2015). Who cares for a dying person also affects where a person may choose to spend the end of life. If the family needs to provide end-of-life care, having a loved one spend their remaining time in a nursing care facility or hospice medical unit is not considered a viable option. This custom stands in contrast to U.S. dominant culture, which emphasizes autonomy and is more accepting of loved ones receiving end-of-life care in nursing care facilities.

Adjustments in medical care are often necessary during the active dying phase. Ongoing medical care is critical to keeping a dying person comfortable. This level of responsiveness can be challenging if the person is not fully conscious or needs help communicating their needs. When pain management strategies must rely on nonverbal cues from the dying patient, attention to cultural differences in expressing pain and discomfort is critical to keeping the patient as comfortable as possible. Culturally responsive medical care providers can help manage pain and discomfort and relieve the stress of family concerns over the comfort of their loved ones.

The active dying process is a time to prepare for death. For the dying person, death's approach can trigger fears and anxiety, a need to put life in order, address relationships, say goodbyes, and tend to their spiritual life. Cultural customs can help alleviate fears, ease anxiety, and aid in navigating these tasks. Respecting a dying person's cultural understanding and beliefs about death can determine whether they find comfort in talking about their impending death or prefer to continue normal activities and conversations as much as possible. Differing cultural views of death can influence whether they find it meaningful for friends and family to come by to share memories, bring gifts or special foods, and say their goodbyes.

Religion provides rituals and practices that comfort the dying person and their loved ones. Religious clergy, priests, and lay ministers are often called to provide prayer and support for the dying person and their loved ones. For example, Catholics may call a priest to offer the Anointing of the Sick (figure 4.5). According to the United States Conference of Catholic Bishops (n.d.), this sacrament heals people from sin and hopes to cure physical ailments. It helps a person prepare for their final journey into the afterlife and brings them peace as the Holy Spirit guides them through the final steps to eternal life. Knowing the person has received this final sacrament can reassure others as they confront losing a loved one.

Hindus observe various rituals and practices rooted in the tenets and beliefs of their faith, which bring comfort to the dying and their loved ones. Common practices include placing pictures of their deity or deities at the head of the dying person, and the family may chant holy verses to create a positive environment. A few drops of holy water from the Ganges River are placed in the mouth, and one Tulsi leaf (holy basil) is put on the dying person's tongue to help the dying attain Moksha—the release from the cycle of eternal rebirth (Chandratre & Soman, 2021).

Figure 4.5. (left) This detail of a fifteenth-century altarpiece shows the Anointing of the Sick, part of *The Seven Sacraments* by Rogier van der Weyden. (right) The Anointing of the Sick in contemporary religious practice is a Catholic sacrament administered by a priest for spiritual and physical healing.

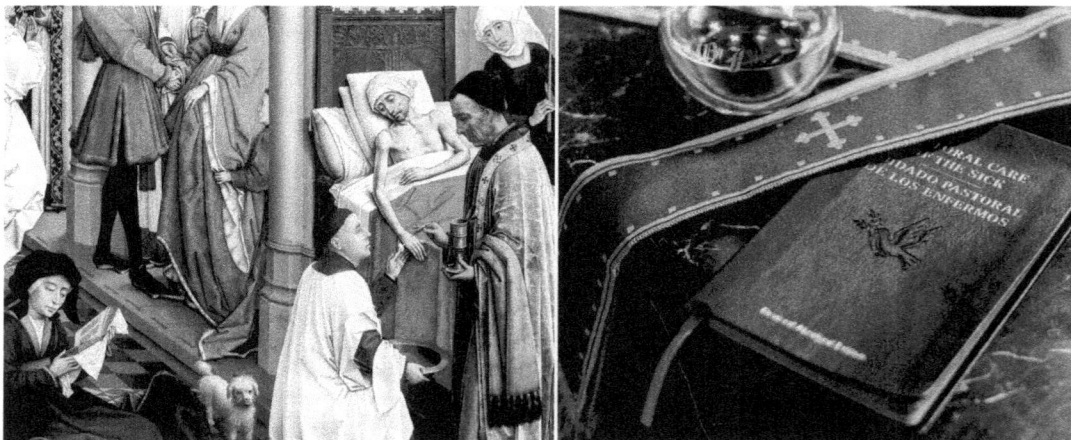

Culture and religion can become intertwined to create death rituals and practices, as seen in the celebration of Día de los Muertos (The Day of the Dead). This celebration combines Aztec cultural traditions centered on honoring and remembering those who have died with Christian traditions. In particular, Día de los Muertos adapts elements of the Catholic holy day celebrations of All Saints Day (November 1) to honor all saints, known and unknown, and All Souls Day (November 2) in remembrance of all the faithful who have died.

In the opening vignette, Linda described some of the ways her family celebrates Día de los Muertos. For example, ofrendas (altars) created in family homes often include traditional Aztec items such as marigolds, whose strong scent is believed to guide souls back home, and replicas of skulls, traditionally displayed to honor those who have died. Altars also contain Christian iconography such as a crucifix and pictures or symbols of the Virgin Mary. Lit candles symbolize the light of God and light the way home for the soul.

Tasks After Death

Cultural practices shape how people mourn, grieve, and adapt to a new reality in various ways and at their own pace. But after a death, some immediate practical matters must be addressed. Notifications of the death need to be sent to family, friends, and other community members, and arrangements for the final disposition of the body and preparations for funerary services or customs need to be made.

Funerary practices are the ways we prepare a person's body after death, how we commemorate their life, and the final disposition of their body. These practices mark the transition between life and death, provide a way to respect and honor those who have died, and reflect our beliefs. This social structure and these specific practices offer a framework but are often modified by family or personal preferences. While taking care of these logistics, loved ones are also experiencing the pain and distress of the death of their loved one, which can tax a family's social, emotional, and household resources. At times like this, our cultural and religious communities often provide a support network to help with whatever tasks need to be done.

Following the immediate flurry of decisions, activities, and customs, friends and family must confront a life without the person who died. For instance, after the death of her partner, Jana returned to work but had to figure out what to do with Piper, their fourteen-year-old golden retriever. Leslie had trained the dog since she was a pup and walked her daily while Jana worked long hours. With a return to daily activities and routines, a person's absence highlights the social roles they held. The hole that's left can be immense.

Notification

Notifying family and friends about a death is one of the first tasks to be addressed after someone dies. Customs impact how information about the death and the plans for rituals and services are shared with others. The information is frequently shared informally from person to person. However, the process may be more structured, whereby traditions and preferences specify who conveys the information, who should be told first, and how it is communicated (in-person, calls, social media, etc.).

For example, a friend described her personal experience surrounding death notification expectations: "When my dad died, I wanted to make sure all immediate family members were contacted before any announcement was made on social media. My aunt, my father's ex-sister-in-law with whom he hadn't spoken in decades, posted about his death on Facebook first and without asking, which felt like a violation of the unspoken rules of notification."

Preparing the Body

The body of a person who has died must then be prepared for final disposition. Beliefs set the context for how and what, if any, rituals should be performed. These practices vary depending on our underlying core beliefs about life and death. For example, Buddhist beliefs stress the importance of treating the body with the utmost respect because the spirit may linger close to the body and can be affected by what happens to the physical remains. Hindu customs emphasize avoiding unnecessary touching of the body because it is considered impure.

Cultural beliefs can prescribe rituals and practices to prepare the body to transition to the afterlife. Greek Orthodox practices include a priest saying the first prayer over the body and lighting a candle. This is repeated forty days later because it is believed the soul roams the earth for forty days before continuing to the afterlife. Customary Islamic beliefs and traditions say that a person should be laid out with their eyes closed, arms crossed over their chest, and body wrapped in a white shroud with their head facing Mecca.

Ceremonies and Rituals

Funerary rituals give people time and a process to remember, honor, and mourn the death of a loved one. They publicly acknowledge the loss and offer a system of support for mourners. Our cultural framework sets out specific practices and ceremonies before **interment**, how the body's final disposition takes place, and the rituals to help process grief.

Death rituals and commemorations take many forms. They may consist of a single ceremony, like a celebration of life or, as in traditional U.S. dominant culture, a funeral. They can involve a series of rituals over a few days, weeks, or months. Ceremonies can be simple and may only entail prayer or brief sharing of memories at the gravesite or a location significant to the person who died.

Alternatively, death rituals can be complex and involve multiple events that require detailed planning and logistics. For example, the traditional practices of the Igbo people who live primarily in southeastern Nigeria have a highly structured death notification process starting with immediate family, then extended family, and finally the community. Completion of the notification signals the beginning of public mourning. Traditionally, a wake includes community members followed by two funerals, each with specific expectations and rituals. The first funeral involves the burial, while the second is a ceremony to ensure safe passage to the world of the ancestors that occurs weeks or months later. Although many Igbo have converted to Christianity or Islam, they often intermingle their traditional rites with the expectations of their religious beliefs and practices (Asad & Nawait, 2018).

Customs often determine where services or rituals take place, how mourners act and dress, the words and music that should be used, and other ritualistic acts that can or should be performed at the funeral or burial. One traditional African American practice is for family and close friends to gather in a family member's home to plan the funeral. African American funerals often blend diverse faith traditions, cultural rituals, and personal touches that reflect the life, passions, and personality of the loved one. The service and burial details often depend on the person's role in their family or community. For example, funerals for matriarchs, patriarchs, ministers, or respected community leaders tend to be elaborate, with great attention to detail. Regardless of the funeral's size or the individual's social standing, services typically follow a familiar sequence of events, including vibrant music, heartfelt eulogies, and communal expressions of grief and celebration (Brooten et al., 2016; Griffin, 2017).

Funerary practices reflect cultural beliefs and frameworks. They symbolize the importance of honoring the person who has died or stress the role of rituals in helping the person transition to the afterlife. For example, followers of Santería, an Afro-Caribbean religion, emphasize the importance of funerary rituals in calming the person's spirit and clearing negative ties to the living or life experiences in preparation for the journey to the afterlife (Irwin, 2022) (figure 4.6). In many Asian cultures, including Chinese and Hmong, performing the funeral rituals correctly and appropriately is as important as the funeral itself because, according to traditional beliefs, the spirits of ancestors can influence the lives of the living. Regardless of the specific funerary practice, these rites mark the beginning of the grieving process.

Figure 4.6. Offerings are placed at the base of a sacred tree in Cuba as part of the Santería funeral rite.

Tasks of Grieving

The grief and loss experienced by the living after a loved one's death create a sense of disorientation and confusion. For example, when Anthony's spouse died, he suddenly became a widower, a single parent, and the sole income earner for his household. The grieving process helps us come to terms with our loss and confront the challenges of a new reality without that person. There can be shifts in statuses, roles, and relationships. Rituals and customs can assist with transitions like this and offer a pathway through mourning.

Expression of Grief and Remembrance

Cultural practices can influence how we express grief and mourn the death of a loved one. For example, in many Middle Eastern cultures, outward expressions of grief such as crying, sobbing, or wailing are more common and socially expected. But in many Western cultures, such as U.S. dominant culture and those in Northern European countries, mourners are expected to remain more stoic, keep grief private, or display subdued grief. Although these are broad generalizations, they demonstrate a significant variation in cultural expectations.

Tradition may also require specific actions that demonstrate grief. Different expectations for these expressions may be based on social factors like gender, age, or status. For example, women may have more latitude in outwardly expressing grief, while men are expected to contain their grief. Cultural beliefs and practices can also determine whether burial sites are considered public or private and who has access to them. In some Native American cultures, burial sites are private and sacred, and tribal cemeteries are only open to tribal members for visitation.

Cultural beliefs about death and mourning also dictate symbols like colors, flowers, and modes of dress. For colors, black is commonly associated with death in Western cultures, while it is white across much of Southeast Asia and purple in Thailand. For flowers, marigolds are frequently associated with death in Mexico and Latin America. In much of Europe, red poppies have represented death since the Roman Empire. These symbols announce a death and identify those grieving who may need help and support.

Remembering and honoring someone who has died is part of the grieving process. Rituals, shared practices, and individual actions are essential in helping us work through grief and adjust to the loss of a loved one. Simple and personal rituals, like visiting a loved one's gravesite, can be comforting. Leaving a symbolic token representative of the person who died or of the visitor's shared experience with that person is common. A Jewish custom is to leave a stone on the grave to show that the dead loved one was visited. Veterans often leave coins at the graves of fellow military service members. The coin's denomination determines who visited: a penny if you are a visitor, a nickel if you trained with them at boot camp, a dime if you served with them, and a quarter if you were there at their death.

In many societies, food has traditionally brought people together and strengthened bonds within the community. After a death, food continues to play a significant role in the rituals and customs that help support and console the bereaved. Prepared meals are often brought to the family so they can focus energy on tending to matters related to the death and the grieving process. It also helps console the bereaved by showing that they are not alone and others are available for support.

Food is also symbolic in many traditions and customs throughout the grieving process. Depending on cultural beliefs and practices, meals may be brought to the graveside to be left for the person who died, or family and friends may share food in communion with the deceased. Within some cultural frames, the deceased's favorite food may be left at the graveside as a symbolic gesture of the connection between the visitor and the person who has died. The use of food as a symbolic connection to, and interaction with, those who have died can be found in cultures throughout the world, from Greece to Vietnam, from Eastern Orthodox countries such as Belarus and Georgia, to the United States.

Time Frame for Grief Process

Grieving is a very personal and individualized process. There is no standard amount of time needed to navigate grief. We often rely on our cultural practices as we deal with the psychological and emotional stress experienced when a loved one dies. Our cultural frame can tell us how long it should take to complete this journey. It provides specific rituals and customs to mark the path and delineate the time needed to move through this process.

Time frames and sequenced events are intended to help us adjust to the loss of a loved one and move forward with our lives after death. They may prescribe the new roles family members are expected to take on. For example, in traditional Northern Tamil Hindu families, when a father dies, the eldest son becomes the family leader or head of the household; if there are no sons, the responsibility falls to the son-in-law. In the customs of many sub-Saharan countries, such as Angola, Ghana, and Uganda, a widowed person may marry their dead husband's brother or cousin.

The timing and sequencing of rituals that honor, mourn, and remember those who have died are shaped by our cultural beliefs. Some rituals address the immediate period following the death of a loved one. For example, in the Jewish faith, mourners sit Shiva after the death of a parent, sibling, spouse, or child. Shiva is a seven-day observance that begins after the family returns home from the funeral. It is a period of intense mourning when family and friends come to the family home to comfort the bereaved. The observance of Shiva involves symbolic customs like the family sitting on low chairs or benches, covering mirrors in the home, lighting a memorial candle, and offering prayers (figure 4.7). These rituals represent religious beliefs and traditions intended to honor the dead loved one, comfort the bereaved, and begin the healing process.

Figure 4.7. A Shiva candle, shown here with the traditional Star of David, is lit for seven days after someone dies.

Cultural expectations can also become institutionalized into our social systems, further perpetuating these beliefs and customs. For example, in the United States, many businesses offer three days of bereavement leave for employees, typically only for the death of an immediate family member. This policy reflects the dominant culture's emphasis on the nuclear family, its ideological roots in a capitalist economy, and the importance of work. U.S. social systems have effectively put a limit on the amount of time we are willing to give people to grieve and for whom. However, to be culturally responsive in your work and interactions, be aware that grieving is not completed in three days, and many cultures prescribe much longer periods of grieving.

Long-Term Remembrance and Grieving

Cultural customs describe practices that happen as time passes after a death. In many belief systems, it's common to perform rituals, ceremonies, or religious services at specified times in remembrance of the death of a loved one. For instance, members of the Greek Orthodox community celebrate a customary prayer service forty days after the death of a loved one and then annually near the anniversary of death. In other cultures, rituals of remembrance may be less structured and more individualized based on family tradition and personal preference.

As time passes, rituals tend to focus more on remembrance. The ongoing ways we honor people who have died are rooted in cultural and personal beliefs. In East Asian countries, Buddhists and Taoists observe a month-long celebration of their ancestors that culminates with the Hungry Ghost Festival. Customary practices include setting out food and symbolic paper offerings to appease the spirits. At the festival, paper lanterns are lit, placed on floats, and released onto bodies of water—the farther the lantern travels before catching fire, the better fortune the family will have during the coming year.

The gravesite often serves as an ongoing memorial to a loved one. Family and friends may decorate the grave to commemorate a birthday, the death date, holidays, or personal life events. Alternatively, visiting a place significant to the person who died can maintain ties with them. People visit specific locations to remember, talk to the person they lost, and share what is happening in their lives. For my brother Greg, visiting Bandon, Oregon, is where he feels closest to our dad. He wanders along the beach, sits at the lighthouse, and walks the jetty. He goes there to honor, remember, and feel connected to Dad.

Religious practices also offer long-term rituals and customs that function as acts of remembrance. The bereaved can include the person who has died in their ongoing prayers or light a candle in their place of worship. In some religions, a request can be made to have a worship day service offered on behalf of a person who has died. For example, in the Catholic Church, a mass can be offered on or near the birthday or death date of a person who has died.

In many countries, the practice of honoring and remembering the dead has been institutionalized into national observance. Often, schools close and work expectations and schedules are suspended so families and communities can come together in commemoration of those who have died. In the United States, the last Monday in May is the national observance of Memorial Day, which is rooted in a cultural tradition of honoring the military who have died in service. Originally called Decoration Day, this day of remembrance involved decorating the graves of family and friends who had died in battle.

In many countries, honoring one's ancestors is a cultural value. Obon, or the Festival of the Dead, is a widely celebrated annual event in Japan to honor deceased ancestors. Their spirits are believed to return to this world to visit their relatives. Paper lanterns are hung to guide the spirits, and food offerings are laid out at altars and temples. In Cambodia, people celebrate the festival of Pchum Ben every October, where the living give back to the dead in return for all their ancestors have done for them. Food is cooked and brought to the Buddhist monks in the belief that this good deed brings positive karma to their ancestors (figure 4.8). This celebration reminds the living about the importance of honoring one's ancestors. Participation in celebrations and commemorations such as these provides another way for the bereaved to remember and honor their loved ones who have died.

Figure 4.8. A group of Cambodians prays during Pchum Ben, a fifteen-day festival that honors deceased relatives.

Practical Applications

When a person is mourning a death, understanding their cultural frame can provide a clearer picture of how to support them through their grief. Cultural beliefs and practices guide how support is offered, accessed, and delivered. However, there are several reasons for variations among members of any specific cultural group. First, culture is both static and dynamic. Some aspects of culture change over time, while others remain steady and consistent. Understanding the broadly shared cultural norms of a given group does not necessarily predict the behavior of an individual member who may not conform to these norms for individual or contextual reasons. Second, a person's membership in multiple subcultural groups, each with its own beliefs and practices, causes additional variations. Therefore, taxonomies (such as "Italians think this way" or "Buddhists prefer that") have limited use; when used alone, these statements can result in misleading assumptions.

The complexity of cultural frames makes it difficult to provide a specific script for how to help support a person affected by the death of a loved one. So, what should or could you do to help someone who is in the dying process or the bereaved after the death of a loved one? **Cultural humility**, an ongoing practice of self-reflection, analysis, and learning about cultural frameworks other than your own, allows you to approach people with openness and authenticity. Regardless of how much you know about another person's cultural framework, being culturally humble will put you on solid ground to take the first step toward offering help and comfort.

When we're not sure what to do, uncertainty often causes us to hesitate and do nothing. We frequently pull back and avoid reaching out, fearful of making a mistake, hurting, or offending someone. If you find yourself in a situation where you don't know what to do or how to comfort someone, try the following: 1) practice compassion, curiosity, and patience; 2) listen actively; and 3) avoid assumptions. The next three sections will explore how to approach someone with cultural humility as you help them navigate the choppy waters of death, dying, and bereavement.

Practice Compassion, Curiosity, and Patience

It can be challenging to know how to reach out and support others who are being impacted by death or the approaching death of a loved one in a culturally respectful way. As you know, understanding death and dying and approaching the tasks associated with death can best be understood through a cultural framework. The first step in helping others is to think about and understand your own cultural frame, although it may feel counterintuitive. It is natural to reflect on your experiences when deciding how to help someone else. We all make assumptions that what worked well for us will be equally helpful for someone else in a similar situation. Awareness of your cultural point of view and how that affects how you see and experience death opens the opportunity to recognize and consider how the same is true for others operating with a different cultural frame.

Our compassion and sensitivity to the emotional suffering of others drive us to want to do something. Compassion is an awareness of someone else's distress along with the desire to ease it, not just telling someone you care. Compassion involves acting before being asked for help, which shows you care. Compassion motivates us to reach out and go out of our way to help. Being compassionate *and* curious can bring us closer to cultural humility.

Curiosity about another person's cultural and religious framework naturally positions you to be culturally humble. When you're aware of your own perspective, feelings, and motivations, you can begin to inventory what you already know about another's beliefs and customs and identify what you need to know to be as supportive as possible. Once you understand what you know about someone's cultural identity, you can also identify what you don't know. Often, what we don't know leads us to make assumptions, and assumptions can cause missteps, hurt feelings, or unintentional exclusion. If you don't know something, ask. Extended family members, friends, or religious or cultural leaders may be able to assist you in identifying ways to offer help and support that align with their cultural beliefs. You may also be able to contact religious or cultural groups, organizations, or networks that can communicate the family's needs.

Patience is a critical practice in bereavement. Recognize and accept that when you reach out to grieving people, the discomfort and awkwardness of not knowing what to say or do is normal. It's okay to acknowledge this discomfort, whether you offer help or receive it. Moreover, if missteps or miscommunication occur, assume good intentions and give yourself and others grace while moving forward. When an offer of help or support is made, there can be multiple reasons why it might be declined. Avoid automatically assuming it is unappreciated or in conflict with cultural practices.

Also, the grieving person may not have an answer to the question, "What can I do for you?" People can be so overwhelmed with emotions and the gravity of bereavement that they may not be able to give you a clear answer. Offering an array of suggestions can be helpful. Even taking on some of their daily tasks, such as walking the dog, picking up some groceries, or taking their child to the park to play, may ease their burden.

Practice Active Listening

One strategy for providing social support to people as they move through the difficult times surrounding death and dying is to listen. Allowing someone to talk about what is happening, what they think, and how they feel can be comforting and reassuring. By verbalizing their thoughts, concerns, and emotions, they can help us understand how to support them in navigating death and the dying process. Moreover, when we listen to others and they are heard, it can validate and reaffirm their experience.

First, let the bereaved person determine when they are ready to talk, how the conversation is structured, or if it takes place. Once you know someone has lost a loved one, make a small gesture to let them know you are available when they are ready to connect. Sending a card, email, or text letting them know you're thinking about them and that you're there for them allows them to reach out in their own time and way. Once they are ready to talk, practice active listening.

Active listening involves being fully present with all your senses, bringing your full attention, and focusing on the person speaking. Nonverbal cues play a significant role in communication. Therefore, active listening includes paying close attention to facial expressions, voice tone and inflections, hand gestures, body posture, and movements. Using open-ended questions and leaving space in the conversation allows the speaker to verbally process their thoughts and decide what they want to say. For instance, asking, "How are you feeling today?" instead of "Are you sad?" encourages a person to think about and describe their feelings. Be patient and wait for the person to open or continue the conversation, and avoid rushing in to fill lulls and silent spaces.

Sometimes, a person might need to express their thoughts and feelings. In these circumstances, it is crucial to provide a safe, judgment-free space for them to express their thoughts and emotions, and to be there to listen and offer support. For example, Becca, an emergency department nurse, was on duty when a coworker brought in her eighteen-month-old child, who had stopped breathing and had no pulse. The ER staff did everything they could, but they were not able to revive the little girl. Becca had to call the official time of death. She told me, "I just needed to vent my frustration over not being able to save the child and the deep sorrow I felt for these young parents and what they were going through. I found an empty room away from the ER to process what had happened, but what I really needed was for somebody to be there and to hear me." Being heard and having your experience and feelings validated is essential in processing grief.

Practice Avoiding Assumptions

We view and understand the world around us through our own cultural lens and life experiences, which provide a knowledge base we reference when responding to situations. We know our experiences to be true, so we often assume our perspective is true for others. However, generalizing our understanding of death and dying to others, especially in a cross-cultural context, can be problematic. You've learned that responses to death and dying vary from person to person within a culture. Individuals often adapt cultural beliefs and practices to meet their needs and circumstances, sometimes putting them at odds with broader cultural expectations (American Society of Clinical Oncology, 2018). Multicultural families may also develop their own set of beliefs and practices.

We make assumptions all the time. It's part of how the human brain makes sense of the world. Once we believe something to be true, we often selectively notice things that appear to reaffirm our assumption, a process called selective perception. This leads us to take actions that align with our assumptions. For example, your assumption that a coworker needs or would welcome outside help as their mother is dying may not be accurate. Their cultural practice might frown on outsiders helping during this time. Therefore, just showing up to offer a meal could be perceived as intrusive during a private time.

In another case, an EMS crew responded to an eighty-year-old woman who had fallen. When the crew arrived, she was conscious and appeared okay, but she needed to be checked and assisted in getting off the floor. Matt, one of the EMTs, checked her vital signs, and he asked the patient's adult child about any existing medical conditions, medications, and if she had fallen before. The woman interrupted, saying, "I can answer for myself if you just give me a chance!" Matt realized that, due to his experience on similar calls where older patients couldn't provide this information, he assumed it would be the same with this woman.

We often base our assumptions and actions on visible symbols. Say your neighbor, Robert, is dying, and while visiting, you see a crucifix on his bedside table. You assume Robert is Catholic and ask if his family has called a priest to come and offer comfort and prayers. Robert tells you that, in fact, he's not Catholic—a friend had left the crucifix. You would likely feel sheepish, and your assumption could affect the quality of your visit with Robert.

Some cultures and religions keep traditions around death private and may not be open to sharing their beliefs and practices with others. For example, for some Native American tribes, many death-related practices are sacred and only talked about within the tribal group. In other situations, there may be times when your help is not accepted or wanted because of cultural traditions or personal preferences that stress the value of self-sufficiency. Checking your assumptions and putting aside your pride allows the focus to remain on the people who need your support.

Case Studies

Patterns of migration and globalization continue to diversify the cultural makeup of nations around the world. In particular, the United States, with its long history as an immigrant nation, continues to attract a significant number of migrants. The resulting cultural groups that make up the United States are far too numerous to be adequately covered in any book, let alone in a single chapter. Therefore, the question then becomes: Which groups are included in a discussion of cultural groups in the United States, and which are not? The following case studies provide a sample of the numerous rich and varied cultural groups that make up U.S. society and are examples of how religion can become so intertwined into cultural beliefs and practices as to be indistinguishable. These examples provide an opportunity to begin learning about other cultures and offer a chance to apply some of the concepts discussed in this chapter.

Russian Old Believers

Russian Old Believers are Russian Orthodox Christians who resisted the reformation of the Church in the mid-1600s and maintained the old liturgy and practices. Old Believers were persecuted by the Russian government and often had to practice their faith secretly or flee the country. Today, Old Believer communities are found within the United States, mainly in Oregon and Alaska, and worldwide, in Canada, Australia, New Zealand, Brazil, Argentina, and Bolivia. Communities also remain in remote areas of Russia and many former Soviet nations like Georgia and Kazakhstan. Old Believers often continue to dress in traditional clothing—women wear long, colorful dresses and scarves to cover their heads, and men are bearded and dress in long-sleeved, high-neck shirts. Both men and women wear braided or woven belts fringed or tasseled at the ends.

Today, Old Believers have varying interpretations of church rituals and practices. However, a shared core of beliefs and practices remains, including common Christian beliefs about salvation, the day of judgment and resurrection, and the afterlife. The rituals marking the transition from life to the afterlife are fundamental to their belief system and integral to their shared identity. Although the funeral practices of Old Believers may vary based on the specific church community, the geographic location, and generational differences, there are commonly shared rituals.

For instance, in Oregon's Old Believer community, when someone dies, the funeral and burial generally occur within twenty-four hours of death. When an unattended death occurs, it is reported to the local authorities, and a church priest is called to perform ritual prayers. Word of the death spreads quickly in this tight-knit community. Family and friends gather around the immediate family and pray over the body, often arriving before local authorities. The funerary rituals begin once the legal process is completed and the body is officially released to the family. Family, friends, and the community are responsible for the preparation and final disposition of the body. The body is washed in the family's home and then placed in a shroud. A plain wooden coffin is built. The body is never left alone. Someone always stays and prays over the body.

Figure 4.9. This headstone shows a Russian Orthodox cross.

The body is often taken by private vehicle to the church for a formal funeral service, typically with an open casket. Mourners approach the coffin and bow to the deceased person out of respect and to seek closure of any unresolved issues. As part of this ritual, attendees often kiss the person on the lips through a translucent veil draped over the head. If the death occurs early in the day, burial is completed by sundown when possible or the next morning when necessary. The coffin is transported to a communal Russian cemetery where a hand-dug grave has been prepared. The coffin is lowered into the grave, prayers are recited, and the grave is covered with dirt by hand. The grave is then marked with a Russian Orthodox three-beam-style cross (figure 4.9). After the burial, all return to the family's home for a funeral dinner. After dinner, the family hands out milostinya (gifts), most often money, to the guests with requests for prayers for the deceased.

The first forty days after death are a time of intense prayer for the deceased. Payments are also given to designated church members, often older women or widows, to continue praying for the dead person during this period. It is believed that on the fortieth day, the deceased is given up to God for final judgment, and, if worthy, their soul enters heaven. After the forty-day observance, final rituals and prayers occur at a church service, and the family may host a final dinner (Morris, 1991; *Old Believers*, n.d.).

The Roma

The Roma are an ethnic group originating in the Punjab region of northern India. Traditionally, a nomadic people, historians believe they migrated through what is now Iran, Armenia, and Turkey, arriving in Europe over one thousand years ago. Today, people of Roma descent can be found worldwide, but the largest populations are centered in Europe, the Middle East, and the Americas. The Roma have often been called "Gypsies" because they were mistakenly said to be from Egypt. Today, this term is considered an insult, and the Roma reject this identification.

Since arriving in Europe, ruling governments have persecuted the Roma. They have been enslaved, sentenced to death, and subjected to racism, expulsion, and genocide. In modern times, the Nazis called the Roma "racially inferior" and killed hundreds of thousands in concentration camps (United States Holocaust Memorial Museum, 2021). In the late twentieth century, they continued to experience discrimination and oppression, especially in the former Soviet Union and its aligned nations. Despite this, the Roma have maintained strong in-group cohesion through their nomadic traditions and shared experiences. Where Roma have settled, they have formed distinct groups called tribes, nations, bands, or family clans.

The Roma tend to adopt the dominant religion in their country of residence but combine it with their cultural traditions and practices. For the Roma, the supernatural world of spirits is a fact of life. Among these spirits are mulo (the spirit or soul of the dead), who return from the other world in human or animal form. Mulo return to deal with unsettled conflicts or insults to their name or property, or if they can't find peace in the other world. They are not necessarily harmful and may return to defend their families. Those who do seek revenge on the living must be warded off by ceremonies and spells (Directorate General of Democracy and Human Dignity, 2023).

For the Roma, end-of-life beliefs, practices, and rituals vary by geographic location, level of assimilation and acculturation, tribe, and band; however, there are commonly shared practices. For example, Roma believe that a dying person should not be left alone, so as death approaches, family and friends will visit often and for long periods. Traditionally, Roma people always died at home, and the visitation and vigil would take place there. Today, many Roma die in hospitals where ongoing visits by large groups of family can be challenging to accommodate in small hospital rooms.

When a person dies, mourning becomes the all-consuming focus until the burial. Traditionally, family members do not bathe, shave, or comb their hair. The body of the deceased person should not be touched to avoid the risk of marimé (contamination) and unnecessary exposure to spirits. The body is brought into the home the night before the funeral, where a wake is held. Funerals incorporate differing religious rites, personal preferences, and specific tribal and clan beliefs. Roma funerals are large gatherings where family and friends gather to honor the deceased person and usher them to the next world. Funeral services may be held at a church, funeral home, community center, or gravesite. Traditionally, mourners wore white for purity or red for vitality, but today, black is often adopted as the color of mourning. Outward expressions of grief, such as profuse crying, wailing, and lamentations, escalate during the service and reach a peak as the coffin is lowered into the grave (Cervank, 2017; Romani customs and traditions, 1997).

Some tribes and clans hold an extravagant dinner called a pomana to mark the end of the funeral rituals. These meals may also be held at intervals during the first year after a death: nine days, six weeks, six months, and one year. Traditionally, the dead person's possessions were burned after the funeral to destroy all material connections to them. With the expenses surrounding death and the cost of a funeral, possessions are now often sold to help alleviate the financial hardship placed on the family.

Rituals are followed to protect and honor the individual's memory. Photographs are placed on the graves to connect family and friends with the spirit of their loved ones. On special occasions, family and friends may bring alcohol and favorite foods to the grave or set a place at the dinner table and share a meal and talk with their loved ones. At holiday celebrations during the first year after death, a place is reserved for the deceased person where food is served as if they were still alive (Romani customs and traditions, 1997; Directorate General of Democracy and Human Dignity, 2023).

Conclusion

As people of all cultures and religions face the end of life, death, and the loss of loved ones, they encounter common tasks. There is no one way to navigate these challenges. The death and grieving experience is often guided by one's cultural framework, where beliefs and practices provide a script and a system of support. When reaching out to share concern, consider cultural differences to make your endeavors more meaningful and helpful. However, cultural and subcultural variations, as well as the confounding effects of personal preferences, can complicate the process of approaching and reaching out to others respectfully. Begin by being culturally humble. Check what you know about a culture's practices, be willing to learn more, and be open to re-evaluating your information base. You can then actively listen, ask questions, and, most importantly, be patient. Allow the time and space for the person who is dying, their loved ones, or the bereaved to share their thoughts, practices, and needs, and then let their preferences guide your support for them.

Summary

» Cultural and religious beliefs and practices offer people guidance and support as they navigate the challenges surrounding death.

» People turn to cultural practices to help them adjust to the changes in social interaction and social relationships that occur after a death.

» Religious beliefs provide people with rituals and a social support system to help them with the grieving process and to restore order to their lives.

» Regardless of religious or cultural frames, common tasks surrounding the death experience include care before death, tasks after death, and grieving the death.

» These common tasks are influenced by cultural and religious beliefs.

» The diversity in cultural and religious frames makes it challenging to know how best to support a person who is dying or who is grieving the death of a loved one.

» Practicing compassion, patience, and a genuine interest in understanding how to best provide support are effective strategies for navigating cultural differences.

» The use of active listening strategies can open channels of communication and offer the bereaved person the opportunity to express their feelings and articulate their needs.

» Practice avoiding assumptions about what a person is feeling or how to best provide support during the death experience—if you don't know or are unsure, ask.

Review Questions

1. What role does religion play in society and culture? Discuss the functions of religion and the interconnected ways that religion and culture influence each other.

2. What factors contribute to the evolution of cultural and religious traditions, and how do individual differences and the reciprocal influences between religion and culture shape these changes?

3. Describe the impact of religious and cultural beliefs on individuals and communities when it comes to core values associated with death. Provide examples from diverse cultural and religious contexts to support your answer.

4. What evidence of assimilation and amalgamation do you see within cultural and religious communities? Consider factors such as heightened self-awareness, multigenerational differences, and geographic variations.

Key Terms

Review these key terms from the chapter. You can find their definitions in the glossary at the end of the book.

» active dying phase	» cultural humility	» profane
» active listening	» culture	» religion
» amalgamation	» funerary practices	» religious framework
» assimilation	» interment	» rites of passage
» cultural framework	» microcultures	» sacred

Chapter 5

—

Navigating Life-Threatening Disease

Vignette **The Ticking Clock**

When my husband was diagnosed with a malignant tumor on his left kidney, the tumor and kidney were surgically removed. His six-month check showed he was clear of cancer, and the prognosis was good. Doctors determined he didn't need follow-up treatment. As we waited for his one-year routine scanning, the tension and anxiety began to build. We knew the futility of worrying, but we struggled to remain calm, hoping for the best and also preparing for the ever-present possibility that the cancer could return.

As my husband and I waited in the exam room, the doctor stuck his head in to let us know that he wanted to take a closer look at the scan and consult the radiologist. Clearly, he was concerned. As he left, my heart sank, and my stomach started turning. Neither of us moved nor said a word, afraid to say anything that might crack open all our emotions, thoughts, and fears. We both wanted to appear calm to reassure the other while we knew the news was likely not good.

At that moment, a surreal, disjointed thought occurred to me—*this is like a movie scene where the patient is waiting for the test results*. You know the one: the viewer can hear the characters' thoughts; the camera focuses on the ticking clock on the wall and then zooms out to show people going about their normal business. It felt exactly like that. I could hear people walking by in the hallway outside, the phone ringing in the outer office, and my husband's slow, controlled breathing.

Questions sped through my mind: What might be happening? What will this mean? How can I make this easier for him? How do we tell the kids? And because I know him nearly as well as I know myself after thirty-five years of marriage, I worried about how he was handling the same barrage of thoughts and emotions.

The doctor's reappearance snapped me back to reality. The scans showed two tumors on my husband's remaining kidney. I reached for my husband's hand and held it tightly. As silent tears streamed down both our faces, I heard the doctor say something about the tumors likely being malignant, that they were intertwined with the kidney, and that he would try to save at least part of his remaining kidney. From that moment on, our lives were forever changed.

Patricia

Introduction

When a person receives the diagnosis of a life-threatening disease, death becomes more immediate, and they are forced to confront their mortality. How someone responds to this reality is affected by the diagnostic process, the nature of the disease, and their cultural and personal understanding of the disease. The diagnostic process can be complex and, at times, lengthy.

From the time a person first experiences physical symptoms or receives abnormal medical test results to the determination of a conclusive diagnosis, it may involve weeks or months of additional medical testing and examination by medical specialists. Once diagnosed with a life-threatening disease, a patient confronts the task of understanding the disease and its likely progression. Patients frequently turn to the internet to learn about the disease, understand how it affects their bodies, and become familiar with medical and health terminology.

Each person approaches these tasks differently depending on their social and cultural frame, as well as their personality and outlook on life. In this chapter, you will examine the journey through the diagnostic process, exploring the experience of facing an unknown sea of possible outcomes.

Learning Objectives

These learning objectives will help you identify what's most important in this chapter. By the end of this chapter, you should be able to do the following:

- » Describe personal and social institutional complexities inherent in the diagnostic process of a life-threatening disease.
- » Explain the role of technology and the internet in accessing health and medical information about a diagnosis.
- » Discuss the role personal and social factors play in shaping the understanding and responses to the diagnosis of a life-threatening disease.

Long-Term Disease Trajectories

A **chronic disease** is a life-threatening condition that can lead to the death of a patient. Many life-threatening diseases, such as cancer, HIV, coronary heart disease, diabetes, and degenerative neurological conditions, affect a person's quality of life and have the potential to limit their life expectancy. The resulting illness may be treatable and remediated, but it may still shorten the patient's life. Chronic diseases can be managed for a time, but eventually, they lead to death. For instance, heart failure can be controlled and treated with a variety of medications. However, the continuing decline in heart function reaches a point where medications can no longer compensate for the weakening heart.

When discussing life-threatening diseases, **biological pathology** refers to the study and diagnosis of a disease. Biological pathology involves using medical procedures and testing to examine biological changes in the body and determine the physiological consequences of these changes. This process is used in the diagnosis of diseases. Once a patient has received a diagnosis, they often have a discussion with their health care provider about the implications of the disease.

A **disease trajectory** describes the likely progression of the disease over time, the manifestation of symptoms, needed treatment regimens, and the overall impact of the disease on their life. A patient's growing awareness of a life-threatening disease develops during the diagnostic process. Symptoms or routine medical testing may trigger initial suspicions of a life-threatening disease. Sometimes, a diagnosis is more complex and takes longer to determine.

Regardless of how the diagnosis is identified, patients receive medical information from their health care provider to help them understand their medical condition once it is confirmed. For instance, after Benjamin's tests indicated he had early signs of Alzheimer's, he met with his doctor to get a better understanding of what to expect over time, discuss treatment options, and what would be needed to prepare for the later stages of the disease. Chapter 6 will discuss end-of-life treatment decisions in more detail.

The meaning of a life-threatening disease includes far more than the biological facts. Interpreting medical information is influenced by someone's personality and psychological makeup, which influences how they experience the disease. In the following sections, you will examine the diagnostic process and its meaning to the patient and their family.

Awareness of the Condition

A doctor can describe what is known and understood about the biology and trajectory of chronic, life-threatening diseases. However, one's personal understanding of the diagnosis may differ greatly from the professional medical staff's understanding. For the patient, their family, and friends, the meaning of a life-threatening diagnosis is not shaped solely by the biological trajectory of the disease. The diagnosis is experienced subjectively within the broader context of the patient's daily reality. When a person finds out they have cancer, the doctor can describe its location and stage of development, recommend treatment options, and provide optimal outcomes of the treatment. But for the patient and their family, the meaning of the diagnosis goes beyond the medical facts: Will they be able to keep working? How will they pay for medical care? Can they still enjoy the hobbies and activities they love?

A patient's understanding and interpretation of a diagnosis impact their overall emotional and psychological well-being and influence how they and their loved ones cope. However, navigating the health care system and gaining access to needed medical diagnostic tests can be frustrating and daunting. Delays inherent in the medical system introduce periods of uncertainty and can slow the flow of information. The diagnostic process can include multiple waiting periods—waiting to see a specialist, waiting for tests to be completed, and waiting for test results. When the patient eventually receives information, it can be overwhelming and challenging to process. Many repetitions of this cycle may occur before the patient receives a final diagnosis. As a result, how someone understands a life-threatening medical condition may morph over time as more information becomes available during the diagnostic process.

The Diagnosis

The awareness and understanding of a chronic, life-threatening disease often begin with a medical **diagnosis**, a determination of a disease or medical condition. A person might experience symptoms or physical changes, suspect the presence of disease, and seek medical help to identify the cause. In some cases, minor symptoms associated with common ailments like a cold, flu, or digestive upsets can indicate a more serious disease. For instance, Matt, a sixty-year-old man, went to the emergency room of a small rural hospital complaining of a persistent cough, thinking he had a bad cold that may have turned into pneumonia. Tests discovered multiple masses in his lungs, and he was referred to an oncologist who confirmed he had lung cancer. Figure 5.1 shows the five stages of life-threatening disease originally proposed by Dr. Kenneth Doka (1993): prediagnostic, acute, chronic, terminal, and recovery.

Figure 5.1. Dr. Kenneth Doka's research proposed five stages of life-threatening disease. The common tasks related to coping with each stage differ.

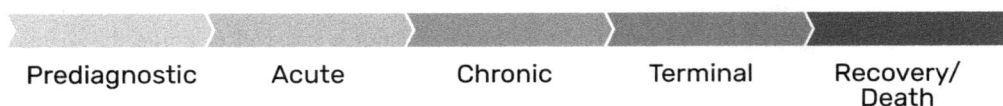

Prediagnostic	Acute	Chronic	Terminal	Recovery/Death

Other times, the underlying disease may go unnoticed, leaving the patient unaware of its presence until it is discovered through unrelated medical exams or testing. This was the case for Ray, who came into the hospital for a possible broken arm. The X-rays of his arm revealed a tumor that was later determined to be bone cancer. Regardless of how the medical journey unfolds, once a patient receives a formal diagnosis of a life-threatening disease, the situation takes on a new reality and meaning.

Sometimes, health care providers can reach a clear diagnosis early in the medical examination process for some patients. For others, no one test or procedure may be definitive, or the results may indicate multiple possibilities that require further exploration. In these cases, more tests and procedures are needed to identify the causes of the condition and develop a specific diagnosis. For patients, an elongated diagnostic process can cause additional anxiety. On top of this, the tests and procedures themselves can be stressful. Understanding what various procedures involve and how they work can help demystify the available options. See box 5.1 for a list of commonly used diagnostic tests.

Diagnostic tests and procedures can also produce conflicting indicators of various conditions, requiring additional testing. For example, Marta presented with severe abdominal pain and received an ultrasound examination that indicated a small mass on the liver. She was referred to her physician, who ordered a CT scan to examine the mass more closely. The CT scan found that the mass was a tumor or cyst on the liver, but it also noted that the spleen was enlarged and there was an irregularity in the shape of the kidney. After an appointment with a specialist, she was scheduled for a PET scan that indicated that the enlarged spleen was likely due to a blood-related condition. More lab work was

Box 5.1: Common Tests Used in the Diagnostic Process

Diagnostic tests can provide information and also conflicting results, further complicating the diagnostic period. The following tests are described in the general order in which a patient is likely to encounter them. As you familiarize yourself with these standard tests, reflect on these questions:

» How might the uncertainty of waiting for results contribute to a patient's anxiety and stress?

» What are the potential physical discomforts associated with going through multiple diagnostic tests?

» What strategies can health care providers use to help patients understand and cope with conflicting or inconclusive test results?

» What financial or logistical burdens might patients face due to the costs of multiple diagnostic tests?

Type of Test	Description
lab work	collection of blood or urine samples to check for changes in health, diagnose medical conditions, and monitor disease progression
EKG/ECG (Electrocardiogram)	evaluation of electrical signals from the heart via electrodes attached to the outside of the body
X-ray	use of external radiation to produce images of internal tissue, bones, and organs
ultrasound	use of sound waves to create an image of organs, structures, and tissues inside the body
CT scan (Computed Tomography)	combination of X-ray images taken from different angles to create cross-sectional images of bones, blood vessels, and soft tissue for a detailed, three-dimensional perspective
MRI (Magnetic Resonance Imaging)	use of a magnetic field and computer-generated radio waves to create images of organs and tissues, especially useful in examining the nervous system
PET scan (Positron Emission Tomography)	use of special dye with radioactive tracers to examine the metabolic or biochemical functions of tissues and organs
scoping	use of a flexible tube with a camera lens on the tip that is inserted into the body to provide a detailed view of any area of concern
biopsy	analysis of samples from tissues, cells, or specific growths removed from the body by scraping the tissue surface, withdrawn using needles, or surgically extracted

ordered, followed by a bone marrow biopsy. After three months of testing and medical procedures, the cyst was surgically removed from her liver, and she was diagnosed with two co-existing chronic, life-threatening blood disorders. The nonmalignant cyst had caused the original pain, but the testing process had uncovered an underlying disease that had yet to become symptomatic.

The Waiting Process

In many cases, waiting for a specific diagnosis is one of the most difficult experiences a person ever faces. Many patients describe the diagnostic process as confusing and stressful, filled with unfamiliar medical terminology and procedures, bureaucracy, and incessant waiting. Megan shared her experience when she went to a medical appointment with her elderly father concerning a mass they had found in his esophagus. As the doctor explained the diagnosis, many medical terms were unfamiliar, and the information was coming so fast she couldn't process what was being said. She described feeling frustrated, angry, and confused as she tried to take notes without knowing how to spell the words. Fortunately, her phonetic spelling got her close enough that an online search when she got home helped her find that he had been diagnosed with adenocarcinoma (cancer that forms in glandular tissue, such as the esophagus).

Beyond the medical process, in the U.S. health care system, patients must navigate the bureaucracy of insurance, scheduling, and approvals, which forces patients and families to wait. There is waiting for the insurance company's pre-approval for medical tests, the test appointment, and the test results, only to find out more tests are needed. If a diagnosis isn't clear, the process begins again. If the patient needs to see a specialist, waiting for a referral and insurance approval takes time, and often, specialists don't have appointments available for several weeks. This process can drag on for weeks or even months before a concrete diagnosis can be made, a prognosis discussed, and treatment plans developed and set into motion. And for the twenty-eight million Americans without health care insurance, the wait can be longer and more complicated due to the complexities of the health care system (Keisler-Starkey & Bunch, 2021).

Barriers to the Diagnostic Process

For many people in the United States, barriers to needed tests, procedures, and specialists complicate the diagnostic process. For example, rural areas of the United States are experiencing a long-standing shortage of health care providers. Sixty-five percent of federal government-identified Primary Care Health Professional Shortage Areas are in rural areas. Local health clinics and small community hospitals continue to shut down because many cannot recruit and retain the needed health care staff, nor remain financially viable. With the closure of these health facilities, medical specialists, diagnostic equipment, and technicians are often no longer locally available (Rural Health Information Hub, n.d.). Access to health care services will be discussed further in chapter 8.

For rural patients needing specialist care, this disparity is even higher. For instance, U.S. women in rural areas travel four times farther to access obstetric care than the average for all women.

In some rural areas, the distance to access hospitals with obstetric units was as high as 143 miles, and the distance to an advanced neonatal care unit was up to 190 miles (Hung et al., 2018; Fontenot et al., 2024).

Often, communities are served by visiting specialists who are periodically available for local care. They often have limited patient openings and hold appointments once a week or sometimes only once a month. This makes it even more difficult for primary care providers to access specialty consultations and streamline referrals, which can further delay medical tests, procedures, and diagnoses (Drew et al., 2006). When a timely diagnosis is essential, delays have obvious medical implications and add challenges and stressors for the patient. Once referrals and appointments are secured, the distance and travel time to the appointments become the next obstacle.

Patients traveling long distances for appointments must arrange time off from work, which can mean losing income. Patients may struggle to secure reliable transportation, pay for fuel, or find someone to take them to the appointment (Rural Health Information Hub, 2022). For instance, in a recent case in rural Oregon, Barbara saw her local doctor for pain in her bladder and blood in her urine. After an initial ultrasound and lab work, she was referred to a urologist for further testing. However, the nearest available urologist with an opening for new patients and who had admitting privileges to the local hospital was seventy-five miles away. She had difficulty lining up reliable transportation and finding someone who could get time off from work to take her to the appointment, causing her to cancel and reschedule several times. These types of cases are familiar to rural health care providers who struggle to provide timely and readily available access to health care for their patients.

Patients in urban and suburban areas may have diagnostic centers and specialists nearby, but many face challenges in accessing these services. Public transportation may be available, but the cost can be a burden. Regardless of location, getting to needed medical appointments can still involve the challenges associated with taking time off from work and the related loss of income. For an illustration of this complex and challenging network of providers, see figure 8.5 in chapter 8.

Accessing Medical Information

Health care providers are cautious about prematurely discussing the full range of possible diagnoses with patients before testing has sufficiently indicated a probable diagnosis. Symptoms, early lab work, and preliminary testing can produce complex information that requires additional testing and analysis of the results to narrow down a diagnosis. Not wanting to worry the patient or provide false assumptions or hopes, health care providers often frame their early communication with the patients in broad, general terms.

Initial lab work can alert a doctor that there is a problem, but there may be multiple possible causes, each leading to different diagnoses and outcomes. Additional testing is often needed to confirm the specific diagnosis. This was the case when Miriam, a fifty-three-year-old patient, was experiencing extreme fatigue and excessive bruising. After some initial testing and referral to a specialist, the hematologist suspected a specific chronic blood disorder, but without further testing, she could not definitively rule out other related conditions. When meeting with the patient, the doctor discussed only what she knew from the initial lab work, telling the patient, "Your red-cell count and platelet numbers are very low, and we need to find out why. We will need to do additional testing to help us find out what is happening." Only when more testing confirmed her suspicions did she begin to talk to the patient about the probable diagnosis of the specific blood cancer she had suspected.

Online Medical Information

Online medical information is instantly available and covers all medical topics and questions. Every year, millions of people rely on online medical information to make health decisions (Fox & Duggan, 2013). Common searches seek advice on when to pursue medical attention, answer questions during the diagnostic process, and access medical and support resources. But if you've ever scrolled through the list of possible illnesses resulting from a search of "I'm sick with a cough, sore throat, fever," you know that easy access to medical information comes with drawbacks (figure 5.2).

Figure 5.2. Many people consult "Dr. Google" as their first step for medical information.

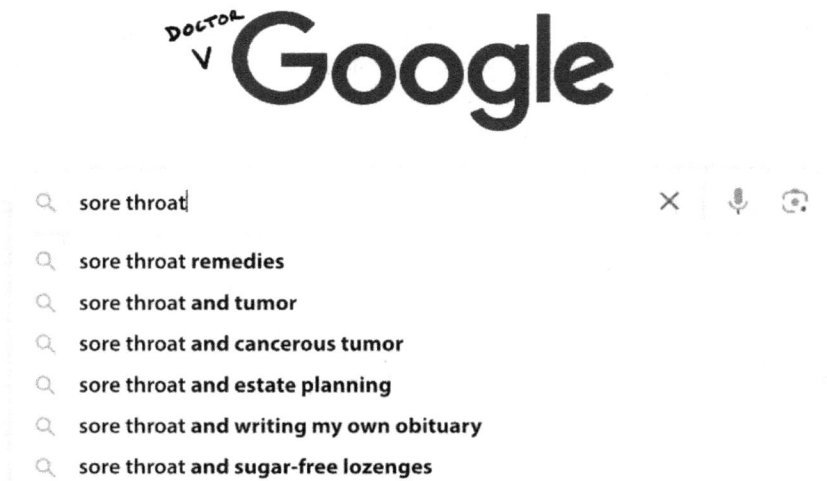

Online information can be a valuable starting point in understanding medical conditions and making health care decisions, but you should approach this information carefully and thoughtfully. The breadth and immediacy of online medical sites can provide clarity in times of medical uncertainty and confusion, but they can also be sources of misinformation. Online searches frequently pull up worst-case scenarios or information so general it points to dozens of possible diagnoses. Both can result in unwarranted panic, stress, and more uncertainty. In other cases, some sites are unreliable, where anyone can claim credibility and expertise (Radionova et al., 2023).

Crowdsourcing is an emerging trend that uses social media platforms to obtain medical information and solicit advice. One recent commenter on a community social media page solicited advice about symptoms she had and whether they warranted follow-up with a health care provider. Many followers recommended she not waste her time and money going to a doctor until she had tried their suggested home remedies. Some would-be medical advisors stated that they or someone they knew had similar symptoms and then described the remedy. This approach to diagnosis is fraught with potential problems. The advice may not only be ineffective, but it can also lead to delays in receiving an accurate diagnosis and needed treatment. In the case of life-threatening diseases, any delay in diagnosis and treatment may have long-term implications on the disease trajectory. Complications from home remedies or adverse interactions with medications the patient may already be taking can result.

Online health information can be an important part of health and disease management, but relying on credible websites is essential to finding the best information. It's helpful to learn more about a diagnosis than your provider has time to tell you in one appointment or about potential treatments to discuss with your provider. Online forums can connect you with others with the same condition to provide support and share emerging medical information. Credible websites are useful in addressing specific medical conditions, but they can also be a good source of general information to help increase your overall awareness and understanding of health care needs, medical issues, and overall well-being.

Cultivating Health Literacy

Most Americans have searched the internet for health information to be informed or learn more during the diagnostic process (Gass, 2021). Online health websites can be vital in increasing **health literacy,** which is the ability to access and use the needed information to make informed health decisions. Basic medical information includes diagrams and explanations of symptoms and causes, the implications of conditions and symptoms, and possible outcomes. With this knowledge, patients can become more active partners in their health, asking relevant questions and developing and implementing a health care management or treatment plan with their providers.

Online health care information quality varies based on the author's background, credentials, and the information referenced (Keselman et al., 2019). Unreliable and biased sources of information can provide outdated, self-serving, self-promoting, erroneous, or harmful misinformation. Therefore, you should take the time to assess and evaluate the information provided. Online health care information can also change quickly, and it is prudent to approach all online sources, even government websites, with a critical eye. It is important to cross-verify information you find online by comparing information from government agencies with data from international health organizations, respected medical centers, and professional associations. Evaluate the citations for the sources of information presented and note the publication dates to ensure it is the latest information.

Even when the website information is accurate, someone without medical knowledge and training can still misinterpret it. Most online medical information is general and can't be specific to an individual patient. Online diagnosis, treatment, and prognosis information doesn't factor in important variables like family history, patient-specific diagnostic data, or other concurrent medical conditions. Without factoring in this information, a self-determined diagnosis and treatment plan can lead to unanticipated and harmful outcomes like medication side effects, drug interactions, and detrimental delays in needed treatment (Radionova et al., 2023).

Sometimes, too much general information is harmful. Using online information to self-diagnose conditions can lead to **confirmation bias**, which is when a patient finds information that reaffirms their existing beliefs. If they later meet with a health care provider, their pre-existing beliefs can make accepting a different professional diagnosis difficult (Radionova et al., 2023). Some patients are so confident in their self-diagnosis that they insist on getting unnecessary testing or specific medications, or they self-medicate, increasing costs and risks of complications.

Although the ease, timeliness, and cost savings of online self-diagnosis or a crowdsourced diagnosis can make online medical information attractive, it cannot replace the professional judgment, resources, and safety of a medical provider or professional medical resources. If you're trying to determine if seeing a medical professional is warranted, consult reliable resources, such as those described in box 5.2, to help make an informed decision.

Box 5.2: Credible Sources for Medical Information

When you're looking for medical information, it's essential to consider the credibility of your source. Below are three sources that are typically reliable. Depending on your situation, one source may suit your needs more than another. When considering the reliability of sources for medical information, look for the following:

» Is the source authored or created by a medical professional?
» Is the information in the source recent or recently reviewed?
» Is the source associated with a medical provider or institution?
» Does the source provide opportunities for further learning and cite their sources?

Patient portals: Many hospitals and clinics provide online accounts where patients can communicate with health care providers. A provider will respond to emailed questions via email or a follow-up phone call.

Nurse hotlines: Many clinics, public health organizations, and insurance companies provide twenty-four-hour hotlines where nurses can discuss symptoms or changes in your health. The nurse will go through a series of questions and advise whether you need to be seen.

Digital medical devices and apps: These tools provide medical and health information in real time so you can determine if medical follow-up is warranted. Medical professionals can also remotely monitor, record, and transmit medical information to assist in preventing, diagnosing, and monitoring chronic conditions. The information gathered can be used to detect anomalies or changes that may need medical attention (Guk et al., 2019).

Coping with Life-Threatening Disease

Everything changes with a diagnosis. Suddenly, you are confronted with unknown outcomes and the possibility of death. A life-threatening diagnosis instantly divides life into a before and after. For instance, my husband's renal cancer diagnosis in 2009 forever changed the way my family thinks about events and memories. Instead of using age or specific years, we often use his cancer diagnosis as a reference point: "Oh, I remember, that was the summer *after* he had cancer."

Even though you get a diagnosis at a single moment, in real time, it often feels like a multifaceted, elongated process. Confirming an initial diagnosis through testing and procedures might take weeks or months. As the disease progresses, subsequent co-existing medical conditions and complications can develop. During this process, the patient and those around them are confronting the psychological, emotional, and social implications of the diagnosis (figure 5.3). The immediate physical symptoms of a condition complicate the process of coping with a new reality. These symptoms are a constant reminder of the diagnosis and the uncertainty of the future.

Figure 5.3. Patients with a life-threatening disease are likely to respond in many ways that involve overlapping social, emotional, and psychological factors.

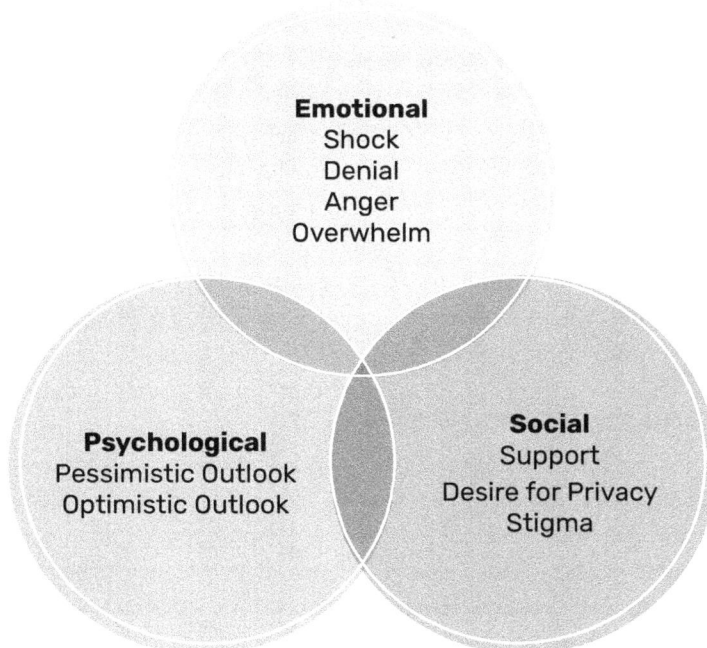

Early Awareness and Responses

The possibility of death brings a heightened awareness of one's mortality that can trigger a variety of responses. The shock of a life-threatening diagnosis can cause a person to freeze or shut down as they struggle to process the sudden change in their life. They can feel overwhelmed, powerless, or out of control, which can lead to tears, anger, or depression. Some patients dwell on the worst-case scenario, while others compartmentalize the reality of the diagnosis and act as if nothing has changed. For some patients, a long-awaited diagnosis can bring a sense of relief by removing the uncertainty and identifying what steps must be taken.

Common emotional responses to a diagnosis include feelings of anger and frustration over the loss of health and the day-to-day aspects of routine life. There can be anxiety, stress, and fear associated with the disease, the future, and the impact on family and friends. People often experience feelings of sadness, hopelessness, and social isolation when grieving the loss of identity and social connections. These varied emotions can occur simultaneously, or people may transition from one to another. Patients may experience mood swings as information about the diagnosis is processed, any new medical information emerges, or the diagnosis and possible prognosis change (Doka, 1993; Valizadeh et al., 2016).

The disease trajectory can affect how a patient adjusts and comes to terms with a diagnosis. The disease's specific symptoms directly impact a person's quality of life, coping strategies, adaptations, and responses to a diagnosis. The manifestation of symptoms associated with a specific disease can also vary from person to person. For example, multiple sclerosis (MS) is a degenerative neurological disease that affects people differently. MS is characterized by symptoms like muscle fatigue, weakness, involuntary muscle spasms, vertigo, dizziness, and vision problems. But the nature of the symptoms, when they appear, how long they continue, and how frequently they appear, is different for each person. The meaning and coping strategies of a disease such as MS will differ depending on how the disease affects a person.

The disease trajectory also affects the patient's treatment options and their overall quality of life. An asymptomatic patient or a patient with minimal symptoms experiences a disease differently than a patient experiencing persistent, disruptive, or debilitating symptoms. Depending on individual circumstances, a person's routine might need to change drastically, or it could remain relatively stable. The ability to continue working or going to school, caring for family, and maintaining social relationships and interests are major factors in a patient's quality of life.

Personality and Psychological Factors

During times of stress, personality traits and psychological characteristics influence adaptation and coping responses. How people respond to a diagnosis and manage their illness is directly connected to how they think and feel about their disease. People with strong negative emotions about their illness are more likely to experience depression and anxiety and have worse outcomes. In comparison, people with an optimistic outlook have more positive coping strategies and better outcomes (Hagger et al., 2017). Patients with a pessimistic perspective tend to focus on the negative aspects of the diagnosis. However, optimistic patients tend to focus on the positive aspects of their diagnosis or what they have control over.

For example, Javier, a patient who had just been diagnosed with advanced heart failure, shared his perspective on his medical condition. He understood the diagnosis and the implications of his failing heart, but told me nothing had changed for him: "My situation is really no different than it was yesterday before I knew I was in heart failure. I'm feeling good today, and I'm focusing on that." Each person's perspective influences their orientation and response to a life-threatening disease.

People who like to be in control often find comfort in using their time to prepare for the later stages of the disease. Attending to finances, childcare, or end-of-life concerns makes patients feel productive and eases stress because they know these matters are addressed. This time can also be used to secure resources that may be needed immediately and those that will be needed later.

Patients often underestimate their potential resources and hesitate to ask for help. Friends, neighbors, coworkers, and community members are essential and frequently underutilized support resources. They can help with daily tasks like grocery shopping, running errands, bringing meals, and driving to appointments, allowing the patient and their care providers to shift more attention to the specific challenges posed by the diagnosis (Doka, 1993).

Health information is an aspect of private life, and people can be reluctant to share it with others for many reasons. Some may be concerned about how others will view them or treat them differently once their diagnosis is known. A **social stigma** can be any attribute, behavior, or characteristic that marks a person as different from the dominant culture; this can include specific diseases and health conditions. For example, a diagnosis of acquired immunodeficiency syndrome (AIDS) or human immunodeficiency virus (HIV) can trigger stereotyped assumptions. In the 1980s and 1990s, many people diagnosed with HIV or AIDS were stigmatized and excluded from their social circles and public life. People living with AIDS faced the loss of employment and housing, were excluded from schools and colleges, and, in some cases, faced targeted acts of violence (Gonsalves & Staley, 2014). Although our understanding of the AIDS virus and its transmission has increased, and there are treatments available to keep the virus under better control, marginalization and discrimination can still impact the lives of people with AIDS.

Sharing health information is a personal decision, and each person will ultimately decide who, when, and with how many others they wish to share their diagnosis. Regardless, utilizing your resources for assistance and social and emotional support is a critical step in coping with a life-threatening illness. While these conversations are difficult, patients and their loved ones often benefit from social support networks where they can share feelings and fears in a nonjudgmental space. As the conversations continue, people can process the information and support each other through the disease's trajectory.

Socioeconomic Factors

Socioeconomic status (SES), generally referred to as a person's social class position, affects all aspects of life and is a primary factor in determining access to resources when dealing with a life-threatening disease. Socioeconomic status considers a person's income, education, and prestige, which all impact the health options available and the decisions a person makes. People in lower socioeconomic groups experience financial struggles, job insecurity, poorer quality housing, food insecurity, and less access to health and social services. Figure 5.4 illustrates how these factors contribute to an individual's ability to cope with a life-threatening diagnosis.

Figure 5.4. This chart shows the socioeconomic factors that contribute to an individual's ability to cope with a life-threatening diagnosis.

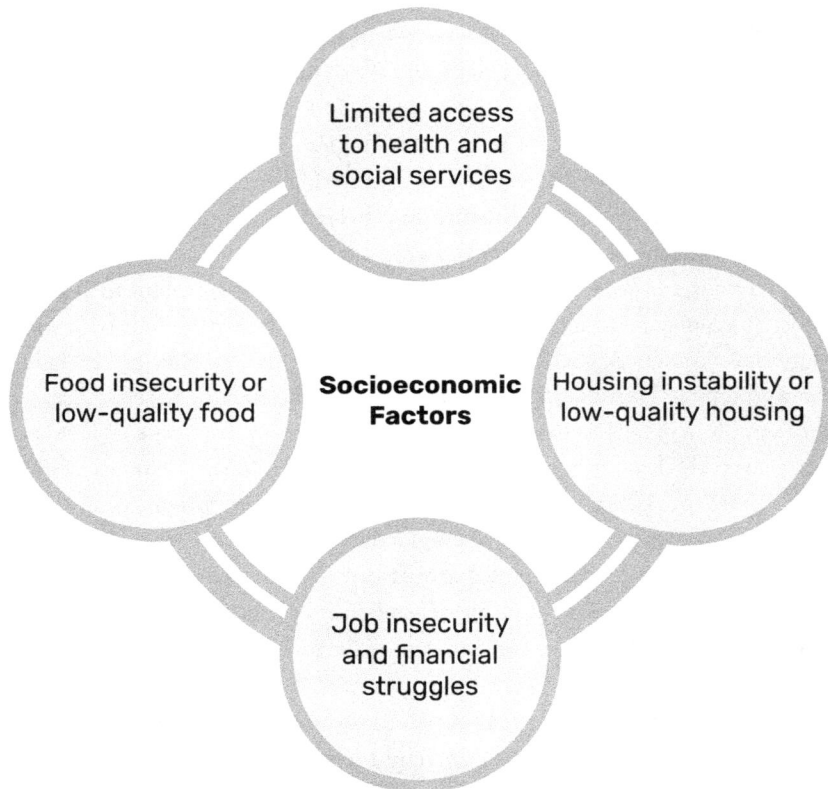

Living with a life-threatening disease often involves struggling with higher medical expenses, symptoms, and physical limitations while coping with a range of emotions. The medical condition may interfere with work, schooling, and daily activities. Experiencing depression, anger, and anxiety affects relationships and social interactions, which may require professional intervention. This burden exacerbates the existing stress of living with fewer available resources while requiring access to additional resources. This cumulative disadvantage can limit a patient's coping options and leave them with greater challenges in acquiring needed support (Van Wilder et al., 2021).

Community resources and services may not be available locally or may not be sufficient to meet community needs. During times of high demand, such as during the COVID-19 pandemic, the gap between the available resources and unmet needs is amplified. People turn to their social network for support, but those around the patient often live with the same life challenges and constraints. Can they take time off from work? Do they have a car and the resources to drive or accompany a patient to appointments? Can they help navigate the health care system? These factors limit people's options when responding to a life-threatening diagnosis.

Cultural and Spiritual Factors

As discussed in chapter 4, cultural and religious beliefs form the foundation for social standards and provide guidance and support to help people overcome challenging times. Being part of a cultural or religious community can provide predictability and a sense of belonging and connection to a social support system. This system becomes critically important when dealing with the uncertainty of a life-threatening disease.

Involvement in religious or spiritual communities can be an important resource in reaffirming or, in some cases, finding meaning and greater purpose in life. Participating in these shared belief systems can address existential uncertainty and provide a social support system from within a religious or spiritual community (Kim & Goldstein, 2017). These contacts and interactions can bring comfort and peace and improve overall quality of life (Young et al., 2015; Tarakeshwar et al., 2006). For those facing a life-threatening disease, spiritual well-being has been positively correlated with higher levels of hope, positive mood states, and overall psychological well-being. It has also been associated with decreased feelings of helplessness, hopelessness, anxiety, and preoccupation with the medical condition (Fehring et al., 1997).

Attitudes and beliefs toward health and disease are understood through a cultural framework. People's responses and approaches to coping with a diagnosis are affected by their cultural beliefs about what constitutes illness and the perceived cause of disease. These understandings then shape perceived options for the next steps based on accepted norms and values (Baider, 2012; Juckett, 2005; Groce & Zola, 1993). For example, if a disease is understood as a form of punishment or if witchcraft or divine displeasure is the suspected cause, medical intervention may be avoided or delayed while the culturally understood cause is addressed. Social support for the person may be half-hearted or lacking if the disease is seen as evidence of their own (or their family's) transgression. When the disease is perceived to be a result of witchcraft, a curse, or an evil spell, people may distance themselves based on the belief that close contact with the person may put them at risk for the same ailment (Groce & Zola, 1993).

Cultural views also influence how people respond to illness and cope with challenges. For example, cultures with a more fatalistic outlook may approach life events differently than those that value personal control and self-efficacy (confidence in one's ability to accomplish tasks and achieve goals). Similarly, in collectivist cultures, people might have different expectations about seeking and receiving support from family and community compared to individualistic cultures that emphasize independence and self-reliance.

Conclusion

We all realize we will die at some point, but receiving the diagnosis of a life-threatening disease forces us to confront that reality in a new, more immediate way. Knowing something is wrong with your body and waiting to find out how serious it might be is mentally and physically draining. You may have to navigate long periods of uncertainty during which other possible medical conditions are ruled out and endure extensive testing and numerous medical appointments before a definitive diagnosis is determined. Receiving the diagnosis of a life-threatening disease is a life-changing event. What that change looks like and how a person responds to the diagnosis is shaped by their social and cultural frame, individual personality, and general outlook on life. In the next chapter, we will explore the challenges and decisions that need to be addressed after a person receives the initial diagnosis of a life-threatening disease.

Summary

» The meaning of a life-threatening disease is a melding of the biological state and the social and personal understanding of the disease.

» The understanding of a life-threatening disease begins during the diagnostic process, where biological information is gathered and analyzed.

» Arriving at a final diagnosis can be a challenging and elongated process involving a series of tests and medical appointments. The process and wait times for a conclusive diagnosis can be frustrating and stressful.

» Patients often turn to the internet for quick and easy access to health information.

» Online medical information should be evaluated based on the credibility and accuracy of the information.

» The medical information concerning the diagnosis is contextualized within any existing religious and cultural belief systems and resource availability.

» Social factors, along with the patient's personality traits and psychological characteristics, come together to make meaning of a disease within the framework of their life. The nature of the disease and its meaning then shape responses and coping strategies.

Review Questions

1. How does the diagnostic process of a life-threatening disease involve both personal and social institutional complexities?
2. In what ways do technology and the internet impact access to health and medical information related to a life-threatening disease diagnosis?
3. How do personal and social factors shape an individual's understanding and response to the diagnosis of a life-threatening disease?
4. What impact does the availability of information through technology and the internet have on the diagnostic process of a life-threatening disease?
5. To what extent do social and institutional factors influence the diagnosis and management of a life-threatening disease?

Key Terms

Review these key terms from the chapter. You can find their definitions in the glossary at the end of the book.

» biological pathology

» chronic disease

» confirmation bias

» crowdsourcing

» diagnosis

» disease trajectory

» health literacy

» social stigma

» socioeconomic status (SES)

Chapter 6

—

End-of-Life Treatment Decisions

| Vignette | ## Running Out of Options

A few years ago, I was diagnosed with a chronic blood condition that causes severe anemia, a low platelet count, and blood thinning, which can lead to severe bleeding from minor cuts. Until recently, it only involved monitoring my platelet count to ensure it didn't drop too low and dealing with the symptoms of anemia like low energy and fatigue. But since my diagnosis, my platelet count has steadily dropped, and I've had greater difficulty controlling bleeding with even small cuts. Simple nosebleeds landed me in the emergency room twice. The fatigue associated with anemia worsened, and I began to limit my daily activities. Lab work showed that my blood condition had worsened, and the anemia needed to be more closely monitored and addressed with medication. I started weekly doctor visits to monitor my condition and to get regular injections to boost my hemoglobin levels.

Every week, my wife drove us to my appointment. At each visit, they tested my blood to see how well the medication was working. As we waited for the results, my wife would always take my hand and reassure me it would be okay. And for months, it was. The numbers bounced around. The platelet counts would be good for several weeks, and then unexpectedly, they'd drop. I'd spend the next week worrying about whether they'd rebound. I tried to take it day by day and live in the moment, but the stress and anxiety of waiting to see if the medication was still working dominated my life.

This treatment and medication regimen worked for nearly two years. But then I developed a severe rash all over my body. The rash welted up, and the itching became so severe that I scratched it until it bled. My wife and I suspected it might be a reaction to the medication, but the doctor was skeptical because a rash wasn't listed as a common side effect of that drug. I was taken off the medication for a week and given steroids. The rash cleared up, and I was put back on medication. I did okay for a few months, but then the rash returned even worse. I was taken off the medication, given a transfusion to boost my blood counts, and given steroids again. After further research, we found that the drug company identified a severe rash as a rare side effect in some patients.

The only other viable medication available for my condition was new and expensive—$15,000 a month. When our insurance denied coverage, we appealed. With the help of the doctor's office, we managed to get insurance to cover the prescription. My wife then had to complete an online education class to administer and monitor the drug protocol. The prescription was delivered overnight, and I started the treatment regimen. Within the first few days, I experienced extreme side effects of a full-body rash, vomiting, and diarrhea. I was instructed to stop the medication. My condition continues to worsen, and I am becoming so weak that even getting to doctors' appointments requires a medical transport. We are now exploring my remaining options.

R. G.

Introduction

R. G.'s experience with a chronic blood condition offers a glimpse into the complexities of confronting life-threatening diseases. Individuals living with chronic ailments often find themselves awash in decisions that deplete their resources and energy. Some of the most significant decisions during this stage focus on developing a treatment plan.

Think of the treatment plan like a nautical chart that lays out vital information about water depths, coastline details, and landmarks that help sailors find their way. Creating a treatment plan is a collaborative process involving a health care team, the patient, and the patient's support network. The treatment plan focuses on what medical professionals know about a disease: the symptoms and conditions associated with how the disease develops and progresses. Like sailing a ship, a treatment plan requires an entire crew to put it into action.

In this chapter, we will examine the factors affecting the development of a treatment plan, including the impact that social and cultural beliefs play in identifying treatment options, treatment goals, and pain management.

Learning Objectives

These learning objectives will help you identify what's most important in this chapter. By the end of this chapter, you should be able to do the following:

» Describe the purpose and components of a treatment plan for a life-threatening disease.
» Discuss how treatment plans can address differences in disease trajectories.
» Discuss how social and cultural belief systems shape treatment goals.
» Explain the impact of a technical imperative and cultural lag in evaluating treatment options.
» Discuss the subjective notion of pain and how belief systems affect the understanding of pain management.

Treatment Decisions for Life-Threatening Diseases

People with life-threatening diseases must manage a series of profound events and decisions. Initially, disease management centers on coming to terms with the diagnosis and eventual prognosis, the predicted course of the disease or ailment. But because life-threatening diseases are, by nature, progressive—meaning they grow, spread, or get worse—they will likely cause or contribute to the patient's eventual death.

With the progression of a life-threatening disease, a person's symptoms and medical conditions change. External factors, such as technological advances, can also lead to new treatments. At other times, existing medications or treatments may no longer be effective or cause side effects that require changes to the treatment regimen, as seen in R. G.'s story. His initially prescribed medication stopped managing his symptoms, which required a reevaluation of treatment options. As you work with people in this chronic phase of disease management, you will see them navigate a series of significant changes.

This period of uncertainty and transition requires adjustments to symptom management, medical treatments, and daily routines in the face of disease. The heightened awareness of life's fragility can also trigger a person's desire to renew or resume relationships, reevaluate priorities, fulfill life dreams, or complete a bucket list of experiences before they die (Doka, 1993). Box 6.1 provides questions to consider when working with people in this challenging phase.

Box 6.1: Questions for the Chronic Phase of Life-Threatening Disease

Consider the following questions when working with people in the chronic phase of a life-threatening disease:

» What challenges do patients and their loved ones face when managing symptoms and side effects and carrying out health regimens?

» How can patients and caregivers prevent and manage medical crises during the chronic phase of a life-threatening disease?

» What sources of stress do patients and their families encounter, and what coping strategies are most effective in managing this stress?

» What strategies can be employed to maximize social support and minimize social isolation?

» In what ways do patients and their families strive to normalize life and manage feelings and fears associated with a life-threatening disease?

» How does a life-threatening disease redefine relationships, and what can be done to maintain healthy, supportive relationships?

» How do patients and their families find meaning in suffering, uncertainty, or decline?

Adapted from the work of Dr. Kenneth J. Doka (1993)

Treatment Plans

When a person is diagnosed with a chronic, life-threatening disease, many challenging treatment decisions need to be made. The disease presentation, emerging symptoms, complexity of individual health variables, and disease trajectory may trigger the need for a plan. A **treatment plan** is developed early in the disease trajectory to best manage a patient's medical conditions and is updated regularly by the patient's care team. This plan allows time for the health care team to gather, process, and evaluate the various options, and it facilitates making complex decisions that may arise during a medical crisis.

Creating a plan involves weighing medical options in response to the current medical conditions and symptoms, forestalling disease progression, and preparing for the needs at the end stage of the disease. The plan should cover specific treatments, the intensity of medical intervention, and advanced care planning. It includes acute short-term issues such as the patient's resuscitation preferences in a hospital setting. However, the plan is especially useful in guiding long-term medical interventions focused on where the individual wants to be and how they want to live the remainder of their life (LeBlanc & Tulsky, 2020; PDQ Supportive and Palliative Care Editorial Board, 2014).

Treatment plans generally include several common elements of patient care, including:

- » patient education
- » scheduled follow-ups
- » ongoing monitoring
- » specialist consultation or referral

For example, Elijah and his health care team created a treatment plan because he hadn't been feeling well and was having intense headaches. At a doctor's appointment, he was diagnosed with diabetes. His blood sugar was dangerously high, which required short-term hospitalization to treat. During his time in the hospital, Elijah, a family member, and his health care provider created a treatment plan. They completed a health assessment detailing his medical history, other existing health concerns, health literacy, and social resources. Elijah set his medical goals of controlling and managing his diabetes. The team set metrics to monitor his progress toward his goal, including blood sugar levels, A1C levels, and blood pressure. Finally, they documented the needed medical interventions like medication, lifestyle changes, regular doctor's appointments, and consultation with a specialist. Implementation of the plan began while he was in the hospital. Elijah learned how to adjust his diet, test his blood sugar levels, and administer insulin. He was also advised to set up a follow-up appointment with an endocrinologist.

As the disease progresses, new needs emerge, and Elijah's care will be coordinated between the members of his treatment team. A health care team frequently includes the patient, family and caregivers, the care manager, and specialists or consultants. The progression of the disease—not the diagnosis alone—guides any needed care, the patient's response to treatment, and a schedule for monitoring and preventive maintenance (Von Korff & Tiemens, 2000).

Treatment Goals

As part of the treatment planning process, the patient, their family, and the health care team should discuss and agree on treatment goals. The nature of the diagnosis may prompt initial treatment goals, but these should be periodically reevaluated and updated. The need for adjustments can be triggered by the progression of chronic conditions, like heart failure, or neurogenerative diseases, like multiple sclerosis. In situations like R. G.'s from the opening vignette, reevaluation may be necessary when stabilizing treatments lose their effectiveness, fail, or when no remaining effective options are available (LeBlanc & Tulsky, 2020).

Treatment options and their outcomes impact the patient's quality and quantity of life. Therefore, talking with the patient about their priorities is essential. **Patient-centered care** allows the treatment team to align care with what's most important to the individual. For example, Angelica, who was living with stage IV pancreatic cancer, opted to receive treatments that could extend her life for many months. But patients who undergo this treatment frequently experience problematic side effects, which is what happened to Angelica. In collaboration with her care team, she decided to continue the treatment and endure the side effects in the hope she would live long enough to see the birth of her first grandchild. Her health care providers could then focus on mitigating the side effects. Whereas Naomi, who faced a similar decision about treatment options, chose to forego the treatment because the side effects prevented her from engaging in her favorite activities during the time she had left. Her health care providers could then focus on addressing the ongoing disease-related symptoms to support her quality of life during her remaining time. Each patient collaborated with their health care team to customize a plan that best met their needs and priorities.

Treatment Considerations

Treatment considerations for any chronic disease will vary based on the disease trajectory, coexisting diagnoses, and an individual's specific life situation. For example, a person who is living with both heart and kidney disease may find it hard to achieve the best outcomes for both conditions. Some medications needed to manage heart failure can intensify the symptoms of kidney disease. Without heart medication, the decline in heart function and the related complications of heart failure cannot be managed as well and may progress more rapidly. The treatment used to intervene in the trajectory of one disease affects the progression and management of the coexisting disease.

People with life-threatening diseases usually don't have stable health conditions in the long term, nor do they quickly get worse in the short term. There may be periods of stability where an individual can maintain their normal activities. However, a chronic, life-threatening disease involves a progression of symptoms and the inevitable health outcomes of that disease. For patients, it can be taxing to meet the challenges of living with the symptoms of the disease, the demands of a treatment regimen, and the ongoing uncertainty of their health.

Advances in research and medical treatments have elongated this period of the disease trajectory. People are living longer with life-threatening diseases. For instance, the cancer survival rate has increased from 49% in the mid-1970s to 68% in 2022 (Siegel et al., 2024). Seventy percent of cancer survivors have lived five or more years after initial diagnosis, and 48% have lived ten or more years (Tonorezos et al., 2024). The length of time people are living with other life-threatening diseases, such as heart disease, has also increased for one-, five-, and ten-year survival rates (Taylor et al., 2019). This trend is prompting an ongoing discussion about balancing the ability to extend life and the quality of that time, which will be discussed later in the chapter. Patients and their health care teams can be more effective in limiting symptoms and managing disease progression by focusing on available medical options, the patient's needs, and their preferences for living with a life-threatening disease.

Disease Trajectory and Treatment Plans

Early in the treatment process, long-term decisions are often limited and influenced by urgent medical issues. For example, Irena was brought to the emergency department at a small rural hospital with an unknown medical condition. The sixty-two-year-old was disoriented, noncommunicative, agitated, and experiencing hallucinations. The presenting symptoms also included weakness on one side of her body, a temperature of 102°F, a rapid heart rate, and general agitation. Lab work revealed the symptoms were related to an extremely high blood sugar reading of over 800 (the normal range is 70–100), which, if untreated, is life-threatening. Doctors found that the cause of her medical emergency was undiagnosed diabetes. After her immediate medical emergency was under control, Irena spent the next few days in the hospital as doctors adjusted her medications and provided patient education to help her manage her diabetes.

Stabilizing the immediate medical concerns and addressing the most pressing symptoms takes precedence over longer-term issues. In Irena's situation, when her immediate medical situation stabilized, the focus shifted to developing a long-term treatment plan for her chronic disease. To minimize the disabling and potentially life-threatening effects of the disease, a long-term treatment plan will often involve ongoing close monitoring by a variety of medical specialists, regular testing and treatments, medication adjustments, and lifestyle changes.

Disease Variations

The nature of the disease and its progression dictate treatment strategy and medication adjustments. Some diseases may be characterized by a slow, steady progression of symptoms that requires regular monitoring and testing to fine-tune, adjust, or change treatment approaches. In the case of emphysema, a chronic lung disease that makes it difficult to breathe, symptoms are progressive as the damage to lung tissue causes the air sacs to weaken and break down over time. To deal with decreased lung function, a patient may need to change the dosage of medications, add new medications and treatments, and alter lifestyle behaviors periodically. For some people, a specific medication or treatment may lose effectiveness, symptoms may intensify, or new symptoms may emerge that require a modification in the current treatment plan.

In addition to the slow, steady progress of long-term disease, other disease trajectories may include periods of stability or remission of symptoms and periods of recurrence or a sudden worsening of symptoms. Living with the irregular trajectory of diseases like Crohn's disease, a type of inflammatory bowel disease, involves ongoing uncertainty of when the next relapse will occur, how intense the recurrence will be, and what adjustments may be needed in the treatment regimen. Any episodic recurrence of symptoms can significantly impact a patient's quality of life and may require an adjustment in treatment.

A life-threatening disease can be stable for a while, but periodic complications can disrupt this stability and lead to treatment adjustments. The progressive nature of heart failure, for example, can lead to swelling in the legs and feet. As the weakening heart struggles to circulate blood to and from the lower part of the body, excess fluid accumulates in the legs and feet. The pressure from the pooling blood in the vessels can force fluid into the surrounding tissue, making the skin more vulnerable to infections like cellulitis and staph. Treating infections frequently involves taking medication, wrapping the legs in absorbent pressure bandages that must be changed several times daily, and keeping the legs elevated for long periods. Although manageable, the treatment regimen significantly impacts the patient's daily activities and quality of life.

One of the most common life-threatening diseases is cancer, a general term to describe a broad array of conditions characterized by abnormal cells that divide without control. Cancer cells can then invade nearby tissues or spread to other body parts. In the United States, over 39% of the population will be diagnosed with cancer during their lifetime (National Cancer Institute, 2020). These rates make it probable that someone you know will, at some point in their life, be diagnosed with cancer. Cancer treatments vary widely depending on type, severity, and prognosis.

In the past, a cancer diagnosis was often viewed as a death sentence. However, regular screenings for many types of cancer have resulted in increased rates of early diagnosis. Early medical intervention can drastically increase long-term survival rates. For example, when localized breast cancer is detected at stage I, nearly all patients survive five or more years; however, the survival rate drops to three in ten when discovered and treated at stage IV (American Cancer Society, n.d.).

The development of more effective treatments means more people diagnosed with cancer go into remission, the stage when signs and symptoms of the disease are reduced or can no longer be detected. This trend is expected to continue with ongoing efforts to raise awareness of cancer and increased funding for research (National Cancer Institute, n.d.). See box 6.2 for commonly prescribed medications and procedures used to treat cancer.

For some types of cancer, an initial treatment regimen can put the disease in remission. In other situations, periodic treatments are needed to keep the cancer under control or in a state of remission. But even in the case of remission, cancer can still reappear weeks, months, or even years later. A recurrence may or may not be related to the first diagnosis and can occur in the same place as before (local recurrence), the same general area (regional recurrence), or more distant parts of the body (distant recurrence).

Recurrence treatment options and regimens may be based on initial treatment decisions and how the patient's body responded to them previously. They may differ based on the type and location of the cancer. Some people will feel the same emotions as they did with the first diagnosis. For others, a new cancer diagnosis can be more upsetting because they experienced the relief of beating it, only to have it reappear. However, medical professionals should encourage patients to rely on their experience and resources to cope with a recurrence diagnosis (Mayo Clinic, 2021). Although common treatments exist to combat a disease, early detection and medical intervention, as well as the differences in individual biology, can impact the effectiveness of treatments.

Box 6.2: Common Treatments for Cancer

As one of the most common life-threatening diseases, cancer has a variety of treatment options (Mayo Clinic, n.d.). Read through the list and consider the following questions:

» What factors might influence the decision to pursue a particular treatment over another?

» Based on what you already know about these treatments, how do different cancer treatments affect a patient's daily activities and routines?

» What role do follow-up care and maintenance therapies play in the long-term management of cancer?

Treatment Options	Description
bone marrow transplant (stem cell transplant)	use of a patient's or donor's bone marrow stem cells to replace diseased bone marrow or allow for higher doses of chemotherapy
chemotherapy	use of drugs to kill cancer cells
clinical trials	investigative studies to find new ways of treating cancer
cryoablation	use of cold to kill cancer cells where tissue is repeatedly frozen and thawed
hormone therapy	removal or blocking of hormones that cause cancer to grow
immunotherapy (biological therapy)	use of the patient's immune system to find, recognize, and fight cancer
radiation therapy	use of high-powered energy beams (X-rays or protons) to kill cancer cells
radiofrequency ablation	use of high-frequency energy to heat the cancer cells until they die
surgery	procedure to remove cancer cells from the body
targeted drug therapy	medication that targets specific abnormalities within the cancer cells

Treatment Adherence

Patients often find treatment regimens for life-threatening diseases complicated and confusing. Treatment schedules, medical procedures, and ongoing monitoring involve a significant commitment of time and can be psychologically and emotionally draining.

For example, Rachelle has end-stage kidney disease that requires dialysis, a time-intensive process that removes waste and excess fluid from the blood when the kidneys stop working properly. Rachelle needs to visit a dialysis center three times a week for four- to five-hour treatments. She considered home treatment, but one option, hemodialysis, would require four to seven treatments per week for two to ten hours each, and a second option, peritoneal dialysis, would involve up to four daily sixty- to ninety-minute treatments. For Rachelle and her care team, visiting the dialysis center provided the best option. Still, it forced major changes to her work schedule, put enormous pressure on her family, and strained her financial resources.

While treatments are critical to an individual's quality of life and the disease trajectory, following detailed and complex treatment processes can be daunting for patients and their caregivers, making it difficult to consistently adhere to treatment routines. **Treatment adherence** refers to how well a patient follows the recommendations of their health care provider. Knowing what must be done does not automatically lead to consistent follow-through and positive outcomes. Patients who view the treatment regimen as too burdensome or disruptive are less likely to follow their doctor's recommendations.

The likelihood of treatment adherence can also be affected by the individual's physical symptoms of the disease, any side effects of treatments and medication they may experience, and the amount of financial burden associated with their medical care. The demands and stresses associated with ongoing treatment can lead to mental and emotional exhaustion, resulting in lower rates of treatment adherence. These factors often intensify for patients who experience medical complications or have more intensive, complex treatment regimens (Chakrabarti, 2014). The lack of adherence to required treatment routines can impact the trajectory of the disease and have dire consequences for the patient.

Health care providers' communication with patients about disease trajectory and treatment adherence should be clear, concise, and open (Sagi et al., 2021). The patient and their support network need basic information about the disease, such as the purpose and importance of treatments, side effects to watch for, and timing of follow-ups. Health care providers can help patients adhere to treatments by providing detailed instructions, prioritizing the most critical elements of the treatment, and working with patients to establish achievable steps to reach their treatment goals.

Limited, clear directions should use straightforward language tailored to the patient's level of understanding. See box 6.3 for guidance on plain language from the Centers for Disease Control and Prevention. An honest dialogue about the severity of the medical condition, the ability of the patient and their support system to carry out the needed treatments, and the resources necessary to overcome any barriers should be a priority. Finally, treatment plans should include a process to evaluate efforts and address unforeseen problems (Atreja et al., 2005).

Box 6.3: Plain Language for Treatment Adherence

Plain language is communication that people can easily understand on first reading or hearing (Plain Language Action and Information Network, n.d.). While plain language is not a requirement for all health professionals, using clear and simple language is an example of a best practice that can help patients follow their treatment plans.

The National Center for Health Marketing (2007) addresses communication barriers in their *Plain Language Thesaurus for Health Communications*, noting that the public often struggles with medical terminology—especially people who do not speak English as their first language and those with limited literacy. To aid in clearer communication, the Health Literacy Council (2022), part of the Centers for Disease Control and Prevention, created *Everyday Words for Public Health Communication*, an online tool to replace public health jargon with plain language alternatives.

Here are a few terms from that online resource:

adhere, adherence: sticks to

chronic disease, illness, or condition: a type of sickness that goes on for a long time and often doesn't go away completely

health care provider: people who take care of you or provide health care

monitor: check, watch

outcome: result

risk: chance, likelihood, reason for a health problem

severe: strong, serious, harmful, dangerous, very bad

Social and Cultural Belief Systems

Culturally based health beliefs and practices determine what health situations are problematic enough to involve the medical health care system. As you read in chapter 4, balancing quality of life and quantity of life is also culturally subjective. Cultural beliefs, values, and preferences impact any possible trade-offs between these perspectives.

For instance, Gary comes from a culture that values physical survival, functional capacity, and the resilience to combat chronic conditions. His way of seeing and understanding life and death means he values extending life and doing whatever it takes to live as long as possible. These cultural values may influence the treatment options Gary chooses and those emphasized by the health care system, which will shape his treatment plan and treatment goals (Singh et al., 2023).

Beliefs about health can vary across different cultures. East Asian cultures, for instance, tend to focus more on living in harmony with the forces of nature; thus, living with progressive medical conditions is seen as a part of the normal cycle of life. Through this cultural lens, death is viewed as a natural part of life. This cultural perspective may lead a person approaching the end of life to opt for less medical intervention and to be more inclined to let nature take its course. Alternatively, a patient may choose to accept comfort care and pain management but decline treatments designed to forestall death (Wang et al., 2024).

Cultural beliefs can affect an individual's decisions about what, if any, treatments they choose (Nilchaikovit et al., 1993). Cultural views can determine whether a person believes a life-threatening disease warrants medical intervention, when and how much to intervene in the course of the disease, and when to let the natural trajectory of death take its course. Therefore, the consideration of cultural beliefs about treatment options and desired goals is an integral part of the treatment planning process.

Cultural Variations in Disclosure and Decision-Making

The U.S. health care system embraces an open-disclosure model centered on the patient's ability to make their own treatment decisions. The **open-disclosure model** involves a frank discussion between the health care provider and the patient concerning the medical facts, available options, and the expected outcomes of the situation. For example, when Imani's medical tests and lab work were completed, she received a copy of the results through her online medical portal and met with her doctor, who explained the results, discussed the implications, and described her treatment options. She asked questions and talked through the options with her doctor to develop a treatment plan. The open-disclosure model reflects a shift in the U.S. health care system toward more patient-centered care.

In some non-Western countries, such as China and India, the open-disclosure approach may be seen as unnecessarily cruel, and family members may make attempts to protect a terminally ill patient from the knowledge of their condition (Wang et al., 2018). Norms of nondisclosure may also be part of an alternative decision-making model that is different than the practice in Western medicine, where the patient is fully informed and participates in their medical decision-making.

Cultural variations may place responsibility for treatment decisions with the family, community elders, the physician, or within a shared family-physician model. In contrast with the open-disclosure model, which is focused on patient autonomy, many cultures embrace a **shared decision-making model**, which emphasizes traditional family-centered choices about health care. In this model, relatives receive information about the patient's medical condition, and treatment decisions are made by the family (Searight & Gafford, 2005). This is the case among many Asian cultures, where disease is understood as an extended family issue, as opposed to an individual concern, and related treatment decisions are a function of the entire family (Candib, 2002). These types of cultural variations should guide health care services and the development of treatment plans, as you'll see in the next section.

Culturally Competent Treatment Plans

Cultural factors influence patients' responses to medical issues and shape the health care provider-patient relationship. U.S. dominant culture practices are woven throughout the country's health care system. Differences between a patient's cultural beliefs and practices and U.S. norms can result in barriers to ensuring the best possible health care outcomes for that patient. Culturally competent health care addresses potential disparities in health care outcomes due to cultural differences.

The American Hospital Association (2013) describes a **culturally competent health care organization** as one that "has the ability to provide care to patients with diverse values, beliefs, and behaviors, including tailoring health care delivery to meet patients' social, cultural, and linguistic needs." Reaching this goal involves examining our health care systems, processes, and services to ensure comfort and support for all patients and their families. Regular assessments are required to identify any disparities in service and care, evaluate efforts to meet the needs of the whole patient, ensure clear communication, and promote equitable access to health care information and resources.

Many professional health care organizations have published guidelines, training materials, and resources to support the cultural proficiency of their members. See box 6.4 for recommendations to promote more culturally competent health care organizations.

Box 6.4: Cultural Competency Guidelines for Health Care Organizations

Cultural competency recommendations address critical elements that promote effective cross-cultural communication, support positive provider-patient relationships, and increase equitable access to services within the health care system. Consider these actions recommended by the American Hospital Association (2013). Reflect on how these steps could promote more effective treatment plans:

» Collect race, ethnicity, and language preference data.
» Identify and report disparities.
» Provide culturally and linguistically competent care.
» Develop culturally competent disease management programs.
» Increase diversity and minority workforce pipelines.
» Involve the community.
» Make cultural competency an institutional priority.

Understanding how cultural differences can impact health care practices and outcomes has become a common topic for medical education and training and ongoing professional development. However, some health care providers may still be unfamiliar with or underestimate how much cultural variations impact provider-patient communication and medical decision-making. Though cultural generalizations may not always be useful or predictive of specific patients (Searight & Gafford, 2005), training information that includes commonly held beliefs and practices within cultural groups can give medical staff a starting point in providing culturally competent health care. However, generalizations often do not fully address the significant diversity within ethnic groups based on subcultural groups, specific family cultures, and religious belief systems.

Variations within a cultural group result from different rates of acculturation, defined as changes in a person's cultural beliefs and practices as they adopt aspects of another culture. For example, after being in the United States for many years, Mei maintains her traditional Chinese belief that medical treatment and care decisions are family decisions. However, she has adopted the U.S. cultural belief that a patient should be fully informed about their medical condition rather than maintaining her traditional beliefs that the patient should be shielded from specific information concerning her medical condition. These differences can affect aspects of treatment planning and treatment goals, such as decision-making processes, preference for disclosure, willingness to forgo treatment, and views of advance care planning (Matsumura et al., 2002).

Choosing and Evaluating Treatment Options

Medical treatments for serious diseases are complex. A patient's biology and personal and cultural beliefs, combined with the availability of treatments, affect the patient's health outcomes. Early treatment decisions are often relatively straightforward, but as the disease progresses, the body responds, and treatment options change, the decision-making process can be increasingly complex. For patients and their caregivers, the rapid introduction of new medical procedures and medications can be overwhelming and complicate the decision-making process. Each treatment option has its own set of advantages and disadvantages, and patients must weigh each of them and choose a path forward.

Treatment Options and Social Expectations

Determining the advantages and disadvantages of treatment options is subjective, shaped by someone's cultural beliefs, desired outcomes, and personal preferences. Each of us has our own comfort level with risk that depends on personality, experience, age, and other factors. To further complicate decision-making, no single treatment is "best" for everyone facing the same disease. For example, Maria, a fifty-seven-year-old woman diagnosed with breast cancer, had the malignant tumor surgically removed. Her doctor proposed three possible follow-up treatments to minimize the risk of the cancer recurring. Each option was effective in preventing the return of cancer, but each came with its advantages, disadvantages, and possible side effects.

For Maria, the first option was a medication with side effects including loss of bone mass and bone density (osteoporosis), development of heart problems, bone and joint pain, mood swings, and depression. The second option was a medication with fewer reported side effects, but its side effects were often more severe, like blood clots, uterine cancer, or stroke. The third option was a series of targeted radiation treatments. Radiation's side effects include skin burns, nerve damage, and skin damage, as well as an increased risk of developing other types of cancer. It would also make later breast reconstruction surgery more difficult. After discussing each option with her doctor, Maria had to weigh these options and decide what to do.

Recent advancements in medical technology have vastly increased the treatment options available to address life-threatening diseases. There are now multiple options for patients like Maria, but each option comes with risks and benefits. New diagnostic procedures, increased effectiveness of treatment options, and greater use of precision medicine have given health care providers more power to intervene in the course of illness and disease. **Precision medicine** focuses on developing effective and safe therapies, medications, and doses tailored to variations in a person's genes. Yet, more options can make it more difficult for patients to evaluate which treatment is best for them.

In the United States and most industrialized nations, technology has become a symbol of progress. Sociologists use the term **technical imperative** to describe the belief that new technologies are both inevitable and essential and that their development and adoption are necessary for the benefit of society. Therefore, progress in medicine is often measured in terms of its technological advancements and the ability to cure diseases and injuries. This ideology shapes U.S. health care policies and medical practice. Providers can feel driven to do everything possible to extend life and forestall the inevitability of death. But it has also led to new challenges in determining when, how, and, ultimately, *whether* medical intervention should be undertaken in various instances of disease and injuries. There are ongoing concerns and questions surrounding the amount of influence exerted by technical advancements and their role in shaping medical decisions.

The technical imperative in health care means that if treatment is possible, it must be done. Since it is possible to keep people alive with a respirator, it must be used. If it is possible to extend life by using chemotherapy cancer treatments, they must be used. As patients become more educated about new treatment options, health care providers face increased pressure to use the latest technology in addition to diagnostic tests, advanced procedures, and the newest drugs. However, overusing new tools and procedures can produce conflicting information, complicating the diagnosis and treatment plan. In some cases, the urge to use every available option can lead to a never-ending cycle of checking for and treating conditions, regardless of how significant they are (Hofmann, 2002).

While advancements in medicine can benefit society, the rapid pace of these changes can also pose challenges. A society's ability to create new technologies often exceeds its ability to understand the technology's implications, which sociologists call a **cultural lag**. Material culture (what a culture makes, creates, and produces, such as architecture, clothing, food, art, goods, and services) tends to change faster than nonmaterial culture (what a culture thinks, such as beliefs, ideas, and ways of being and doing).

The cultural lag between what medicine can do and what it *should* do occurs as we consider the social implications of new medical treatments and the development of the medical, legal, and procedural guidelines for their use. For example, a vaccine to prevent cervical cancer caused by the human papillomavirus (HPV) was first recommended for preteens ages eleven to twelve, teens, and young adults by the Centers for Disease Control and Prevention in 2006. However, many youths are still not vaccinated. Ongoing resistance to this vaccine stems from concerns about its necessity, safety, side effects, lack of physician recommendations, and parents' beliefs that their teens don't need it because they are not sexually active (Beavis et al., 2018; White et al., 2023).

Similarly, new drugs and treatments can extend life, but what is the trade-off? In some cases, ethical considerations influence how people view medical advances. For example, some people object to using stem cells in medical research because they may have come from aborted fetuses. In other cases, quality of life is a critical consideration. A cancer patient may have access to a specific new drug or treatment that can extend life. But is gaining a few months worth the significant financial costs, debilitating side effects, and decreased quality of life just because a treatment is possible and available? The next section will introduce decision-making models and other strategies to help answer these challenging questions.

Decision-Making Models

Many health care decision-making models exist to help patients weigh the risks and benefits of treatment options. The Ottawa Decision Support Framework provides a structure to help individuals evaluate medication and treatment options (Ottawa Hospital Research Institute, 2021). Based on this model, the Ottawa Personal Decision Guide provides a series of questions to clarify decisions to be made and identifies information needed to assess the risks and benefits (Ottawa Hospital Research Institute, 2015). The guide includes prompts to flesh out individual and cultural values to identify resources and help the patient arrive at the best possible decision to meet their needs and preferences (see box 6.5).

Box 6.5: Questions to Guide Decision-Making

The Ottawa Personal Decision Guide is a four-step process that helps people make health or social decisions based on the knowledge, values, certainty, and support they have (Ottawa Hospital Research Institute, 2015). Here's an overview:

1. Clarify your decision: What decision do you face? What are your reasons for making this decision? How far along are you in making a choice?
2. Explore your decision.
   a. Knowledge: List the options, benefits, and risks you know.
   b. Values: Rate each benefit and risk using stars to show how much each one matters to you.
   c. Certainty: Choose the option with the benefits that matter most to you. Avoid the options with the risks that matter most to you. Which option do you prefer?
   d. Support: Who else is involved? Which option do they prefer? Is this person pressuring you? How can they support you? What role do you prefer in making the choice?
3. Identify your decision-making needs.
4. Plan the next steps based on your needs.

Common risks and side effects from medications and treatments are well-documented and should be considered in the decision-making process. For newer medications and procedures and those still in trial studies, only preliminary information about the risks and benefits may be available. But the likelihood and severity of any unwanted side effects can also vary from individual to individual.

Possible side effects can be minimized when patients talk with their health care provider about possible interactions with any other prescriptions, over-the-counter medications, and dietary supplements being taken. Carefully following directions for the medication and asking a pharmacist about precautions (e.g., whether to eat beforehand, foods to avoid, dosing, and timing) may also reduce unwanted side effects. Patients should be encouraged to report side effects that become too problematic, as their health care provider may be able to change their medications or offer a different treatment option if one is available.

Weighing the risks and benefits of specific treatment options involves more than assessing the physiological dimension of a medication or treatment. What is important to an individual and their quality of life is rooted in personal and cultural values. As discussed earlier, cultural beliefs not only shape the understanding of illness and related expectations about daily life and social interactions but also affect what may be considered acceptable risks and benefits of treatments.

How specific medications and treatments impact the ability to fulfill social roles (such as the ability to work, take care of children, and tend to the ill) or the potential impact they have on family, friends, and work life (the cost, timing, and logistics of treatments) can play a significant role in assessing the risks and benefits. Individuals' circumstances differ, and their beliefs and values shape the decision-making criteria. For example, if cultural values stress the responsibility of a parent to provide for their family, and the prescribed treatment involves missing work or the side effects leave the person unable to work, a patient may forgo the recommended treatment to be able to fulfill social expectations. These factors also affect perceptions of pain and pain management, which the next section explores.

Pain and Pain Management

Pain often accompanies chronic disease and end-of-life illness. Therefore, treatment plans should include short- and long-term strategies for pain management. The strategies will vary based on the disease pathology and an individual's specific symptoms. As the disease progresses, it may become necessary to update a treatment plan and make changes in pain management strategies.

While medical professionals rely on standardized pain-rating scales, each of us experiences pain differently. What one person may experience as unbearable pain, another might accept as uncomfortable but tolerable. Health care providers must rely on the self-reported experience of pain and customize pain management strategies accordingly.

People also describe their pain within their cultural frameworks and life experiences. In the United States, patients often use words like "sharp," "shooting," "aching," "piercing," "throbbing," or "cutting" to describe pain. These terms are commonly understood ways to describe variations in pain in the U.S. dominant culture, but for other cultures, these terms may have little to no meaning when describing pain. For instance, tribal cultures may rely on symbols and stories to relate what they are feeling or use examples that come from meaningful imagery within their cultural context: pain might be described as feeling like lightning, fire, the bite of a snake, or radiating like a spider's web (Galanti, 2015).

Having a clear understanding of a patient's pain is an integral part of the diagnostic and treatment process. Pain indicates a problem in the body. Finding the source of that pain and identifying the type of pain helps facilitate successful pain management. A health care provider may ask a patient to describe their pain and prompt the patient with descriptors. They may ask questions such as "Is the pain sharp or dull?" or "Does it radiate down your leg?" If these descriptors are not culturally meaningful, the patient may struggle to communicate what the pain feels like, which can be a barrier to effective pain management. One tool for understanding a patient's pain level is the pain scale shown in box 6.6.

Box 6.6: Medical Pain Scale

Health providers use pain charts to help patients describe their pain levels. Charts often include a numbered scale: zero being no pain all the way up to ten being the most severe pain. The scale also includes a series of faces to represent the numbered level of pain. Figure 6.1 is an example of this type of chart.

Figure 6.1. This chart shows a variation of a pain chart known as the Wong-Baker Pain Rating Scale.

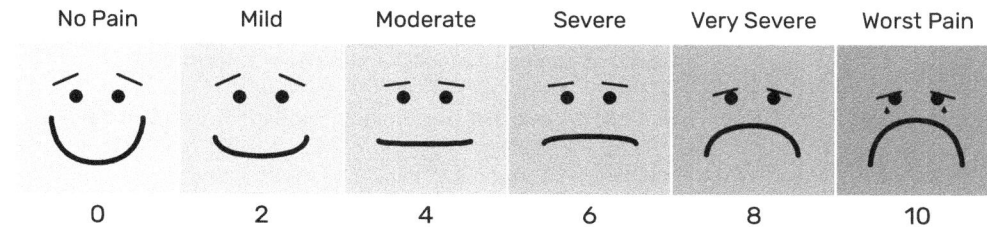

No Pain	Mild	Moderate	Severe	Very Severe	Worst Pain
0	2	4	6	8	10

Using numbers and faces to describe pain may not work for everyone. Some cultures have negative or positive beliefs about specific numbers that can affect whether they would use a particular number to describe their pain. For others, a smiling face does not always suggest happiness or well-being. In many Asian cultures, a smile can indicate embarrassment, anger, or social discomfort (Fang et al., 2020).

Neurodivergent patients, including those with autistic spectrum disorders, may have difficulty communicating pain, making these charts less effective in determining their pain levels. In these situations, health care providers can use multiple approaches to assess pain, including verbal expressions and sounds, facial expressions and gestures, and behavioral observations by family and caregivers (Johnson et al., 2023).

The Management of Pain

Pain is a multidimensional, complex concept that includes a variety of sensory experiences characterized by discomfort and suffering. The presence of pain can bring on other physiological symptoms such as nausea, diarrhea, weakness, and fatigue. See box 6.7 for descriptions of different forms of chronic pain.

A reciprocal interaction exists between some psychological conditions and physiological pain. Anxiety, stress, and depression can trigger pain as well as exacerbate existing pain. A person's lifestyle, activities, relationships, and independence are affected by the presence, level, and duration of their pain. For example, Chris, who was being treated for bone cancer, had been managing his symptoms. As the cancer spread to his spine and hips, the pain became more intense, and he found it harder to get through his daily activities. He could no longer meet his friends for golf, enjoy his favorite hobbies, or play with his four-year-old granddaughter. His doctor continued to adjust his medications. Some days were better than others, but the medication's side effects made him feel groggy and disconnected, and he was still experiencing breakthroughs of intense pain. Worn down by chronic pain, Chris began to withdraw socially.

Box 6.7: Forms of Pain

There are many ways to classify and talk about pain. The following descriptions identify specific kinds of pain.

Type of Pain	Description
acute	pain that comes on quickly and lasts for a short time
breakthrough	periodic flare-ups of pain while the patient is already medicated
chronic	ongoing pain that persists over a longer period
idiopathic	pain without a known physical or psychological cause
neuropathic	pain that occurs when the nerves are not properly functioning due to nerve irritation or nerve damage
psychogenic	pain caused by psychological disorders; the pain is real, but it does not usually have a clearly identifiable origin
somatic	pain that is detected by sensory nerves in the muscle, skin, and soft tissues; pain messages are sent to the spinal cord and brain
visceral	pain that is detected by sensory nerves in the internal organs with pain messages sent to the spinal cord and brain

---

Pain is often one of the most challenging symptoms associated with life-threatening disease and end-of-life illness, whether it's part of an anticipated disease trajectory or an unavoidable side effect of treatment. Since pain often develops or intensifies as a disease progresses, treatment plans frequently include pain management strategies. Specific pain treatment decisions are based on the type of pain and its cause, the medical options available, and the patient's beliefs and expectations. Pain relief is often the desired outcome, but in some cases, the elimination of pain may not be possible without complete sedation. In this situation, treatment goals focus more on reducing pain, maximizing functional ability, and improving quality of life.

Pain management approaches vary based on several factors, including the specific type of pain. Acute pain, an immediate indicator of injury or physical harm to the body, is often addressed using a PRN (pro re nata: give as needed) protocol. When a patient feels pain, medication is taken as needed to relieve the pain. In the case of chronic pain, medication may be administered according to a scheduled protocol to provide more consistent relief. This can improve the outcome when medications that need to reach a stable level of concentration in the bloodstream are used to maximize their efficiency.

At times, a scheduled pain management approach may be augmented with a different medication to address periodic pain breakthroughs.

The Language and Culture of Pain

While pain is fundamentally a physiological phenomenon, the meaning and interpretation of pain are influenced by social and cultural factors. Our upbringing affects how we understand the nature, intensity, and duration of pain. Cultural expectations shape our understanding of acceptable pain levels that are just part of life and pain that needs to be addressed as a medical issue (Rogger et al., 2023). For instance, researchers found that back pain was common in a rural Nepalese community, yet no one sought medical care for the pain at a local medical facility. Researchers found that back pain was considered a normal part of aging in this community and wasn't considered a medical issue (Anderson, 1984).

Social expectations structure how people verbally and nonverbally convey the presence of pain. Some cultural beliefs and values encourage the suppression of outward pain behavior. In some communities, children are socialized early in life to "be brave" and not cry when in pain. This cultural expectation is often gender specific, with boys and men being socialized to "tough it out" and not seek help when they're hurting. Specific occupations, such as military, first responders, construction, and agriculture, encourage workers to be stoic, not express pain, and minimize the need for medical pain relief. In contrast, other cultures are more emotive and encourage the open expression of pain, just as they would openly demonstrate other feelings in daily life.

Beliefs and values affect perceptions of the effectiveness of pain treatment, which can mimic the well-documented placebo effect. The **placebo effect** in this context refers to changes in physical or mental health attributed to a treatment or medication, regardless of whether the change or the correlation to the treatment is real. Some cultures, including many found in Central Africa, believe that more intrusive or unpleasant treatments are more effective. Therefore, intravenous injections may be preferred over oral tablets, even if the tablets are highly effective. Foul-tasting medicine may be believed to work better than medicine that tastes pleasant, and bigger pills are perceived to work better than smaller pills. These beliefs can affect whether a prescribed pain medication is taken and how effective it is perceived to be (Murdan et al., 2023; Eibs et al., 2020).

Cultural expressions of pain and beliefs about pain treatments can affect how a patient reports pain, what the patient expects, and whether a prescribed treatment protocol is followed. To avoid underdiagnosis and undertreatment of pain in cross-cultural interactions, health care providers must anticipate pain needs and initiate conversations, explain the rationale for pain treatments, and offer possible options when they are available (Galanti, 2014).

Conclusion

Whether you are a care provider or facing a diagnosis yourself, the uncharted waters of a life-threatening disease can feel daunting and, at times, overwhelming. There is so much unknown to navigate. You might be able to find plentiful information about the general trajectory of a disease and what others have experienced, but your journey will be unique. How a disease affects the body, the effectiveness and availability of the treatments and medications, and how an individual physically and psychologically responds to the disease and treatments can vary from person to person. The way someone adapts to declining health, periods of normalcy, and sudden unexpected changes is affected by social, cultural, and personal attributes.

A medical treatment plan outlines the steps to manage a disease over time. Developed in collaboration with your health care provider and your family, a treatment plan ensures that a patient's medical preferences and goals guide the treatment process. It also identifies contingencies to address changes in the patient's symptoms and medical condition as the disease progresses. Although there may be little a person can do to prevent the eventual progression of a disease, creating and implementing a treatment plan allows the patient to have some control over their response to the disease.

Summary

» Life-threatening diseases are progressive and will either be the eventual cause of or a major contributing factor to death.

» Living with a life-threatening disease poses challenges as one comes to understand what it means to live within the context of a specific disease.

» During the chronic phase of a life-threatening disease, there are often periods of medical stability and normalcy punctuated by critical medical changes and acute medical crises.

» Early in the disease progression, a treatment plan is developed to outline treatment options and treatment goals.

» Treatment decisions are collaboratively developed by the health care providers, the patient, and the patient's social support network.

» The treatment plan is informed by medical needs and health care provider recommendations, but it is also shaped by the patient's cultural beliefs and personal priorities.

» Pain management strategies within the treatment plan address the patient's subjective experience of pain that is informed by their cultural notions of pain.

» Across the disease progression, the treatment plan may need to be updated and adjusted when a patient's medical condition changes, new medical technology advancements create new treatment options, or personal preferences change.

Review Questions

1. What is the main aim of a treatment plan for a life-threatening disease, and what does it include?
2. How do societal and cultural beliefs influence the objectives of treatment for a life-threatening disease?
3. What is the impact of advancements in technology and cultural beliefs on the assessment of treatment options for a life-threatening disease?
4. How do personal beliefs shape the understanding of pain management in the treatment of a life-threatening disease?
5. What role does the concept of cultural lag play in the evaluation of treatment options for a life-threatening disease?

Key Terms

Review these key terms from the chapter. You can find their definitions in the glossary at the end of the book.

» cultural lag
» culturally competent health care organization
» open-disclosure model
» patient-centered care
» placebo effect
» precision medicine
» shared decision-making model
» technical imperative
» treatment adherence
» treatment plan

Chapter 7

The Dying Process

Vignette **The Call of Honor**

In my second year of medical school, while preparing for my first medical board exam, nightly calls with my mom about my father's deteriorating health had become a tradition. They lived five hours away, and he had been in COVID isolation for the last fourteen months because his cancer left him severely immunocompromised. The chats with Mom covered symptom management, wound care, supplies, and logistics. They also circled around dealing with the loneliness and pressures of caregiving in isolation and the uncertainty of how much longer she could care for him alone.

Dad was rapidly losing his mobility and needed more help with daily activities. Over the last few weeks, he'd lost the ability to walk without falling. Now, he mainly stayed in his living room chair, and Mom slept beside him on the couch. The nights had been long. He was in terrible pain and experienced violent side effects from chemotherapy. Between the pain, oxygen deficiency, and lack of sleep, he'd had a night of confusion and uncontrollable PTSD from a lifetime of first-responder trauma. Knowing how drastically he was deteriorating, I called the next day to check in. Mom was in tears from a horrible night of having to keep Dad safe by restraining him while he relived past traumatic events. That was the moment I knew I had to be with them.

One of Dad's greatest worries was that his health situation might distract me from my upcoming board exam. From the outside, this seemed ridiculous, but it was so incredibly important to both of my parents that I didn't push the issue. After this conversation with Mom, I knew they were no longer okay. I had that deep, gut-gnawing, nauseous feeling that you just can't ignore. I called my husband, and he confirmed what I already knew—I needed to be with them now.

Knowing Mom would be upset that I was coming to help, my husband advised, "Tell her when you get to the end of their driveway." I don't remember much of that drive through the desolate night. As I passed through the last town with an open store, I called Mom to ask how she was doing. She said that they had just had their first hospice visit and now had a hospital bed to use. She was relieved to finally have some support but was unsure how she would get him into it and properly adjusted. I told her not to worry because I would be there to help in about thirty minutes. She started crying again, saying I shouldn't have come with my test only a week away. While her words said I shouldn't have come, the relief in her voice told me it was the right decision.

When I arrived, Dad was sprawled across the new hospital bed, and he looked at me without saying much. I hugged them both and made a plan with Mom to get him and his bedding sorted out. He was mildly coherent most of the evening, but at one point, he asked why I was there. I could tell he was worried, so I told him I was on break from school. I spent the rest of the night on the floor next to his bed, studying and helping Mom with his intermittent pains and disorienting moments. Throughout the night and the next day, we worked together to find the right combination of medications to control his pain as his body was shutting down.

By morning, he could no longer drink or talk, and we needed a new pain medication from hospice that could be taken without swallowing. Though he could no longer speak, he woke at one point and looked at me. With a solid stare and furrowed brow, he motioned with his two fingers, pointing from his eyes to mine, like he used to do to say he's got his eyes on me. Then he gave me his trademark smirk that always made me laugh. That smirk turned out to be our last interaction. We called our dearest family friend/auntie and my sister-in-law to give my mom a break while we found a priest to offer last rites. Shortly after the priest left and the four of us sat talking around his bed, Dad passed away peacefully, surrounded by people who loved him dearly.

No words can describe how important this time was for me. I'd never felt such a strong emotional pull toward what I should be doing as when I traveled to be with my family. I had no idea how quickly Dad would transition from talking and taking a few bites of his favorite foods to taking his last breath, but I do know that those few days forever changed who I am and how I feel about end-of-life care. I feel passionately that there are few honors greater than being able to help someone transition peacefully into death. That time was truly a gift I could never have imagined wanting.

S. C. A., 2021

Introduction

Dying begins well before death actually occurs. Understanding the trajectory of the dying process can help reduce the fear of uncertainty and inform end-of-life planning. Nothing is inevitable about the end-of-life trajectory and timeline. Everyone experiences the dying process differently. However, the ability to recognize the typical physical, mental, and emotional changes that occur as death approaches helps us navigate these complex and challenging waters.

As a person's end of life approaches, they and their caregivers need to decide on numerous medical and care issues. Decisions often include whether to continue medical treatments, when and if to shift to comfort care, and how to manage symptoms and pain. The kind of care that will best support the dying person and their loved ones depends on personal preference, cultural and spiritual beliefs, and the availability and accessibility of options. These options, however, may be affected by where someone lives. In much of rural America, for instance, medical services that fulfill personal or cultural preferences for end-of-life care and support can be difficult to access.

This chapter will explore the process of dying, end-of-life care issues and options, and the factors that shape personal choices concerning end-of-life decisions. By understanding the process of dying, we can cultivate compassion, make informed decisions, and support both individuals and their loved ones during this crucial transition.

Learning Objectives

These learning objectives will help you identify what's most important in this chapter. By the end of this chapter, you should be able to do the following:

- » Discuss the meaning of a "good death" and the factors that shape this construct.
- » Explain the Death with Dignity movement and both positions in the debate.
- » Discuss end-of-life care options and the access barriers to these services.
- » Describe common death trajectories, and discuss the implications for end-of-life care.
- » Describe the typical physical, mental, and emotional changes at the end of life.

Sociocultural Dimensions of Dying

My neighbor recently told me that her elderly cousin had passed away. As we talked, my neighbor said her cousin had lived a long life and, gratefully, it had been a "good death." But what does "good death" really mean, and how can death ever be described as good? Does it mean dying peacefully with family and loved ones at your side, as described in the opening vignette, or enjoying a long, full life before taking your final breath? Does a "good death" have a definition?

Figure 7.1. Three dimensions (physical, psycho-emotional, and sociocultural) affect an individual's definition of a "good death."

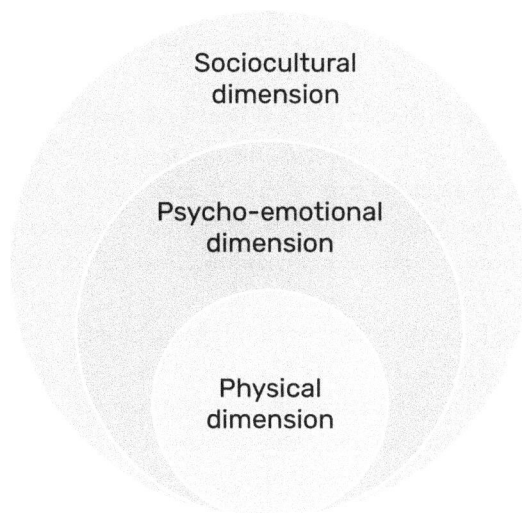

Sociocultural dimension

Psycho-emotional dimension

Physical dimension

Death experiences can vary based on the specific circumstances leading up to the end of life and at the time of the death event. A **good death** is defined by the qualities of the experience for the dying person and their loved ones. Depending on the cause of death, this experience can involve the terminal end-of-life phase, which may last for an extended period, and the nature of the final death event. Whether a person's death is perceived as good or not is subjective, which means it is based on one's own experience rather than objective facts. The meaning of a good death, then, is based on personal preferences and shaped by cultural beliefs.

The meaning of the death experience centers on three primary dimensions, as illustrated in figure 7.1. The physical dimension focuses on managing pain and ensuring care aligns with the individual's specific needs during this critical time. Equally important is the psycho-emotional dimension, which seeks to alleviate unnecessary stress and suffering while preserving the person's dignity. Finally, the sociocultural dimension highlights the role of social relationships and cultural expectations, recognizing how these factors influence the experience of dying and support systems.

In this section, we'll discuss sociocultural factors. For example, someone who is dying may want to fulfill social obligations, complete life goals, avoid burdening others, or participate in cultural or spiritual rituals. This is the case for Nona, who is dying from liver cancer. As she nears the end of her life, Nona considers a "good death" to include being independent, caring for herself until death, and fulfilling her bucket list of adventures. For others, receiving religious blessings or being surrounded by family and friends may be an important determinant of a good death.

Some people prefer the phrase "dying well" instead of a "good death" because they believe there is nothing inherently *good* about death. Instead, they emphasize the quality of a person's experience during the dying process. They assert that death is a natural biological process with no inherent value other than the cultural value we assign to it. Whether you consider anything about death to be *good* depends on your experience and cultural understanding of death. Does death represent the end of pain and suffering? Does it represent a transition to eternal peace? Does it lead someone to a better existence? Your cultural values shape how you answer these questions. To balance multiple perspectives on the topic, both "good death" and "dying well" are used interchangeably in the discussion that follows.

Cultural Beliefs and Practices

Cultural expectations set the standards and provide the social processes by which one is expected to navigate the dying process. Common themes associated with dying well include the desire for comfort, social connection, and maintaining a sense of dignity; however, cultural views on what constitutes a good death may vary. These differences in attitudes, perceptions, and preferences directly impact a person's choices for end-of-life care and how they define quality of life. Cultural beliefs may influence choices regarding the preferred level and type of medical interventions, the information communicated to the patient, and who makes the medical decisions.

As discussed in chapter 2, death fears and anxiety are shaped by cultural beliefs. A person who belongs to a culture that fears death may use every possible treatment or medication available to prolong their life. Another whose culture views death as a natural part of the life cycle may choose treatments focusing on their quality of life rather than extending life. These beliefs influence decisions about specific treatment options, such as whether someone uses resuscitation and feeding tubes during end-of-life care.

During the dying process, cultural beliefs influence people's behavior toward one another, manifesting as patterns of social interaction. Preferences concerning who should be with the dying person, how end-of-life decisions are made, and who is responsible for the decision-making are formed within a cultural context. For instance, in traditional Chinese culture, an adult child is responsible for the parents' end-of-life care and is expected to do whatever can be done to prolong their life. However, the discussion of death and dying is also a cultural taboo, and initiating a discussion of death can be considered disrespectful (Lee et al., 2014). When a person is actively dying, cultural expectations around discussing death have a significant impact on the ability to make end-of-life medical decisions.

Cultural expectations also impact which emotions are expected and allowed, and whether emotional displays are public or private. In some cultures, publicly showing emotions at the time of death or during the dying process is expected. Wailing, flailing, and outward emotional displays of torment are demonstrations of love for the person who is dying or has died. At the same time, in other cultures, it is important not to show emotions. For example, in Egypt, where cultural patterns of communication are open and emotive, it is considered normal for women to weep and wail at the death of a loved one in a demonstrative display of grief. While in many Buddhist cultures, demonstrative displays of grief are less the norm because death is seen as a liberation from this life and a transition to an existence of happiness and peace. In U.S. dominant culture, a grieving person is expected to process their emotions quickly, based on the culture's emphasis on speed, efficiency, and the minimization of discomfort (Mintz, 2024). As discussed in chapter 4, when considering how culture shapes a person's beliefs and behaviors, we should be mindful of how cultural practices change in response to the dominant culture, a process known as acculturation (Carteret, 2010).

Social Status and Expectations

Dying is a profound process of transformation and transition. During the dying process, previous social status expectations, such as the norms and behaviors we expect of others based on their social position, change as society and the individual respond to the eventual death and prepare for the loss of a contributing member of society. Whether as a mother, father, worker, student, or child, the person may no longer be able to fulfill the social responsibilities associated with their specific social positions.

The understanding of a good death and the relative importance of the factors affecting the death experience also vary across different social roles. What is important to the dying person may differ from the concerns of their loved ones and the priorities of health care providers (Meier et al., 2016). For example, Jeannie, a mother who is dying, wants to remain alert for as long as possible so she can interact with her family right up to her death. To allow for this, her care team decreased her pain medication, but she now experiences more pain. Jeannie's family, on the other hand, wants to keep her as comfortable as possible, and her pain management is their priority. The complexity of factors affects the meaning of a good death and can lead to competing preferences. In the United States, where a patient-centered approach to health care is common, a patient's preferences drive treatment and care decisions (Massachusetts Medical Society, 2017). Therefore, regardless of competing perspectives, the patient's needs and desires always take primacy.

As a person approaches the end of life, they may take on the master social status of "a dying person." A **master status** is a social position that supersedes all the other social statuses a person may hold. In a sociological context, master status refers to the primary status position of an individual that shapes their interactions and relationships with others in a particular context; it does not imply someone having power over another person. Yet, because the word "master" can have associations with oppressive systems of slavery and colonialism, some scholars have advocated for a different description, such as primary status or dominant status. At this time, no alternatives have taken hold; "master status" remains the widely accepted term to describe this established sociological concept.

As first described in chapter 1, social status is a person's social position or ranking in relation to other people within society. This shift can be seen in the case of Barbara, who is dying from brain cancer. She holds many social statuses, as figure 7.2 shows. She is a Black woman, mother, wife, daughter, professor, volunteer, singer, gardener, and much more, but her master status has become that of a dying person. The people around her and her self-perception are shaped by this master status. Her status as a person dying of cancer has a significant impact on her life and dominates how others interact with her.

The status transition to that of a "dying person" is often accompanied by a perceptual and behavioral shift away from worldly everyday activities to more existential issues. During the terminal phase of life, a person may reflect on their life's works and experiences within the context of a greater purpose. This often involves searching for meaning in life and death, seeking sources of peace and comfort, and deepening engagement in religious practices.

Figure 7.2. Barbara's master status as a person dying of cancer dominates all other roles and aspects of her identity.

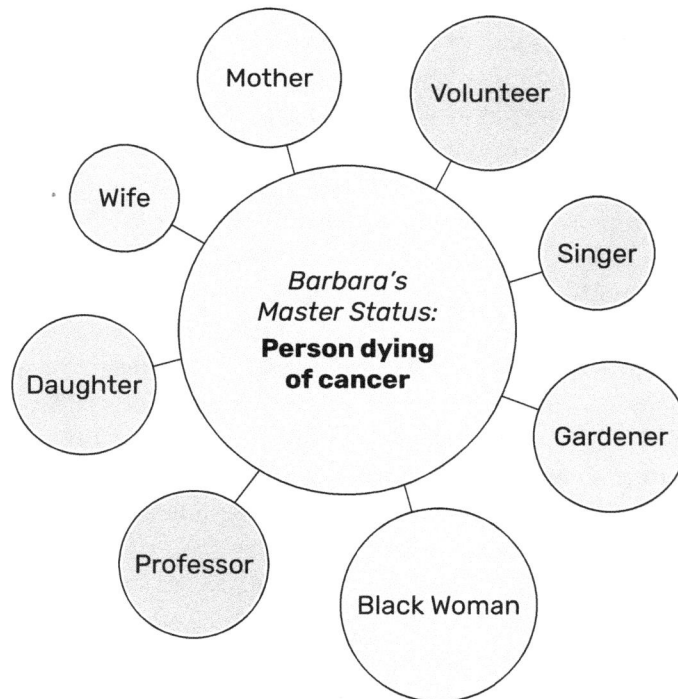

Religious Beliefs and Practices

For many people, spiritual belief systems offer answers to difficult questions, provide comfort through rituals, and foster a supportive community. Religious practices can give reassurance, solace, and a sense of peace during the dying process. People may find comfort in their religious or spiritual rituals, such as the lighting of religious candles, participating in prayer, or receiving a blessing or anointing. For others, it might be reassuring to receive holy sacraments, make a religious offering, or complete a pilgrimage to a sacred location.

Spiritual and religious belief systems play a key role in helping people confront death and manage challenges during the dying process. Each religion's beliefs define what constitutes a good death and the social expectations of the dying process. For instance, Christianity offers guidance for people who are living with dying. Christian denominations believe in the resurrection of the dead, everlasting communion with God after death, and God's ultimate wisdom. Therefore, the end of life is a time to trust in God's wisdom, accept the eventuality of death by letting go of the mortal body, and continue following the teachings of their faith. Even within the diverse practices of Christianity, Christians understand life as a sacred gift; therefore, many denominations oppose medically assisted death or the termination of life support efforts. Christians may also stress the importance of end-of-life rituals and want visits from church representatives to pray over the dying and their loved ones, bestow blessings, or perform end-of-life rituals.

In contrast, a common Hindu belief is that the family has the duty to perform end-of-life rituals and may wish to protect loved ones from the prognosis of death. When the prognosis is dire, any unnecessary prolonging of life is avoided and viewed as interfering with karma and reincarnation (Choundry et al., 2018). Hindu practices and traditions vary more widely, and no single religious authority or standard set of rules prevails. However, a widely shared belief is the importance of preparing for death to ensure good karma, the sum of one's choices and actions that determines one's next phase of life. Traditional practice may include turning the head of the person who has died to the east to face the gods and placing holy water on their lips. Some may prefer to die while lying on the floor, as a bed is seen as a barrier between the earth and the sky.

These examples help illustrate how religion can influence end-of-life practices. Religious and spiritual beliefs guide people through this challenging time. Although various religions may have differing beliefs and practices, a primary function of religion is to help explain the meaning of life and provide an understanding of death. Religious rituals also guide the transition between life and what comes after death. Religious and spiritual practices prescribe what should be done to prepare for death. They explain the role of these practices in easing a person through the dying process and preparing them for what will come.

End-of-Life Care Options

Chronic disease or age-related physical decline at the end of life can be accompanied by pain and distressing symptoms. To improve the quality of life and relieve pain and suffering, **palliative care**, sometimes referred to as comfort care, provides specialized treatment for people living with serious illnesses and medical conditions such as heart failure, cancer, or neurological diseases. Palliative care focuses on anticipating, preventing, and treating physical, psychological, and emotional pain and relieving symptoms. The benefit of palliative care is not limited to patients with a particular diagnosis or projected prognosis. This type of supportive care can begin at the time of diagnosis or any point throughout the disease trajectory. However, the end-of-life phase is when many patients benefit from palliative care. Palliative care is separate from hospice care, which will be discussed later in this chapter. Figure 7.3 illustrates the commonalities and distinct features of these two end-of-life care options.

Figure 7.3. Palliative care and hospice care both focus on symptom management, though the timeframe and types of intervention differ.

	Palliative Care	Hospice Care
Diagnosis	Serious illness, not necessarily terminal	Terminal illness
Timeframe	At any stage of illness	Typically in the last six months of life
Treatment Approach	Relief from symptoms and ongoing treatment	Relief from symptoms without curative treatment

Consider the case of Phil, who was diagnosed with heart failure several years ago. During the early stages of the disease, he only had minor symptoms with little disruption to his daily activities. As the disease progressed, he became weaker and more fatigued. Now, as the end of life approaches, he spends much of his time in a recliner or bed. Phil is experiencing increased pain, stiffness, and muscle weakness that limit his mobility and ability to engage in daily activities without assistance. His medical care team has adjusted his treatment plan to improve the quality of his remaining time, including palliative services from a physical therapist, a massage therapist, and a counselor to address his depression related to his pain and loss of mobility.

Access to Palliative Care

Access to palliative care benefits the patient, daily care providers, and the health care system. Patients who have their comfort care needs identified early and addressed promptly have less pain, fewer symptoms and complications, and a reduction in hospital stays. The use of palliative care services at an earlier stage of a disease or medical condition can improve a patient's physical, functional, emotional, and social well-being and increase coping skills (Temel et al., 2010).

Community-based palliative care programs lower health care costs and reduce the need for hospitalization (Weng et al., 2022), including programs for life-threatening medical conditions such as organ failure, pulmonary diseases, Alzheimer's disease, and cancers. Receiving palliative care at the community level has distinct advantages. These programs and the facilities are often easier for a patient to access and visit. They may be closer to a patient's home, with some offering home health visits.

Specialized medical staff can help bridge the various services a patient may need. These programs also minimize the time and stress for a caretaker who needs to help a loved one access services. A patient's use of a community-based palliative program can reduce the time, effort, and transportation required to access these services through the hospital system.

Community-based palliative care can also influence how often and when patients go to the hospital. When palliative care is closely coordinated with the patient's care team and health goals, locally based medical providers can regularly monitor the patient, adjust medications, and access additional services as needed. This alignment of services increases the likelihood that emerging situations can be addressed before they become serious and require a more intensive response, which may keep patients at home and out of the hospital. If patients also feel they are receiving the care they need, they are less likely to visit the hospital for care and, therefore, spend less time in the hospital overall (Spilsbury & Rosenwax, 2017).

Hospital admissions and hospital stays are reduced when patient needs are aligned with the most appropriate and effective level of care. Reduction in overall health care costs minimizes the strain on health care resources and an overburdened hospital system. A patient's age, gender, socioeconomic status, and location affect all aspects of a person's life, including the dying experience. For example, U.S. rural populations tend to be older, have higher mortality rates, suffer more from chronic diseases, and be disproportionately poorer than urban populations. They also have less access to palliative care (Rural Health Information Hub, n.d.-b). In the United States, approximately 66% of urban hospitals with more than fifty beds have palliative care available (Dumanovsky et al., 2016); whereas in rural areas, only 17% of comparably sized rural hospitals provide palliative services (figure 7.4) (WWAMI Rural Health Research Center, n.d.). Data also indicate that caregivers for the medically fragile who live in rural areas often spend more time providing care and are more likely to care for multiple people than in urban or suburban areas.

These disparities in palliative care access are especially concerning considering the important role these programs play in supporting the patient's caregivers and loved ones. In addition to the direct care of the patient, palliative care providers can also assist a caregiver in the coordination between doctors, helping the family understand treatment regimens, building a support team, and identifying and accessing resources and respite care options.

Figure 7.4. This chart compares the availability of palliative care in urban and rural communities in hospitals with more than fifty beds. Adapted from WWAMI Rural Health Research Center, n.d.

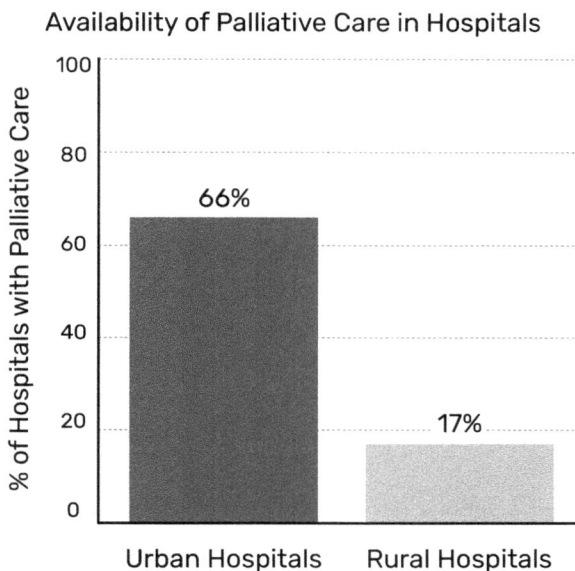

Availability of Palliative Care in Hospitals

For example, Pam, a sixty-eight-year-old grandmother, is caring for her sister who is in end-stage kidney failure due to complications from diabetes. But she is also responsible for the care of her frail, aging mother and two young grandchildren. Living in rural Oklahoma, they are thirty miles from her sister's specialists and the nearest major hospital. Fortunately, a nearby community clinic has a palliative care outreach program. When a home health nurse makes his weekly visit, he notices Pam is exhausted, seems overwhelmed, and is having trouble following her sister's medication protocol. He takes the time to review the information and dosage with Pam and her sister and leaves written instructions with the clinic's twenty-four-hour contact information in case of any questions. On the way out, he speaks with Pam to assess her well-being and then connects her with a local resource that offers support for caregivers, including options for short-term respite care.

One reason rural areas face significant barriers in providing palliative care is that more sparsely populated regions lack sufficient patient numbers and medical resources to maintain these programs. These areas are hindered by geographically dispersed patients, significant travel and driving time, the lack of rural hospitals and medical specialists, and difficulties with recruiting and retaining trained health care providers (Weng et al., 2022). For many patients in rural areas, palliative care services are not an option.

Nursing Care and Home Health Care

Nearly 25% of people in the United States are in a care facility at the end of life (National Center for Health Statistics, 2017). Many residents may have already been in a care facility for some time, while others transitioned to a care facility as they approached the end of life. For example, sixty-three-year-old Lily suffered a debilitating stroke six years ago and has been a resident at a nursing care facility since then. Recently, she was diagnosed with advanced lung cancer and is now receiving end-of-life care. In contrast, seventy-nine-year-old Dominick was recently admitted to the care facility when his end-stage emphysema and declining health left him unable to care for his personal and medical needs. In both situations, these residents will likely spend the remainder of their lives in a care facility, an average of two to three years, according to market research.

Nursing care facilities, also known as nursing homes, are residential centers designed to provide health and personal care services for individuals who are no longer able to care for themselves. These facilities offer a broad range of services:

» Assisted living settings help residents with meals, medication, and housekeeping.
» Skilled nursing care facilities focus on medical care, including rehabilitative services like physical, occupational, and speech therapy, and complete support with daily activities.

Seventy percent of nursing care facilities are for-profit, while 13% are nonprofit, and only 7% are government-operated (Michas, 2022). These numbers highlight the predominance of for-profit nursing care facilities, which have implications for the organization and delivery of care. Differences in ownership models—such as for-profit, nonprofit, and government-operated facilities—may influence priorities, resource allocation, and access to services.

Nursing care facilities can be essential end-of-life options, but they are often unavailable for rural residents. Rural nursing care facilities face many of the same challenges as rural palliative care programs. Rising operational costs due in part to the lower number of patients, distance to resources, and difficulty in finding and retaining trained staff have resulted in a high rate of nursing facility closures across rural America. Compared to urban and suburban areas, as well as mid-sized cities, a higher number of rural counties lack nursing homes. Only 82% of rural counties in the United States have a Medicare/Medicaid-certified nursing home, with most of the underserved counties located in the West, Midwest, and South. Even in rural counties that may have a nursing home, the distance to the facility and transportation barriers can be problematic. Rural residents who do need to leave their community, family, and friends to access these services face the additional stress of relocation and isolation (Rural Health Information Hub, n.d.-b; Rural Policy Research Institute, 2022).

Accessing at-home care can address some end-of-life medical and social service needs. **Home health agencies** reduce hospital admissions by providing medical services that help patients stay in their homes. Home health care providers may administer medication through IVs, give injections, care for wounds, monitor health conditions, and make immediate referrals for emerging health conditions. They can also connect patients to other essential nonmedical care, like social services or home care aides.

End-of-life health care delivered in a patient's home can be less expensive, more convenient, and just as effective as services provided in hospitals or nursing care facilities. However, rural residents have limited access to these services, which may be located fifty to one hundred miles away with few openings or long waiting lists. In many instances, options for specialized medical needs, occupational or physical therapy, or mental health support may not be available. To reach their patients, rural area home health workers often travel long distances on poor roads or in inclement weather, leading to delays or interruptions in care. These challenges can also make it difficult for hospital patients who are discharged to follow their instructions and receive these services (Rural Health Information Hub, n.d.-a; WWAMI Rural Research, 2021).

When the health care provider and the patient are at different locations, telemedicine can help fill service gaps by providing remote clinical services, including diagnosis and treatment, in both audio and visual formats. Research indicates that telemedicine can improve access to health care professionals for at-home patients and allow them to develop genuine relationships with their providers (Steindal et al., 2020). The use of virtual appointments to monitor medical conditions, manage emerging symptoms, adjust medication, and ascertain when in-person visits are necessary can relieve the burden of long-distance travel and expense for patients and their families.

However, for rural residents, limited cellular coverage and internet access can negate this option. One-fourth of rural Americans and nearly one-third of Americans who live on Tribal lands do not have access to broadband internet services, limiting their ability to use telemedicine (Vogels, 2021; Bureau of Indian Affairs, n.d.). Some areas have unreliable cell connectivity or, in some cases, zero cell phone access—even in places relatively close to busy highways and towns. For example, drive just ten miles east of the major highway that connects cities along the Oregon coast, and you are suddenly out of cell phone range and without broadband internet service. This lack of reliable access leaves millions of Americans unable to use telemedicine to receive health care services (Pew Research Center, 2024).

Hospice

An important option for end-of-life care is **hospice**, specific care intended for terminally ill people at the end of their lives. The goal of hospice care is to support the patient and their loved ones while fostering the highest quality of life possible for whatever time the patient has left rather than curing the disease or medical condition. To qualify for hospice services, a physician or primary health care provider must verify that the patient is terminally ill with six months or less to live. A patient's enrollment can be extended as many times as necessary to support a patient until the end of life. Patients can disenroll at any time or request re-enrollment whenever they choose.

Hospice programs focus on reducing pain and keeping the patient as comfortable as possible. They address overall well-being during the end of life, including attention to physical, psychological, social, and spiritual needs. To address these needs, a hospice team may involve doctors, nurses, other health care providers, social workers, counselors, and volunteers. See box 7.1 for descriptions of the different kinds of service providers in hospice programs.

Box 7.1: Hospice Team Members

Hospice care teams provide end-of-life care for patients and support for their families or caregivers (Mayo Clinic, 2021). They typically include the following:

  » **bereavement counselors**: licensed professionals who offer support and guidance after the death of a loved one in hospice
  » **doctors**: a team of health care professionals, including a primary care doctor and a hospice doctor or medical director, who oversee care
  » **home health aides**: care providers who give extra support for routine activities, such as dressing, bathing, and eating
  » **nurses**: health care professionals who come to your or your relative's home or another setting and are responsible for the coordination of the hospice care team
  » **pharmacists**: health care professionals who provide medication oversight and suggestions regarding the most effective ways to relieve symptoms
  » **social workers**: licensed professionals who provide counseling, support, and referrals to other services
  » **spiritual counselors**: chaplains, priests, lay ministers, or other spiritual counselors who provide spiritual care and guidance for the entire family
  » **therapists**: speech, physical and occupational therapists can provide therapy if needed
  » **volunteers**: trained assistants who offer company or respite for caregivers and help with transportation or other needs

---

Depending on patient preference, hospice programs may include access to aromatherapy, therapeutic massage, or art, music, and pet therapy. These services complement pain management and contribute to the patient's psychological well-being and comfort (Dingley et al., 2021; Hospice Alliance, n.d.).

Most hospice services are provided at home to the patient, with a family member acting as the primary caregiver. With home-based care, staff make regular visits and are on-call around the clock. In some areas, respite care may be available to relieve the family member or caretaker periodically. If only a short break is needed, a relief caretaker may come to the home for a few hours or the day. However, if longer breaks are required, the patient may be transferred to a hospice facility for care when resources become available. Hospice programs may be available in some hospitals, nursing homes, and designated hospice facilities. The patient will reside in these facilities for ongoing end-of-life care in these situations. The cost for both in-home and residential facility hospice programs is financially supported by the patient's Medicare, Medicaid, Department of Veterans Affairs, or private insurance benefits. However, most hospice services are often based on a patient's need rather than their ability to pay (Mayo Clinic, 2021).

Although hospice programs are increasingly available nationwide, less than 20% of hospices operate in rural areas (Rural Health Information Hub, 2021). Rural hospice programs face many of the same barriers as the other previously discussed end-of-life care options. Due to lower patient numbers, staffing shortages, high staff turnover, and long driving distances, they operate under lower cost margins, making them more financially vulnerable and limiting available services. In addition, home-based hospice relies on a family member or friend to serve as the primary caregiver, which can be difficult to arrange. Adult children have often relocated to other cities or states, or other possible caregivers live long distances away, making it difficult for the dying person to be cared for in their home (Parker, 2021).

With limited access to hospice services, many rural patients who need immediate end-of-life care are left with no other option than to be admitted to rural critical access hospitals. These hospitals are small facilities with limited in- or out-patient beds, often fewer than twenty. In these instances, swing beds that are regularly used for both acute care and skilled nursing care are temporarily shifted to patients who need end-of-life medical comfort care (Centers for Medicare and Medicaid Services, n.d.). With resources and staff limitations like those of other rural medical care services, these hospitals do their best to support end-of-life patients. Still, they have a broader primary mission, operate under different regulations and restrictions, and are unable to offer many of the comfort care and family support services provided by hospice.

Factors in End-of-Life Choices

People make end-of-life care decisions based, in part, on their general orientation toward life. A **sanctity-of-life perspective** holds that all life is a sacred gift with intrinsic meaning. Many who hold this perspective believe that God or a higher power grants life, and only this divine source can decide when it ends. In this view, everyone has a right to life, and it should be valued and protected. A **quality-of-life perspective** involves an individual assessment of one's life based on a personal standard of health, comfort, happiness, and purpose. This multidimensional evaluation considers a person's overall emotional, psychological, and social well-being and the satisfaction they find in relationships, activities, and experiences.

For example, Paige recently met with her doctor concerning the side effects of her ongoing chemotherapy for terminal blood cancer. The treatments had slowed the progression of the disease, but severe side effects had become difficult to manage. She had been experiencing tingling in her arms and legs, extreme nerve pain, and numbness in her legs and feet that limited her ability to walk, work, tend to daily activities, or sleep. Unrelenting pain, lack of mobility, and sleep deprivation made her miserable and depressed. With no other viable options, she could choose to continue treatments to prolong her life or stop them to improve the quality of her day-to-day life, knowing death would likely come more quickly. She is currently weighing this decision, and her choice will rest partly on her orientation to the meaning of life.

An individual's perspective affects their willingness to intervene in the dying process. Someone who sees life as a sacred gift may be inclined to undergo treatment to extend life for a few weeks or months despite debilitating side effects. Someone who prioritizes quality of life may forgo further treatments to maximize their enjoyment of the time they have left. In addition to these personal views, the following sections will discuss other factors that influence end-of-life choices, such as someone's financial resources and racial and ethnic identity.

Financial Resources

As discussed, where you live affects your care options, constraining and shaping your choices for end-of-life health care. While urban and suburban communities may have greater variety and access, these services may not be financially or logistically attainable for many residents, regardless of location. Many people, especially those who belong to the working class or who live at or below the poverty line, may encounter financial barriers to the end-of-life care they need or would prefer. Those with limited financial means often struggle to pay for end-of-life care and have trouble arranging for someone to help them secure needed services.

Those who rely on government programs for health care also face limitations and restrictions on what services are covered. For instance, Medicare does not generally pay for custodial care such as feeding, toileting, and other assistance in daily care offered by many nursing care facilities and home health care providers. In other situations, individual states can opt out of or limit access to federal programs such as Medicaid, which provides health care to low-income households (Wachterman & Sommers, 2021). Even with private or employer-based medical insurance, most policies offer limited, if any, coverage for end-of-life care services. Medicare, Medicaid, and private health insurance will be discussed in greater detail in chapter 8.

The middle class, which generally has more financial resources than the working class, can still face challenges in accessing end-of-life care. For example, Theresa's husband Paul died ten years ago after a long and expensive battle with cancer. They spent much of their savings on his care because he did not qualify for any government assistance, and their health insurance did not cover many of his medical needs and long-term nursing home care. Theresa is now facing her own end-of-life care decisions. She will pretty quickly go through the rest of her savings because of the $4,000–$9,000 per month bills for assisted living and eventual nursing home care. Once she spends her resources and qualifies for Medicaid, her options will decrease because many nursing care facilities do not accept Medicaid reimbursement or have a limited number of Medicaid placements available. These types of difficult situations and choices often disproportionately impact women because they statistically live longer than men.

Racial and Ethnic Identities

People are increasingly using hospice at the end of life, as a growing number of patients are choosing to die at home. However, health disparities, defined as unequal and unjust health outcomes and access to health care services experienced by different racial and ethnic groups, exist in end-of-life treatment, including the use of hospice, as they do in all areas of health care.

Research shows Black patients are less likely to access hospice, more likely to have multiple emergency visits and hospitalizations, and more likely to undergo intensive treatment in the last six months of life compared to White individuals. These differences in end-of-life care are consistent with a broad range of racial disparities in health care use and outcomes (Ornstein et al., 2020). Commonly shared beliefs, preferences, and values among many Black patients may contribute to lower rates of hospice care. Black patients and their families tend to prefer life-sustaining treatments, are less comfortable discussing death, and are more likely to distrust the health care system than patients from other racial groups. The long-standing distrust of the health care system is an especially important factor since hospice focuses on palliative care rather than curative care (Johnson et al., 2008).

Social and personal factors also influence a person's use of hospice care, including financial limitations based on social class, how health care resources are distributed in the United States, and how the U.S. health care system works (Wheeler et al., 2013). Racial disparities in health care are also impacted by personal and cultural factors. These factors include individuals who prefer more aggressive care, mistrust the health care system, lack in-home resources, or do not have adequate information about treatment options (LoPresti et al., 2014).

For instance, Hispanic patients are less likely to choose hospice services at the end of life. Hispanic Americans are now the second-largest racial or ethnic group in the United States and one of the fastest-growing groups (Funk & Lopez, 2022). The Hispanic American community uses multiple terms to describe themselves—Hispanic, Latino, Latina, Latinx, Latine, etc.— which reflect diverse perspectives, linguistic preferences, and cultural identities. For consistency and to align with Census data and related sources, this chapter uses the term "Hispanic" as an umbrella term for all members of this community. The Hispanic population is not only growing but also aging rapidly (Peña et al., 2023), yet hospice care remains underutilized by these families (Cardenas et al., 2023).

Historically, Hispanic families have used hospice less than other racial or ethnic groups. As a result, they are less likely to have prior experience with hospice and may know little or nothing about it before they need it. Language barriers between families, medical staff, and hospice workers can also lead to misperceptions and complicate sharing information about available end-of-life options and how to access services. Additionally, the uninsured rate among Hispanic patients is more than double that of non-Hispanic patients. A lack of medical insurance can hinder access to hospice services, making them a less viable end-of-life option (Kreling, n.d.; U.S. Department of Health and Human Services, 2021).

While the Hispanic population nationally represents a racially diverse group, this demographic group shares some cultural norms and expectations about end-of-life care. While non-Hispanic families receiving hospice services generally value information about what to expect in the last days of life, Hispanic families often avoid direct discussion of the prognosis and do not want to discuss the actual death. This runs counter to the open, frank discussion of death and what to expect, which is a foundational element of hospice care. Many hospice agencies are incorporating strategies to help navigate these types of cross-cultural interactions and preferences to ensure that hospice care is inclusive and a viable choice for those nearing the end of life. For example, hospice agencies may use staff who are bilingual or trained in cultural competency to use sensitive terminology when possible (e.g., "future care" instead of "terminal care"), assess the family's preferences in communication, and identify a family member or community member who is familiar with the family to act as a sounding board for guidance about communication (Kreling et al., 2010).

Death with Dignity Movements

In recent decades, the movement to ensure that individuals have the autonomy and agency to control their own end-of-life decisions, including the right to die, has grown. Autonomy and agency refer to a person's ability to live according to their values and control their own decisions and actions. Social institutions, such as health care, medicine, and government, have long set the standards, accepted practices, and legal statutes concerning end-of-life options. But these options may conflict with personal preferences, highlighting a fundamental question: Who has the ultimate right to decide how and when an individual's life ends?

For many people, the right to decide what a good death means and what constitutes quality of life belongs to the individual. This decision may include how much pain, suffering, and debilitating symptoms they should endure at the end of life. Across the United States, advocacy groups work to pass **right-to-die legislation** (also referred to as physician-assisted suicide or medically assisted death), which are laws that provide the option for terminally ill patients who meet specified legal criteria to end their life by taking medication prescribed by a doctor.

Oregon enacted the first right-to-die law in the United States in 1997 (Oregon Health Authority, n.d.-a). Oregon's Death with Dignity Act (DWDA) allows a terminally ill individual to end their own life with a self-administered lethal dose of medication prescribed by a physician for that purpose. The Oregon law outlines a structured procedure with specific requirements and criteria that must be met for an individual to utilize this option, as shown in box 7.2. As more states pass right-to-die legislation and many others consider the issue, debates continue over this type of legal protection for self-determination at the end of life.

Supporters of legal access to medically assisted death assert that the right to die is a fundamental human right when a person is facing a terminal disease. They support patient autonomy and choice over government restrictions and contend that if patients have control over their medical treatment, they should also have control over the circumstances of their death. Those who advocate for right-to-die laws also note that most legislation lays out specific criteria and a regulated, structured process to safeguard against possible abuses of the laws (Dugdale et al., 2019).

Box 7.2: Oregon's Death with Dignity Act Criteria

Oregon's Death with Dignity Act has survived multiple legal and political challenges and has become a model for many other states that have sought out this protection as an end-of-life option (Oregon Health Authority, n.d.-b). As of March 2022, Oregon is no longer enforcing the previous residency requirement. As you read through Oregon's requirements, consider the reasons behind each of these criteria, the role of health care providers, and the cultural and religious perspective that might influence one's view of this law.

Participants must be:

>> at least eighteen years or older
>> capable of making and communicating their own health care decisions
>> diagnosed with a terminal illness that will lead to death within six months
>> able to self-administer and swallow the medication or self-administer via a feeding tube

Procedural and core criteria include:

>> two oral requests to the physician at least fifteen days apart
>> a written request to the physician be signed by two witnesses
>> confirmation of the diagnosis and the prognosis by two physicians
>> verification by a physician that the patient is capable of making and communicating their own health care decisions
>> information on feasible alternatives presented by a physician

Opponents of this legislation fear a lack of oversight. They cite concerns that if a person is too ill to speak for themselves, others will make this life-ending choice for the patient. Opponents worry that adopting right-to-die laws will be a slippery slope, opening the door to greater access to medically assisted death provided by the current law. For example, the law requires patients to self-administer the medication. Some want to expand the definition of "self-administer" to include the right of a patient to identify another person to administer the end-of-life prescription. However, opponents argue that normalizing medically assisted death will lead to patients feeling responsible for relieving the burden their care places on their loved ones. Many believe physicians should alleviate suffering, not the patients themselves (Dugdale et al., 2019).

As this discussion continues, eleven jurisdictions (California, Colorado, Hawaii, Maine, New Jersey, New Mexico, Montana, Oregon, Vermont, Washington, and the District of Columbia currently have right-to-die laws or court rulings that support right-to-die options (Buchholz, 2022), and many others are considering some type of legislation to protect this end-of-life option.

Navigating the Death Experience

Many changes occur as a person approaches the end of life, but some changes are more anticipated than others. People expect physical changes with a life-threatening disease or a terminal medical condition. They know symptoms are likely and physical decline is inevitable, even though the timeline differs based on the disease or condition and a person's unique biology.

However, people are often less aware of the changes in social interactions that occur during the end-of-life stage. Physical limitations can lead to shifts in the frequency and occurrence of social interactions. Knowing that the end of life is near can also affect what people discuss and how they express it. The following sections will examine the biological patterns of death and the impact of death awareness on social interactions.

Death Awareness and Social Interaction

Communication and interactions with people who are terminally ill play a critical role in providing comprehensive medical and social support during the end-of-life stage. Clear communication between the patients and their support network helps them meet their care needs. In the 1960s, sociologists Barney Glaser and Anselm Strauss (1965) began writing about the dying experience, focusing particular attention on the social interactions between the dying person and the people around them. They observed that the details about a patient's condition, their prognosis, and who knows this information can shape communication. Based on what the people interacting know and how they understand the implications of the information, they enter into a social agreement about what they will say openly.

In sociology, **awareness contexts** refer to the different levels of knowledge and acceptance of a medical situation, particularly in the terminal stages. Glaser and Strauss (1965) identified four ways awareness contexts can influence communication and social interaction when someone is dying:

» **Closed awareness**: The dying person is not aware of their impending death, but others may know. The patient may not understand their condition or choose not to accept the reality of their situation. This context is often short-term and unstable as people pick up on subtle cues and become aware of their circumstances.

» **Suspected awareness**: The dying person deduces they are dying, but no one around them confirms it. Patients may not come out and directly ask others about their prognosis. Instead, a patient may indirectly prompt and prod others to see if they will confirm their suspicion.

» **Mutual pretense awareness**: Participants side-step the issue, avoid direct communication, and pretend that things are normal. Unspoken, implicit agreements maintain the illusion that the patient is getting better. When the topic arises, participants change the subject or become dismissive or angry.

» **Open awareness**: Participants fully acknowledge the prognosis. An honest environment encourages the expression of emotions and frank conversations about people's needs and how others can provide support. The reality of death is acknowledged and discussed as part of everyday life.

Each of these awareness contexts sets up a specific environment that shapes patterns of communication. But that context can change as a person's situation changes. For example, although Audrey was in end-stage liver cancer, she and her husband interacted in a mutual pretense awareness context and did not talk about her prognosis. But as her physical condition declined and her symptoms worsened, they could no longer ignore her reality. They eventually shifted to an open awareness context where they found comfort in being able to talk about her condition and reach out for additional support.

Death Trajectories

Death trajectories can predict what is likely to happen and when, but they are not determinative. Factors like individual physiology, variations of the disease, and specific lifestyle choices can alter the disease's progression and trajectory. However, trajectories help map the likely course of decline, the distinctive path of decline, and the speed at which the condition progresses. This information assists in planning treatment and care, determining the level and timing of medical intervention, and developing coping strategies.

Current models of the dying trajectory commonly identify four distinct disease paths that map the course of decline across the dying process: sudden death, terminal disease, major organ failure, and frailty (Lynn, 2004). The following sections provide an overview of the four death trajectories, describing their likely occurrence, interventions, and key characteristics. Figure 7.5 provides a chart to help you compare the four paths.

Figure 7.5a. This chart shows the four major death trajectories, their progression, treatments, and complicating factors. Adapted from Lunney et al., 2022.

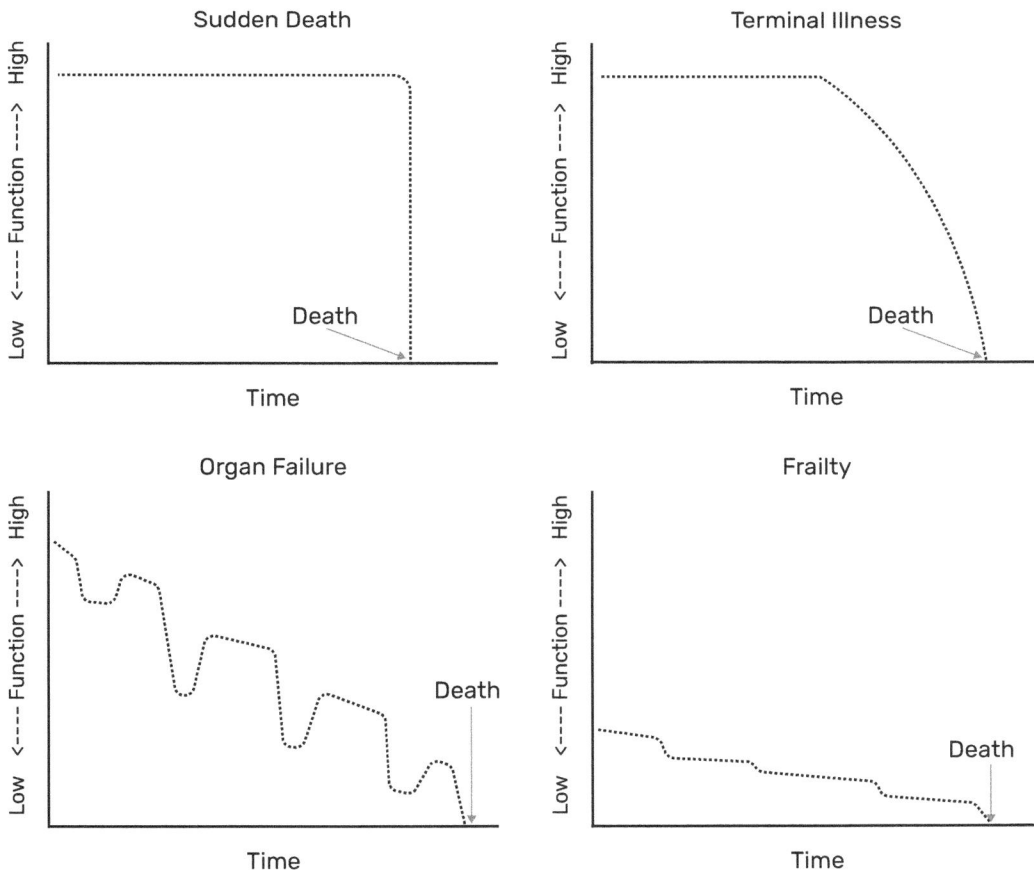

Figure 7.5b. This chart shows the four major death trajectories, their progression, treatments, and complicating factors.

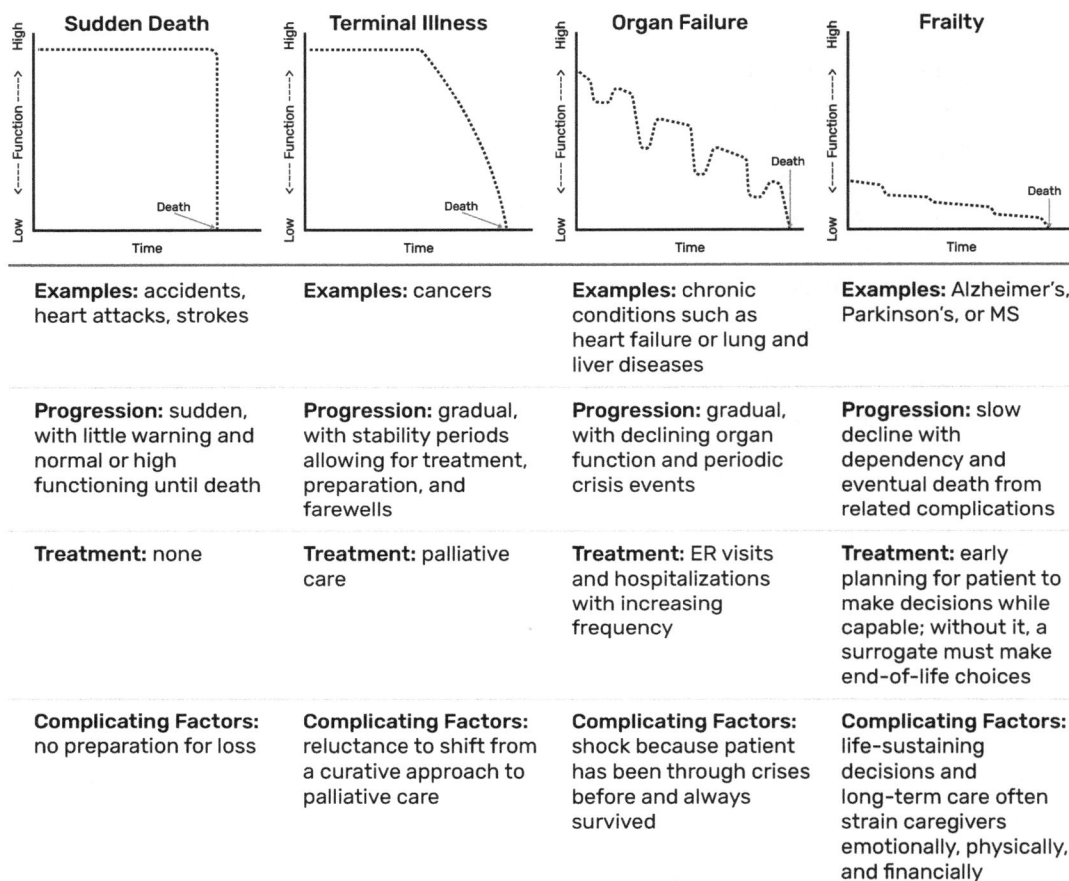

Sudden Death	Terminal Illness	Organ Failure	Frailty
Examples: accidents, heart attacks, strokes	Examples: cancers	Examples: chronic conditions such as heart failure or lung and liver diseases	Examples: Alzheimer's, Parkinson's, or MS
Progression: sudden, with little warning and normal or high functioning until death	Progression: gradual, with stability periods allowing for treatment, preparation, and farewells	Progression: gradual, with declining organ function and periodic crisis events	Progression: slow decline with dependency and eventual death from related complications
Treatment: none	Treatment: palliative care	Treatment: ER visits and hospitalizations with increasing frequency	Treatment: early planning for patient to make decisions while capable; without it, a surrogate must make end-of-life choices
Complicating Factors: no preparation for loss	Complicating Factors: reluctance to shift from a curative approach to palliative care	Complicating Factors: shock because patient has been through crises before and always survived	Complicating Factors: life-sustaining decisions and long-term care often strain caregivers emotionally, physically, and financially

Sudden Death Trajectory

Sudden death occurs with little or no apparent warning that death is imminent, and the person has a normal or high level of functioning right up to death. This trajectory includes death from accidents and health conditions such as heart attacks, strokes, aneurysms, and brain bleeds.

» **Occurrences:** This trajectory often occurs outside health care facilities or during routine activities.

» **Interventions:** Medical intervention may only involve responding EMS personnel, emergency room staff, or bystanders performing CPR.

» **Characteristics:** Marked by shock and lack of preparation, this trajectory leaves no chance to say goodbye, complete bucket-list goals, or take care of end-of-life legal issues (e.g., wills, life insurance).

Terminal Disease Trajectory

Due to medical advances in treating life-threatening diseases, the duration of the terminal disease trajectory has lengthened. Disease progression may stabilize or slow with effective treatments, but eventually the progression of the disease exceeds the ability of medical treatment to control the condition, and the decline to death continues. Examples of this trajectory include many types of cancers.

» **Occurrences**: Periods of stability or control of the disease allow time to develop treatment plans, understand the nature of the disease trajectory, and prepare end-of-life plans.

» **Interventions**: While health care providers can often identify the turning point from management to accelerating decline, there may be reluctance of both patients and providers to shift from a curative approach to palliative care. Advance care preparation should include a plan for palliative care and needed social support as the end of life approaches.

» **Characteristics**: This trajectory allows time for the patient and loved ones to process the meaning of the diagnosis, say their goodbyes, and attend to end-of-life details.

Major Organ Failure

Major organ failure is frequently characterized by a slow, gradual onset, accompanied by declining organ function and periodic crisis events caused by eroding organ function or an acute condition brought on by the disease progression. This trajectory is common to chronic, progressive conditions such as heart failure, kidney disease, or lung and liver diseases.

» **Occurrences**: This trajectory often involves emergency room visits and hospitalizations. Acute events become increasingly rapid in succession. Any acute event may result in death or recovery to a new, more tenuous condition.

» **Interventions**: Individuals become more dependent on others for support, frequent access to medical help, and assistance with daily needs as their condition deteriorates. Medical and end-of-life choices should be in place.

» **Characteristics**: The individual rarely thinks of themself as "dying," and loved ones are surprised by their death because the patient has been through crises before and always survived.

Frailty Trajectory

The frailty trajectory involves a slow decline over a long period, with changes in a person's condition that can take many years. Health crises are rare, and the trajectory is frequently seen in cases of Alzheimer's and neurodegenerative diseases such as Parkinson's or multiple sclerosis.

» **Occurrences**: Many patients suffer from cognitive decline and continuing physical deterioration, and they often experience a decline in multiple physiological systems. Individuals often die of complications associated with being completely dependent on others in all activities of daily living.

» **Interventions**: Early treatment and care planning allow the patient to make decisions about their ongoing care while they are still able to be part of the process. This involves assessing the patient's quality of life, especially during the end stage as overall decline reduces the effectiveness of medical interventions. Eventually, decisions concerning the withholding or withdrawal of life-sustaining treatments may need to be made.

» **Characteristics**: Without a long-term plan in place, a surrogate decision-maker will need to make end-of-life decisions for the patient. The intensive care needed over a long period takes an emotional, physical, and financial toll on caregivers and treatment decision-makers (Ballentine, 2018).

Active Phases of Dying

Each person's path to death is unique. Some may experience a steady decline, while others fade quickly. **Active dying** is the final phase of the dying process. Common changes take place as the body starts shutting down, but predicting precisely when death will occur is still difficult.

Understanding what is happening during the active phase of dying and why it is happening can reduce fears and help people prepare for death. This knowledge may be especially helpful for family and friends in providing comfort and reassurance, as well as taking action to help maintain the dignity of their loved ones.

Two to Three Months Before

In the two to three months before a person's death, you may notice the following changes:

» **Physiological changes**: Their body begins to slow down. No longer needing much energy, they stop feeling hunger and thirst, which is normal. Although they may sleep more and lose weight, they are not suffering by not eating.

» **Psychological changes**: They may experience a sense of mild euphoria, well-being, and happiness. They may use this phase as an opportunity to reflect on and review things they regret.

» **Behavioral/social changes**: They may start to withdraw, thus beginning the separation from others and the world. They may say no to visitors. Even when they're open to seeing people, the interaction may be difficult because of their withdrawal, and visitors may feel rejected and struggle to connect.

One to Two Weeks to Days Before Death

The dying process moves faster during this phase. A notable acceleration can be frightening, but it is common as the end of life draws closer. Here are some changes you may notice in the one to two weeks before someone's death:

» **Physiological changes**: Their body has a hard time regulating itself. They may experience fluctuations in body temperature, lower blood pressure, and increased sweating. Swallowing becomes more difficult, and bowel movements become smaller and less frequent.

» **Psychological changes**: As oxygen decreases to their brain, they may be unresponsive or have bouts of agitation, confusion, or hallucinations. They may interact with those who have died, see and reach for people and items that are not there, or relive past experiences. Some people understand these as medically based hallucinations, while others interpret them as religious experiences or manifestations of the transition between life and death. It can be unsettling when the dying person is hallucinating and saying things that don't make sense. Rather than correcting or dismissing their experience, it is more comforting to listen and offer support.

» **Behavioral/social changes**: The person often communicates less and sleeps much of the day. Family and friends may want to wake them, but it is often best if they are allowed to sleep. At this stage, providing comfort often means simply being present with the person rather than focusing on doing things for them.

Just Before Death

As death approaches, the person enters the final phase of active dying. You may notice these primarily physiological changes:

» Breathing becomes more irregular and may stop for twenty to thirty seconds at a time. Guppy-like breathing efforts, coughing, and a gurgling or rattling sound caused by secretions settling in the back of the throat (often referred to as a "death rattle") may be observed.

» Skin color frequently becomes pale, lips and nail beds appear bluish, and mottled-purplish coloration starting in the hands and feet may spread up the arms and legs.

» The dying person can experience sudden leg and arm movements, run a temperature, or have an irregular pulse rate.

At death, a person's breathing and heartbeat stop, and they can't be roused. Their eyes may close or be partially open with a fixed stare, their mouth may fall open, and waste matter in the bladder and rectum may be released.

Conclusion

When people talk about the dying process, they most often focus on the biological aspects of death. There are changes in the body, treatments, and symptoms to navigate, as well as the long-term impacts on daily activities. As death nears, more time and resources are needed to provide medical support and keep a loved one comfortable. This may require families to assess the many options available for end-of-life care. Knowing what these options are can help the patient and their family make the best possible decision.

But dying is also a social process. The dying process affords the patient and their loved ones the chance to show their love for one another, cement the bond they have, and say goodbye. This step involves having the opportunity to make those last social connections with the people we love. In the opening vignette, the daughter described how important it was for her to help care for her dad and to be there for her mom. She knew her dad was dying, and it was her last chance to see him. By going home to be with him, she was able to have that final connection before he died as he shared their father-daughter gesture: *I have my eyes on you.*

Summary

» Observable physical, mental, and emotional changes occur as death approaches.

» When the dying person and their loved ones know what to expect and recognize what is happening, it can help alleviate fears and prepare everyone for what is coming.

» Understanding the dying trajectory enables the dying person to engage in medical and care decisions early in the process and helps family and loved ones make informed decisions for end-of-life care when the dying person may no longer be able to participate in the decision-making process.

» Understanding the death trajectory makes it easier to identify what services and supports might be needed and to pre-position available and accessible resources and options in case they are needed. The dying person and their loved ones can also make decisions about how to spend their time and what is important to accomplish.

» End-of-life customs and rituals may take priority for some people, while others may prioritize spending time connecting with loved ones and saying goodbye.

Review Questions

1. What is meant by a "good death," and what elements contribute to this concept?
2. What is the Death with Dignity movement, and what are the differing opinions on this issue?
3. What options exist for end-of-life care, and what barriers prevent access to these services?
4. How do death trajectories impact end-of-life care, and what are the typical physical, mental, and emotional changes that occur during this time?
5. What is the significance of physical, mental, and emotional changes in the context of end-of-life care?

Key Terms

Review these key terms from the chapter. You can find their definitions in the glossary at the end of the book.

» active dying
» awareness contexts
» death trajectory
» good death
» home health agency
» hospice
» master status
» nursing care facility
» palliative care

» quality-of-life perspective
» right-to-die legislation
» sanctity-of-life perspective

Chapter 8

—

Complexities of the U.S. Health Care Model

| Vignette | **Trapped by the System**

In October 2021, my dad was an eighty-nine-year-old widower who maintained his own home, cooked simple meals, and kept his clothes and himself impeccable. When my brother found him struggling to breathe one day, he took him to the emergency room, but my brother wasn't allowed to accompany Dad due to COVID-19 protocols. Because Dad was so weak and hard of hearing, the emergency room staff eventually allowed my brother into the ER as his health advocate. Imaging and testing revealed he had pneumonia, multiple large blood clots in his lungs and heart, and gastrointestinal bleeding, and they removed a liter and a half of fluid from around his lungs. My brother was told that our father had signed a DNR (Do Not Resuscitate) order, and he was transferred to a lower care level bed in another hospital about twenty miles away. My sister and I learned of Dad's transfer after he had already been moved.

We were given pamphlets about hospice care and advised to start preparing for final goodbyes. We repeatedly asked the hospital staff to allow us to speak with the doctor or to give us a more detailed explanation of Dad's prognosis. Because Dad hadn't chosen a designated health representative, we were told they were unable to speak with us. I finally got the name of the hospital care coordinator and began discussions about Dad's next steps. Because he didn't have any health insurance, his case manager began the process of getting him Medicaid coverage. She said that Medicaid would provide rehabilitation and placement after discharge, but with COVID-19 raging, it would be difficult to find a placement. She told us they would be unable to send Dad home unless he had twenty-four-hour care, but he had no savings or insurance coverage for a caregiver.

I kept trying to reach his hospital doctor to discuss his prognosis, but my messages went unreturned. I called for nightly updates, letting the nurses know that he was hard of hearing but too proud to mention it. I was happy to hear they wrote a reminder of this on his wallboard. The nursing staff, a revolving list of names, did everything they could to provide the best care. I left messages for his case manager, asking for an update on the Medicaid application. Nothing. We couldn't visit the hospital due to COVID-19 and had no answers as to what our next steps would be. Later, we found out the case manager had been on vacation, and no one was available to take over her caseload.

One day, I got a report that Dad had been restrained. Concerned about his changing trajectory, I spoke to the charge nurse for an overall update and told her that I still hadn't heard from Dad's doctor. I soon had a call from the hospitalist (a physician who manages the care of patients from admission to discharge), who explained Dad's prognosis. He had heart failure with only about 15% heart function left. Here it was, finally, an answer. Dad wasn't expected to recover enough to live on his own without medical care. He wasn't strong enough to be released, and there were no rehabilitation rooms available as we waited for Medicaid to be approved. Dad was losing his race against time while dealing with the reality of his failing body all alone. He wanted so badly to get out of bed. His lack of mobility led to anxiety. His nurse wrote on his board: "Talk to him like you would your grandfather." One day, a nurse who had cared for him over several shifts called to report a sudden deterioration. I understood the urgency. My sister and I raced from different states to be with him as he took his final breaths.

This was not what my dad would have wanted. All the expense and heartache of extensive medical care only caused him more confusion and anxiety as he tried to process what was happening to him without our support. The situation was partly due to him not having insurance, a designated medical power of attorney, or an advanced directive in place. But it was also affected by our complex, bureaucratic patchwork of health care options. Health care and hospital rules, regulations, and policies made it difficult for us to get information and support Dad at the end of his life. The arduous and cumbersome process of accessing medical insurance exchanges and Medicare/Medicaid overwhelmed my dad and slowed our ability to secure needed resources. And beyond anyone's control, everything was amplified by a global pandemic and its stresses on an already overburdened health care system.

S. J. M.

Introduction

Where a person dies has a significant impact on their death experience. Whether death occurs in a hospital, care facility, hospice center, or at home, the location determines access to medical care, support services, loved ones, or the comforts of home and familiar settings. As in S. J. M's vignette, although the situation was amplified by the COVID-19 pandemic, her dad's end-of-life care in a hospital setting was very different from what it might have been had he died at home.

Given a choice, seven out of ten Americans would prefer to die at home, and only 9% say they would prefer to die in the hospital (Hamel et al., 2017). When asked, 41% believe it's likely they will die in a hospital, and recent data show that 35% of all deaths in the United States occur in a hospital (Centers for Disease Control and Prevention, 2020). The number of people who die in hospitals includes deaths involving accidents, violence, or the sudden onset of a medical condition. Still, many people with end-stage chronic medical conditions will spend their last days in a hospital. Recent data indicate that 20% of people who die in the United States have been admitted to an intensive care unit (ICU) at or near the time of death (Kruser et al., 2019). Most critically ill patients who are hospitalized, including those sent to ICUs, are admitted through the emergency department. Of the older Americans who were seen in the emergency room during the last month of their life, 77% were admitted to the hospital, and most of those who were admitted died there (Smith et al., 2012).

Patients may intend to receive end-of-life care at home, but severely ill patients who are approaching the end stage of life frequently seek medical help in hospital emergency rooms. These acutely ill patients may arrive in severe pain and with worsening symptoms. Yet, emergency departments are not designed to provide end-of-life care. Emergency departments tend to be overcrowded and expensive, and the frenzied pace of the ER can aggravate the stress that patients and their families already feel. By default, emergency department staff often determine care pathways, including the balance between palliative care and life-sustaining treatments (Smith et al., 2012). Throughout this chapter, we'll examine how hospital usage, the organizational structure of health care, and other factors add to the complexity of the health care system in the United States.

Learning Objectives

These learning objectives will help you identify what's most important in this chapter. By the end of this chapter, you should be able to do the following:

- » Discuss the dying experience in U.S. hospitals.
- » Describe the complex structure of the U.S. health care system.
- » Discuss the multifaceted approach used to pay for health care in the United States.
- » Examine the challenges that doctors, nurses, and hospital bureaucracies face in communicating with patients and their loved ones about the dying experience.

Understanding the U.S. Health Care System

The United States prides itself on having the most advanced medical systems in the world, with some of the most highly trained doctors and the most modern facilities. This country spends far more on health care than any other wealthy nation. In 2016, the United States spent 17.8% of its Gross Domestic Product (GDP) on health care, compared to an average of 11.5% for other comparative nations. Policymakers typically attribute this spending disparity to the U.S.'s overuse of medical services and underinvestment in social services. The difference in spending also appears to be driven partly by high prices for health care services. The United States has a lower rate of insurance coverage, spends over two times more on pharmaceuticals per person, and spends nearly three times more on health care administration tasks like planning, managing, and regulating. Most notably, despite this extensive spending, it does not achieve better overall health care outcomes (Papanicolas et al., 2018).

Many Americans access numerous medical services and spend time in the hospital in their final days. The complexity of the U.S. health care system can make it difficult to ensure that these patients receive appropriate and timely medical care and support. Understanding the structure and organization of the health care system can provide valuable information and insights to locate and access needed medical services. This knowledge can be especially useful during the end stage of life when health care issues are more likely to be complex, change rapidly, and involve coexisting medical conditions.

Inside the U.S. Health Care System

Health care in the United States is delivered through a loosely structured system organized at the local level that can be opaque and difficult to understand. Think of the health care system as a computer system made up of many different parts—such as a processor, memory, and storage—that work together to process and display information. When one or more of the parts are not functioning or interacting with each other as they should, the computer may freeze up or fail to work. Similarly, the health care system also consists of different parts, such as hospitals, health care facilities, clinicians, and insurance plans that need to work together to deliver consistent, timely, and quality health care.

Figure 8.1 illustrates how the U.S. health care system is composed of a combination of public programs and private insurance. Currently, U.S. health care is not a well-integrated system. Rather, it operates as an array of loosely connected components, which limits its ability to provide health care efficiently.

Figure 8.1. The U.S. health care system's complexity is partly due to its mix of public and private funding, varied insurance programs, decentralized administration, and the influence of diverse stakeholders with competing interests.

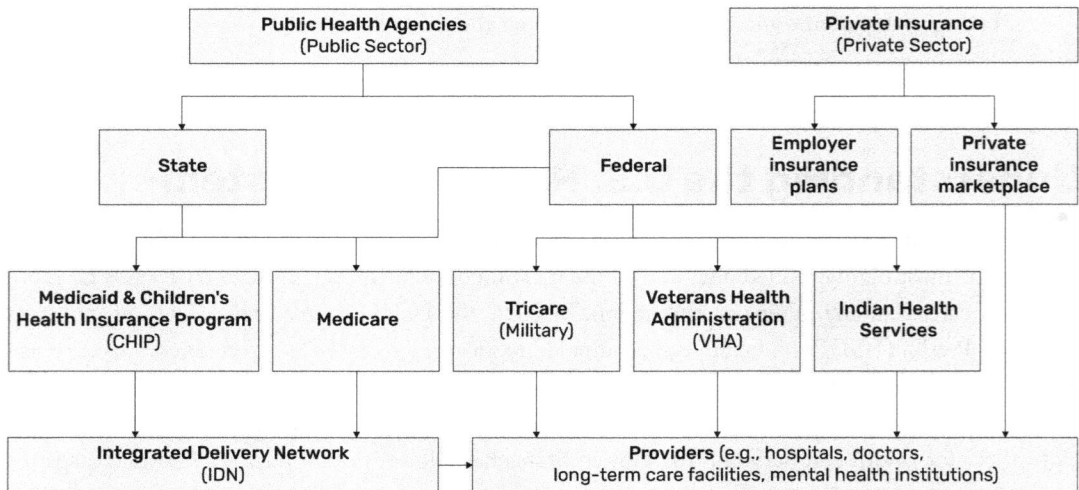

Elements of the system operate in various configurations that include loosely connected health care provider groups, provider networks, and independent medical practices.

Large sections of the health care industry are gathered under the umbrella of several corporate enterprises, with varying degrees of integration between each of the corporations' facilities. An

integrated delivery network (IDN) is a health care organization that aligns hospitals, physicians, and other providers under one system to deliver coordinated care. HCA Healthcare, for example, is one of the largest IDNs in the health care industry. HCA provides a broad range of primary, acute, and home health care services that include 175 hospitals across twenty states, psychiatric and rehabilitative hospitals, surgical centers, diagnostic and imaging services, oncology therapy, physical therapy, community-based care, and hospice services. Other large IDNs, such as Universal Health Services, Encompass Health, and Ascension Health, have similar health care facilities (Yang, 2024). At the same time, a significant number of other providers operate independently or are nonprofit organizations with shifting work relationships to other independent providers and provider networks.

Although large health care networks, such as HCA, provide a continuum of services, they operate in cities and communities where other IDNs and various independent providers also offer health care services. Doctors, both inside and outside a network, can have admitting privileges at a network-based hospital or can refer a patient to a network-operated diagnostic or treatment facility. Depending on the health care structure in a particular community, a patient may only be able to get the specific care they need by accessing a different provider network. This was the case when Judy's primary care provider referred her to the only urologist in the community for a procedure. The urologist was affiliated with one health care network, but he had privileges at the local hospital that was part of a different provider group. As Judy's example shows, overlapping provider networks shape patient care and often require individuals to navigate multiple systems to access necessary treatments.

The United States does not have a nationally coordinated system for health care networks and professionals to communicate and share information about patients. This lack of coordination complicates the sharing of patient records, insurance information, and other relevant data, thereby slowing access to and delivery of care. This decentralized system makes it difficult for medical providers to collaborate, coordinate, and plan. It also makes the system frustrating and difficult to navigate for both patients and physicians. The burden of navigating this complex system falls on patients and their loved ones. Patients using multiple health care networks and providers often struggle to ensure records and medical information are shared on time while communicating between various clinicians and insurance coverages.

Market Forces in Health Care

In addition to this unwieldy kaleidoscope of providers and services, the entire health care system operates within the **open market**, where businesses compete to set prices without market barriers or government interference. In this economic environment, profit-oriented entrepreneurs generally provide the products, equipment, and many of the services necessary to deliver health care. Hospitals open and close their doors according to community resources and the dictates of market forces (De Lew et al., 1992; Frakt, 2019). When hospitals cannot generate enough revenue to balance their books or make sufficient profits to satisfy investors, particularly in the case of for-profit facilities, they often close, leaving many communities across the country without a local hospital. When hospitals close, a community may struggle to retain physicians, paramedical professionals, and diagnostic and treatment facilities.

Nonprofit groups typically operate most hospitals, while others are managed by government or public nonprofit organizations, such as community hospitals, veterans' facilities, or hospitals on Native American reservations. However, a growing number of hospitals are owned by private for-profit companies or private equity groups. Currently, nearly half of all U.S. hospitals are for-profit, one-third are nonprofit, and the remainder are government-operated (De Lew et al., 1992; Welch et al., 2022).

Hospitals that operate as nonprofit organizations are accountable to their donors, founders, and service recipients. In the case of public nonprofits, they answer to the funding government entity and the service recipients. Typically, the primary objective of nonprofit hospitals is to develop the most effective methods for delivering patient care. Revenue is generated to cover operating costs, and any surplus revenue goes back to fund organizational goals and objectives. Many nonprofit hospitals also receive additional donations to help fund their operations and expand services.

In contrast, for-profit hospitals are designed to provide needed medical services to consumers while making a profit. For these organizations, the goal is to maximize profit and increase their market share by generating new customers. Inherent in this market-based model is the drive to dominate the market and minimize the competition. The management of for-profit hospitals is accountable to its owners and investors; the profits are used to grow the organization, increase revenue, and any excess revenue is distributed to the owners and investors. Figure 8.2 compares these two models.

Figure 8.2. Whether a hospital is nonprofit or for-profit shapes how it responds to market forces, which ultimately impacts its purpose, revenue sources, and accountability to stakeholders.

Non Profit Hospital	**Vs.**	**Hospice Care**
Develops the best ways to provide medical services for patients	Purpose	Provides medical services to consumers while making a profit
Covers operating costs; surplus revenue and donations fund organizational goals and expansions of services	Revenue	Uses a market-based system in which profits are used to grow the organization to increase revenue; excess revenue is distributed to owners and investors
Accountable to donors, the founders, and the service recipients; for public nonprofits, accountable to the funding government entity and the service recipients	Accountability to Stakeholders	Accountable to owners and investors

Physicians and Health Care Professionals

Contact with the health care system usually begins with a physician, physician's assistant (PA), or nurse practitioner (NP) who provides direct medical services. For some, this means visiting the local doctor's office, where the physician has been practicing in the community for years. However, less than half of all physicians work in private practice clinics that they own outright. Physicians are increasingly coming together to form larger, jointly operated clinics that can deliver health care services more efficiently and help minimize increasing operating costs. For instance, several family physicians may share clinic space and support from shared physician assistants, nurse practitioners, registered nurses, medical assistants, basic diagnostic and equipment techs, and office support.

These joint ventures can take a variety of forms. Nearly 40% of physicians work directly for a hospital or a practice at least partially owned by a hospital or health care system, and less than 6% work as independent contractors (Kane, 2021). Independent contract doctors typically utilize office space, exam rooms, or procedure areas within hospital facilities, often under a contractual arrangement. For instance, at a local community hospital, an independent contract cardiologist has office space, admitting privileges, and access to hospital staff and services. Their patients are billed separately for the doctor's and the hospital's services. This arrangement enables a cardiologist to be available to the community while also helping the hospital financially support specialized equipment and associated services. Contracting physicians maintain control over their medical decisions and practices, but they also bear the responsibility for any repercussions, such as malpractice claims resulting from errors in diagnosis or treatment.

Shortage of Health Care Providers

The increasing shortage of health care providers has become a public health care crisis that has significant implications for those needing end-of-life medical care. This shortage of medical professionals reaches across the health care workforce, from physicians, nurses, and medical assistants to medical techs and home health care assistants. It affects all sectors of the delivery system, including hospitals, clinics, surgical centers, diagnostic and treatment services, nursing care facilities, and hospice care.

Due to provider shortages, patients often face long wait times for medical appointments or procedures. This was the case for George when his general physician left his medical practice. After weeks of making phone calls to various clinics, George finally found a doctor who accepted his insurance and had an opening for new patients. Even then, his first appointment was three weeks away. After his exam, he was referred to a neurologist, but because his medical issue was not an emergency, he waited over three months for an appointment and another month for an appointment for tests. George's experience highlights how provider shortages can lead to significant delays in care, affecting timely diagnosis and treatment.

This staffing crisis is partly fueled by an aging workforce, high rates of burnout, and a shortage of teaching facilities and faculty (Orlowski, 2022). The increased needs of both a growing and aging population are further complicated by the large number of people leaving the health care workforce. The combination of these factors leaves large swaths of the population without enough medical staff to provide emergency care, treatment for chronic illness, and end-of-life medical care. These shortages are widely felt across the United States, but their impact varies from region to region. Nationwide, an estimated eighty-three million Americans lack sufficient access to a primary care physician or family care physician (American Medical Association, 2023).

Physicians, Physician's Assistants, and Nurse Practitioners

Scheduling an appointment with a medical care provider can be one of the greatest challenges in navigating the U.S. health care system. As with George's experience described in the previous section, many people encounter this problem, and the situation is getting worse. If you don't have a doctor, the first hurdle is finding one who is currently accepting new patients, which can be difficult because many doctors have full or overburdened patient loads. Once you find a new doctor, or if you are fortunate enough to have one already, the next hurdle is to schedule an appointment. Depending on the situation's urgency, patients can wait several weeks or months to see a doctor. For those at the end of life, when time is an important factor and physical, psychological, and emotional resources are already taxed, fighting to simply make an appointment can be even more exhausting.

Unfortunately, the shortage of doctors and other health care professionals is expected to continue. Over the next decade, the American Medical Association (2023) projects a shortage of more than 100,000 doctors, with the greatest shortfall expected in the fields of general and family medicine. Many Americans will find it harder to locate a family doctor with openings for new patients, and they will wait longer to see a specialist. General and family physicians are, in many cases, the initial entry point into the health care system and are indispensable in making needed referrals to appropriate specialists. For individuals with chronic diseases and end-of-life medical needs, these primary care providers play a crucial role in monitoring ongoing treatments, medications, and care.

In response to the growing shortage and uneven geographic distribution of physicians, the health care industry has expanded the use of nurse practitioners (NPs) and physician assistants (PAs) over the last several decades. NPs and PAs are trained and licensed to diagnose, treat illness, and prescribe primary, acute, and specialty care medication. Although they do not possess the same level of education, training, and expertise as physicians, and are limited in their scope of responsibility and the types of medical care and treatments they can provide, NPs and PAs fill a critical role. They frequently focus on primary and acute care, including wellness care, long-term care, and the monitoring and management of treatment. However, an increasing number of NPs and PAs are training in specialty areas of medicine such as pediatrics, obstetrics, cardiology, or gerontology.

Individual state laws regulate the extent to which NPs or PAs can independently provide health care services and may require additional training to practice without oversight by a physician. In some underserved communities, NPs and PAs are employed to help bridge the physician shortage gap, ensuring more widespread access to health care, particularly for primary care (National Nurse-Led Care Consortium, 2021). They can augment the number of local physicians working in the same clinic, allowing more patients to be seen or staff clinics as the sole local health care provider. In both cases, they regularly consult with a physician, either in-clinic or virtually, as needed. Increased reliance on these health care professionals means that these providers experience the same stress and burnout issues as physicians.

Recruiting and Retaining Nurses

The health care system is also struggling to recruit and retain nurses. This shortage has plagued the health care system for decades and will be slow to resolve. Despite the growth in people entering the nursing field, the numbers will not be sufficient to fill the gap. In 2025, estimates show a 10% (78,000) shortage of nurses. Only slight improvements in the shortage (64,000) are expected by 2030 (National Center for Health Workforce Analysis, 2022).

The shortage has been exacerbated by an increase in nurses leaving the field since the beginning of the COVID-19 pandemic. In 2020–21, over 100,000 registered nurses (RNs) left the profession, many of whom were under the age of thirty-five (American Association of Colleges of Nursing, 2022). This decrease represents the largest drop in RNs in over forty years; it is not a temporary situation, nor is it solely a result of the pandemic. Many contributing factors have plagued frontline nurses for years. Although the pandemic brought many of these issues to a head, the recruitment and retention of nurses has long been a growing system-wide issue.

The difficulty in retaining nurses in the profession is a significant factor contributing to the nursing shortage. Those who leave nursing, as well as those who are considering leaving nursing, consistently cite stress, burnout, and workload as primary issues. Specifically, nurses note the impact of long shifts, high patient-to-nurse ratios, constant pressure, and feeling undervalued. These factors are further exacerbated by chronic insufficient staffing (Muir et al., 2024). Attrition rates—the percentage of individuals who leave a group or organization over a specific period—are particularly problematic for those entering the profession. After several years of education and clinical training, research shows that nearly one-third of nurses leave the profession within the first two years. Nurses who leave their careers early cite the same issues as factors in their decision to leave the profession (Tate, 2022).

The overall staff shortages across the health care system are self-perpetuating. Due to the nursing shortage, nurses are experiencing a rise in patient-to-nurse ratios. At the same time, health care support staff shortages also mean nurses must spend more time doing non-nursing work such as cleaning, procuring supplies, and clerical duties. While struggling with their expanding workload, hospital nurses described feeling a lack of empathy and support regarding the challenges of their current work situation, including the prevalence of aggressive behavior by patients and their families. Research indicates that 25% of nurses reported being physically assaulted, and 50% were verbally abused or bullied by patients and their families and friends (Al-Qadi, 2021).

Nurses also described the impact that staff shortages and an overloaded health care system have on patients and their families. These shortages can lead to medication errors or delays, more patients returning after hospital discharge, and patients leaving the ER because the wait was too long. This increasing burden on nurses only adds additional stress to an already demanding profession.

To address the critical nurse shortages, some hospitals are increasing pay and offering signing bonuses, providing mental health resources, and implementing flexible scheduling. Research conducted by McKinsey & Company, a global management consulting firm, highlights a need to redesign care models that affect how nurses spend their time. Recommendations include delegating tasks to technicians or support staff and optimizing technology that can automate routine tasks (Berlin et al., 2023).

For instance, health systems such as Trinity Health are using virtual nurses to support on-site teams, helping to free up nurses' time for direct patient care (Boyle, 2021). These types of strategies aim to reduce workload and prevent burnout, ultimately improving patient outcomes and staff retention in a challenging health care landscape.

Medical Care Costs: Who Pays?

End-of-life medical care is, on average, the most expensive care a person will receive. Recent data indicate that during the last three years of life, a person will incur an average of $155,000 in medical expenses. Approximately $80,000 is expended during the last year of life, with the highest costs occurring in the last three months. Most of these medical expenses involve hospital-related services and direct-care medical providers.

Figure 8.3 shows how these expenditures are paid for by various federal programs, private insurance policies, and individual out-of-pocket funds (French et al., 2017; Arapakis et al., 2022). Out-of-pocket expenses can be so high that, on average, 3% of all end-of-life charges go unpaid.

Medical services in the United States are financed through a complex mixture of private insurance, individual payments, and public payers, including federal and state government agencies. Unlike many other high-income nations, the U.S. does not have a nation-wide health insurance system. Most Americans rely on employers to voluntarily provide health insurance coverage or purchase private insurance on the open market. Government programs are also in place to provide health care for some Americans. However, these programs mainly enroll people over the age of sixty-five, those in the military, individuals with disabilities, or those with low incomes. Some people have both government and private insurance, as in the case of Medicare and supplemental insurance policies, but other people have no coverage (De Lew et al., 1992).

Figure 8.3. This chart shows the cumulative average in health care spending during an individual's last year of life (based on 2014 U.S. dollars). Adapted from Arapakis et al., 2022.

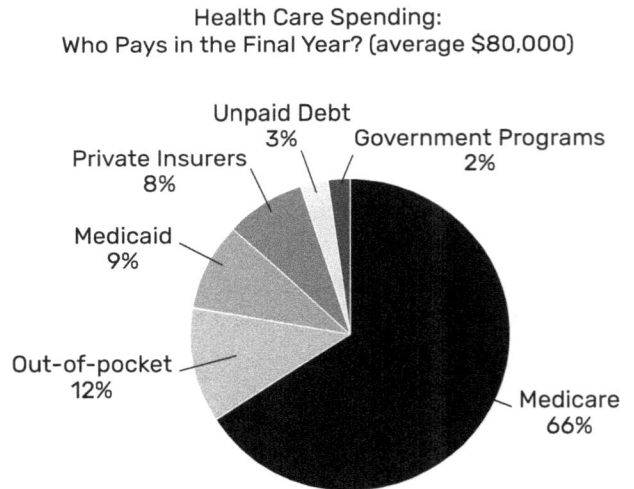

Health Care Spending: Who Pays in the Final Year? (average $80,000)

- Unpaid Debt 3%
- Government Programs 2%
- Private Insurers 8%
- Medicaid 9%
- Out-of-pocket 12%
- Medicare 66%

The terminology around insurance can be difficult to understand for several reasons. Not only are there multiple types of insurance, but each policy has its own set of rules and exclusions. Insurance companies tend to use abbreviations and acronyms, such as HMO (Health Maintenance Organization),

PPO (Preferred Provider Organization), and EOB (explanation of benefits), which can be confusing if you've never encountered them before. Additionally, the policies and the language used to describe them change frequently, making it even harder to keep up. Box 8.1 includes frequently used terms and their definitions.

Box 8.1: The Language of Insurance

Insurance terminology can sound like a foreign language to those who are new to these concepts. Here are a few definitions provided by HealthCare.gov, the official website of the U.S. Centers for Medicare and Medicaid Services.

> » **coinsurance**: the percentage of costs of a covered health care service you pay (20%, for example) after you've paid your deductible
> » **co-pay/copayment**: a fixed amount ($20, for example) you pay for a covered health care service after you've paid your deductible
> » **deductible**: the amount you pay for covered health care services before your insurance plan starts to pay
> » **out-of-pocket costs**: your expenses for medical care that aren't reimbursed by insurance
> » **premium**: the amount you pay for your health insurance every month

---

Private Health Insurance

Most Americans rely on private health care insurance to cover medical care costs. In 2022, 65.6% of Americans had private insurance, and over two-thirds received benefits from their employer (Keisler-Starkey et al., 2023). Some employers offer no health insurance coverage or only offer it to certain employee groups. When health insurance is offered, the types of policies and the coverage amounts vary significantly from workplace to workplace. Some offer a choice of policies, while others offer only one option. Some employers contribute a specific dollar amount toward a policy they offer, while others provide a stipend for employees to purchase insurance on the open market. Yet, about 14% of U.S. employers do not offer any type of health insurance benefits, resulting in the majority of the uninsured (and their dependents) being employed without health care coverage (Grundy et al., 2024).

Public Health Insurance

To increase access to health care insurance, the **Affordable Care Act (ACA)** was passed by Congress and signed into law in 2010, taking effect in 2014. The passage of the ACA, commonly referred to as Obamacare, marked a major national effort to provide health insurance coverage for as many people as possible and make substantial reforms to the overall health care system.

The ACA has three primary goals:
> » to make affordable insurance available to more people and provide financial assistance to pay premiums and out-of-pocket costs based on financial need

» to expand Medicaid to help low-income households access health care

» to support innovative medical care delivery methods to lower health care costs

The ACA is founded on a shared responsibility model. This means the government facilitates access to health care, but individuals must choose and secure coverage. In practice, this meant that states set up insurance exchanges to help people purchase insurance on the open market. These insurance exchanges are virtual marketplaces where consumers and small businesses can shop and purchase private insurance coverage. The websites help potential customers compare and evaluate qualifying private plans and access information about eligibility for financial assistance in paying premiums (U.S. Department of Health and Human Services, n.d.).

ACA insurance exchanges can be helpful when people try to navigate the maze of insurance options and choices. In 2022, more than 1,100 private insurance providers offered a vast array of health care policies with different benefit structures, premiums, and rules (National Association of Insurance Commissioners, 2022). These companies operate in an open market economy, where they can sell insurance and where prospective customers can buy policies with few restrictions or regulations from government agencies. Most people with private insurance are covered for inpatient hospital and physician services, but the breadth and depth of other services depend on the specific policy. Home health care and long-term care for chronic conditions and frailty related to aging are not generally covered by private or public health insurance. Although some companies offer long-term care insurance policies, they can be expensive and have limited coverage (De Lew et al., 1992).

How the responsibility for co-pays, out-of-pocket expenses, and deductibles is shared by the insurance company and the insured person differs across policies and companies, which directly impacts the cost of the policy. Generally, the higher the co-pay, out-of-pocket costs, and deductible the policyholder pays each time they use their insurance, the lower the cost of the insurance policy. Therefore, many people frequently opt for lower premium costs, hoping they will not have any major health problems that would cause them to pay these additional costs not covered by their insurance. However, lower-cost policies have higher co-pays, out-of-pocket costs, and more restrictions on what medical care services are covered. These policies often leave people **underinsured**, meaning they have insurance, but the coverage is insufficient to cover the full cost of a claim or loss.

The level of coverage and the rate at which a policy will cover medical care can also be affected by provider network coverage. Individual insurance companies and individual policies may limit which doctors, testing and diagnostic facilities, and hospitals they will cover. Any providers a person uses that are out-of-network or outside the designated provider network may only be partially covered or not covered at all.

Medicare

Publicly funded insurance programs are also available to help cover medical costs for eligible people. **Medicare** is a national health insurance program for people over sixty-five or people with qualifying disabilities, end-stage renal disease, or ALS (Lou Gehrig's disease). Medicare helps with the cost of health care, but it does not cover all medical expenses or the costs of most long-term health care facilities. This program covers more than 18% of the population, with 20% of all Medicare expenditures directed toward medical care during the last year of life (Keisler-Starkey et al., 2022; Arapakis et al., 2022).

Since its inception in the 1960s, Medicare has expanded and grown more complex. With more options and choices, coverage may be provided through government-private business partnerships. Medicare is divided into several parts—each covering different types of health care services—to meet diverse needs:

» Part A (the original Medicare) is provided at no cost for those who qualify and covers hospital-related costs: inpatient hospital care, limited time in a skilled nursing care facility, some home health care, and hospice.

» Part B helps meet the medical costs for doctors and other health care providers, outpatient care, home health care, durable medical equipment, and some preventive health care services. Part B is optional; you can sign up and pay a monthly premium for this coverage.

» Part D helps cover the cost of prescription drugs. Anyone who qualifies for Medicare can purchase this optional coverage, which is only provided through private insurance companies approved by the federal government.

Numerous policy options are available on the open market, and Part D costs and coverage may vary from plan to plan. Choosing the best plan for your individual needs can be daunting and, at times, overwhelming.

Medicare recipients can also choose to enroll in Medicare Advantage policies, sometimes referred to as Part C, which bundles Parts A, B, and usually D. They may have lower out-of-pocket costs and extra benefits beyond the original Parts A and B, such as coverage for vision, hearing, and dental. Although these policies are offered through private insurance companies, the insured still has Medicare and receives most of their Part A and Part B coverage through the Medicare Advantage Plan. Regardless of the specific Medicare options a person chooses, co-pays, deductibles, and expenses often result in substantial out-of-pocket expenses for the patient. Additional insurance policies can be purchased on the open market through private providers to help with these expenses. Supplemental coverage, also known as Medigap policies, can be purchased on the open market from private insurance companies.

Deciding which options and combinations of policies offered by private insurance companies work best for you or a loved one can be difficult. The standard recommendation is to examine your current health condition and base the decision on which options best meet those needs. With over seventy Medicare Advantage and Part D stand-alone options available as of 2023 (Cubanski & Freed, 2022), the already daunting process of choosing the best policy for your needs is further complicated by the limited enrollment period. Each year, in the late fall, Medicare has an eight-week open enrollment period during which recipients can join, switch, or drop a plan. However, your medical needs and medications can change frequently throughout the year and may or may not be covered by your current policy. At the end of life, acute incidents like a stroke or heart attack, abrupt changes in chronic conditions, or rapid shifts in overall health are common. These issues can leave patients with insufficient medical coverage and large medical debt.

Medicaid

Medicaid is a federal health care program that covers medical costs for qualified people based on their limited income and available resources. Medicaid and Medicare are both government health programs in the U.S. with similar names that provide essential health coverage, yet they are different in eligibility, funding sources, and the specific populations they serve, as figure 8.4 shows.

Figure 8.4. This diagram shows two government-funded programs, Medicare and Medicaid, that aim to improve access to health care and reduce financial barriers for eligible individuals.

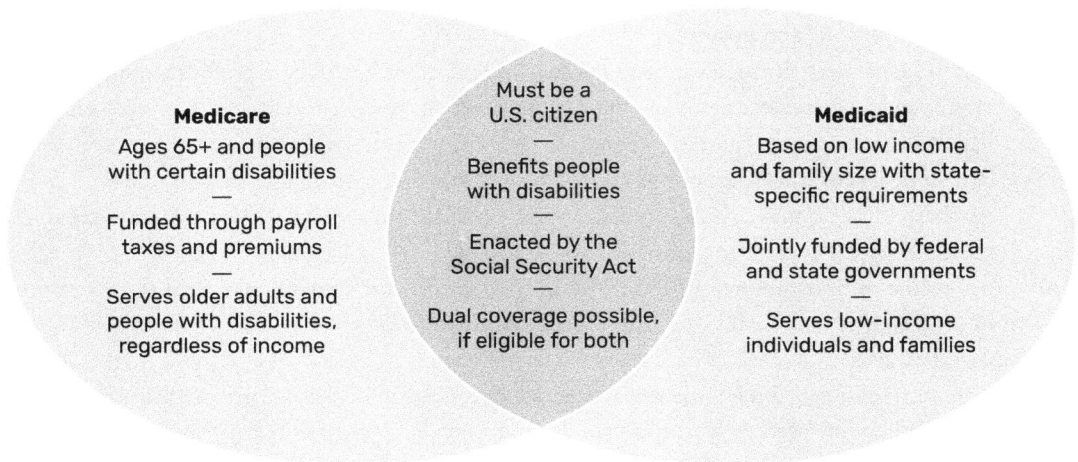

Medicare

Ages 65+ and people with certain disabilities

—

Funded through payroll taxes and premiums

—

Serves older adults and people with disabilities, regardless of income

Must be a U.S. citizen

—

Benefits people with disabilities

—

Enacted by the Social Security Act

—

Dual coverage possible, if eligible for both

Medicaid

Based on low income and family size with state-specific requirements

—

Jointly funded by federal and state governments

—

Serves low-income individuals and families

Although individual states design and administer their own programs, they must comply with federal guidelines to receive funding. Eligibility and coverage can vary from state to state; however, low-income individuals and families must meet eligibility criteria commonly recognized by federal and state laws. Medicaid recipients generally pay nothing for covered medical services; however, in some situations, they may be required to pay a small co-payment for certain items and services. If you qualify for both programs, Medicaid may help pay your Medicare Part B premium and cover some deductibles and co-pays.

Medicaid does cover skilled nursing care facilities, rehabilitation facilities, and long-term care facilities. In most cases, 100% of the direct care cost (expenses tied to diagnosing, treating, or managing a patient's health condition) is covered when a patient is a Medicaid recipient and in a Medicaid-certified nursing care facility. The recipient may have to pay for extras like a private room, personal comfort items, special meals outside dietary medical requirements, books, social events, or other services and amenities.

In most states, to qualify for this nursing care facility option, a person must meet the income and asset eligibility criteria, which include countable resources (wages, Social Security benefits, Veterans' benefits, bank accounts, stocks/bonds, trusts/annuities, property, life insurance, and other assets). Most states also consider your income over a five-year period. Any assets you transferred out of your possession during that period may count toward your total financial resources. If you live in a nursing home funded by Medicaid, you get full care but must give up most of your countable resources and income, except for a small amount of money you're allowed to keep each month (Centers for Medicare and Medicaid Services, 2015).

Military Health Care Coverage

The U.S. Department of Defense offers health insurance options for its military personnel through **Tricare**, a health insurance program that covers nearly ten million current and former military members and their dependents. This program ensures access to health care in almost every part of the world. Much like private sector health insurance options, Tricare has numerous plans to choose from with differing fee structures that cover hospital care, doctors, prescriptions, and other health care services. The Tricare program is available to current uniformed service members and their families, including those in the National Guard and retired military personnel, although it is generally not available to those who have left military service before retirement (Military Benefit Association, n.d.).

The **Veterans Health Administration (VHA)** provides health benefits to U.S. Armed Services veterans, including Reserve Units and the National Guard, who have met minimum service requirements. The VHA is America's largest integrated health care system, serving over nine million enrolled veterans through regional medical centers and outpatient sites. Qualified members can receive coverage for most medical care and services, and some will qualify for additional services depending on their priority group and any recommendations from a VHA primary care provider. A veteran's service history, disability rating, and income will determine their priority group rating, which affects how much, if anything, they pay toward health care. Veterans' health benefits can be used outside VHA facilities if none exist in your state or U.S. territory or if the service is not available. The VHA offers various benefits to address long-term care needs, including physical therapy, respite care, assistance with daily tasks, nursing care facilities, and memory care (U.S. Department of Veterans Affairs, n.d.).

The VHA is experiencing the same stresses as other health care providers. Staffing shortages are straining the system's ability to provide timely access to the veterans who need medical care. An increasing number of aging veterans rely on these services and usually have complex medical conditions. Since 2015, the VHA has been scrutinized by Congress and the U.S. Government Accountability Office (GAO) after veterans shared stories of waiting four to eight months to get appointments and diagnostic tests or of being unable to get timely medical care at all. For example, veterans like Lin, a former Army medic, have reported waiting over six months for a routine checkup at their local VHA clinic. With few VHA facilities in her state, Lin often had to seek care outside the system but still struggled with long delays due to the referral process. Concerns remain about the accuracy of VHA administrative reporting processes regarding the actual conditions and wait times for care (GAO, 2019).

Health Insurance Realities

Universal access to affordable and adequate health insurance remains elusive in the United States. Despite private insurance options and publicly funded programs' efforts to provide nationwide comprehensive health care coverage, over thirty-one million people did not have health insurance in 2020 (Cha & Cohen, 2022). The uninsured, especially those who have been without insurance for a year or longer, are disproportionately young, Latinx/Hispanic, poor, sicker, and living in the South. Even those with insurance experience gaps in coverage, co-pays, or out-of-pocket costs that affect access to medical care. Over 40% of working-age adults are inadequately insured, meaning their coverage doesn't provide them with affordable access to health care. Nearly half of the respondents in a recent survey reported skipping or delaying care due to the cost, and four out of ten stated they had difficulties paying medical bills or were paying off medical debt (Collins et al., 2022).

Dying in the U.S. Health Care System

The U.S. health care system is fragmented and lacks meaningful standardization or coordination. Patients and their families navigate a disjointed system to locate, match, and access insurance coverage across different providers and networks that may or may not communicate with each other. As a result, patients must find a health care provider that accepts their insurance, secure an appointment, transfer previous records and test information to another system, and then address in-network and out-of-network co-pays and deductibles. Figure 8.5 illustrates the many hurdles one patient encountered when seeking care.

Some parts of the system are highly organized within the patchwork of independent health care providers. The structures of hospital networks, individual hospitals, and medical centers are based on standardized rules, processes, and procedures that use a hierarchical chain of command to make decisions and control the flow of information.

Within the hospital setting, however, people can become locked in a maze of rigid rules and processes that affect health care delivery. For example, in end-of-life medical care, the hospital structures also impact the dying experience for the patient, their loved ones, and the attending medical staff. As you've learned, dying is a complex human experience, not merely a biological medical occurrence. As a person goes through this emotional, human event in a hospital, they can be confronted and constrained by an impersonal and rule-oriented bureaucracy.

Dying is one of the most personal and emotional events that regularly takes place within a highly bureaucratic system. Health care staff are trained to follow standardized rules and processes, which can feel impersonal and dismissive of a unique situation. At the same time, staff are expected to meet the needs of individual patients. The contrast—between death as a deeply individual experience shaped by relationships, emotions, and personal meaning and the standardized, structured nature of the health care system—can make the death event feel impersonal and dehumanizing. These competing outcomes pose challenges for hospitals and the people working within them as they provide medical care and emotional support at the end of life.

Figure 8.5. This chart shows the actual distances one patient had to travel for various appointments and specialists.

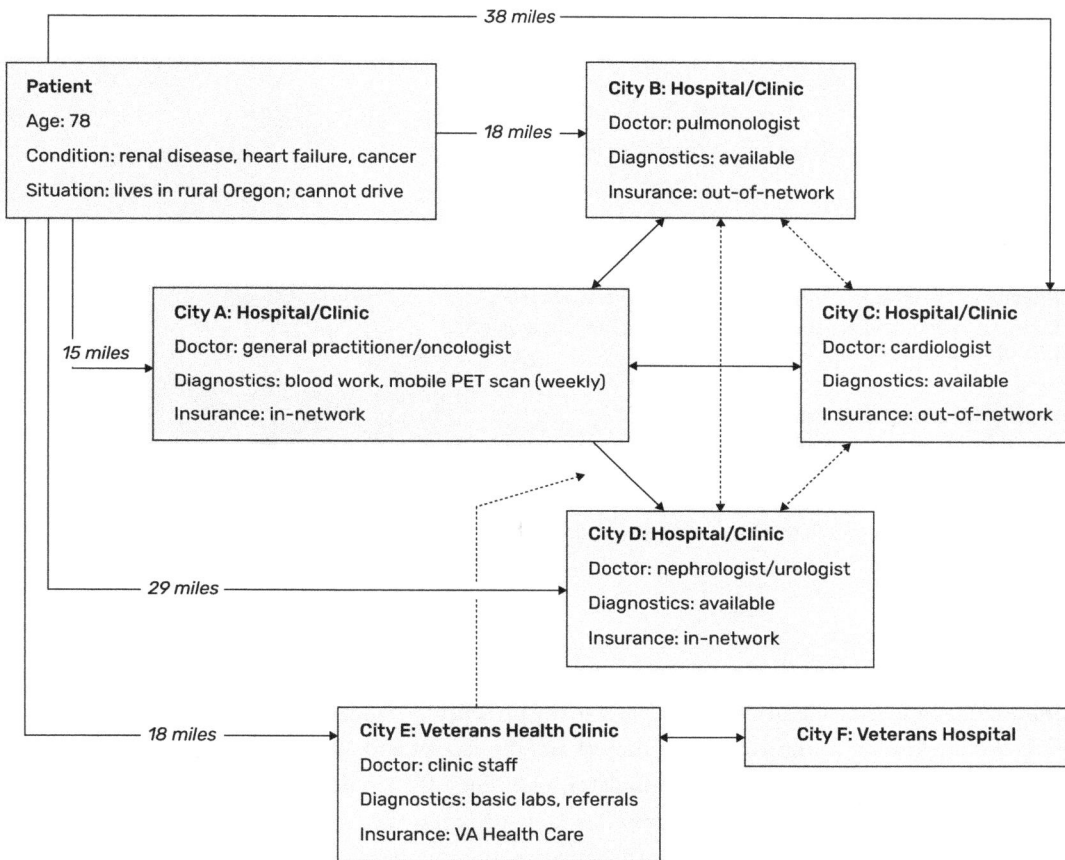

Bureaucracy in Hospital Facilities

Hospitals and large medical complexes are highly organized bureaucracies that deliver health care services. A **bureaucracy** is an organization structured to function rationally and effectively, with a clear chain of command and uniform, consistent outcomes. Hospital bureaucracies have a clearly defined division of labor and specialization of job duties: administrators, doctors, nurses, physician assistants (PAs), nurse practitioners (NPs), certified nursing assistants (CNAs), and support staff. Each work area has a hierarchy of authority and scope of responsibility. For instance, doctors are the ultimate authority in medical decisions, nurses carry out doctors' orders, and CNAs perform the associated basic supportive services for daily care (figure 8.6).

Figure 8.6. Hospitals use a highly structured division of labor to deliver specialized patient care within a complex health care environment.

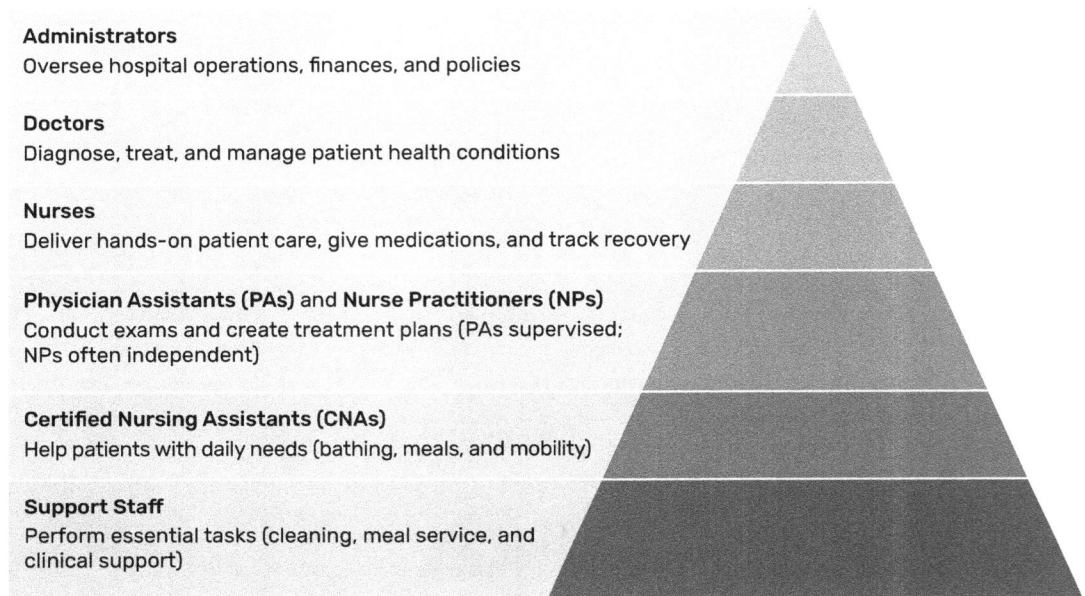

Administrators
Oversee hospital operations, finances, and policies

Doctors
Diagnose, treat, and manage patient health conditions

Nurses
Deliver hands-on patient care, give medications, and track recovery

Physician Assistants (PAs) and **Nurse Practitioners (NPs)**
Conduct exams and create treatment plans (PAs supervised; NPs often independent)

Certified Nursing Assistants (CNAs)
Help patients with daily needs (bathing, meals, and mobility)

Support Staff
Perform essential tasks (cleaning, meal service, and clinical support)

Tasks in a hospital facility are completed by adhering to rules and procedures. For example, a doctor prescribes a specific medication for a patient, the prescription is sent to the pharmacy, the pharmacy sends the medication to the nurse, who then charts the receipt and administration of the medication, and the information is copied to the administrative billing office to be sent to the insurance company or patient. Every step is tightly orchestrated and rigidly controlled through policies and procedures. The organization is designed to coordinate activities for large numbers of people in pursuit of organizational goals, specifically to achieve desirable medical outcomes and ultimately to facilitate the patient's release.

Bureaucracies are notorious for being impersonal and machine-like, but informal structures exist within medical facilities to humanize their operations. Interpersonal relationships and social ties between patients and medical professionals change or bypass the formal structure and rules. In hospitals, this may involve a nurse or medical professional making a minor change in a process to address a patient's personal and emotional needs.

For example, Marta had been in a rural hospital for symptoms of end-stage heart failure and was ready for discharge. She had decided to enroll in hospice care, and her son was there to take her home. He only had an hour before he had to return to work, and the nurse told him it might take a couple of hours to complete all the paperwork to release his mom. After learning about the situation, another nurse used her break time to walk the paperwork all over the hospital to get the required information and signatures to ensure Marta was discharged in time for her son to take her home. This was not part of a nurse's job responsibilities, nor did it follow a specific protocol. The nurse circumvented the bureaucratic process to better meet Marta's needs and her son's situation.

Formal processes in hospitals ensure the consistent delivery of medical services. However, many rules, processes, and documentation are in place to protect the organization against possible complaints and lawsuits. The tension between these standardized processes and the informal structures that try to prioritize the patient's overall care and well-being is especially poignant at the end of life. Think back to the opening vignette as S.J.M. struggled to navigate the bureaucratic maze of rules and the hierarchical authority that controlled access to information about her dad's declining condition. Out of compassion and an understanding of the specific situation, the staff bent the rules to get her timely information so she could get to her father's bedside before his death. When entering her dad's hospital room, she was both relieved and touched by the note reminding staff to "talk to him as if he were your grandfather."

Hospitals and the Dying Patient

The organizational structure of hospitals and the interactions with the health care staff influence the death experience for the patient and their loved ones. Hospital rules and procedures define possible options, set expectations, and control how communication takes place and information is shared. This overarching structure affects who controls the various factors that influence decision-making for medical providers, patients, their families, and loved ones. The number of deaths that occur in hospitals and the increase in life-prolonging medical treatments and options make it necessary to examine how hospital processes and staff training shape the death experience.

Hospitals' organizational subcultures can be different from the organizational culture. This culture influences how processes and procedures address the medical needs of patients who can then be released. The work focuses on diagnosing, treating, and improving medical conditions. From this perspective, the most frequent response to critical illness or injury in hospitals is **curative care**, which attempts to try to preserve life, restore health, and avoid death. Increasingly, this curative role lives side-by-side with the growing need for palliative end-of-life care. Yet, overall, hospital culture and the organization's primary purpose are still focused on its curative function (Kaufman, 2005). Many aspects of hospitals are misaligned and struggling to effectively meet their expanded role in delivering end-of-life care.

Providing end-of-life palliative care, also called comfort care, necessitates a shift in focus and health care services compared to curative care. As you learned in chapter 7, palliative care tries to improve the overall quality of life. It stresses the importance of providing practical social and emotional support in addition to needed medical care. Each person needs different supports to improve their quality of life as death approaches. Meeting these personalized needs can be time-intensive and involve services and specialized staff that traditionally have not been considered part of hospital-based medical care. End-of-life preferences such as massage, music, continuous bedside comfort, and an unrestricted flow of visitors are difficult to accommodate within medical facilities structured to provide standardized, curative medical care.

Meeting the holistic needs of dying patients—considering their physical, emotional, psychological, and social well-being—is further complicated by hospitals' financial processes. Payments from insurance companies are structured as reimbursements for medical care intended to restore or maintain health. Therefore, medical insurance policies, including government programs such as Medicare, are far less likely to cover comfort care services to support quality of life rather than prolong life (Kaufman, 2005).

Doctors and Difficult Conversations

The shift from curative to palliative end-of-life care can be stilted, tenuous, and unclear for hospital staff. Hospitals are geared to direct everything and everyone toward lifesaving treatment, even when staff, patients, or their families may not support prolonging the dying process. Sharon R. Kaufman, a cultural anthropologist who spent two years mapping the experiences of dying patients, their families, and medical staff in hospital settings, noted that end-stage diseases and injuries are typically treated until no positive physiological responses occur: "Only then is death expected. Only then does it 'need' to be acknowledged by hospital staff" (Kaufman, 2005, p. 29).

When doctors see that the curative approach is no longer effective and death is inevitable, they must decide how to best support the patient's end-of-life care. For patients and their families to maintain autonomy and make informed decisions, they require clear and explicit information about their medical condition. Patients are typically unfamiliar with medical terminology, and the numerous treatment options can be confusing and difficult to evaluate. Doctors are under increasing time pressure from growing administrative tasks, which impact how much one-on-one time they can spend with patients.

Varying levels of language proficiency and health literacy also impact the patient-provider relationship. The importance of communication between doctors and patients and their families is stressed throughout medical school and practiced during medical training rotations. Doctors are familiar with the issues and are mindful of the ways information is delivered to patients and families (Drossman et al., 2021). However, these honed communication skills are not always directly transferable from curative medical situations to palliative end-of-life care.

Learning about death is an expected part of medical school training and is commonly integrated across the four years of the curriculum. Yet, medical schools are not required to include end-of-life care as part of a student doctor's rotations, where they receive practical experience in multiple specialties. Organizations that accredit medical schools, such as the Liaison Committee on Medical Education (LCME), generally operate with a minimal baseline of required end-of-life training. Student doctors rarely care for dying patients in their core training rotations. They may not have had the opportunity to formally debrief or reflect on any end-of-life medical situations and discussions they experienced (Williams et al., 2022), though some schools have opted to offer or require a geriatric or palliative care rotation. Since doctors may not have received specific training and experience in death and dying during their medical education, some practicing physicians are acquiring additional professional training in this area (Blau, 2017).

Due to a lack of training and other factors, doctors may be evasive and avoid mentioning death when talking with patients who are approaching the end of life and their families. The doctor who talks candidly with a patient about death before visible signs of dying are evident is more the exception than the rule (Kaufman, 2005). This evasiveness may be partly due to the disproportionate number of lawsuits U.S. doctors face when a patient's family is dissatisfied with medical outcomes or when a patient dies (Carroll, 2015). Other countries with universal health care systems tend to have fewer malpractice lawsuits because of differences in their regulations and legal systems. A recent study suggests that miscommunication is a significant factor in malpractice claims, with 53% of claims involving patient-provider communication (Humphrey et al., 2022).

A detailed and direct conversation about end-of-life care and death is confounded by the difficulty in determining the death trajectory for each patient, as you read in chapter 7. Each patient's unique biology and individual personal factors can make it difficult to predict when a patient will die (Chen, 2013). Some diagnoses support a specific prognosis, but we are each on a unique timetable. When doctors disagree about treatment strategies and a patient's death trajectory, predicting the end of life can be even more difficult (Kaufman, 2005).

Individual variations in the end-of-life trajectory cause physicians to overestimate the survival timeline, usually giving the patient the best possible scenario. Many physicians prefer to deliver the "bad news" in a staged format as symptoms and medical conditions change (Kaufman, 2005). This format involves explaining the expected decline while also offering options to treat medical symptoms and conditions as they arise. But even when no viable options for curative treatment remain, doctors often indirectly explain the situation by telling the patient that there is "not much more I can do" rather than explicitly discussing approaching death (Chen, 2013).

In contrast, patients say they are reassured by having their options clearly described and knowing that their doctors are giving them all the latest medical information. Patients also indicate that they prefer doctors to be direct and refrain from using euphemisms (indirect words meant to soften the negative effect of the information). When the doctor is comfortable discussing end-of-life options, patients feel more at ease. Although many patients express a preference for doctors who are direct and clear, some patients are more likely to perceive doctors who use a direct communication style regarding end-of-life issues as poor communicators (Chen, 2013). This contradiction may contribute to the tendency of physicians to skirt the issue of approaching death or avoid direct and explicit information.

Determining the best approach for open and direct discussions varies from patient to patient and can also be impacted by family dynamics, especially when the family is not in agreement about medical decisions. Doctors frequently navigate existing strained family relationships that are under the additional stress of the situation, often at the bedside of the dying patient. Therefore, doctors with existing relationships with their patients, such as family doctors or long-standing specialists, may be better able to align their approach with a patient's preferences and navigate complex family relationships.

Nurses and Difficult Conversations

Nursing focuses on providing and coordinating ongoing medical care while keeping patients as comfortable as possible to ensure the best outcome. Nurses monitor medical conditions and symptoms, assess and observe patients, and administer medication and treatments. They play an essential role in transferring information among the health care team members and between the health care providers, patients, and their families. At the end-of-life stage, nurses provide medical care in a variety of settings, including hospitals, long-term care facilities, hospices, and patients' homes.

Though nurses are trained to provide general medical care that usually includes palliative care, research shows that many nursing schools only lightly cover death and dying. Some nursing schools focus on more meaningful coverage of end-of-life care, including topics like approaches to communication, working with families, navigating family dynamics throughout end-of-life care, and standard palliative care training (Farmer, 2019). Bachelor of Nursing programs are more likely to have upper-division courses on death and dying in their curriculum. These courses teach students what to expect and what to do for a patient who is actively dying. Instruction includes end-of-life symptom management, postmortem care, and how to work with grief-stricken families and loved ones (Tyler, 2017). Nurses in specialty areas such as oncology, cardiology, or intensive care units typically have additional end-of-life care training, though many report feeling unprepared (Farmer, 2019).

More than most other health care professionals, nurses tend to spend more time with dying patients and their families. As a result, they field medical and prognostic questions from the patient and their loved ones. In the opening vignette, when S. J. M. was unable to contact a doctor or her calls to them went unanswered, the nurses were her only source of information about her dad's condition. However, due to the distinctly different roles and training of doctors and nurses, nurses may be reluctant to discuss a prognosis and instead only directly answer questions about the patient's condition and treatments. Like doctors, nurses can also be evasive about the end of life and avoid directly mentioning death (Tyler, 2017).

Helping people medically is one thing. Knowing how to support a dying patient or a bereaved family is another skill entirely. Many nurses are not formally trained in this specialized skill set. Yet, it is most frequently nurses who are at the bedside of a dying patient as their loved ones ask the hard and emotional questions: Is he dying? Can you do anything for her? How long does he have? Should I tell the family to come to say their goodbyes? Nurses are expected to provide emotional support and information, but they are often left to acquire these skills on the job.

Conclusion

Most Americans will spend a substantial amount of time in and out of the U.S. health care system as they approach the end of life, and many will die in hospitals. As a person nears death in a hospital, their quality of life and death experience are influenced by the structure and organization of the health care system. Navigating this complex system can overwhelm patients and their families, especially at the end of life when emotional and psychological stress is heightened. The bureaucratic rules and procedures of health care facilities and the standardized training of medical professionals may facilitate the effective delivery of medical care. They can also create barriers to meeting the needs of individual patients at the end of life. For S. J. M.'s family, hospital rules and processes shaped her father's end-of-life experience and made it different from what they would have hoped. But to this day, S. J. M. is grateful for the staff who worked around the system, found alternative ways to provide the family with information, and allowed them to be with him in the end.

Summary

» U.S. health care is delivered through a loosely structured yet complex system.
» Health care is organized at the local level, but large segments of the industry are controlled by extensive integrated delivery networks (IDNs)
» The shortage of physicians and nurses harms their work life, the health care system, and patient access.
» Health care is funded through a complex maze of private health insurance companies, public health insurance programs, and an individual's funds.
» Public insurance programs include Medicare (based on age or ability), Medicaid (based on income), and military health care (based on military service).
» Hospitals tend to operate using a bureaucratic organization model that involves standardized rules, processes, and procedures.
» When people die in a hospital, the standardized rules and organizational processes may conflict with the individual nature of the dying experience.
» Doctors and nurses must regularly have difficult conversations with patients and their loved ones but do not always receive formal training to discuss end-of-life issues.

Review Questions

1. What is the typical experience of dying in U.S. hospitals?
2. How is the U.S. health care system structured, and what makes it complex?
3. Can you describe the different methods used to pay for health care in the U.S.?
4. What are the difficulties that health care providers face in communicating with patients and their families about the dying experience?
5. How do doctors, nurses, and hospital bureaucracies navigate these challenges in their interactions with patients and their loved ones?

Key Terms

Review these key terms from the chapter. You can find their definitions in the glossary at the end of the book.

» Affordable Care Act (ACA)

» bureaucracy

» curative care

» integrated delivery network (IDN)

» Medicaid

» Medicare

» open market

» Tricare

» underinsured

» Veterans Health Administration (VHA)

Chapter 9

Violent and Traumatic Death

Vignette **Seeking Peace**

"My reality is starting to bend."

My beautiful daughter Hannah said this to me in September 2015. She was having a mental health breakdown and was suicidal. She needed to get to the hospital as soon as possible.

* * *

My daughter was born in unique circumstances. The first seven-and-a-half months of my pregnancy with her were in a foreign country during an emotional, stressful, and unstable time. Exactly two months after I arrived home, she was born. She was beautiful, sweet, healthy, and safe. She was inquisitive and playful, and I adored her. Her siblings called her the "Peacemaker," and she truly was our family's peacemaker.

We were all floored in 2013 when she was diagnosed with schizophrenia. She never displayed any of the signs or symptoms of having mental health issues. She was a brilliant young person throughout her elementary, high school, and college years until the illness seized her. We were determined to stand by and support her no matter what. All of us loved her beyond measure. For three years, she fought long and hard to overcome her illness.

On April 10, 2016, my beautiful daughter took her life. She took a walk and ended her pain and torment. My other daughter and her husband found her. They hadn't realized she was in crisis until they came upon her and started CPR. It wasn't until the paramedic's flashlight shined on her face that they realized she was gone. I was at the beach for the weekend when the call came. My daughter said, "Mama, my sister has been hurt, and you must come home now."

Nothing could have prepared me for what I came home to. My three young adult children were sitting on the sofa with a detective. A chaplain was consoling them. My world fell underneath me when the detective said, "Your daughter is not at the hospital. She has passed and is with the coroner where she died." I looked into the eyes of my children and husband. The hurt and heartache I saw were unfathomable for a mother and wife. My heart told me to be strong and not let them see Mama break down. So, I turned to the detective and chaplain, saying, "I need a moment with my family."

* * *

I turned back and said to my family, "The Devil has not had victory over our family tonight, and your sister is in the arms of Jesus." I continued, saying, "Your sister loved God, and he knows she was sick. God does not punish his children who are sick. This is not your fault, and we need to band together as a family with love and care. I love each of you with all my heart, and nothing will ever change that."

The next day, I went to the funeral home. I had already decided that she would have the most beautiful and loving celebration of life we could give her. We couldn't give her a beautiful wedding, but she would have a beautiful celebration filled with love and hope. I stood in the coffin display room, choosing a coffin for my daughter. My husband held onto me and quietly guided me around the showroom as my legs kept buckling under me. It was all I could do not to scream out in agony. My heart and soul were shattered. But I couldn't break down. My three children were with me. I needed to show them we, as a family, could get through this.

* * *

At the celebration of life, our family, church family, friends, community, and coworkers came, supported us, and showed their love for our beautiful girl. After the celebration of life, I told myself, "You need to be strong and lean on God." My faith has grown, our family is closer, and the love still flows.

My last words to her were, "I love you, sister," and she responded, "I love you too, Mama." I carry this with me every day. I don't focus on her death. Instead, I focus on her life and the beautiful and loving contributions she gave to all of us.

Linda, 2023

Introduction

Many years ago, my grandfather died in a car crash. He and my grandmother were driving over the Cascade Mountains when his vehicle inexplicably left the road and crashed, killing him and critically injuring my grandmother. So many questions about the crash remain unanswered. Why did his car leave the road? Was there something on the road? Did he have a medical event? What *really* happened? I was very close to my grandfather, and it took me years to accept his death, the way it happened, and the fact that I'd never really know the answers to all my questions.

The death of a loved one is heartbreaking, no matter when and how it happens. But when a person dies by suicide, a violent or traumatic accident, or a mass casualty event, the sense of loss and grief is compounded. The suddenness and unexpectedness of a traumatic death challenge our understanding of reality and complicate the grieving process. Before grieving can begin, we must grapple with the questions surrounding these deaths. What happened? How did it happen? And the most perplexing and often unanswerable question: Why? These natural reactions and questions complicate the grieving process for families and friends when a loved one dies from sudden and traumatic causes.

In this chapter, we'll discuss several types of sudden traumatic death, including suicide, homicide, accidental deaths, and mass casualty incidents. These situations pose unique challenges for those navigating the grieving process. Whether you are directly affected or supporting someone else, understanding the additional factors inherent to violent deaths can help you chart a course through a traumatic death experience.

Learning Objectives

These learning objectives will help you identify what's most important in this chapter. By the end of this chapter, you should be able to do the following:

» Understand the risks of trauma, the methods for addressing trauma, and the reasons it may lead to challenges during the grieving process.

» Describe the disparities of suicide, the grief reactions to traumatic loss, and

» suicide prevention strategies.

» Explain how the methods, location, and legal process of homicides impact the grieving process.

» Identify the most common types of accidental death and how these accidents affect the grieving process.

» Relate the features and challenges of mass casualty incidents to experiences of secondary trauma and the grieving process.

Trauma and the Grieving Process

The American Psychological Association (n.d.) defines **trauma** as "an emotional response to a terrible event like an accident, crime, natural disaster, physical or emotional abuse, neglect, experiencing or witnessing violence, death of a loved one, war, and more." In a clinical context, trauma refers to an emotional response to a deeply distressing or disturbing event that overwhelms an individual's ability to cope, causes feelings of helplessness, diminishes their sense of self, and limits their ability to feel a full range of emotions and experiences.

The impact of trauma can be long lasting and affect a person's mental, emotional, and physical well-being. For professionals working in hospice care, grief counseling, or funeral services, understanding trauma is crucial. Individuals facing death, whether their own death or that of a loved one, may experience significant trauma. This can be due to the circumstances of the death, unresolved issues, or previous traumatic experiences that resurface during the grieving process.

Trauma-informed care (TIC) is an approach in health care and other service sectors that acknowledges the widespread impact of trauma and integrates this understanding into all aspects of service delivery. The six principles of trauma-informed care, according to the Substance Abuse and Mental Health Services Administration (SAMHSA), emphasize the following: 1) safety, 2) trustworthiness and transparency, 3) peer support, 4) collaboration and mutuality, 5) empowerment, and 6) attention to historical, cultural, and gendered contexts.

For example, one summer evening, Sharon and her husband Marv were downtown for dinner when an armed man attacked them. Marv was killed, and Sharon was injured. On the way to the hospital, a police officer accompanied her and explained the need to gather details about the attack for immediate dissemination to other officers. Though Sharon's injuries appeared minor, she was deeply traumatized and struggled to focus on the officer's questions. Recognizing her distress, the officer used a trauma-informed approach—calmly explaining the need for information, showing compassionate patience, and offering to call someone to support her at the hospital.

In this scenario, the officer's actions align with the six principles of trauma-informed care, as shown in figure 9.1. The officer stayed with Sharon during transport to the hospital (safety) and explained the need for immediate information (trustworthiness and transparency). The officer responded with sensitivity and patience by offering to call someone to be with Sharon (peer support) and respecting her need to process what just happened (collaboration and mutuality). The officer allowed Sharon to focus on what she could manage at the time (empowerment), ensuring that the interaction was sensitive to Sharon's unique needs (cultural, historical, and gender issues).

Figure 9.1. The six principles of trauma-informed care are part of a framework designed to recognize the impact of trauma and support healing through respectful and responsive practices. Adapted from Substance Abuse and Mental Health Services Administration (SAMHSA).

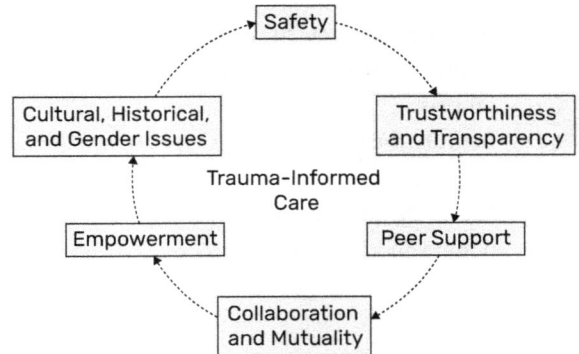

Sudden Traumatic Death

The death of a loved one, regardless of the cause, involves the challenges of grief, sorrow, and adjustment. **Sudden traumatic death**, when a death occurs unexpectedly and violently, brings with it additional challenges. The abruptness of traumatic death can leave family and friends unprepared to face the grieving process and often draws outside attention from bystanders or the media. People often perceive traumatic deaths as preventable, yet these deaths occur daily without warning. For instance, over 21,000 homicidal deaths occurred in 2022—that's fifty-seven dēaths each day (Korhonen, 2024).

The suddenness of traumatic death often leaves survivors with no time to prepare for the loss of a loved one. In other types of death, there may be time during the dying process for loved ones to engage in anticipatory grief, where they can begin processing feelings of sadness, anxiety, anger, and even guilt before a loss happens. This preliminary grief work is delayed in the case of sudden death and then compounds the conventional grief work that occurs upon the death of a loved one. Chapter 11 discusses anticipatory grief in more detail.

After a sudden death, family and friends must also deal with losing what could or should have been: Could it have been avoided? Why did this happen? These questions often lead to painful speculation from loved ones and sometimes from outsiders and the media. Families dealing with traumatic death may face social assumptions and judgments of the events that led to the death. Families beset by grief must give a social explanation of a private event that can shake their sense of safety and security.

As the grieving process unfolds, outsiders make judgments about what the deceased person "should have done or not done" or how they "should have prepared" for their loved one's sake by getting life insurance, writing a will, or making other financial preparations. However, it is complex and challenging to think about and prepare for a sudden death event. Therefore, it is often not attended to, and families are left making these decisions while also handling the emotional fallout.

Secondary Traumatic Stress

Exposure to human tragedy and loss of life can place a person at risk for a condition known as **secondary traumatic stress (STS)**, a natural stress response to knowing about or helping someone who has experienced a traumatizing event. It can affect a wide range of people, including those who have been indirectly exposed through family members and friends of people who have experienced trauma, and people who work with victims of trauma or around trauma scenes. Consuming high levels of media coverage of trauma, especially visually intense and graphic content or prolonged coverage of trauma events, can also trigger secondary trauma (Comstock & Platania, 2017; Lamba et al., 2023).

Secondary traumatic stress produces observable emotional and behavioral symptoms like post-traumatic stress disorder (PTSD). Symptoms can include:

- » feeling overwhelmed, hopeless, helpless, or powerless
- » difficulty in focusing and making decisions
- » feeling anger, irritability, sadness, and anxiety
- » feeling hypersensitive or insensitive to the stories we hear
- » emotional, psychological, or physical exhaustion or feeling numb
- » difficulty sleeping, experiencing nightmares, and social withdrawal and self-isolation (Centre for Addiction and Mental Health, n.d.)

Trauma-informed care uses what is known and understood about the impact of trauma on people's lives, recognizes the signs and symptoms of trauma, and avoids re-traumatization (Substance Abuse and Mental Health Services Administration, 2014). A trauma-informed organization can then integrate this information into its processes, procedures, and policies.

Trauma-Informed Practices

Trauma-informed practices are often incorporated into health care, education, and emergency services organizations. Even if an organization has not officially adopted this approach, employees may be trained to apply these fundamental principles within their existing policies and procedures whenever possible. As employees go about their work, trauma-informed practices can help them perform their tasks while supporting individuals affected by trauma.

Secondary trauma can affect anyone working in helping professions where people work with others who have experienced trauma, such as health care providers, emergency first responders, psychotherapists, human service workers, and counselors. Ongoing work-related trauma can have negative effects on a person's mental and physical health, social and personal relationships, and job performance. These symptoms may appear after one situation or exposure, gradually develop with repeated, prolonged experiences, or be triggered by a single event after cumulative exposure. See box 9.1 for strategies for dealing with secondary traumatic stress.

Box 9.1: Managing Secondary Traumatic Stress

Recognizing early symptoms of secondary trauma in oneself or others can be challenging, but strategies exist to prevent, reduce, and manage its effects. Workers can:

» participate in seminars and trainings on traumatic stress and burnout;
» prioritize self-care, such as eating healthy, staying hydrated, exercising, and getting adequate sleep;
» be aware of mental, emotional, and physical health, and watch for signs of burnout and traumatic stress;
» develop a buddy system with coworkers, watch out for each other, and avoid isolating and disconnecting from others; and
» take breaks at work and away from work.

In many of these professions, it can be difficult in the middle of a trauma event or during a string of events to take a break. But even stepping away for a few minutes can make a difference (CDC, 2018).

Suicide and the Grieving Process

Suicide touches the lives of people from all walks of life, ages, backgrounds, and professional settings. Individuals who work with people who are dying or grieving, such as health care professionals, therapists, counselors, clergy, first responders, and hospice workers, may encounter suicide in several ways. All of us must have access to resources for ourselves and those around us. As you explore this topic, be sure to take note of the available suicide prevention resources and support (see box 9.2).

Suicide is a complex public health problem with no single cause. **Suicide**, defined as death caused by self-directed injurious behavior with the intent to die, is the eleventh leading cause of death in the United States. According to the Centers for Disease Control and Prevention (CDC), suicide was the leading cause of death in 2022 for people ages 10–14 and 25–34 and the third leading cause of death for ages 15–24 in the United States (CDC, n.d.). The CDC calls it a "serious public health problem," and since 2000, suicide rates have increased by 36%. In 2022, there were 49,476 suicide deaths, which is about one death every eleven minutes (CDC, 2024c).

Box 9.2: Suicide Prevention Resources

"Far too many individuals have the false belief that their loved ones would be better off without them. . . . Many we have lost to suicide are some of the most courageous persons I have ever known. They are holding on until they just can't anymore." — Wendy Martinez Farmer, licensed professional counselor and vice president of 988 Strategy, Grants, and Clinical Standards (Enochs, 2024).

988 SUICIDE & CRISIS **LIFELINE**

Access more information on suicide prevention at these websites:
- » 988 Suicide & Crisis Lifeline: https://988lifeline.org/
- » CDC Suicide Prevention Resources: https://www.cdc.gov/suicide/factors/index.html
- » National Institute of Mental Health – Suicide Prevention: https://www.nimh.nih.gov/health/topics/suicide-prevention

The number of people who experience **suicidal ideation**, which is thinking about, considering, or planning suicide, or who act on a suicide attempt, is significantly higher. The CDC reported that in 2022, over 13.2 million American adults seriously thought about suicide, 3.8 million planned a suicide attempt, and 1.6 million attempted suicide (CDC, 2024a).

Most of us have been affected by suicide. Recent research finds that between fifteen and thirty people are severely impacted by a single suicide death. However, on average, up to 135 people are affected to some degree by a suicide death when counting all people who knew the deceased person (Cerel et al., 2018). No single cause of suicide exists, but situations that lead to feelings of hopelessness, despondency, sorrow, and distress can be risk factors. Risk factors typically fall into four domains: individual, relationship, community, and societal. Individual risk factors include a history of suicide attempts, a family history of suicide, mental illness, depression, financial or legal troubles, substance use, and experiences of victimization. Relationship-related risks involve the loss of connections, social isolation, or bullying. At the community and societal levels, factors such as discrimination, suicide clusters, and easy access to lethal means also contribute to risk (CDC, 2024b).

Suicide affects people beyond family and social networks, and grief can be experienced across a community. Social media can broaden the awareness of a suicide death, which can extend feelings of loss and grief far beyond the local community. The broadly felt impact of suicide can be seen in the death of Nex Benedict, a nonbinary teenager who was found dead in their home after an earlier altercation at school. Having been bullied because of their gender identity, Nex was assaulted by a group of classmates in the bathroom at an Oklahoma high school. Their death was later determined to be caused by suicide. This story is enmeshed in larger political issues, but their death touched many others far beyond their family and friends. It also stirred the emotions of community residents, members of the LGBTQ+ community and their families, parents whose kids have been bullied by or have bullied other kids, and people who learned of Nex's story through media reports and social media platforms.

Disparities in Suicide

Suicides occur across all demographic groups, but some suicide rates vary by age, gender, race, ethnicity, marital status, and other social factors, including occupation. For example, older adults have traditionally higher rates of suicide than those who are middle-aged. Suicide rates for men are substantially higher than those for women. By race and ethnicity, suicide rates are highest among non-Hispanic American Indian/Alaska Native people. Higher-than-average rates also occur within specific groups, such as veterans, people living in rural areas, and those working in certain industries. Young LGBTQ+ people have more suicidal thoughts than their heterosexual and cisgender peers (CDC, 2024a). In the following sections, we'll explore how demographic factors influence suicide rates.

Age

Suicide affects people of all ages and is a leading cause of death in the United States (CDC, 2023a). Historically, the rates of suicide have been the highest among older adults. While rates have declined since 1999, they remain high. Many older adults are living with chronic illness, and this age group has high rates of undiagnosed or untreated depression. With age comes a greater likelihood of experiencing loneliness due to the loss of a spouse and social isolation, which are commonly identified risk factors. Suicides by older adults also tend to be carefully planned and are more likely to be successful than attempts in younger age groups. Due to age and health-related factors, it's also harder for older adults to recover from or survive a suicide attempt.

Young adults face an increasing risk of suicide, with suicide rates for youth and young adults rising 52.2% between 2000 and 2021. Research also indicates that 20% of American high school students reported thoughts of suicide. In 2021, 9% reported that they had attempted suicide in the previous twelve months (CDC, 2023a). Physiological and social development factors contribute to teens' and young adults' suicide risk. The brain's prefrontal cortex, which controls executive functions like impulse control, does not fully develop until a person's mid-20s. This means that judgment and decision-making skills are still developing in teens and young adults, which impacts the ability to weigh risks and consequences and evaluate values and decisions (Fleisher, as cited in Cohen, 2022). They are more prone to risky, impulsive behavior and experimentation with drugs and alcohol, which are often involved in suicide attempts.

Teens and young adults often have fewer meaningful social connections than older adults, who often have a spouse or significant other, family, and work relationships. Young adults also face major life changes and future decisions as they think about college, careers, and other adult concerns. Without strong social support and coping skills, these significant issues place additional pressure on young adults that they may be unprepared to handle.

In addition, as suicide rates among young adults have risen, so has social media use. The prevalence of smartphones has increased young adults' access to the internet. At this challenging time in their life, social media increases exposure to additional stressors. While social media can provide access to positive influences, it also exposes young people to cyberbullying, imposes idealized standards of beauty and performance, and amplifies the forces of peer pressure. The significant amount of time young adults spend on social media increases their likelihood of social isolation, and the resulting decrease in sleep and exercise can lead to poor mental health or exacerbate any existing mental health condition (Balt et al., 2023).

Gender

Significant gender differences exist in suicide rates for both adults and adolescents. In 2021, the suicide rate for men was four times higher than the rate for women. Although men make up approximately 50% of the population, they account for 80% of suicide deaths in the United States (CDC, 2023a). Women, in contrast, have higher rates of suicidal thinking and are three times more likely to attempt suicide than men (Crosby et al., 2011). Sociologists describe this predictable and measurable difference in suicide deaths between men and women as the **gender paradox of suicide**, which refers to the fact that women are more likely to attempt suicide, but men are much more likely to die of suicide.

Multiple factors may contribute to the gender paradox of suicide, including the methods commonly used by men and women. Men often choose more violent and lethal methods like firearms, hangings, and jumping, while women are more likely to self-poison, by overdosing on medications or drugs, or exsanguination, which is when a person bleeds to death from a cut (Callanan & Davis, 2012). These differences might come from gender-based familiarity with and access to each method. For example, men are more likely than women to be familiar with and have access to firearms and, therefore, are more likely to choose this method.

Understanding how suicide rates differ between genders is challenging because research looking specifically at LGBTQ+ identities and suicide rates is limited. LGBTQ+ is an umbrella term for people from a wide range of sexual orientations and gender identities and expressions; this abbreviation includes lesbian, gay, bisexual, transgender, and queer people. The plus sign recognizes the diversity of gender identity and sexual orientation beyond those listed as part of the umbrella term. Demographic data reported at the time of death through official documents such as death certificates or hospital, police, and EMS reports do not systematically include the sexual orientation or gender identity of people when they die. This makes it challenging to examine causes of death for LGBTQ+ people and to understand and address any mortality disparities (Haas & Lane, 2015).

Some research has found that rates of suicidal thoughts and suicide attempts are higher among lesbian, gay, and bisexual adults when compared to heterosexual adults. In the 2015 U.S. Transgender Survey, which is the largest survey of transgender adults in the nation, over 48% of respondents reported seriously thinking about suicide in the past year, 40% reported attempting suicide in their lifetime, and over 7% reported attempting suicide in the past year (James et al., 2016). In another study, although LGBTQ+ people were overall more likely to report suicide-related thoughts, plans, and attempts within the past twelve months, the risks varied depending on the intersection between sexual identity and other demographic variables, such as gender, age, race, and ethnicity (Ramchand et al., 2021).

LGBTQ+ teens and young adults are particularly at risk for suicide and suicide attempts. In 2021, LGBTQ+ high schoolers were five times more likely to report attempting suicide than their heterosexual and cisgender peers (CDC, 2023a). Other national research has found similar data. The Trevor Project's 2022 National Survey on LGBTQ Youth Mental Health found that 45% of LGBTQ+ youth seriously considered attempting suicide in the previous year. LGBTQ+ youth of color, particularly Native or Indigenous youth, were more likely than White youth to attempt suicide (The Trevor Project, 2022). Gender-based victimization, discrimination, rejection, and bullying have been associated with the increased suicide rates among the LGBTQ+ community. For example, youth who experienced rejection by their families because of their sexual orientation or identity had an attempted suicide rate 8.4 times higher than those who had more family support and acceptance (Ryan et al., 2009). However, LGBTQ+ youth with at least one accepting adult in their life were 40% less likely to report having a suicide attempt during the last year (The Trevor Project, 2023).

Geographic Location

Where someone lives impacts their risk of suicide, and suicide rates vary substantially across geographic regions. In the United States, suicide rates increase as population density decreases and an area becomes more rural. In 2021, rural areas had a suicide rate of 21.7 deaths per 100,000 people, while large metropolitan areas had a suicide rate of 11.6 deaths per 100,000 (CDC, 2023a). A person's place of residence and social environment are important factors in understanding suicide risks.

What is it about rural communities or social environments that can account for these higher rates? Some research has shown that rates of suicide among men seem to be especially affected by living in rural areas, while suicide rates among women seem unaffected by rural living. Several factors may contribute to this issue, including limited social interaction and less frequent close contact with family and friends, greater access to lethal means, societal stigma surrounding mental health challenges, and insufficient availability of mental health services (Casant & Helbich, 2022).

In rural America, the logistics of life, like long distances, lack of transportation, and poor internet or cell service, can make it harder to socialize. Living in sparsely populated areas, miles from others, can make getting together with friends and family difficult. Another stress factor in more homogeneous rural communities can be the social pressure to conform and fit into standard behaviors and social roles (Chinni, 2021). Rural residents often have less access to mental health services due to chronic shortages of mental health professionals in rural areas. Even when services are available, people in rural communities may face an increased stigma associated with accessing mental health services. In small, tight-knit communities with few mental health professionals, the lack of anonymity increases and can lead to concerns about confidentiality.

Occupational Risks

Much of our adult life is spent in the workplace, and our occupation is a major part of our social identity. Our work environment and conditions can contribute to mental health risk factors. For instance, certain industries and occupations have significantly higher suicide rates when compared to the general U.S. population. Construction, mining, oil and gas extraction, quarrying, agriculture, forestry, and other service industry jobs (a huge sector of the economy from fast food workers to hospitality to delivery workers) had the highest suicide rates for men, while women working in arts, design, entertainment, sports, media, law enforcement, and health care support were at greater risk. For both men and women, occupations with the lowest rate of suicides were found in education, training, and library services, including jobs such as teachers, professors, and archivists (CDC, 2023a). In the next sections, we'll look closely at the high suicide rates in three occupation groups: military personnel, first responders, and health care workers.

Military Service

While the suicide risk for active-duty military personnel is similar to the civilian population, veterans who have separated from the military are 1.5 times more likely to die by suicide than nonveteran adults (DeAngelis, 2022). Suicide rates among veterans compared to nonveterans began to increase sharply in the early 2000s. In 2002, the veteran suicide rate was 12.1% higher than for nonveterans but had grown to 66.2% higher in 2017. In response, the Department of Veterans Affairs (VA) launched the National Strategy for Preventing Veteran Suicide in 2018. While the comparative rate has dropped slightly, in 2020, the veteran suicide rate was 57.3% higher than nonveterans. Suicide is now the second leading cause of death among veterans under age forty-five (U.S. Department of Veterans Affairs, 2022).

Veterans face many unique increased risk factors for suicide, including high exposure to trauma, stress and burnout, social isolation, easy access to and familiarity with guns, and difficulty reintegrating into civilian life (DeAngelis, 2022). For many veterans, these challenges are exacerbated by a lack of access to needed medical and mental health care services, high rates of unemployment, and homelessness. Military service, including combat and frequent deployments, has long been assumed to increase suicide risk. However, recent research was unable to find an independent association between military-specific variables and suicide risk, noting the research and data analysis limitations of previous military suicide studies (LeardMann et al., 2013).

The U.S. Department of Defense (DOD) and the VA have identified suicide risk and suicide prevention as their highest clinical priority. In 2022, the government established an independent review committee to seek input and recommendations from military personnel and civilian employees to help in their efforts to prevent veterans' deaths by suicide. The committee aims to develop and fund public health services to address health issues, encourage healthy lifestyles, and expand and enhance mental health services, such as community services and veteran-to-veteran support services and programs (DeAngelis, 2022). The goal of these efforts is to foster a more supportive environment, improve the delivery of mental health care, and address the stigma of mental health and other barriers to care (U.S. Department of Defense, 2023).

First Responders and Emergency Services

Jobs that involve high-stress duties, life-and-death responsibilities, and hazardous work environments can amplify factors associated with a higher risk for suicide. These conditions describe the day-to-day reality for first responders and emergency services personnel, such as law enforcement officers, firefighters, emergency medical services (EMS), and 911 telecommunicators. With every shift, first responders must be prepared for anything, from everyday emergencies to major trauma, along with the stress of these situations. Traumatic scenes, high-risk safety situations, or large-scale emergencies magnify the stress. Work schedules that involve shift work and being on-call also impact family and personal relationships, which must be strong to help remediate job stress. In general, acute stress from specific incidents and chronic stress from daily responsibilities are linked to an increased risk of suicidal behaviors.

Suicide is a serious risk for people in these occupations. Police officers and firefighters are more likely to die by suicide than in the line of duty. EMS personnel are 1.3 times more likely to die by suicide than the general population. Research on suicide risk for 911 telecommunicators has lagged that of other first responders, even though they are often the first to engage with people in crisis. Studies have found high rates of post-traumatic stress disorder (PTSD) and depression among 911 telecommunicators, which are risk factors associated with suicide. Even with what is known about the high rates of suicides among first responders and emergency service personnel, the numbers are likely underreported, and more research is needed. This is especially true for those who have multiple jobs or work as volunteers (Tiesman et al., 2021a).

Medical Professions

Historically, the suicide rate for health care workers has been disproportionately high. Health care workers like doctors, nurses, and even veterinarians face challenging work conditions with long hours and rotating, irregular shifts, which have frequently been identified as contributing factors to suicide. Medical workers experience stress associated with being exposed to infectious diseases and workplace injuries, dealing with emotionally difficult interactions with patients and their families, and confronting human suffering and death routinely. These working conditions and the responsibilities of health care workers put medical professionals at an increased risk for suicidal behaviors (Tiesman et al., 2021b).

Physicians, particularly women who are physicians, have a significantly increased suicide risk. For men who are physicians, the suicide rate is 1.4 times that of the general population, while for women, the suicide rate is 2.3 times that of the general population. Some specialties within medicine are also at higher risk, with anesthesiologists, psychiatrists, general practitioners, and general surgeons being the most at risk (Dutheil et al., 2019). Overall, doctors also report suicidal ideation at nearly double the rate of the general population: 7.2% compared with 4% (Laboe et al., 2021).

Higher rates of depression, a substantiated risk factor for suicidal behaviors, appear to start early in medical training. Incoming medical students are less depressed than other recent college graduates, but they experience more burnout and suicidal thoughts within months of starting medical school (Dyrbye et al., 2014). The demands and expectations of medical school training appear to impact students' quality of life and the emergence of mental health conditions associated with higher stress levels. This trajectory continues into residency and medical fellowships.

Medical training encourages stoicism (an emphasis on rational behavior over emotional response) and focuses on the importance of decision-making. Students learn to avoid errors and meet exacting standards. Patients always come first, even when it affects the trainee's well-being. In this highly competitive environment, student doctors may believe they will be faulted for showing vulnerability. The demands and expectations during medical training virtually guarantee high levels of stress and burnout (Kalmoe et al., 2019).

Once medical students become physicians, exposure to high levels of personal and professional stress continues. Physicians make life-or-death decisions for patients daily while dealing with non-medical stressors of a business-oriented health care industry. Physicians spend significant time completing documentation requirements and updating electronic health record systems. They are more likely to face high-stakes conflicts with administration or colleagues over medical decisions and financial processes. Malpractice claims can impact their professional reputation and financial stability. Work demands and work schedules take a toll on personal relationships and overall quality of life, which can lead to issues at home. Compounding these stresses, physicians are experiencing increased regulation and oversight, leading to decreased autonomy, which has been linked to decreased job satisfaction and burnout (Kalmoe et al., 2019).

Nurses also face a higher risk of suicide. Nurses make up the largest segment of the health care workforce and have a significantly higher suicide risk than the general population. This is a newer phenomenon. While nurses of all genders are at greater risk of suicide, women have been at higher risk since 2005 and men since 2011 (Davidson, as cited in Carr, 2020). Nurses who are women were at twice the risk for suicide as compared to women in the general population and 70% more likely than physicians who are women (Davis et al., 2021). Data on suicide risk for men who are nurses, approximately 12% of practicing nurses, are less clear (McElroy, 2023).

In the overburdened U.S. health care system, physician welfare garners significant focus, while nurses face similar pressures with less attention. Nurses provide most of the bedside care and face long shifts filled with stressful work, staff shortages, workplace violence, and musculoskeletal injuries associated with patient care. Nurses' suicide risk factors can be exacerbated by long hours and less autonomy. The COVID-19 pandemic further amplified many of these stressors. Even after COVID, nurses continue to struggle with many of these risk factors, which have been exacerbated by staff shortages fueled by the large numbers of nurses leaving the profession.

Suicide Contagion

Evidence shows that suicide can be "contagious," meaning that exposure to information about suicides can lead others to engage in suicidal behavior. **Suicide contagion** refers to situations when direct or indirect knowledge of suicide increases the likelihood of subsequent suicides or contributes to suicide risk factors (Gould, 1990). The widespread use of social media makes it easy to share information about suicides. As a result, many people beyond the person's immediate community see the posts and then repost them, which can trigger copycat suicides and increase suicide rates (Calvo et al., 2024). In this digital age, one person's suicide can cause spikes in suicide rates far beyond the local area, creating suicide clusters anywhere. A **suicide cluster** refers to a greater increase in suicide attempts than expected occurring close in time or geographic location.

The rapid spread of information through the internet and social media can increase suicidal behavior in at-risk individuals, especially teens and young adults. Research shows that direct or indirect exposure to suicidal behavior often precedes this increase. While exposure doesn't cause suicide, it can trigger those already at risk. Factors like mental illness, substance abuse, past suicide attempts, and stressful life events, like relationship issues, illness, job loss, or financial problems, make some people more vulnerable. Social factors like bullying, grief, or isolation also increase the risk (Walling, 2021).

Increases in suicide rates can follow media reports of real or fictional suicides in movies, TV shows, or books (Gould & Lake, 2013). Evidence shows that the impact depends on how the story is told. Frequent stories, dramatic headlines, and detailed descriptions of the suicide method can raise suicide rates (Gould, 1990; Gould & Lake, 2013; Michel et al., 1995). Media coverage that glamorizes or normalizes suicide can influence vulnerable people, while media coverage that includes suicide prevention information and resources may encourage others to reach out for help (Hoffner & Cohen, 2017; Colman, 2018). Implementing media guidelines to reduce and carefully frame reports can help mitigate these effects (Gould, 2001). An individual's connection to the deceased person, whether a family member, friend, or admired public figure, can also affect their susceptibility to media influence.

Suicide Prevention

Suicide prevention focuses on multiple ways for us, as individuals and as communities, to support people in emotional distress (figure 9.2). Suicide often results from a combination of internal factors, such as personal and psychological characteristics, and external socioenvironmental influences. Aspects of a person's overall physical, psychological, and emotional well-being can be risk factors associated with suicide. Social issues such as relationship problems, financial and legal issues, or experiencing social isolation may also be contributing influences (Tiesman et al., 2021a).

Figure 9.2. The National Institute of Mental Health provides resources for suicide prevention.

To address the wide range of risk factors, suicide prevention often focuses on person-to-person contact and support; the development of community-based programs; and national policies to support families, stabilize housing, ensure living-wage jobs, and improve access to health care and mental health services. On an individual level, the National Institute of Mental Health's five action steps can help someone you know who's experiencing emotional pain: ask, keep them safe, be there, help them connect, and stay connected.

More broadly, we should all know the warning signs of suicidal behavior, understand the risk factors associated with suicide, and be aware of resources, as shown in box 9.3.

Box 9.3: Suicide Prevention Basics

Warning Signs

- » talking about wanting to die or about killing themself
- » talking about feeling empty, hopeless, or trapped and seeing no solution
- » feeling unbearable physical, psychological, or emotional pain
- » socially withdrawing from friends, family, and regular activities
- » saying goodbye to friends and family, giving away important possessions
- » planning and looking for ways to kill themselves

Risk Factors

- » previous suicide attempts or exposure to suicide
- » depression and other mental illness
- » serious illness, declining health, or chronic pain
- » substance use
- » employment, financial, or legal problems
- » experiences of violence or bullying
- » relationship problems
- » social isolation

Help Available

- » Safety plans: Develop a list of coping strategies and support people to contact if needed in a crisis; limit access to lethal means such as firearms, pills, or poisons.
- » Psychotherapies and medications: Work with health professionals to address psychiatric disorders, behavioral conditions, and mental health needs such as depression, stress, and anxiety.
- » Collaborative care: Seek a team-based approach involving psychiatric, primary health care, and mental health specialists to provide coordinated supportive care (U.S. Department of Health and Human Services, n.d.; Centers for Disease Control and Prevention, 2022).

Homicide and the Grieving Process

Homicide, the killing of one person by another, is the ultimate crime. Homicide deaths carry unique challenges and concerns for the surviving family, friends, and community. The sudden loss of a loved one because of the actions of another may cause feelings of helplessness and senselessness that complicate the grieving process. Survivors may feel anger along with the desire for justice. They may feel fear and confusion as they grapple with the loss.

Homicide has ripple effects that go beyond the loss of human life. While homicide immediately impacts the lives of the victim's family, it also affects the community and its members, who can be described as indirect victims. Homicide creates a violent environment that hurts society, the economy, and government institutions. Homicide is not limited to people living on the margins of society, as is popularly believed. It can affect anyone regardless of age, sex, race, ethnicity, or socioeconomic background.

Recognizing the collective grief that results from homicide, some agencies, such as the Violence Prevention Alliance (VPA), a global network coordinated by the World Health Organization, aim to prevent and reduce the impact of violence on communities. VPA advocates for support systems for survivors of violence and families affected by violent death. Grief resources and counseling help individuals navigate the emotional and psychological aftermath of loss. In addition to promoting evidence-based interventions, agencies like VPA incorporate grief support into a broader mission of violence prevention, helping communities heal while striving to prevent future tragedies. In the United States, the CDC takes a public health approach by funding violence-prevention research, programs, and initiatives.

Homicide definitions vary based on the perpetrator's actions and the crime's context. Legal definitions and laws differ by country and among states within the U.S. However, homicides are generally divided into two types: criminal homicide (an unjustifiable killing that leads to criminal charges) and noncriminal homicide (a justifiable killing, such as by law enforcement or in self-defense).

The International Classification of Crime for Statistical Purposes from the United Nations Office on Drugs and Crime (UNODC) defines homicide as the "unlawful death inflicted with intent to cause death or serious injury" (UNODC, 2015). Intentional homicide includes three elements: killing a person, intent to kill or seriously injure, and unlawfulness of the act. Intentional homicide is always illegal, and the perpetrator is fully liable for criminal prosecution. This definition makes homicide different from suicides, justifiable killings like self-defense, and deaths caused by reckless or negligent actions without the intent to kill.

Occurrences, Method, and Location

In the United States, one out of every ten people will experience the death of a loved one due to homicide. This is a staggering statistic. Beyond the immediate family, each homicide death directly affects at least three to ten other people closely connected to the victim, often referred to as co-victims (Bastomski & Duane, 2018; Center for Victim Research, 2018). The homicide rate in the United

Figure 9.3. This chart compares homicide rates among G7 Nations. Adapted from Dyvik, 2023.

Homicide Rates by Region

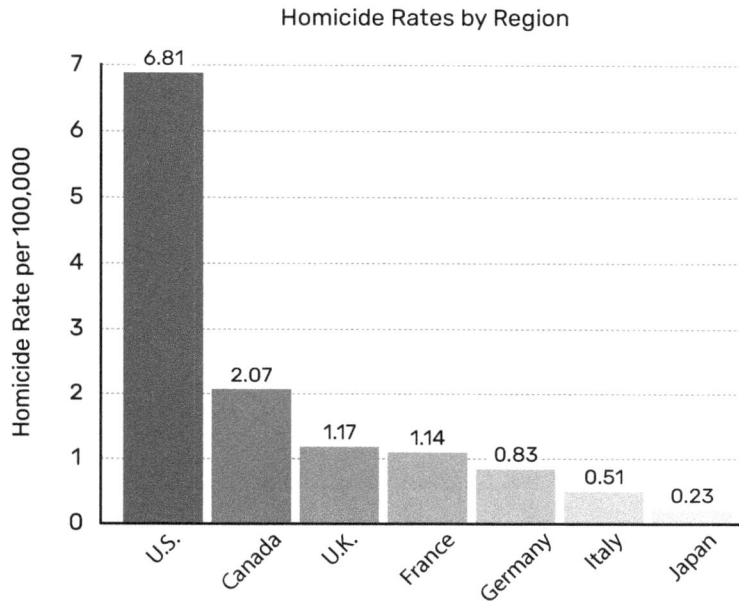

States is significantly higher than in other comparative nations, as you can see in figure 9.3. For example, U.S. rates are three to five times higher when looking at countries with similar political, economic, and value systems, such as Canada, France, and the United Kingdom (Dyvik, 2023).

Homicide rates vary significantly depending on the geographic location. Each year, as new crime data are released, headlines flash the names of the states and cities with the highest homicide rates. But what does the data say, and how can we make sense of this information? First, homicide data are often presented at a rate per 100,000 people, which allows us to statistically compare states and cities regardless of their size. Once the rates are determined, the states are often ranked from highest to lowest. The data are then used for further research and development and delivery of services, resources, and prevention strategies. The data may seem overwhelming, but consider what this information represents. These numbers are people, family and friends, coworkers and neighbors, community members, and fellow human beings. The data describe how sadly common it is for families and friends to face the challenges of losing a loved one to homicide.

In rate-based comparisons, small numbers of homicides in low-population states can drastically affect the state's ranking. Conversely, it can take greater numbers of homicides to have the same effect on the ranking of higher-population states. For example, the homicide rate in California is 6.4 per 100,000 people, but because of its large population, this represents 2,495 deaths. However, Mississippi, with a smaller population, has a rate of 23.7 per 100,000, representing 656 deaths

Figure 9.4. This chart shows the states with the highest homicide rates. Adapted from CDC, 2022a.

Homicide Rates by State

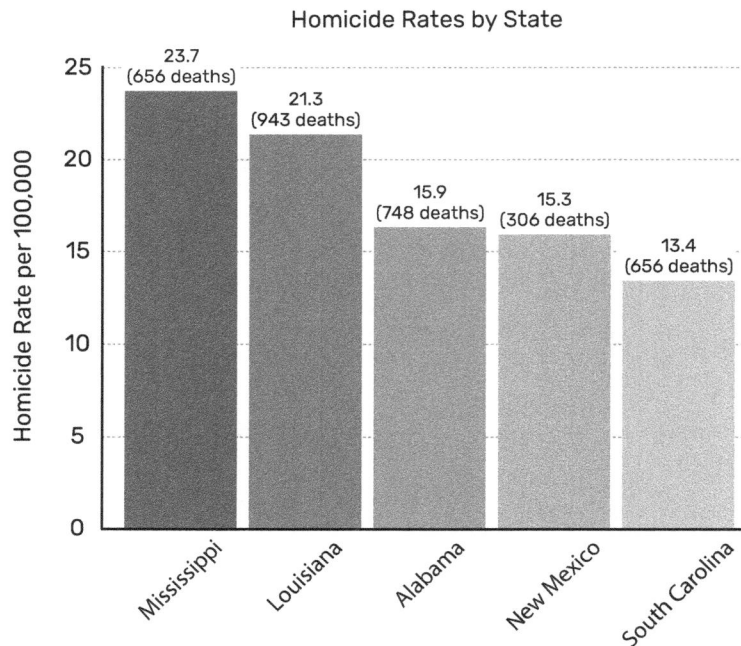

(CDC, 2022a). The data do not account for variations in homicide rates across different regions of the state or differences between urban and rural areas. Figure 9.4 shows the states with the top five highest homicide rates by population. An intentional homicide occurs every thirty-two minutes somewhere in the United States (FBI, 2019). The overwhelming majority (76%) of homicide deaths are a result of firearms.

Victim-Suspect Relationship

The relationship between a victim and perpetrator is a significant factor in homicide. The death of a person by homicide poses many of the same challenges for family and friends during the grieving process as other types of sudden traumatic deaths, such as a lack of time to prepare for the death and begin the grieving process. However, when a loved one is killed by someone they know, have known, or interact with regularly, it can shatter their sense of trust and security.

Family members are often shocked when someone close to their loved one—and possibly to them—is responsible for the death. Grief becomes even more complicated if the perpetrator regularly interacted with the victim's family and friends. People may take sides, supporting either the victim's family in their grief or the perpetrator's family, who may deny the charges. These divisions can fracture families, strain friendships, and split communities, leaving individuals isolated from the very support systems they need to navigate their grief.

In 2019, victims were killed by someone they knew in more than 41% of homicides. In these cases, 28% of the perpetrators were nonfamily members, like friends, acquaintances, dating partners, neighbors, schoolmates, or coworkers, while 13% were family members (FBI, 2020). Women are substantially more likely to be murdered by their intimate partner, and most female homicide victims are killed by a current or former male intimate partner with a firearm (Tobin-Tyler, 2023). Homicide is also the leading cause of death during pregnancy and postpartum (Wallace et al., 2022). Box 9.4 offers resources for people experiencing intimate partner violence, which includes physical, psychological, or sexual harm within the context of an intimate relationship.

Box 9.4: Addressing Intimate Partner Violence

Survivors of intimate partner violence (IPV) may experience ambiguous grief as they mourn the loss of a relationship, even though it was harmful. Survivors may face stigma or judgment from others who do not understand the complexities of IPV. This stigma can make it harder for someone to access support networks or feel validated in their grief. Many resources are available, including:

» National Coalition Against Domestic Violence (NCADV): Advocates for policies and provides resources to support survivors of domestic violence.

» National Domestic Violence Hotline: The Hotline can be accessed via the nationwide number 1–800–799–SAFE (7233) or TTY 1–800–787–3224 or (206) 518-9361 (Video Phone Only for Deaf Callers). Website: https://www.thehotline.org/

Americans spend much of their adult lives in the workplace, interacting with coworkers, customers, and the public. Some occupations and employee positions have higher rates of work-related homicide. The highest rates are reported in retail sales, transportation, management, construction, extraction, and production. Retail workers are at the highest risk because their work environments make them more vulnerable to robbery. Risk factors include sites where employees work alone, stores that are open late or twenty-four hours a day, isolated locations, readily available cash, or proximity to major highways or freeways (CDC, 2023b). Taxi and rideshare drivers have some of the same risks: handling cash, working with the public, working alone, and working late at night or early in the morning.

Most workplace homicides involve men (81%) between the ages of twenty-five and forty (44%) and occur in retail (33%) (CDC, 2022c). Firearms are commonly used, with 40% of non-law enforcement workplace shootings linked to robberies and 48% non-robbery related. In robbery-related cases, 95.6% of the perpetrators are unknown. Most non-robbery shootings stem from arguments, often involving customers, coworkers, or people with personal ties to the employee (Doucette et al., 2019). These deaths involve people just doing their jobs. Surviving families must not only grieve the death of their loved one, but they also do so with the additional stressor of losing a source of income.

Children, Teens, and Gun-Related Deaths

Any homicide is tragic, but the senseless death of a young person who has their entire life ahead of them is especially difficult and traumatic for family, friends, and their community. In 2022, an average of seven youths (ages nineteen and under) died each day by homicide in the U.S. The overwhelming majority of these homicide deaths involved firearms (Korhonen, 2024; KFF, 2024). The United States' firearm death rate for young people is by far the highest among comparative nations, a staggering 9.5 times higher for children and teens than the next country, Canada, as seen in figure 9.5.

Figure 9.5. The U.S. has the highest child and teen gun-related mortality rate. This chart compares the number of gun-related deaths among children and teens in the U.S. (2021) and peer countries (2019). Adapted from KFF, 2024.

Gun-Related Deaths Among Children and Teens in U.S. and Peer Countries

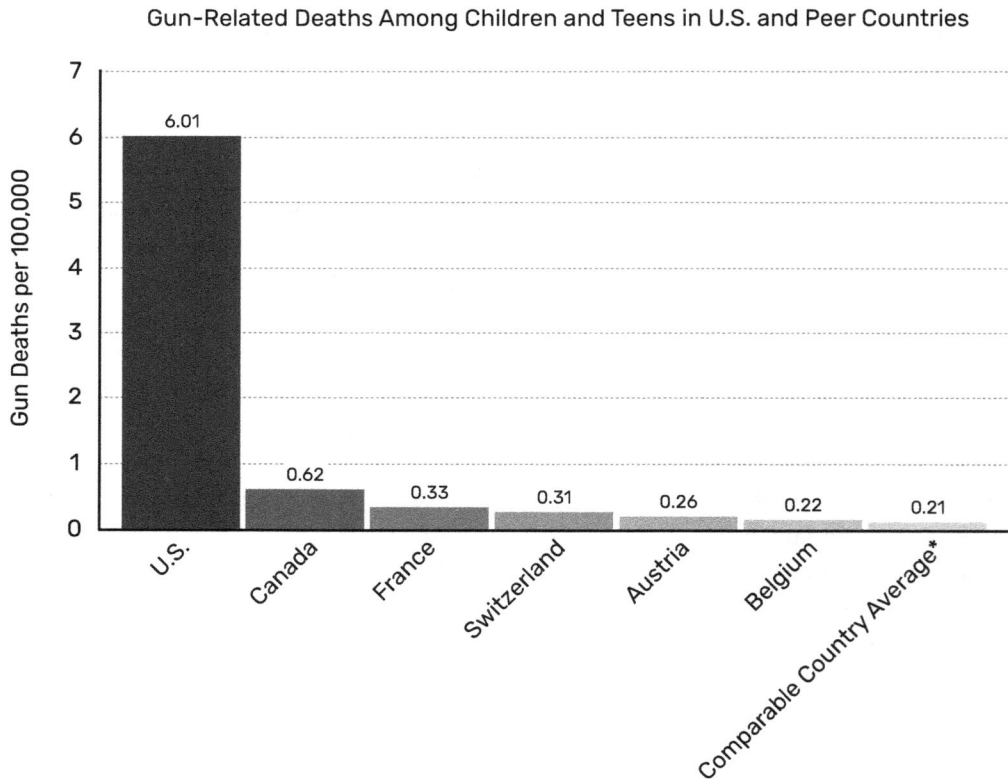

In 2020, firearms became the leading cause of death for American children and teens, making guns the cause of more deaths of young people than any other injury or illness. From 2019 to 2021, firearm-related deaths of children and teens increased by 50%. In other high-income nations, firearms are not even listed among the leading causes of death (McGough et al., 2023).

Within the United States, firearm death rates vary significantly from state to state. Generally, states with stricter gun laws have lower rates of child and teen firearm deaths. Louisiana has the highest rate (17.6%), while New York and New Jersey have the lowest (2.1%). But even those states have rates significantly higher than those of comparative nations (McGough et al., 2023). In the U.S., most youth firearm-related deaths are homicides (60%), followed by suicides (32%), and accidents (5%). In contrast, suicides accounted for the majority (55%) of adult firearm deaths in 2021 (Gramlich, 2023).

Youth from historically marginalized communities carry a disproportionate burden associated with gun-related deaths. For example, in 2021, Black youth were five times as likely as White or Hispanic youth to die by gunfire (Gramlich, 2023). Racial and ethnic differences also appear when looking at the types of gun deaths involving children and teens, as seen in figure 9.6.

Figure 9.6. According to 2021 Pew Research Center data, Black children and teens are five times more likely to die by gunfire. Adapted from Gramlich, 2023.

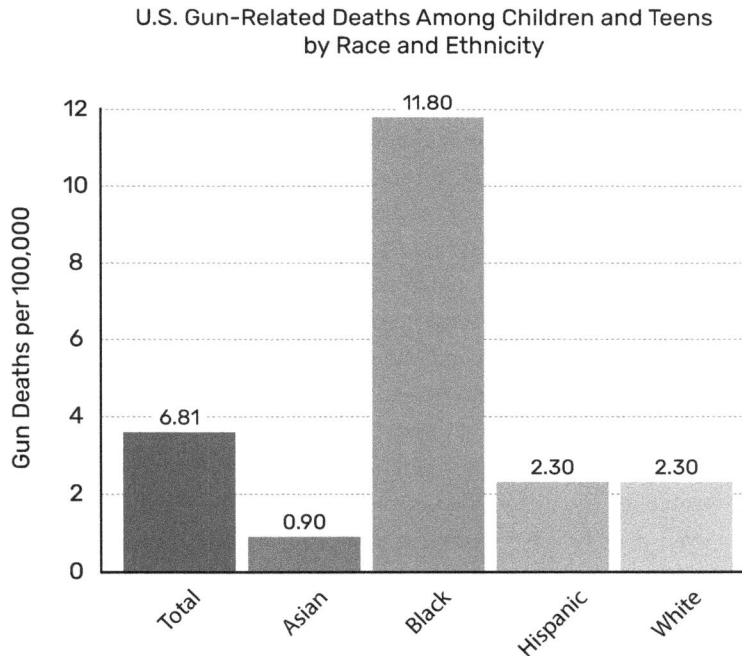

U.S. Gun-Related Deaths Among Children and Teens by Race and Ethnicity

Among Black youth, 84% of gun deaths were homicides, while 8% were suicides. For White youth, 66% of gun deaths were suicides, and 24% were homicides (Gramlich, 2023). More broadly, homicide is the leading cause of death for African American youth, the second leading cause of death for Hispanic youth, the third leading cause of death for American Indian/Alaska Native youth, and the fourth leading cause of death among White and Asian/Pacific Islander youth (Youth.gov, n.d.). Box 9.5 highlights two organizations addressing gun violence in the United States.

Box 9.5: Addressing Gun Violence

The data around gun violence can be disheartening, but hope exists in the form of organizations working to reduce gun violence and its toll on communities. Here are two organizations that show how grassroots and policy-driven efforts can reduce harm and save lives.

» **Everytown for Gun Safety**: Advocates for stronger gun laws and supports victims of gun violence.

» **The Brady Campaign to Prevent Gun Violence**: Focuses on advocacy and education to end gun violence.

Legal Process and Homicide

As you have read, the loss of a loved one from a sudden and traumatic death presents challenges when working through the grieving process. After the nonviolent death of a loved one, a relatively small number of people (10–15%) experience significant challenges while working through their grief, while in the case of a violent death, almost half of all bereaved people experienced prolonged and complex grief (Lundorff et al., 2017; Nijborg et al., 2024). Certain characteristics of sudden traumatic deaths point to increased difficulty in working through grief. The sudden and unexpected nature of these deaths leaves the bereaved psychologically and emotionally unprepared. Survivors struggle to make sense of death caused by violence, which is substantially different from death due to natural causes. When sudden traumatic deaths are reported by the media and posted on social media, the added exposure invites curiosity, misinformation, and assumptions. This attention may erode survivors' trust in the public, leaving them more socially isolated in their grief.

Traumatic deaths frequently involve some type of legal investigation and court proceedings to determine the specific cause of the death and any criminal actions. This process can be lengthy and stressful for everyone involved. Detailed investigations often include information from the death location, interviews with witnesses, and an autopsy to determine the exact cause of death. When the information has been gathered, a prosecutor determines if the individual will be criminally charged or held civilly responsible for the death. If a person is criminally charged or a civil lawsuit is filed, it can take months or even years before a trial takes place. During that time, investigators will continue the investigation, conduct interviews, and gather evidence in preparation for a criminal or civil trial. During the court process, family and friends can experience significant distress. Enduring days of testimony about their loved one's death, they may have to face the accused, hear accusations about the deceased, and watch the media rehash what took place in the courtroom.

If the accused person is convicted, the family and friends of the deceased may be allowed to present a victim's impact statement in court before sentencing. A victim's impact statement (VIS) allows people who have been affected by a crime to describe in their own words the emotional, mental, physical, and financial damage they have suffered. This information may be presented in a court sentencing hearing or submitted to the court. The VIS is entered into the court record and considered by the court when determining the appropriate sentence for the offender.

Delivering a VIS in court can impact the grieving process (Nijborg et al., 2024). Whether or not to make a VIS is a personal decision. Some family and friends have found delivering a VIS to be a positive experience that helps in the grieving process. It may help them process emotions and trauma, feel empowered, and regain a sense of agency and control in a situation where they previously felt helpless. It may also influence the sentencing of the offender. However, it can also be emotionally difficult, potentially re-traumatize those affected by the crime, and raise concerns about the privacy and safety of those providing the statement. Therefore, people should work with a victim advocate when considering whether to make a statement.

Accidental Death and the Grieving Process

Like suicide and homicide, a sudden, violent, and random death caused by an accident is a traumatic experience for loved ones and communities. Accidental deaths are challenging in their randomness: sometimes, the victim was simply in the wrong place at the wrong time. Sense-making, which can help the bereaved accept death as a part of life, becomes more complex (Currier et al., 2007). For families, there is no time to psychologically prepare for the death or gather resources and a support network. A violent crash can also damage a person's body so much that identifying the deceased becomes more difficult, and funeral and interment options can be limited, inflicting more trauma on the family.

Car Crashes

Most people don't think about the possibility of dying in a car crash while running errands or visiting friends. Yet, most fatal crashes happen within twenty-five miles of home and at speeds under forty miles per hour (National Highway Traffic Safety Administration, n.d.). Victims are usually on familiar roads, going to work, or doing everyday activities when these tragic, often human-caused, accidents occur without warning. In fact, motor vehicle crashes are common in the United States, with over six million reported in 2021, leading to nearly 2.5 million injuries (National Center for Statistics and Analysis, 2023). Despite their frequency, crashes remain one of the leading causes of unexpected deaths.

News and social media often quickly report crash-related deaths, spreading personal and private information more than the family may wish. In the case of Sylvia's daughter, who died in an early morning crash on her way home from her bartending job, media attention fueled rumors and speculation about whether alcohol had been involved in the crash, causing Sylvia and her family even more distress. Such attention can invade the privacy of grieving families and disrupt their ability to mourn.

Families already grappling with grief often face significant financial strain due to crash-related deaths. Medical costs can be high if the victim is transported by ambulance or airlifted to a medical facility and receives care before death. Vehicle repairs or replacement might not be fully covered by insurance. These situations pose additional challenges if the vehicle is the family's only means of transportation.

Crash-related deaths can bring about legal challenges. Law enforcement or attorneys may investigate or interview those involved in the crash to determine who is at fault, often leading to lengthy and public court trials. When the responsible party is someone the victim knew or if the victim caused harm to others, the situation can be even more heartbreaking. Family and friends of the deceased person often must endure court proceedings and ongoing media coverage regarding the crash, which can drag out for months and sometimes years. Hearings frequently involve testimony going over every detail of the crash and how their loved one died. The re-opening of their emotional wounds can stall the healing process and prolong the grieving process.

Bicycle and Pedestrian Deaths

In a vehicle-bicycle crash, the bicyclist is extremely vulnerable to severe injury and possible death. In the United States, bicycle trips represent only 1% of all trips taken on today's roadways but account for over 2% of the people who die in vehicle-related crashes. Most bicyclist deaths happen in urban areas. However, nearly two-thirds occur away from intersections on roads with higher speeds. About one-third of bicyclist deaths involve alcohol use by the driver or bicyclist. Adolescents and young adults have the highest rates of serious bicycle injuries, while adults between the ages of fifty-five and sixty-nine have the highest death rates. Gender is also a factor, with male bicyclists having a death rate six times higher than female bicyclists (CDC, 2022b).

Pedestrian deaths have been increasing faster than other traffic-related fatalities. Between 2010 and 2021, pedestrian deaths increased by 77%, while all other traffic deaths increased by 25%. The most recent data indicate a continuation of this upward trend, with a 19% surge in the deaths of people walking between 2019 and 2022. In 2021, nearly 8,000 pedestrians were killed in crashes involving a motor vehicle. That number equates to one death every sixty-six minutes. Rates can vary significantly from state to state; however, most pedestrian deaths occur on high-traffic, higher-speed urban roads and streets, and nearly half involve alcohol use by the driver or pedestrian. Pedestrian deaths disproportionately occur among adults over sixty-five, while American Indian/Alaskan Native and Black people have the highest pedestrian death rate among all racial and ethnic groups (CDC, 2023c; Governors Highway Safety Association, 2023). Deaths resulting from pedestrian, bicycle, and motor vehicle accidents are a persistent public health concern, and several organizations are working to address traffic fatalities, as box 9.6 shows.

Box 9.6: Addressing Traffic Fatalities

For those who survive crashes or lose loved ones, the aftermath often involves significant physical, emotional, and financial challenges that shape the experience of grief and recovery. Efforts to address this issue are supported by organizations and initiatives dedicated to making roads safer for all:

» **Mothers Against Drunk Driving (MADD)**: Advocates for policies to end drunk driving and support crash victims.
» **National Highway Traffic Safety Administration (NHTSA)**: Implements safety standards and educational campaigns to reduce road accidents.
» **Vision Zero Initiative**: An international effort to eliminate traffic fatalities through safer road designs and stricter enforcement of traffic laws.

Mass Casualty Incidents and the Grieving Process

Advances in telecommunications technology have produced a heightened awareness and increasing public focus on **mass casualty incidents (MCI)**, which are events that result in many injuries or deaths and overwhelm the local health care and emergency response systems. MCIs can be caused by natural disasters like earthquakes or hurricanes, human-made events such as terrorist attacks or mass shootings, or large-scale accidents like train derailments or industrial explosions. The key characteristic of an MCI is the need for additional resources and coordination to effectively manage and treat the affected individuals. Despite the low odds of being involved in an MCI, many people worry about the increasing dangers in the world and fear for their own or their loved ones' safety.

Defining an MCI by a specific number of deaths is challenging due to factors like the event's cause, location, and available resources. Therefore, MCIs are often defined as any number of injuries and casualties that exceed locally available resources. This definition emphasizes local capacity to handle the situation, considering the number and severity of injuries and fatalities.

Mass casualty incidents can be human-made or natural. Human-made events include terrorism like the 9/11 attacks and 2001 anthrax mailings; accidents like building collapses and industrial fires; and mass shootings in public places like schools, malls, and theaters (U.S. Department of Justice, 2010). Domestic terror attacks can also result in mass casualties, such as the 1984 mass Salmonella poisoning of salad bars in rural Oregon by members of an armed religious group (Torok et al., 1997). Though nobody died, over seven hundred people were poisoned, and many were hospitalized in what is known as the largest bioterrorist attack in U.S. history.

Natural disasters like earthquakes, tornadoes, hurricanes, and wildfires can cause MCIs, with each U.S. region facing specific threats. For instance, earthquakes are frequent in California and Alaska, tornadoes in the Midwest and Southeast, and hurricanes along the Gulf and East Coast. As population density increases in these areas, the likelihood of an MCI from natural events rises. Climate change is also causing more frequent and severe weather-related disasters. Life-threatening weather events are occurring with increasing regularity as we experience more frequent droughts, torrential rains, and intense windstorms. These events, in turn, lead to more wildfires and floods, severe thunderstorms spinning off stronger tornadoes, and extreme low-pressure systems producing more powerful hurricanes.

Features and Challenges

Mass casualty incidents share standard features, issues, and challenges that must be addressed regardless of the type, size, and location. Since an MCI is, by definition, an event that overloads local systems and resources, the most immediate challenge is to get people, equipment, and supplies where they are needed. This effort often necessitates a multiagency response that can include federal, state, and local law enforcement agencies, fire departments, search and rescue units, government agencies, medical staff and facilities, and private equipment and resources. Box 9.7 shows how two organizations, the American Red Cross and the Federal Emergency Management Agency (FEMA), respond to large-scale emergencies. Effective communication and coordination of personnel and resources are essential to address these situations.

The process used to collect the remains of the people who have died in an MCI is affected by the number of deaths involved, the type and location of the incident, and the available resources. Large numbers of deaths and injuries that will need care can quickly overtax rescue and retrieval resources and slow the recovery process. However, smaller numbers of victims in rural or remote locations can have the same effect. The location and difficulty reaching victims can also pose safety concerns for first responders. In situations such as a building collapse caused by a natural gas explosion or earthquake, specialized equipment and strategies may be needed to locate and retrieve a victim safely. The process for the retrieval of the victims' bodies can be affected when there is an investigation of the incident. The need to gather and preserve material evidence can constrain the methods used and slow the efforts to retrieve victims.

Problems in locating and collecting the victims' remains can lead to identification issues. Trauma to the body caused by severe force or delays in reaching the victim can cause degradation of the body, making timely identification difficult. When visible identification is impossible, families may need to produce medical and dental records of their loved ones and provide DNA samples to aid identification. When this happens, family and friends are left in limbo, and the grieving process is disrupted while they await final confirmation of the fate of their loved one.

Delays in body retrieval and lengthy or complex victim identification can create challenges in securing adequate morgue facilities to store the remains of victims, especially in the case of large numbers of fatalities. Finding sufficient funeral, cremation, and burial services can also be an issue. Official death certification can be delayed if personnel who complete the process and paperwork aren't available. In such cases, the family must wait for the necessary documentation to complete the body's final disposition and take care of legal and financial matters. These logistical shortages can have a widespread impact on families and friends, making it difficult for communities to assist each other.

Box 9.7: Responding to Disaster: Two Approaches

Organizations like the American Red Cross and the Federal Emergency Management Agency (FEMA) play critical roles in responding to mass casualty incidents. The aftermath of large-scale emergencies often involves grief, trauma, and the challenge of rebuilding lives, highlighting the need for robust support systems and resources. Consider the complementary roles these two agencies play in disaster management:

» **FEMA**: A government agency that coordinates disaster response and recovery efforts, offering financial assistance, rebuilding programs, and resources to help communities prepare for and withstand catastrophic events.

» **The Red Cross**: A humanitarian nonprofit that provides immediate aid, including emergency shelter, medical assistance, and emotional support for survivors. Their focus on community resilience extends to preparedness programs that help mitigate future risks.

Secondary Trauma from MCIs

Mass fatality incidents profoundly impact families and the community. The effects of an MCI reach far beyond the immediate circle of family and friends of those injured or killed in the incident. These tragedies also touch the lives of all who help on-site, support survivors and the bereaved, and assist the community in recovering.

Mass casualty incidents are often short-duration, high-intensity events. However, longer-term incidents such as wildfires, plane or train crashes, or complex structure collapses can last many days or weeks. During a long response, the extra demand for staff can be tough to manage and adds stress on workers. Those involved, like first responders and recovery teams, endure extended shifts with minimal rest and constant exposure to severe devastation, placing them at risk for secondary traumatic stress.

This was the case after the devastating floods from Hurricane Helene that killed ninety-six people (North Carolina Department of Health and Human Services, n.d.). In September 2024, parts of western North Carolina received as much as two feet of rain in a matter of hours, washing away homes and entire communities. Emergency personnel worked around the clock for days, searching through floodwaters, landslides, debris flows, and destroyed buildings to locate survivors. In this high-pressure environment—where time was critical, the destruction was widespread, and the impact on people's lives was clear—these workers faced the additional challenge of recovering the bodies of the deceased, putting them at risk of secondary traumatic stress.

Beyond first responders, community members in close physical proximity to an MCI can be at higher risk of stress and anxiety (Abrams, 2023). When an incident occurs nearby, you are more likely to know and identify with someone directly affected by the deaths. People recognize the similarities between themselves and those impacted by the MCI and draw a comparison. For example, when a tornado destroyed a neighboring town and several residents died, Sandra thought, "That could have been here. We could have lost our home or a loved one. Tornadoes happen every year, it could be us next time." Increasing evidence shows that even people far from the MCI location can experience anxiety, stress, and mental health issues if exposed to media coverage of the incident (Comstock & Platania, 2017).

Frequent exposure to media coverage of disasters can increase people's anxiety about the possibility of similar events affecting them or their loved ones. This heightened alertness may lead to avoidance behaviors and a generalized fear. Others may become exhausted by the never-ending stream of tragic news in the media. This negative information overload can overwhelm people, leading to inaction and disengagement (Abrams, 2023). In addition, a feedback loop between media exposure and anxiety can develop. Consuming media about mass casualty events can increase the desire to seek out more coverage, leading to heightened distress, thus perpetuating the cycle (Thompson et al., 2019).

Conclusion

We rarely consider that a loved one might die suddenly and traumatically, without warning—let alone that it could happen to you. It isn't supposed to happen that way; in our minds, death occurs in old age. And it's true—most people will die from age-related factors. Therefore, most people are unprepared for violent death when it does occur.

For bereaved family and friends, the traumatic death of a loved one can be especially difficult. Without time for their loved ones to put their affairs in order or for family and friends to say good-bye, survivors wrestle with unanswered questions. People in their support system may have the same questions and minimize contact, not knowing what to say or fearing they might say the wrong thing. The grieving process can also be disrupted, delayed, or elongated by legal processes and ongoing media coverage of the death event.

Regardless of the type of traumatic death, those who have been impacted face challenges in accessing support and finding their way through the grieving process. In the opening vignette, Linda shared how her family started their journey through their grief. Family, friends, and her church community came together to support one another, and with strength from their religious faith, they began navigating the grieving process. Their experience highlights the importance of community, resilience, and tailored interventions in helping survivors cope with traumatic loss. For professionals working with grieving individuals and communities, understanding these complexities is essential for providing compassionate support that acknowledges both the personal and structural dimensions of loss.

Summary

» All death is challenging, but sudden, traumatic death can be more trying, disconcerting, and stressful. It comes out of nowhere and could happen to anyone, regardless of age, race, or social class.

» Traumatic deaths are often covered by the media, making a personal event a public issue, which can complicate the grieving process.

» Workers who address violent death are at increased risk for secondary trauma.

» Disparities in the rates of suicide are based on social factors and personal characteristics and behaviors such as age, gender, geographic location, occupation, mental illness, and individual behavioral decisions.

» Suicide prevention strategies and resources can play a role in reducing suicide rates.

» Homicides in the U.S. are significantly higher than in comparative nations and are overwhelmingly committed with firearms, with one in ten Americans impacted by a loved one's homicide.

» Traumatic deaths are often followed by lengthy legal and court processes that can delay, stall, or prolong the grieving process.

» Mass casualty incidents increase the risk of secondary trauma for those who work in emergency and social service occupations, as well as for people who witness the scope and human tragedy of these events.

Review Questions

1. What are the risks associated with trauma, and how can trauma be effectively addressed? Why might trauma result in chronic or complicated grief?
2. How do disparities in suicide manifest, and what are the complex grief reactions to traumatic loss? What strategies can be employed for suicide prevention?
3. In what ways do the methods, location, and legal processes of homicides impact the grieving process?
4. What are the most common types of accidental death, and how do these accidents influence the grieving process?
5. How do the features and challenges of mass casualty incidents contribute to experiences of secondary trauma and affect the grieving process?

Key Terms

Review these key terms from the chapter. You can find their definitions in the glossary at the end of the book.

» gender paradox of suicide
» homicide
» mass casualty incidents (MCI)
» secondary traumatic stress (STS)
» sudden traumatic death
» suicidal ideation

» suicide
» suicide cluster
» suicide contagion
» trauma
» trauma-informed care (TIC)

Chapter 10

—

Government, Economics, and the Business of Death

| Vignette | **Drowning in Paperwork**

In the days after my husband's death, I was like a boat adrift in fog. I met with the funeral director to handle paperwork, including filing for a death certificate. It was a surreal, almost out-of-body experience to go over the details of my husband's life and his death. I kept thinking, "This must be a bad dream ... it can't really be happening." The funeral director asked a series of questions: my husband's parents' names, birthplace, educational attainment, occupation, and location of death. The funeral director also needed a copy of his service record (DD-214) if I wanted military honors at his service. I was advised to order six to eight copies of his death certificate in short and long formats. I didn't even know there were long and short versions, nor did I understand why I needed to order so many. I would soon find out.

Three weeks later, the copies of his death certificate arrived in the mail. When I opened the envelope, seeing his name in the box marked "deceased" took my breath away, triggering another wave of tears and a gut-wrenching sense of loss. With these death certificates in hand, my journey through the legal and economic reality of death began. I met with our attorney, my head swimming with legal requirements: register his death with the county, change the name on the deed to our house, begin a claim on his life insurance, and initiate the actions laid out in his will. A copy of his death certificate had to be sent to Social Security, Medicare, and his retirement pension to stop his benefits. Credit card information had to be updated, his cards needed to be canceled, our vehicle titles changed, and our bank accounts updated. Each action required an explanation of my husband's death, proof of my relationship to him with our marriage certificate, and a copy of his death certificate.

Most tasks started with a phone call, and occasionally, the person on the other end would make the requisite "I'm sorry for your loss" statement, and then the business transaction would begin. I understood how government and business worked, but that didn't help the sensation that I was drowning. The love of my life had been reduced to a number and a document to be processed. All I wanted and needed along the way was a lifeline—to have people acknowledge that all the paperwork represented a beloved person who had been lost.

Patricia

Introduction

Even when a couple makes end-of-life plans together, as the opening vignette shows, the actual arrangements can be daunting. While navigating loss, the person left behind must grapple with many documents and decisions as they journey through the bureaucratic sea of government and private business rules, regulations, and procedures. A loved one's death is a deeply personal experience that consumes psychological and emotional energy, yet it is also a regulated process shaped by governmental policies.

In the United States, the social institutions of government and the economy regulate and structure how people are expected to behave and the activities they should engage in regarding death. For instance, before someone can get their financial affairs in order after the death of a loved one, they must obtain an official certificate to verify that a death has occurred. The social context of death intertwines the intimate human experience with the bureaucratic, legal, and economic frameworks that govern it. As you explore in this chapter how laws regulate the funeral industry and shape business practices across the economy, you'll also learn how societal values, cultural traditions, and historical narratives determine how and where we bury our dead.

Learning Objectives

These learning objectives will help you identify what's most important in this chapter. By the end of this chapter, you should be able to do the following:

» Explain how the U.S. government certifies a death and describe how the bureaucratic, legal, and economic dimensions of this process reflect the interaction between societal systems and personal loss.

» Discuss the funeral industry from a sociological perspective, considering the economic, cultural, and social factors that shape its practices.

» Describe the options for burial and disposition of the body after death, examining how customs, traditions, religious beliefs, and economic and environmental considerations influence these choices.

» Discuss the different types of cemeteries commonly found in the United States, highlighting how these burial grounds reflect societal values, historical narratives, and urban planning.

Government Regulation

During the seventeenth century, legal systems in Europe, particularly in England, began to formalize processes for declaring a person legally dead. These processes were crucial for settling estates and transferring ownership of property. Without a legal death declaration, the property could remain in legal limbo, preventing heirs from claiming their inheritance. As settlers migrated from England to the

Americas during this period, they brought processes that influenced the legal principles in what would eventually become the United States.

As the U.S. legal system began to take shape during the eighteenth century, so did the need for documented evidence of death. Death certificates became a formal legal document to prove an individual's death, essential for the execution of wills and the transfer of assets. In addition to documenting an individual's death, government records for births, marriages, and deaths tracked important population data. A **register of death** is an official document of the deaths of individuals within a specific jurisdiction and typically includes the deceased person's name, date of death, place of death, age at death, and often the cause of death. Figure 10.1 shows a register of death from the nineteenth century. Death registry information is now typically gathered by each state and is accessible through state vital records offices. At the national level, state records are also aggregated in the Social Security Death Index records.

Figure 10.1. This register of death from the nineteenth century documents the deaths of community members and provides an official recognition of loss.

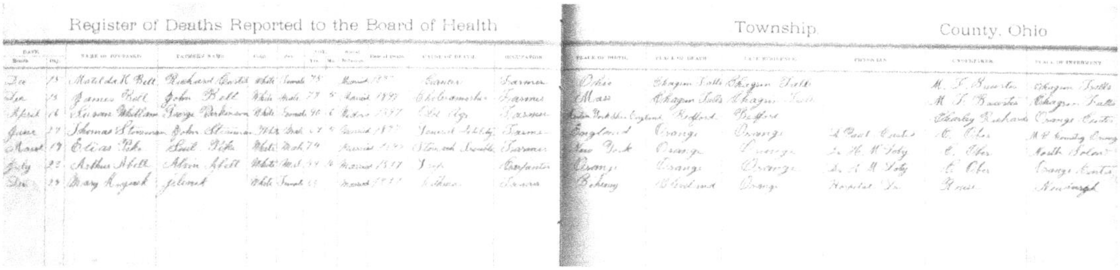

During the nineteenth century, the United States used registers of death to address public health concerns by tracking **mortality rates**, the number of deaths in a population over a specific time. With increased industrialization and urbanization, mortality rates provided critical data that allowed the government to take a more active role in regulating health and safety. By the mid-nineteenth century, the newly established American Medical Association (AMA) began advocating for using mortality statistics, including trends in mortality rates over time and comparisons between groups, to understand how living conditions impacted people's health. For example, information about deaths from typhus, yellow fever, and cholera epidemics significantly impacted support for sanitation reforms and promoting public health in general. The increasing use of mortality statistics in public health led to a broad-based call for each independent registration area to adopt a standard death reporting form (the first "U.S. Standard Certificate of Death") by January 1, 1900 (National Center for Health Statistics, 2009).

The history of government regulation informs how death is handled today. Deaths that occur in the United States must be registered with the government. This process involves verifying that a death has occurred, establishing the cause of death, and issuing official documentation of the death. Typically, individual states or cities, such as New York City and Washington, DC, have the legal authority and responsibility for documenting and registering deaths. These data are then collected by the National Center for Health Statistics (NCHS), which Congress requires to compile vital statistics each year, including data on deaths. The following section takes a closer look at the official government documents and roles involved in verifying a death.

Certifying Death

A **death certificate** is an official document issued by the government that includes information about the cause, time, and location of death. The certificate includes identifying information about the person who has died, called the **decedent** in legal contexts. A standard death certificate contains a medical and nonmedical portion. A physician or government official usually completes the medical portion of the death certificate. After the pronouncement of death, the funeral director can complete the nonmedical part of the death certificate. Death certificates are available in long and short forms. Long-form death records include the manner of death, cause of death, or any medical information. Short-form death records only include the fact of death and demographic information.

State laws vary on who can obtain a copy of a death certificate. Informational copies used for personal records are usually more freely available. However, access to death certificates may be restricted until several years—typically twenty-five or more—have passed since the individual's death. Certified copies of a death certificate bearing an official stamp are needed to carry out legal tasks after death. Depending on the state, certified copies may be limited to immediate family members, executors of the estate, and people who can prove they have a financial stake in the estate. However, each state defines who is considered immediate family. In Oregon, for instance, immediate family members can order short-form death records from the county or state office, including spouses, children, parents, siblings, grandparents, and grandchildren. However, only spouses, children, and parents can order long-form death records unless they have notarized permission from an eligible family member to receive them (Center for Health Statistics, 2018). Box 10.1 describes the three main sections of the standard death certificate and describes who is eligible to complete each section.

Box 10.1: Completing the Death Certificate

Individual states can use their own version of a death certificate form, but most comply with the U.S. Standard Death Certificate issued by the CDC's National Center for Health Statistics (NCHS), as shown in figure 10.2.

A death certificate is commonly divided into three sections:

» demographic data, such as name, age, birthplace, race, marital status, educational achievements, and occupation (usually completed by the funeral director)
» place of death and disposition of the body (usually completed by the funeral director)
» record of who pronounced the death (emergency services personnel, law enforcement, medical providers, etc.) as well as the time and place of death

Figure 10.2. The U.S. Standard Death Certificate ensures accuracy and reliability in the recording and reporting of deaths. Source: CDC, NCHS.

U.S. STANDARD CERTIFICATE OF DEATH

LOCAL FILE NO.   STATE FILE NO.

1. DECEDENT'S LEGAL NAME (Include AKA's if any) (First, Middle, Last) | 2. SEX | 3. SOCIAL SECURITY NUMBER

4a. AGE-Last Birthday (Years) | 4b. UNDER 1 YEAR — Months / Days | 4c. UNDER 1 DAY — Hours / Minutes | 5. DATE OF BIRTH (Mo/Day/Yr) | 6. BIRTHPLACE (City and State or Foreign Country)

7a. RESIDENCE-STATE | 7b. COUNTY | 7c. CITY OR TOWN

7d. STREET AND NUMBER | 7e. APT. NO. | 7f. ZIP CODE | 7g. INSIDE CITY LIMITS? ☐ Yes ☐ No

8. EVER IN US ARMED FORCES? ☐ Yes ☐ No | 9. MARITAL STATUS AT TIME OF DEATH ☐ Married ☐ Married, but separated ☐ Widowed ☐ Divorced ☐ Never Married ☐ Unknown | 10. SURVIVING SPOUSE'S NAME (If wife, give name prior to first marriage)

11. FATHER'S NAME (First, Middle, Last) | 12. MOTHER'S NAME PRIOR TO FIRST MARRIAGE (First, Middle, Last)

13a. INFORMANT'S NAME | 13b. RELATIONSHIP TO DECEDENT | 13c. MAILING ADDRESS (Street and Number, City, State, Zip Code)

14. PLACE OF DEATH (Check only one: see instructions)

IF DEATH OCCURRED IN A HOSPITAL: ☐ Inpatient ☐ Emergency Room/Outpatient ☐ Dead on Arrival | IF DEATH OCCURRED SOMEWHERE OTHER THAN A HOSPITAL: ☐ Hospice facility ☐ Nursing home/Long term care facility ☐ Decedent's home ☐ Other (Specify):

15. FACILITY NAME (If not institution, give street & number) | 16. CITY OR TOWN, STATE, AND ZIP CODE | 17. COUNTY OF DEATH

18. METHOD OF DISPOSITION ☐ Burial ☐ Cremation ☐ Donation ☐ Entombment ☐ Removal from State ☐ Other (Specify) | 19. PLACE OF DISPOSITION (Name of cemetery, crematory, other place)

20. LOCATION-CITY, TOWN, AND STATE | 21. NAME AND COMPLETE ADDRESS OF FUNERAL FACILITY

22. SIGNATURE OF FUNERAL SERVICE LICENSEE OR OTHER AGENT | 23. LICENSE NUMBER (Of Licensee)

ITEMS 24-28 MUST BE COMPLETED BY PERSON WHO PRONOUNCES OR CERTIFIES DEATH | 24. DATE PRONOUNCED DEAD (Mo/Day/Yr) | 25. TIME PRONOUNCED DEAD

26. SIGNATURE OF PERSON PRONOUNCING DEATH (Only when applicable) | 27. LICENSE NUMBER | 28. DATE SIGNED (Mo/Day/Yr)

29. ACTUAL OR PRESUMED DATE OF DEATH (Mo/Day/Yr) (Spell Month) | 30. ACTUAL OR PRESUMED TIME OF DEATH | 31. WAS MEDICAL EXAMINER OR CORONER CONTACTED? ☐ Yes ☐ No

CAUSE OF DEATH (See instructions and examples) | Approximate interval: Onset to death

32. PART I. Enter the chain of events—diseases, injuries, or complications—that directly caused the death. DO NOT enter terminal events such as cardiac arrest, respiratory arrest, or ventricular fibrillation without showing the etiology. DO NOT ABBREVIATE. Enter only one cause on a line. Add additional lines if necessary

IMMEDIATE CAUSE (Final disease or condition ----> resulting in death) a. _____
Due to (or as a consequence of):

Sequentially list conditions, if any, leading to the cause listed on line a. Enter the UNDERLYING CAUSE (disease or injury that initiated the events resulting in death) LAST
b. _____ Due to (or as a consequence of):
c. _____ Due to (or as a consequence of):
d. _____

PART II. Enter other significant conditions contributing to death but not resulting in the underlying cause given in PART I | 33. WAS AN AUTOPSY PERFORMED? ☐ Yes ☐ No
34. WERE AUTOPSY FINDINGS AVAILABLE TO COMPLETE THE CAUSE OF DEATH? ☐ Yes ☐ No

35. DID TOBACCO USE CONTRIBUTE TO DEATH? ☐ Yes ☐ Probably ☐ No ☐ Unknown | 36. IF FEMALE: ☐ Not pregnant within past year ☐ Pregnant at time of death ☐ Not pregnant, but pregnant within 42 days of death ☐ Not pregnant, but pregnant 43 days to 1 year before death ☐ Unknown if pregnant within the past year | 37. MANNER OF DEATH ☐ Natural ☐ Homicide ☐ Accident ☐ Pending Investigation ☐ Suicide ☐ Could not be determined

38. DATE OF INJURY (Mo/Day/Yr) (Spell Month) | 39. TIME OF INJURY | 40. PLACE OF INJURY (e.g., Decedent's home, construction site; restaurant; wooded area) | 41. INJURY AT WORK? ☐ Yes ☐ No

42. LOCATION OF INJURY: State: — City or Town:
Street & Number: — Apartment No.: — Zip Code:

43. DESCRIBE HOW INJURY OCCURRED: | 44. IF TRANSPORTATION INJURY, SPECIFY: ☐ Driver/Operator ☐ Passenger ☐ Pedestrian ☐ Other (Specify)

45. CERTIFIER (Check only one):
☐ Certifying physician-To the best of my knowledge, death occurred due to the cause(s) and manner stated.
☐ Pronouncing & Certifying physician-To the best of my knowledge, death occurred at the time, date, and place, and due to the cause(s) and manner stated.
☐ Medical Examiner/Coroner-On the basis of examination, and/or investigation, in my opinion, death occurred at the time, date, and place, and due to the cause(s) and manner stated
Signature of certifier: _____

46. NAME, ADDRESS, AND ZIP CODE OF PERSON COMPLETING CAUSE OF DEATH (Item 32)

47. TITLE OF CERTIFIER | 48. LICENSE NUMBER | 49. DATE CERTIFIED (Mo/Day/Yr) | 50. FOR REGISTRAR ONLY- DATE FILED (Mo/Day/Yr)

51. DECEDENT'S EDUCATION-Check the box that best describes the highest degree or level of school completed at the time of death.
☐ 8th grade or less
☐ 9th - 12th grade; no diploma
☐ High school graduate or GED completed
☐ Some college credit, but no degree
☐ Associate degree (e.g. AA, AS)
☐ Bachelor's degree (e.g. BA, AB, BS)
☐ Master's degree (e.g. MA, MS, MEng, MEd, MSW, MBA)
☐ Doctorate (e.g. PhD, EdD) or Professional degree (e.g. MD, DDS, DVM, LLB, JD)

52. DECEDENT OF HISPANIC ORIGIN? Check the box that best describes whether the decedent is Spanish/Hispanic/Latino. Check the "No" box if decedent is not Spanish/Hispanic/Latino.
☐ No, not Spanish/Hispanic/Latino
☐ Yes, Mexican, Mexican American, Chicano
☐ Yes, Puerto Rican
☐ Yes, Cuban
☐ Yes, other Spanish/Hispanic/Latino (Specify) _____

53. DECEDENT'S RACE (Check one or more races to indicate what the decedent considered himself or herself to be)
☐ White
☐ Black or African American
☐ American Indian or Alaska Native (Name of the enrolled or principal tribe) _____
☐ Asian Indian
☐ Chinese
☐ Filipino
☐ Japanese
☐ Korean
☐ Vietnamese
☐ Other Asian (Specify) _____
☐ Native Hawaiian
☐ Guamanian or Chamorro
☐ Samoan
☐ Other Pacific Islander (Specify) _____
☐ Other (Specify) _____

54. DECEDENT'S USUAL OCCUPATION (Indicate type of work done during most of working life. DO NOT USE RETIRED)

55. KIND OF BUSINESS/INDUSTRY

NAME OF DECEDENT — For use by physician or institution

To Be Completed/ Verified By: FUNERAL DIRECTOR

To Be Completed By: MEDICAL CERTIFIER

To Be Completed By: FUNERAL DIRECTOR

REV. 11/2003

The third component of the death certificate form is used to record pertinent information about who pronounced the death (emergency services personnel, law enforcement, medical providers, etc.) as well as the time and place of death. Most of the questions in this section are dedicated to the chain of events that directly caused the death (disease, injury, complication) and the manner of death (natural causes, accidental, suicide, homicide).

State law determines who is eligible to complete this section. Most states require medically trained personnel to answer these questions, though some states may allow coroners without medical training to complete the section. Funeral directors typically complete the first two sections and ensure the cause of death is provided by the responsible party. The completed form is submitted to the government agency responsible for vital statistics to be officially registered (Miller Temple, 2018).

Death Certificates

A death certificate serves as the legal record needed to settle the affairs of the person who has died. It is often used as proof of death for legal and business purposes. Government agencies and private businesses may require proof of death to change, distribute, or manage benefits and business or retail accounts. A death certificate is often required to access pension benefits and Social Security survivor benefits for a spouse or children, or to notify an agency or company to stop paying benefits. It may also be needed to claim a life insurance payout, administer investment and bank accounts, change legal property ownership, or manage credit cards and other accounts (Miller Temple, 2018).

Government-regulated legal issues also require a death certificate. The executor of a will or trust needs a death certificate to manage and distribute the deceased person's estate, arrange for a funeral, or finalize the disposition of the body. A surviving spouse may be required to provide proof of death before remarriage or when addressing custody or child-support issues for underage children. Death records can also be relevant in criminal and civil liability proceedings. For example, in the criminal court system, the death certificate may provide specific evidence relevant to a crime or be used to establish proof of death. In personal injury cases in civil court, a death certificate can be used to prove who or what is responsible for the individual's death, including any previous medical conditions that might have contributed.

Death certificate information is confidential and restricted for a specified number of years (usually fifty years). However, public health officials regularly use county, state, and national death record information from populations to identify needs, assist in program development, and complete public health research. They rely on death certificate mortality data as a primary information source about the causes of death and illnesses preceding death. For example, death certificates help data analysts track the number of people who died from cancer, heart disease, or complications associated with diabetes. The information from each death certificate can be analyzed, and the aggregated information can be published without identifying individuals. These data are then used to identify public health challenges and determine federal and state funding and research priorities to improve public health and prevent premature deaths (Kelmar, 2022).

Documenting Death

Deaths must be reported to the responsible government agency, most often at the county level. Although the process varies from state to state, the area medical examiner or coroner is typically responsible for certifying a death.

The **medical examiner** is usually an appointed official. They are physicians trained in pathology who investigate deaths that occur under unusual, unattended, or suspicious circumstances. They may also perform postmortem examinations as needed and initiate a legal inquiry as to the cause of death. These highly trained medical professionals can complete autopsies, interpret toxicology and other laboratory testing results, and integrate these findings with information gathered at the death location. Their training prepares them to assess immediate and earlier medical history, collect and document evidence, and provide expert testimony in legal proceedings (Fierro, 2003).

A **coroner** is usually not a physician and may or may not have any medical background, training in forensic medicine, or experience in forensic science. Usually, coroners are elected government officials, but they may also be appointed depending on state and county laws. They typically have no specialized professional training and may also work in law enforcement or the prosecuting attorney's office. Since coroners are rarely pathologists, they often employ contracted forensic pathologists for autopsies and medical expertise to support the coroner's investigations when required (Fierro, 2003).

Whether a death is certified by a medical examiner or coroner, one important distinction in the documentation process is whether the death was attended or unattended. The phrase "attended death" conjures images of family and friends around the bedside of a loved one. However, in legal terms, an **attended death** is one where a person dies in a hospital, medical setting, long-term care facility, hospice care, or at home under a doctor's care. In these situations, a physician can attest to the presence of an extended disease, illness, or injury. Definitions and state legal codes vary, but an attended death typically does not require the doctor to be at the patient's bedside, only that a provider-patient relationship exists (Franklin County Coroner's Office, n.d.). An **unattended death** occurs when no health care provider-patient relationship exists at the time of death. In rare cases, the deceased person may not be found for days, weeks, or even months. This situation is more common with people of advanced age and those who live alone, or it may occur after an accident, suicide, or homicide.

Medical Examiners and Coroners

The first step in the documentation process is completed by a person with medical training who can determine death, such as a physician, nurse, certified health care provider, emergency services personnel, medical examiner, or medically trained coroner. For out-of-hospital deaths, emergency medical services, paramedics, or law enforcement may pronounce death in consultation with a physician, medical examiner, or medically trained coroner. Some states use medical examiners, some use coroners, and others may employ both roles depending on the local jurisdiction.

As described earlier, the training and expertise of medical examiners or coroners are critical in documenting death. However, the expertise and credentials of those who document death vary widely. These positions might be an elected or appointed person as young as eighteen or a highly trained physician. Medical examiners are typically doctors who have completed residencies or advanced medical training in forensic pathology. While some coroners may have little to no experience or training, others have acquired advanced training and certifications in their profession. For example, North Dakota requires a coroner to be a licensed physician; some states, such as Kansas and Louisiana, require coroners to be certified as forensic pathologists; and in Georgia, coroners must be twenty-five or older, have a high school education, have no felony convictions, and complete a weeklong death investigation course (How qualified, n.d.). Some death investigators work for an elected sheriff, while others own funeral homes, introducing a possible conflict of interest (Young, 2022).

Increasing professionalization of death investigation careers and more precise science around death have led to a nationwide shift from the coroner system to a medical examiner system. However, this move is affected by rising costs and the limited availability of medical examiners to fill these positions. Across the country, roughly eighty of the 750 full-time pathologist positions remain vacant. Only around forty new pathologists receive certification each year. With many pathologists retiring or leaving the field, the expense and time needed for training medical examiners after medical school pose challenges for local governments that want to switch to a medical examiner system. Reforms currently focus on improving the training and certification of coroners and giving them more independence from other government agencies.

History of the Funeral Industry

Before the Civil War (1861–65), families or local communities mostly handled funerals. Due to the high number of battlefield deaths, the Civil War ushered in the beginnings of the American funeral industry with advancements in techniques and practices that continue today. One concept that emerged during this period was the **funeral home**, a facility that provides services for handling a deceased person's body and burial. By the early 1900s, early funerary practices and beliefs solidified into standardized services, gaining economic prominence by the middle of the century and expanding into today's billion-dollar funeral industry.

While the funeral industry has weathered scathing public attacks in recent years for taking advantage of grief-stricken people, local funeral homes across the country have established themselves as trusted places of business. Tasked with the final disposition of a deceased person's body and comforting bereaved families, the funeral industry continues to adapt and change to meet contemporary trends and preferences. In the next section, we'll examine the development of the funeral industry in the United States and its impact on contemporary funeral practices.

Emergence of the Funeral Industry

The practice of **embalming**, a chemical process that preserves the body from decay, gained increased acceptance in the United States during the Civil War. For the first time, military families with the financial means could have their loved one's remains shipped home from the battlefield so the body could be viewed before burial. Families began to hire death specialists to prepare the body for the long journey. The demand for these services spurred the development of improved body preservation methods, including the injection of chemicals to preserve the body. Embalming gained wider acceptance after the death of Abraham Lincoln. In 1865, the president's well-preserved body traveled by train (figure 10.3) for nearly two weeks on a cross-country journey, viewed by hundreds of thousands of people (Klein, 2022).

Figure 10.3. Engine "Nashville" hauled the funeral train of assassinated President Abraham Lincoln in April 1865. A portrait of Lincoln is mounted on the front of the locomotive.

Through the end of the nineteenth century, embalming techniques continued to improve. Representatives of chemical companies traveled across the country, offering local undertakers instruction on the latest advances in embalming. Undertakers who completed this coursework earned diplomas to demonstrate their expertise. Simultaneously, public health theories supported embalming and argued that embalmed bodies posed less of a threat to public health. In addition, many American undertakers had connections with furniture makers who made finer quality caskets with polished wood and intricate detailing than the traditional plain wood or metal coffins. A growing emphasis on aesthetics in the nineteenth century led Americans to prioritize the appearance of the body, driving demand for finer quality caskets designed for display before burial (Laderman, 2003).

Origins of the Contemporary Funeral Industry

Americans' emphasis on funeral aesthetics during the early twentieth century led to an increase in funeral homes. The specialized work of embalming and funeral preparation made it more efficient for the body to be transported to a business site rather than prepared at home. Neighborhood funeral homes were often located in the undertaker's home, where they prepared the bodies and assisted in other funerary services. Professional organizations were also formed at this time, along with educational facilities for the training of undertakers. As the industry professionalized, undertakers became known as funeral directors to recognize the expanded services associated with funeral homes.

Governmental regulations introduced in the 1970s and 1980s significantly impacted the U.S. funeral industry, especially the requirements for full disclosure of pricing and services by funeral homes. In 1984, the Federal Trade Commission Funeral Rule was enacted to respond to consumer complaints about deceptive practices and misleading pricing within the funeral industry. For example, before the Rule's enactment, families were often charged a fee for embalming without permission, required to purchase a casket from a funeral home before their loved one was cremated, or required to purchase goods and services, such as flowers, memorial cards, music, and transportation for the family, to access the funeral home's broader services.

The Funeral Rule stopped these practices and was revised to further protect consumers in 1994. This rule applies to all funeral providers, including any person or business that sells or offers to sell funeral goods and services to the public. Funeral providers do not have to be licensed funeral directors, and the business does not have to be a licensed funeral home to be covered by the Funeral Rule. Cemeteries, crematories, and other businesses can also be considered "funeral providers" if they market both funeral goods and services (Federal Trade Commission, 2015).

Over time, the funeral industry has adapted to shifts in public preferences for funerary rites and rituals. In the late twentieth century, traditional practices like open-casket viewings became less common despite being popularized by funeral directors in the first place. For instance, fewer people are choosing formal funerals with an open casket where the embalmed body is made to look as if they are asleep on a satin bed and pillow. Instead, people are increasingly opting for a celebration of life, which can be held weeks or months after someone dies. More people are also choosing cremation. Although cremation has been commercially available since the late 1800s, it became more acceptable in the late 1960s. This trend coincided with the growing acceptance by more Christian church leaders, increased concern about the environmental impact of the chemicals used in the embalming process, and the rising cost of embalmment and casket burials in comparison to cremation. Cremation continues to gain popularity, and by 2023, more than 60% of people who died were cremated in America (National Funeral Directors Association, 2023).

Initially, the funeral industry saw the increase in cremations as a threat to their business. Cremations do not involve embalming and often do not include a viewing or religious service. Many funeral directors didn't have the facilities, training, or resources to do the cremation themselves. To respond to this cultural shift, funeral homes began building crematoriums or contracting with other facilities for these services. They adapted their services to include cremation and ceremonies to honor the deceased person and the final disposition of the ashes. As they had in the past, funeral homes promoted new rites and rituals to meet the needs of their customers. Suppliers produced a range of stylized urns and products created from the ashes to memorialize loved ones, such as lockets, statuary, and artificial diamonds. At the same time, cemeteries built **columbaria**, which are buildings, rooms, or freestanding walls designed to hold urns (figure 10.4).

Figure 10.4. A columbarium, such as this one at the Lawton Cemetery, is a structure with niches designed to store urns containing cremated remains.

The U.S. Funeral Industry

Despite changes in American funeral rituals, funeral homes continue to fulfill a critical role in assisting families and friends when a loved one has died. The funeral services industry in the United States is valued at $23 billion and includes funeral homes, funerary goods and supplies, crematoriums, and cemeteries (Hawryluk, 2022). The industry continues to expand its selection of specialized services and goods and now includes casket and cremation urn manufacturers, florists, memorial suppliers, mortuary cosmetologists, transportation companies, videographers, headstone manufacturers, and many other peripheral suppliers. Box 10.2 describes some of these unique roles within the funeral industry.

Box 10.2: Funeral Industry Workers

The funeral industry encompasses a diverse range of roles dedicated to supporting individuals and families through the complex processes of honoring and memorializing loved ones. As you read through these descriptions, consider how the different roles provide both logistical and emotional support for grieving families.

» **Funeral concierges** help plan and coordinate end-of-life services. They assist in pre-planning for services and addressing the impending or immediate need for funeral service. These concierges communicate with funeral homes or vendors for the customer, schedule and coordinate services, and negotiate prices.

» **Funeral directors** are usually a high-level manager or coordinator and may own and operate the funeral home. They manage funeral logistics, mortician duties, and administrative aspects of the business.

» **Mortuary cosmetologists** use make-up and hair styling to make the deceased person look as natural and lifelike as possible. Some are restorative artists who specialize in reconstruction of the body after severe trauma. These workers may be funeral home employees or independent contract workers.

» **Undertakers** were what people used to call this profession, but morticians is the term more commonly used in the United States today.

About 19,000 funeral homes operate in the United States, and approximately 90% are small businesses or family-owned and operated by local funeral directors or small regional chains (Bohne, 2024). The remaining 10% are owned by large funeral home chains and private equity-backed firms. Although most funeral homes continue to be independently owned and operated, large corporations and private equity groups have taken an increased interest in what is becoming known as the "death care" industry. Over the last few decades, multinational corporations and private equity investment groups that pool funds from investors to generate higher profits have been buying up independent, family-owned funeral homes at an increasing rate. This trend has been fueled, in part, by the Baby Boomer generation (born 1948–1964), whose numbers represent a larger potential market and an opportunity for industry growth and increased profit (Hawryluk, 2022).

Some argue that a lack of local ties and an emphasis on generating revenue make corporate funeral homes more concerned with their shareholders and investments and less concerned with the needs of grieving families. Consumer advocates have voiced concerns that private equity groups will raise the prices for funeral goods and services, as has been the case with many other large, publicly traded companies that control chains of funeral homes (Hawryluk, 2022).

In addition to funeral homes, more companies are entering the death care industry. Start-ups, wholesale manufacturers, and big-box stores now sell funeral goods directly to consumers. Nowhere is this more evident than with the increased online sales of caskets and urns. Caskets are often the largest funeral cost, with funeral homes marking up the retail price 290% on average (Boring, 2014). Customers have turned to retailers like Costco, Walmart, Sam's Club, and Amazon for lower-priced caskets and urns. In addition, many casket and urn manufacturers now sell directly to consumers at much lower costs (Passy, 2017). Under the FTC's Funeral Rule, funeral homes are legally required to use a casket or urn purchased from another seller without charging the customer to do so. However, many funeral homes find they need to increase their prices on other funeral goods and services to make up for the revenue lost when customers provide their own caskets or urns purchased elsewhere.

Problems and abuses continue to challenge the industry. Despite the Funeral Rule requirements, some companies have a poor reputation for consumer abuse and questionable sales tactics. Frequent consumer complaints include the high costs of funeral goods and services, misrepresentation of prepaid funeral plans, sales of unnecessary products, and concerns about environmental pollution at cemeteries. Some funeral homes continue to use misleading practices, such as showing the most expensive caskets before more affordable models and employing high-pressure tactics to sell unnecessary items at inflated costs, such as rubber gaskets for sealing caskets (Crawford, 2017).

While the funeral industry has received criticism, it is equally important to recognize the compassionate and specialized care that many funeral professionals provide. Most families will need to access funeral services at one of the most emotional and vulnerable points in their lives, and they should feel supported during the process.

American funerary practices include end-of-life rites and rituals that mark the social transition from life to death and the afterlife. These practices bring people together to confront death and provide a way to express condolences and sympathy. Societies typically have ceremonial practices to honor those who have died, a process for the final preparation of a person's body, and a means for expressing grief. Funerary rituals are grounded in philosophical, cultural, and spiritual beliefs and provide a support network to help cope with grief and loss.

Funeral practices in the United States have evolved to reflect societal changes. The emphasis on individualism in U.S. dominant culture has resulted in funerary rituals that address individual and community needs. Increasingly, Americans craft personal funeral ceremonies that represent the life and personality of the deceased person. In the last several decades, the funeral industry has embraced an "adaptive" funeral concept by expanding the range of goods and services available at local funeral homes. Funeral directors continue to play a central role in interment, but more progressive funeral directors now facilitate customized services. The sections that follow show how rites and rituals serve multiple social functions, from expressing grief to reinforcing community bonds to celebrating the legacy of loved ones who have died.

Visitation, Processional, and Interment

Since the mid-nineteenth century, the traditional funeral in U.S. dominant culture has included the embalmment and placement of the body in a casket or coffin and a period of viewing or visitation, which is then followed by a formal funeral service and interment. The viewing or visitation is usually held at a funeral home or chapel, where the body of the deceased person is displayed in an open or closed casket. During this ritual, people can view the body, pay their respects, and express condolences. This event also provides a time for loved ones to reflect and begin to process their loss and grief.

Formal funeral services usually involve a social gathering where readings, music, prayers or religious scripture, a eulogy, and personal remembrances are shared in the presence of the person's remains. Traditionally, these services are somber events centered on religious or spiritual rituals, but increasingly, funerals are becoming more individualized. Many traditional funerals in U.S. dominant culture include displaying the casket, using pallbearers to carry or escort it, sending flowers, and wearing black or dark clothing.

The service may involve a funeral processional to move the body to the funeral service site and, after the service, to the burial or interment location. An officiant leads the processional, followed by the pallbearers who carry or escort the casket or urn, and then the immediate family. After the service, the procession escorts the casket to the hearse. The procession of cars to the cemetery is usually led by the funeral director and staff, followed by the hearse carrying the remains, and then the immediate family. Other family members, friends, and mourners drive behind to create the rest of the procession.

At the grave site, the officiant or attendees may recite prayers, sing songs, or share readings and poems. Afterward, the casket is lowered into the ground, or the remains are placed in a crypt or columbarium. Religious rituals to sanctify and bless the final interment site are common, and in many cultures, attendees shovel dirt into the grave or place a symbolic item at the site. Grave and interment site rituals can also act as the funeral service. After the funeral and interment, a reception may be held where family and friends gather. This gathering usually involves food and beverages and offers the chance to connect around the shared loss.

Memorial Service and Celebration of Life

A memorial service or a celebration of life may be held instead of or in addition to a traditional funeral. These social gatherings typically occur days or weeks after the final interment or disposition of the body. This delay gives family and friends more time to plan the event and allows attendees time to make travel arrangements. While many of the rituals may be the same as at a funeral, the event's tone can be quite different, with a more customized and personal feel.

A **memorial service** typically refers to an end-of-life gathering where the loved one's remains are not present or that takes place after the final disposition of the body. The service may include some of the elements of a funeral and have a somber tone. A memorial service can occur at any point, not just immediately after the person's death. For example, some families hold an annual memorial service to honor their loved ones on the anniversary of their passing. In other instances, a memorial service may be secular or open to the community, as with the death of a public figure or beloved community member.

A **celebration of life** is a more joyous and upbeat celebration that focuses on the positive aspects of a person's life rather than a ceremony dedicated to mourning. Many families use the term to indicate that the gathering will have a different focus and tone than a traditional funeral. Some families may even encourage guests to wear bright, colorful clothing. Often, celebrations of life are held after burial or cremation in casual settings like a park or a place special to the deceased person. The service is usually less formal and structured, and attendees are encouraged to celebrate the deceased person by sharing stories, happy memories, and accomplishments. The ceremony may include symbolic gestures, such as the release of butterflies or balloons, personal messages, poetry, or the planting of a tree or flower.

Body Disposition

Many people make plans for what will happen to their bodies after death. **Body disposition**, how a person's body is dealt with after death, is an individual choice, but religious beliefs, cultural practices, personal philosophy, and financial considerations influence the decision. Historically, Americans have overwhelmingly chosen burial for their final disposition, but today, cremation is the most common choice.

The many options mean people need to provide clear and detailed instructions about what they want to happen to their body after death. Confronting one's mortality by stating one's wishes about final disposition can be empowering. Advance planning can relieve family members from having to make difficult decisions while they are grieving. The following sections will explore how customs, traditions, religious beliefs, and environmental factors affect this decision.

Burial

Burial is a common choice for many people. There are two primary types of burials: traditional burial and direct burial. In a **traditional burial**, the body is prepared and placed in a casket that is present at the funeral service and then interred in the ground or a mausoleum. For traditional burials and services, preparing the body often begins with embalming, a two- to four-hour process that involves removing organic fluids and gases from the body and replacing the fluids with a chemical solution to preserve body tissues. Cosmetics are then applied to restore a person's life-like appearance. The body is dressed and placed in the casket for viewing or the funeral service. Embalming is useful when there is a long period between death and the viewing. It is generally not legally required if final disposition occurs within two days of death; refrigeration is a viable alternative under most state regulations. However, many funeral homes require embalming before an open casket viewing or funeral.

After the funeral service, the casket is transported to the interment site, which can be purchased before or after the death. For in-ground burials, the casket is usually lowered into an excavated space in the ground fitted with a vault or burial container. It is then covered by soil. Most states do not require burial vaults and caskets, but individual cemeteries set their own rules. Most graves are at least four feet deep, but no federal rules determine this. Above-ground burial in a mausoleum or crypt is another, though more expensive, option. The casket is carried into the mausoleum and sealed in a crypt. Mausoleums can be constructed to house a single casket or multiple caskets (figure 10.5).

Figure 10.5. The Mellon mausoleum in Pittsburgh's Homewood Cemetery is a grand neoclassical structure housing the remains of the prominent Mellon family.

In a **direct burial**, entombment takes place quickly, generally without many of the typical funeral rites, such as a viewing or visitation. The body is buried in a simple container or a burial cloth, although most cemeteries require a grave liner or burial vault. Because embalming is not required for a direct burial, the cost is far less than a traditional full-service funeral. However, depending on the specific situation, local regulations, and personal preferences, a direct burial in a cemetery may still require a casket, cemetery plot, fees to open and close the grave, a cemetery endowment for upkeep, and a marker, monument, or headstone. Even with these requirements, a direct burial is often chosen because of its simplicity and affordability.

With a traditional or direct burial, the final interment generally takes place in a public, private, or nonprofit cemetery. However, some people are buried on private property, depending on state and local regulations. For instance, some states require that burial plots be a specific distance from buildings, property lines, underground utilities, streets and sidewalks, or bodies of water. Living in particular areas, such as densely populated communities, may limit the option for home burials (Bauer, 2021; Green Burial Council, 2022). For home burials, caskets and burial vaults are rarely required by law.

Cremation

Cremation, the thermal process that reduces human remains to cremains or ashes, is now the most frequently chosen option for final disposition. This choice represents a significant shift away from burials driven by lower costs and more options for the final placement of the ashes. Some who choose cremation opt for a formal funeral service or memorial, while others prefer a more individualized service, memorial, or remembrance ritual. Increasingly, families contract with online cremation services rather than a local funeral home. Once the cremation is completed, the cremains can be picked up or delivered directly to the family (Marsden-Ille, 2023).

The cost of cremation varies based on location, type of funeral services accompanying cremation, and final disposition of the ashes. Although costs can change quickly, the median cost in 2024 for a cremation in the United States was $2,000–$5,000, although in some states, the cost can be as low as $800. The average cost of a cremation with a funeral service is $6,000–$8,000. The least expensive option is a direct cremation conducted immediately after death and including no service. The cremated remains are then returned directly to the family. Cost is also affected by whether the family purchases or provides the cremains container. If cremains are to be buried, some cemeteries have specific requirements regarding the type of container to be used. Funeral costs accompanying a cremation are affected by the type of services requested, transportation to a cemetery, and the choice of interment.

The cremation process generally takes one to two hours. The body of the deceased is placed in a cremation container made of combustible material such as cardboard or particleboard, although a wooden or decorative casket can be chosen. Small sentimental items can be cremated with the deceased if they don't interfere with the cremation process. The cremation container is then placed in the cremator chamber. Flames and heat in the chamber reduce the body to bone fragments that are then mechanically reduced to small particles called cremains or ashes (Cremation Association of North America, n.d.-b).

Cremains can be disposed of in many ways. Cemetery options include in-ground and above-ground burials or placement in a columbarium. The niches in columbaria are usually purchased, but others may offer lease options for ten to twenty-five years. A niche includes a plaque for the name and personal information and spaces to put small tributes, mementos, and flowers. Ashes can also be buried in natural settings like woodland burial sites that offer interment, similar to a traditional cemetery. Each burial site has rules outlining allowed ceremonies, types of urns, markers, headstones, or other memorials like benches, statuary, or plants (Kewley, 2021). Many people keep their loved ones' ashes at home, so they are always nearby. It's common to divide the ashes into individual urns or sentimental containers given to family or friends. Scattering the ashes at a meaningful location is also a popular option.

Today, many creative and innovative options exist to honor your loved one, their personality, or their values. Keepsake glass figurines, pendants, other jewelry, and stained-glass suncatchers can be made by mixing ashes with molten glass. Diamonds and other gems can be manufactured from your loved one's cremains and turned into jewelry that memorializes your loved one and creates a family heirloom. Cremains can be mixed with concrete to help form a marine reef and support marine life. Cremains can also be mixed with fireworks so that your loved one can go out with a bang. You can even place your loved one's cremains aboard a spacecraft to be shot into space to be a part of the cosmos forever (Cremation Society of America, 2019).

From a sociological perspective, the expanding number of options available for the final disposition of a loved one's ashes can be seen as a reflection of individualism, a key value in U.S. dominant culture. Instead of following a single, socially accepted burial practice, it is becoming more common to choose the option that is most meaningful for the deceased person and their loved ones. The available options continue to grow as business entrepreneurs respond to this cultural shift toward individualized choices.

Environmental Options

Concerns about human impact on our planet have increased interest in eco-friendly options for the final disposition at death. A **green burial** involves caring for someone's body after death with minimal environmental impact. Green burials minimize the consumption of nonessential goods, use biodegradable options for items like caskets, shrouds, and urns, and forgo the use of toxic products like embalming fluid, herbicides, pesticides, and fertilizers in cemeteries to support land conservation and preservation (Green Burial Council, n.d.). In practice, this could mean that the body is not embalmed, placed in a nontoxic, biodegradable container, and buried in designated natural spaces. Green burial site fees typically range from $500 to $2,000, generally less than a traditional cemetery.

Natural organic reduction (NOR) is an emerging eco-friendly option for final disposition, commonly referred to as human composting. NOR creates conditions that facilitate decomposition so that the body's nutrients can be returned to restore forests and nourish gardens and natural habitats. As of 2024, NOR is legal in twelve states: Arizona, California, Colorado, Delaware, Maine, Maryland, Minnesota, Nevada, New York, Oregon, Vermont, and Washington. Despite pending legislation in other states, NOR remains controversial and faces political and religious opposition from those who believe the process doesn't adequately respect human remains.

In the NOR process, the body of the deceased is sealed in a container filled with organic material like wood chips, alfalfa, and straw, where it decomposes for four to six weeks. The human body contains the bacteria needed to break down tissue. However, a mix of bacteria, fungi, and protozoa can be added to the container to speed up the composting process. When the process is complete, the remaining bones are mechanically reduced, the composted material is heated to kill harmful pathogens, and a sample is tested to ensure it is safe for use. Once it is declared safe, the compost is given to the deceased person's family, who can deposit it in a place special to the person who died. Some NOR companies can use the compost for designated land conservation and restoration projects. The entire NOR process takes about two months and costs $4,000 to $7,000 (Dembosky, 2024).

A third option, **aquamation**, often called water cremation, uses alkaline hydrolysis to dispose of a person's body. This process takes twelve to eighteen hours and uses heated alkaline water under pressure to decompose the body into a skeletal form. The remaining bones are mechanically reduced, similar to the cremation process. With a smaller carbon footprint than thermal cremation, aquamation is considered an eco-friendly alternative, but it has been slow to gain acceptance. Although aquamation has long been used for animals, and many medical schools currently use it to dispose of the remains of bodies donated for research and training, many people are put off by the imagery associated with the process. Aquamation is legal in many states, but individuals should check with their local regulations because current legislation could affect this choice (Cremation Association of North America, n.d.-a).

Body Donation to Science

Another alternative to burial is **whole body donation**, the agreement to give one's entire body to science after death for research and education. Many people choose to be organ donors at the time of their death, but donating your entire body to science is also an option. Donated bodies contribute to scientific research, medical breakthroughs, and medical education. Whether decided by the individual in advance or chosen by the family after death, the whole body donation process must happen quickly. Having the decision documented is essential to facilitate the process. Bodies can be donated directly to public, private, or nonprofit universities, research institutions, or **non-transplant anatomical donation organizations (NADO)**. NADOs include both not-for-profit organizations and for-profit companies that make money by providing bodies or specific anatomical specimens to facilities and medical institutions that use them for training, education, and research.

Most people are eligible to donate their bodies to science. Medical and research institutions accept donations from all ages, races, and locations, and past medical conditions or surgeries do not generally prohibit body donation. However, eligibility may be affected by factors such as severe bacterial or viral infections, kidney failure or jaundice, severe obesity, or when the death is a result of severe trauma. Once a donated body is received by the research institution or body donation company, the anatomical specimens will be removed and sent to medical schools and research institutions. Many institutions offer the option of having cremated remains returned to the family.

The body donation industry varies widely from state to state and organization to organization. With minimal federal oversight and state regulation, it's important to get as much information as possible before choosing whole body donation. For-profit companies actively advertise online and work with funeral homes, hospitals, nursing homes, and hospices to solicit bodies to be sold. However, they often also sell additional services to the donors, such as transportation of the body, cremation, and return of the cremains. While universities, medical schools, and state-run anatomy programs publicize their programs, they do not aggressively solicit donors, may offer fewer services, and have more donor eligibility restrictions (Shiffman & Grow, 2017).

American Cemeteries

Cultural beliefs and norms guide the rituals and processes of burial, while geographic terrain and physical location affect the sites and methods used. In early U.S. society, these factors often meant a ground burial aligned with sociocultural rituals to honor the person who died and mark their transition between life and death. Cemeteries, also called graveyards or burial grounds, serve social and personal functions. Socially, they provide a physical and symbolic separation of the living from the dead. They offer a place where people can visit, remember, honor, and maintain a connection to their dead loved ones while leaving the demands of daily life behind (Reimers, 2003).

Cemeteries reflect the social stratification, segregation, and social order among the living. A person's social position, based on social indicators such as economic class, race, ethnicity, religion, gender, or age, often affects the choice of cemetery, the location and size of the burial plot, the type of grave marker, and the information inscribed on the marker. Some cemeteries are open only to members of a specific religious or ethnic group. Historically, people were legally segregated in death as well as in life. Laws and social norms forced Black Americans to be buried in segregated cemeteries.

Segregation often limited burial options for people of other racial and ethnic backgrounds, such as Native Americans, Latinx/Hispanics, and people of Asian descent. Even within cemeteries open to all, sections are sometimes dedicated to specific groups based on social status. It is common to find an area of a cemetery reserved for infants and children, military veterans, religious affiliations, community or political leaders, or celebrities. The following sections show how burial grounds reflect societal values, historical narratives, and urban planning.

Traditional Native American and Colonial Cemeteries

Traditional Native American burial customs vary based on the diverse cultural beliefs of distinct tribal groups. Burial practices often reflected the seasonal movements of nomadic societies or the ways of life in settled communities. In some tribal groups, burials frequently included various forms of encasement of the deceased person—some were walled in caves with rocks, placed in stone sarcophagi, or wrapped in animal skin and placed on the ground to be exposed to the forces of nature. Many tribal groups preferred below-ground interments, such as individual grave sites or underground burial mounds, while others placed their dead in trees or on scaffolding that decayed over time (Nordin, n.d.). Regardless of the method, an ongoing practice across many Native American cultures is to lay out personal items of the deceased person with the body or leave symbolic items on the grave sites.

Many of these traditional practices have changed over time and through contact with other cultures. During the colonization of their ancestral lands, Native Americans adopted new burial practices or had them imposed through religious proselytizing, intermarriage, edict, and the enforcement of laws and regulations. For instance, Spanish colonists and the Roman Catholic Missions changed burial practices among Native American tribes in Texas and parts of the Southwest. The Catholic Missions introduced the concept of church-consecrated graveyards, where converted Native Americans were to be buried following Church doctrine and practices. Many local Native Americans continued their traditional burials but felt the need to do so in secret to avoid social repercussions (Potter & Boland, 1992).

Contemporary Native American burial practices continue to reflect the intermingling of varied tribal traditions and cross-cultural influences. The preferred burial method may be affected by the location of ancestral lands, whether the deceased person or their family lives on-reservation or off-reservation, and their proximity and interaction with the dominant culture. Practices may also differ based on the person's religious affiliation, age, traditionality, and personal preference. It is not unusual to have multiple cemeteries and diverse burial practices on one reservation: church-affiliated, secular, dominant culture, and traditional.

The burial customs associated with the U.S. dominant culture can be traced to the early English, Spanish, and French colonial settlements on North America's eastern and southern shores. English colonial settlements replicated the familiar practices of burying their dead in consecrated ground close to local churches, and the use of churchyard cemeteries became the preference across much of New England. In an exception to this practice, the early Puritans rejected churchyard burials. Instead, towns often set up secular community graveyards or used family burial plots in more rural areas. In the Middle Atlantic and South, family cemeteries were more common in rural areas than in larger towns. Towns were farther apart, and often, a single church served large areas. The terrain made transportation difficult, and most travel was by ship. The distance between family plantations and churches led to the widespread use of family cemeteries on the plantation grounds (Potter & Boland, 1992).

In the late eighteenth and into the nineteenth century, Russian occupation of parts of Alaska further diversified burial customs in what would become part of the United States. As Russian settlements grew in support of the Northwest fur trade, they brought their cultural and religious burial practices to the area and established Russian Orthodox missions among the Native populations. The Native Americans of the area, the Dena'ina, an Athabascan people, had traditionally cremated their dead and left the ashes out in nature so the spirit could leave and take the final journey. However, the Russian Orthodox church required a ground burial and forbade cremation. When local Native Americans converted to the Russian Orthodox faith, a blending of burial practices and beliefs emerged. Miniature gable-roofed wood buildings were built over the graves to provide a place for the spirits to go so they would not bother the living until they were ready to make the final journey (see Chapter 2, figure 2.3). The graves are lined up in regular rows, each covered by a brightly painted spirit house with comb-like crests and fronted by Greek crosses (Flintoff, 2012).

Rural Cemeteries

As the United States grew and urbanized in the 1800s, its towns and cities became more densely populated. So, too, did its cemeteries. Overcrowded urban churchyard cemeteries became a public health concern. In response, the rural cemetery movement gained popularity to address deteriorating urban conditions and quality of life. **Rural cemeteries** were park-like spaces located beyond the urban environment, close enough for people to visit but removed enough to provide an escape for people to experience the emotional relief of nature as they remembered their lost loved ones.

This new kind of American cemetery was inspired by romantic notions of nature and art popular at the time. These cemeteries were often designed by botanists and horticulturalists (MacLean & Williams, 2003). Located on elevated ground at the city's edge, rural cemeteries gave visitors a sweeping, picturesque view of the surrounding countryside (figure 10.6). With an emphasis on landscape design, the cemeteries featured expansive natural settings, greenery and foliage, and decorative obelisks, mausoleums, crypts, and headstones. Families could visit on Sundays for leisurely walks and peaceful picnics. The additional space allowed extended families to buy a large burial plot as the final resting place for many generations. Often, fenced plots contained a monument or obelisk with the family surname and the given names of everyone buried there.

Figure 10.6. This bird's-eye view of the Laurel Hill Cemetery emphasizes its serene, rural setting.

GENERAL VIEW OF LAUREL HILL CEMETERY.

Lawn-Style Cemeteries and Memorial Parks

In the twentieth century, a new standard in burial-ground design combined natural settings with business-like efficiency. Characterized by a pastoral, grassy open space with strategically placed trees and shrubs dotting the landscape, **lawn-style cemeteries** are more formal and rationally organized than the picturesque rural cemeteries of the nineteenth century. In a lawn-style cemetery, gravesites are arranged in rows, with single headstones or smaller monuments marking each plot. Technological developments in the late 1800s allowed craftspeople to make more standardized headstones of durable materials like marble, granite, and bronze, contributing to a uniform appearance. Although generally smaller in scale than the park-like rural cemeteries, the lack of irregular, large monuments and obelisks makes lawn-style cemeteries feel more open and expansive.

A concern with efficiency dominated late-nineteenth and early twentieth-century thought, and the lawn-style cemetery's design reflected this thinking by streamlining management and maintenance. Minimal landscaping, standardized layout, and a preference for flat, ground-level grave markers made maintenance easier, quicker, and less expensive. The lower costs of cemetery upkeep, the increased willingness of people to pay for grave plots, and the sale of site-maintenance services led to an increase in for-profit cemeteries.

The lawn-style cemetery led to a new design used in modern cemeteries and recently opened sections of older lawn or rural-style cemeteries. **Memorial parks** have a spacious, natural appearance, with landscaping limited to evergreens and shrubs along the edges. Above-ground headstones are not allowed, but these cemeteries may contain a few strategically placed artistic centerpieces, such as military, patriotic, or religious symbols. Designated cemetery sections may be devoted to specific religious affiliations, ethnic groups, or social status groups, such as the military or an area for infants and children.

Cemetery management is a major financial component of the funeral industry. The business focus on efficiency and profitability has shaped the design and management of memorial-park cemeteries. These cemeteries maximize available space and usually only allow ground-level or tablet-style grave markers of a specific size to ensure easier, lower-cost maintenance for groundskeepers. Strict guidelines regarding the type and configuration of grave markers, personal items left on grave sites, and when they will be removed are common. The design and use of these cemeteries are affected by business management strategies, for-profit interests, and the marketability of these perpetual care memorial parks.

Military Cemeteries

The first officially sanctioned U.S. military cemeteries were established in the Civil War era (1861–1865). As the war raged on, surviving soldiers often buried their dead comrades quickly in fields, churchyards, local cemeteries, or near the battlefields where they died. As the death toll from the war mounted, President Lincoln signed legislation to purchase land for the burial of soldiers who died serving their country. These cemeteries were first set aside for the burial of those who died in battle, but several years after the end of the Civil War, national cemeteries were opened to all honorably discharged veterans of the Union forces. Not until the early twentieth century were Confederate soldiers, whose graves were marked with the Southern Cross of Honor, an emblem issued by the Department of Veterans Affairs, allowed to be buried in national cemeteries (Lucas, 2021; National Park Service, n.d.).

At the end of World War I, national military cemeteries were opened to American veterans with any wartime service. Later, eligibility was expanded to include all veterans of the U.S. Armed Forces, American war veterans of the Allied Armed Forces, and veterans' spouses and dependent children. There are 171 national military cemeteries in the United States and twenty-six outside of the country. These cemeteries are typically managed by the Department of Veterans Affairs, the Department of the Interior, or the Department of the Army (Office of Public and Intergovernmental Affairs, n.d.).

Qualified veterans are entitled to a gravesite in a national cemetery with available space. The opening and closing of the grave, a headstone or marker, and perpetual care for the grave are provided at no cost to the veteran's family or heirs. A U.S. flag is also provided to drape the casket or accompany the urn of a deceased veteran who served honorably. Headstones are standardized, and the length and type of information permitted on military grave markers in national cemeteries is limited. Inscriptions generally include name, date of birth, date of death, and if applicable, the service branch, war service, rank, specialty, and Medal of Honor insignia. Families may also choose a symbol or sentiment, such as "in loving memory" or "beloved spouse," from a prescribed list of options. Cremated remains can be placed in national cemeteries with the same honors and benefits as casketed remains.

Segregated Cemeteries

Cemeteries and burial sites reflect the social stratification and social divisions of society. Segregated cemeteries based on race, ethnicity, religion, and social status have long been a part of our history and continue in many ways to this day. African American cemeteries are the clearest example of how segregation followed people from life to death. Enslaved Africans were first transported to North America in 1619, but their burial sites were often not marked or only marked using materials that did not survive over time.

City and community officials further segregated African American burial sites by designating separate cemeteries for free Black individuals and enslaved people. Individual enslavers made the decisions about practices, final disposition locations, and maintenance of the burial sites for enslaved people. Due to their marginalized status within society, African American burial sites were often ignored, built over, paved over, and eventually forgotten. Many of these cemeteries have been subsequently located through historical record searches or discovered during building or road construction excavations. Some early African American cemeteries have gained historical recognition and preservation status (MacLean & Williams, 2003). For example, in 2023, the Pierce Chapel African Cemetery was identified as one of the eleven most endangered historic sites in the United States by the National Trust for Historic Preservation (Montoya, 2023). The National Trust is a nonprofit organization founded by a congressional charter to empower and support local preservation efforts. The cemetery in Harris County, Georgia, covers about two acres and holds the remains of an estimated 500 enslaved or formerly enslaved Africans. This designation and public awareness are intended to help bolster the ongoing reclamation efforts to restore and preserve this historic site.

Arlington National Cemetery is one of the most well-known and recognizable military cemeteries in the United States. This final resting place for the men and women of the Armed Forces provides a glimpse into our past and present, including when segregation was the law of the land. At first glimpse, a visitor to Arlington sees row upon row of white marble tombstones that appear uniformly to honor and acknowledge those who have served this nation regardless of social status. However, visitors to sections twenty-three and twenty-seven will encounter headstones engraved with the initials for the United States Colored Troops, the name of the regiments of Black soldiers in the Civil War (figure 10.7). Although they fought side by side with other Americans, they could not be buried beside them. This segregated section was later expanded to include Black military veterans from other wars (Schalkham, 2006).

Segregation was also evident in cemeteries across the country, from large cities to rural America. Contemporary U.S. history is full of examples of cemeteries that denied burial based on a person's race or ethnicity, including the case of Sergeant John R. Rice, a Korean War veteran killed in combat whose burial was stopped in mid-process in 1951. As a member of the Winnebago tribe, Sgt. Rice was denied burial in a local cemetery because of a clause in the sales contract for the burial plot that stated the cemetery reserves burial privileges for Whites only. In the 1990s, a church cemetery in Thomasville, Georgia, requested the removal of a recently buried baby because the father was Black. In 2016, a local cemetery association in Texas refused to bury the remains of a man because he was Mexican. In both

Figure 10.7. This view includes seven headstones for unidentified members of the U.S. Colored Troops, Arlington Cemetery, Virginia.

situations, public pressure and court litigation reversed these attempts to maintain a "Whites only" policy for burial in these cemeteries (Sherman, 2020). These cases represent countless others known only to the bereaved families and friends who were directly impacted. People denied equal access to burial options have been forced to endure years of litigation, face public humiliation and scrutiny, and, in some cases, delay or relocate the burial.

Ethnic and Religious Cemeteries

Unlike the forced segregation of cemeteries discussed in the previous section, ethnic and religious cemeteries reflect a personal or family preference. These cemeteries form when members of a community choose to be buried in a cemetery or a specific section of a cemetery near others with a similar background. Having loved ones buried near others who share life experiences, culture, and traditions can help maintain a connection to one's homeland and heritage.

Ethnic cemeteries reaffirm and leave an enduring record of the contributions made by members of a cultural community. They also enhance a sense of connectedness and belonging as part of the fabric of this nation. The preferred design of an ethnic cemetery, its location, and the geographic orientation of the graves may reflect traditional practices. The form and shape of the grave marker, the symbols and epitaphs on the grave marker, and inscriptions in a specific language frequently differ from what is found in dominant culture burial plots, as do grave decorations and remembrance practices.

Religious cemeteries are owned and operated by religious groups or orders to serve a specific religious community. Reminiscent of historical churchyard burial sites, these cemeteries are frequently located on consecrated or blessed grounds and are reserved for the followers of that church or religious affiliation. In some cases, the religious burial site may be a specific section of a cemetery that is otherwise open to all. Depending on the particular religious group, the cemetery may require strict adherence to prescribed religious practices, while others operate according to loose guidelines and principles of belief. Some religious cemeteries are open to all, regardless of beliefs.

Potter's Fields

A **potter's field**, sometimes called a potter's cemetery, is a dedicated space for people who are unknown, whose remains are unclaimed, or whose families cannot afford to bury them. The term potter's field can be traced back to the Bible. In the New Testament book of Matthew (27:3–27:8), priests buy a potter's field for the burial of strangers, criminals, and the poor. In biblical times, a potter's field described land unfit for agriculture and suitable only as a source of clay for making pots. Although early potter's fields generally referred to a section of existing cemeteries, they are now more likely to be separate cemeteries.

No uniform system exists in the United States for the final disposition of unclaimed, unknown, or impoverished people. The resulting patchwork approach varies by state, city, or local jurisdiction. For instance, in urban areas, mass graves have often been used where the bodies of the indigent (the legal term for people who cannot afford burial costs) and unclaimed were buried in simple wooden coffins, usually marked with numbers, not names. New York City continues this practice, burying hundreds of coffins each year on Hart Island, where about one million people have been interred (Hennigan, 2020; *New York allows*, 2016). Other states and jurisdictions cremate unclaimed bodies. The ashes can then be buried in large mass graves or placed in a columbarium, lowering the government's costs and decreasing the space needed for final disposition. Even in areas that choose cremation, the process varies in terms of how long the body is held before cremation, how cremains are stored, where ashes are scattered, or how cremains are buried in mass ceremonies (What happens, 2019).

Conclusion

The loss of a loved one is such a personal experience that we may not notice the significant effect government and business have on our experiences of death until we are confronted with legal regulations, bureaucratic processes, and the funeral industry. Some requirements, such as filing a death certificate to verify that a death has occurred, are needed before business issues for the deceased person can be completed. Navigating the funeral industry and the marketing of burial, interment, final disposition, and funerary options can be confusing and overwhelming.

Social forces also shape our options and decisions concerning end-of-life rituals and final disposition. Our social position and cultural traditions impact our choices concerning when, where, and how we handle our loved ones' bodies. These differences affect how we interact with the business of death, yet this universal experience connects us. The proverb "as we are in life, so are we in death" is a sentiment that can be found in many traditions and speaks to the human desire for continuity with one's values, even unto death.

Summary

» A death must be recorded with the appropriate government agency, typically at the county level, where a death certificate is issued, detailing the cause, time, and location of death, demographic information, and the method and place of body disposition.

» A death certificate is needed for a survivor to manage the legal and business affairs of the person who died.

» The U.S. funeral industry emerged during the Civil War era and has developed and adapted over time to reflect ongoing social and cultural changes.

» Increased regulation of the funeral industry addresses consumer concerns and criticisms of coercive business practices.

» Traditionally, U.S. dominant culture end-of-life rituals have included a funeral service, memorial service, or celebration of life, but people are increasingly opting for more individualized rituals.

» The final disposition of a body after death reflects social, cultural, and personal beliefs.

» In U.S. dominant culture, more people are choosing cremation over traditional embalmment with a ground burial.

» Interest in alternative means of body disposition after death, especially more eco-friendly options, is growing.

» The location and design of cemeteries, as well as who can be interred, reflect social values, cultural practices, and historical narratives.

Review Questions

1. How does the process of government certification of death work, and how do its bureaucratic and legal aspects demonstrate the interplay between societal systems and personal grief?

2. Looking through a sociological lens, how do the structures and practices of the funeral industry reflect economic, cultural, and social factors?

3. When exploring the options for handling the body after death, how do customs, traditions, religious beliefs, and environmental concerns contribute to the decision-making process?

4. In what way do different types of cemeteries frequently seen in the United States reveal insights into societal values, historical stories, and urban planning approaches?

Key Terms

Review these key terms from the chapter. You can find their definitions in the glossary at the end of the book.

» aquamation
» attended death
» body disposition
» celebration of life
» columbarium/columbaria
» coroner
» cremation
» death certificate
» decedent
» direct burial
» embalming
» funeral concierge
» funeral director
» funeral home
» green burial
» lawn-style cemetery

» medical examiner
» memorial park
» memorial service
» mortality rates
» mortuary cosmetologist
» natural organic reduction (NOR)
» non-transplant anatomical donation organization (NADO)
» potter's field
» register of death
» rural cemetery
» traditional burial
» unattended death
» undertaker
» whole body donation

Chapter 11

—

Bereavement, Grief, and Mourning

| Vignette | **Reflections on Grief**

My first significant losses were my grandparents. I remember the sadness and tears and how much I missed them. But my family didn't talk openly about death. Without a model, I didn't know what to do or how to get through the grieving process.

As the years clicked by, I encountered more loss: classmates and friends, aunts and uncles, my mother-in-law. And the deaths kept coming: a niece, a nephew, cousins, a beloved friend and colleague, my father, sister, mother, and most recently, my husband. Through these experiences, I gathered from other people's reactions that I was supposed to mourn differently depending on my relationship with the person and the circumstances surrounding their death.

Similarly, the social support I received corresponded to the perceived or expected closeness of the relationship. For instance, people gave me more support after my mother's death compared to my mother-in-law's death, even though I had been estranged from my mother for many years and had a much closer relationship with my mother-in-law.

My grief was also very different when my niece died in childbirth. The intense sorrow at her loss mixed with the profound joy at the birth of her beautiful baby boy. Those in my social circle supported me as I worked through the shock. But soon after, people stopped checking in and changed the subject whenever I spoke about my struggle to make sense of her death. Even after my husband's death, I felt there was a limit on how long I was supposed to grieve. Three years later, many people seem to think I should move on with my life.

There's no right way to grieve; we each get through loss in our own time and way. Still, social expectations mark the boundaries for acceptable grieving. Interactions with friends, family, and colleagues send subtle messages. Social support wanes, and people get uncomfortable.

I've seen people's faces when I try to talk about my feelings. When someone falls outside the social conventions of acceptable grieving, they risk being marginalized, invalidated, or cut off from social support. My experiences have helped me understand that it's okay to take whatever time you need to work through your grief. And when others are grieving, it is important to support them for however long their journey through grief might take.

Patricia, 2024

Introduction

Grief, bereavement, and mourning are universal experiences that each person navigates in their own way, shaped by cultural, social, and personal factors. This chapter explores how grief is experienced, expressed, and understood through various frameworks and models. We will examine how social expectations and personal experiences guide behavior in bereavement, how different types of grief manifest, and how external factors, like the nature of the death, influence the grieving process. By understanding these complexities, we can better appreciate the diverse ways people process loss and honor the memories of those they've lost, both privately and publicly.

Learning Objectives

These learning objectives will help you identify what's most important in this chapter. By the end of this chapter, you should be able to do the following:

» Distinguish the differences between grief, bereavement, and mourning.
» Analyze various frameworks that describe how people move through grief.
» Classify the different types of grief and explain how these relate to the experience and expression of loss.
» Evaluate how the circumstances of sudden, violent death, and accidental death affect the experience of grief.
» Examine how people use memorials, both personal and public, to remember those who have died.

The Language of Loss

The language of loss offers people a way to talk with others about their experience when a loved one dies. Words are symbolic representations of thoughts, ideas, beliefs, and feelings that allow us to communicate and share our experiences. If we have words to describe our loss, others are more likely to understand and support us. Although experiencing loss after the death of a loved one is universal, the way we express it, both verbally and nonverbally, varies across cultures and individuals.

Health care professionals use academic or scientific terminology guided by conceptual frameworks to describe a person's grief, while bereaved individuals often use more personally relevant words to describe their experiences. These differing approaches can cause dissonance and miscommunication, which may lead health care providers to distance themselves from the individuals' pain. When a grieving person starts using the standardized health care language, it can also distance them from addressing the nuances of their individually experienced grief (Corless et al., 2014). These caveats do not negate the importance of having a shared vocabulary to express the experiences of loss; if people don't have the words, they can't talk about it.

Bereavement, grief, and mourning are three terms frequently used when discussing the death of a loved one. These words are barely adequate to capture the full depth and breadth of what we experience after the death of a loved one. It can be challenging to articulate the complexity of feelings, thoughts, and experiences associated with the loss of a family member or friend. However, a clear understanding of these terms and recognition of their social contextual meanings can help us give voice to this human experience. Although bereavement, grief, and mourning are often used interchangeably in various contexts, each expresses a unique component of loss.

Bereavement

Bereavement refers to the state of having lost a significant other to death. The death of a loved one can feel as if a piece of us has been suddenly torn away. This normal human experience can be marked by sorrow and distress that trigger social, cognitive, and emotional disruptions in one's life. The bereavement period is the time after a loss when these emotions are most pronounced.

During the bereavement period, social expectations guide the survivors as they learn to live without the person who died. For instance, family and friends of a recently widowed mom with small children may bring meals and help with daily tasks during this transitional time. They may offer to watch her children or have them stay for a sleepover to give the mom some time to mourn and plan for the next steps. But these offers taper off over time as she is expected to work through the grieving process, adapt to the loss, and gradually move into her new social role as a widow and a single parent. For those who occupy the bereavement role, these expectations grounded in social and cultural norms guide their behaviors, actions, and emotions associated with death.

As discussed in chapter 4, cultural and religious beliefs and customs structure expectations as people grieve. Bereavement practices, such as tossing a handful of dirt onto the lowered casket or scattering ashes at a special location, help provide closure so survivors can begin to move on with their lives. Cultural and social norms surrounding grief map out what deaths should be acknowledged, who should express grief, how long to mourn, and how the deceased person should be remembered.

Variations in belief systems affect the long-term aspects of remembrance and memorials and how these are privately experienced and publicly expressed. In the United States, bereavement norms often conflict with the standards embodied in our social institutions. For example, institutional expectations, such as a workplace's policy for bereavement leave, can limit individuals' bereavement practices. Laws and legal processes (government), the workplace (economy), and the health care system (health and medicine) regulate daily activities, including bereavement practices. The underlying beliefs and attitudes of these practices may place implicit constraints on bereavement through social expectations and social pressures (Oyebode & Owens, 2013).

Grief

While bereavement is the state of being after the death of a significant other, **grief** refers to the personal reaction to that loss. Grief is a normal response to death. It is a universal human reaction, but it is also personal and individual in how each person experiences the loss. The grief experience is not a static state, but rather, it is a process that varies from person to person and across time. Grief reactions can ebb and flow from day to day, but sometimes, the pain of loss can feel overwhelming. A survivor may experience a range of complex and unanticipated emotions, from shock or anger to disbelief and profound sadness.

The intensity, duration, and expression of grief are also influenced by the nature of the death and the survivor's relationship to the deceased person. For example, the death of an elderly grandparent may be experienced very differently from the sudden, unexpected death of a teenage sibling in a car crash. While it is difficult to specify the duration of the grieving process, most people report that they recover adequately within a year after the loss; others, however, may experience an extended period of grieving (Mughal et al., 2022).

Grief can involve both physical and psychological responses. Most people experience one or more physical symptoms associated with grief, such as tightness and heaviness in the chest or throat, digestive distress, headaches, muscle weakness, fatigue, and reduced immune function. When someone is grieving, they are envisioning their new reality and internally processing an array of emotions and thoughts. Grief can be mentally and emotionally exhausting, making daily activities difficult to complete. Survivors may experience feelings of disbelief, difficulty in concentrating, and preoccupation with the death event and loss. There can be sleep disruptions, hallucinations, and a loss of interest in daily activities. A person may cycle through a range of feelings, including shock, numbness, sadness, denial, anger, guilt, helplessness, depression, and yearning. A person can become more aggressive or irritable and may cry when triggered by a significant item, song, movie, or at random for no apparent reason (Mughal et al., 2022).

Mourning

As previously discussed, grief refers to the personal, internal reactions to death, but **mourning** is how people express that grief. Mourning is the public, social acknowledgment of a death and its impact on survivors. The expression of loss and pain is shaped by cultural, spiritual, or community-based expectations. Mourning may also reflect family death traditions or individually unique practices. People can express their grief by crying, talking about the death, or revisiting memories of the deceased person. The mourning process even includes the ceremonies we choose to honor those who have died and how we handle their body after death.

Mourning behaviors and rituals have a clear purpose. They externalize people's pain and confusion. Mourning rituals, such as leaving an empty seat and place setting at the family's dinner table, acknowledge sadness, promote acceptance, and offer a way to channel and process intense feelings. For some, these rituals and practices can provide emotional comfort, offer closure, and mark the loss formally. Mourning rituals can also help people adjust to the loss of a loved one and give a sense of order and control around their grief.

Mourning customs often acknowledge the social loss of a loved one or community member. As social beings, survivors use mourning rituals to honor loved ones who have died. Traditions, such as visits to the cemetery, serve as an act of remembrance and can promote an ongoing connection with the deceased person. Gathering with those who are mourning can help create a connection with one's community and support system. These customs facilitate re-entry into the social world after the loss. Communal support is an important aspect of processing grief.

The Grieving Process

Grief is an integral part of the healing process after a death. The grieving process is a personal journey that we each experience and navigate in our own way. At times, it can feel lonely, even when we have support. But working through grief helps us move beyond the initial reaction to the loved one's death. It provides the time needed to acknowledge the difficulty of this life event, honor the depth of emotions, and process sorrow. When a person dies, we lose that social and personal connection. Grief provides a way to process that loss. It can help us detach from the person we have lost and force us to confront a world without them. The grieving process moves us forward so we can navigate this change, adapt to a new reality, and manage without our loved ones.

Stages of Grief

The **stages of grief model** introduced by psychiatrist Elisabeth Kübler-Ross in 1969 marked a sociocultural shift in the understanding of psychological and emotional experiences of death and dying. Historically, the subject of death was often avoided in medical and care settings. Medical professionals did not always involve dying patients in their care decisions or even tell them of their terminal diagnosis. Up until the second half of the twentieth century, many health care professionals believed that withholding the truth of someone's diagnosis was better than causing emotional distress (Testoni et al., 2020).

Kübler-Ross's insights on the experience of dying based on interviews with terminally ill patients changed how people understood the psychological and emotional experience of death and dying. Kübler-Ross's research delineated five commonly experienced end-of-life stages: denial, anger, bargaining, depression, and acceptance (figure 11.1).

Figure 11.1. The Kübler-Ross grief model, developed in 1969, was first introduced by Elisabeth Kübler-Ross in her book *On Death and Dying*.

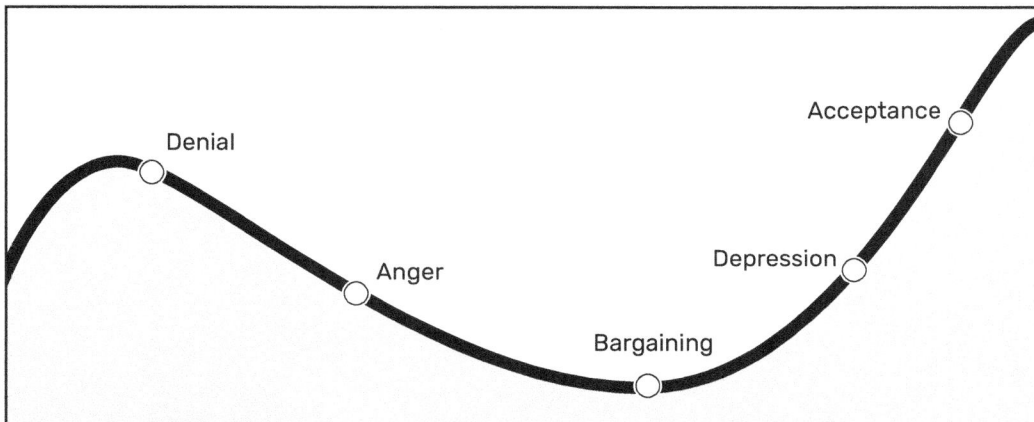

The Kübler-Ross Grief Cycle

Denial

Anger

Bargaining

Depression

Acceptance

The stages of grief model and the importance of patient-led care have changed how medicine and popular culture view end-of-life care. Kübler-Ross and others have subsequently applied this model to other types of loss, as in the case of survivors' experiences of loss and grief after a death (Tyrrell et al., 2023; Ross Rothweiler & Ross, 2019). Box 11.1 describes the Kübler-Ross Change Curve, which was developed in the 1990s as a reinterpretation of Kübler-Ross's original grief model. Like the original stages of grief, people do not experience the emotions as a linear progression. The journey to acceptance and adaptation is dynamic, complex, and often cyclical.

Box 11.1: Kübler-Ross Change Curve

Based on in-depth interviews with terminally ill patients, Kübler-Ross gained a deeper understanding of common behaviors, thoughts, and emotions experienced by patients facing the end of life. Her stages of grief model and the change curve based on her original research are useful in supporting the needs of people who are grieving. Figure 11.2 shows the common emotional responses in the Kübler-Ross Change Curve.

Figure 11.2. The Kübler-Ross Change Curve begins with shock and moves toward integration.

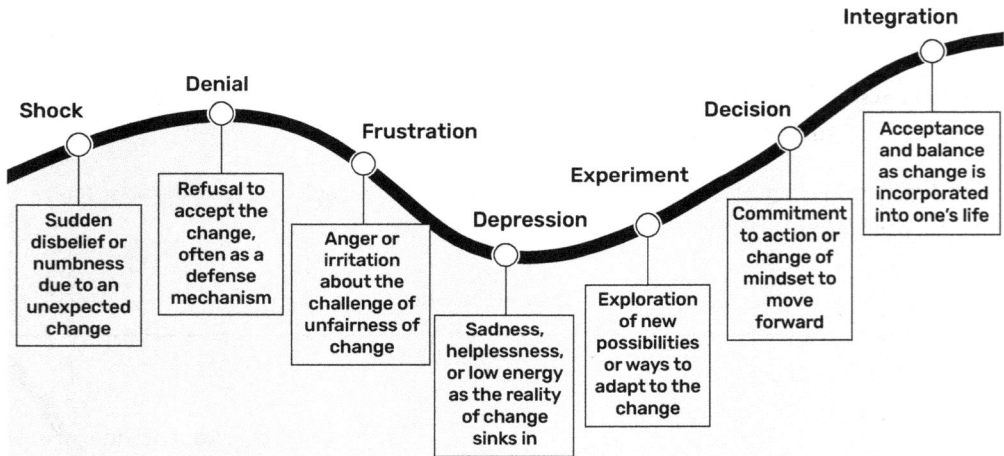

The stages of grief model has been increasingly criticized in recent years. Some question the model's use of specific stages that have not been validated empirically, and they have concerns that these stages are applied too rigidly. Some people have interpreted the five stages of the model too strictly, with the expectation that patients must move sequentially through each stage to reach the goal of "acceptance." In response to the criticism, supporters explain that the stages of grief model is grounded in qualitative research focused on the experiences of patients approaching the end of life.

Kübler-Ross herself remarked that the model was meant to be personal, subjective, and more descriptive rather than prescriptive. Everyone will have a unique experience in their grief process and may express each stage differently, if at all. The experience can be fluid as a person moves from stage to stage in a nonlinear fashion. Individuals may shift back and forth and, at times, revisit a previously experienced stage. It is also not unusual for a person to occupy more than one stage at a time. Regardless of the variability of an individual's experience, the deeper understanding of the end-of-life experience provided by this model is an important tool in helping support the terminally ill patient, caregivers, and those experiencing grief and loss (Tyrrell et al., 2023; Ross Rothweiler & Ross, 2019).

Tasks of Mourning

Grieving assists people in working through their reactions to death. The path through the grieving process varies and can be influenced by factors such as a person's age, gender, and relationship with the person who died. One's personality, previous experiences, coping skills, social support, culture, and religion are also factors.

While people's reactions may differ, they often have the following experiences in common:
- » **thoughts and actions**: disbelief, yearning, a constant focus on the deceased person, confusion, disruptions in sleeping and eating patterns, and social withdrawal
- » **physical and emotional well-being**: physical exhaustion, muscle weakness, feelings of sadness, anger, loneliness, crying, restlessness, and numbness
- » **spirituality**: feeling lost, searching for meanings, or questioning beliefs (Worden, 2018)

These types of reactions are expected and not unusual unless they are exceptionally intense, persist long-term, or adversely impact a person's ability to perform daily activities. Some people might have one reaction, while others may experience many. Strong reactions might lessen over time, or they might persist for a long time. The duration of these reactions differs for each person, depending on the circumstances.

Regardless of the variations in experiences, working through grief responses often takes longer than expected. For many, grief and related responses do not steadily decline. People are more likely to experience ebbs and flows in intensity as their responses fluctuate over time. Grief reactions can also come in waves for months or even years. Anything can trigger these episodes: a movie, song, possession, location, or even a specific date can conjure up the memory of a loved one. The first year after a death is often the most intense, as the grief reactions tend to decline in frequency, intensity, and duration over time.

William Worden, a renowned expert in the field of life-threatening illnesses and a founding member of the Association of Death Education and Counseling, proposed a framework used to understand the nature of grief work and specific tasks to be accomplished to adjust and adapt to the loss. His framework identifies the importance of addressing the following four tasks in working through the grieving process:

» **Task 1: Accept the reality of the loss.** The grieving process involves facing the finality of death; the person is gone and will not come back. Avoidance behaviors may include denying the facts or retaining the possessions of the deceased person as if they will return.

» **Task 2: Process the pain of grief.** Survivors must go through the pain at some point. Delays in experiencing the pain only prolong the grieving process. Attempts to escape and numb these feelings may include the use of alcohol and drugs, avoiding reminders of the deceased person, and changing geographic locations to avoid focusing on the emotions of grief.

» **Task 3: Adjust to a world without the deceased person.** Three primary adjustment areas during the grieving process include external, internal, and spiritual adjustments. External adjustments are often connected to the loss of the roles the deceased person played in the survivor's life. For example, the death of a close friend can mean a loss of social support, companionship, and a confidant. A death may also necessitate survivors to make internal adjustments in the understanding of self (who am I?), self-esteem (sense of self-worth and value), and self-efficacy (confidence in one's ability to control and respond to one's environment). For instance, a surviving wife, partner, or parent must reassess who they are by confronting their ability to fill vacant roles and addressing gaps left by their loved one's death. Additionally, a person's spiritual framework may require adjustments when searching for meaning in the loss of a loved one. A death can challenge beliefs and assumptions about the world, the way it works, and how we fit into this new reality without the deceased person.

» **Task 4: Find a way to remember the deceased person while moving forward with life.** This task focuses on defining and reconfiguring an ongoing bond with the deceased person. The challenge is to find meaningful ways to remember the deceased person without obstructing daily life. Many people find this to be the most challenging task, often holding on to past attachments in ways that prevent them from forming new ones (Worden, 2018).

Worden's framework emphasizes that the grieving process is not a step-by-step linear process. Work may take place on multiple tasks simultaneously, and tasks may be revisited and reworked over time (figure 11.3). Someone who is mourning may accomplish some of these tasks and not others and may not fully adjust and adapt to the loss (Worden, 2018).

To understand the differences in how people navigate grief tasks, Worden stressed the importance of being attentive to various factors that can affect how these tasks are carried out. Common factors include the survivor's kinship connection to the deceased person, their attachment, the quality of their relationship with the deceased person, and how the person died. The personality qualities of the bereaved, pre-existing mental health issues or substance use, any current stressors, as well as the social supports available, can also play a role in how they respond to the loss and navigate the tasks (Worden, 2018; Khosravi, 2021).

Figure 11.3. Worden's four tasks of mourning help people think concretely about the experience of grief.

Types of Grief

Grief is multifaceted and can be varied and complex depending on the specific individual and the nature of the loss. The grieving process can also be affected by the particular type of grief a person is experiencing. When supporting someone who is grieving, it can be helpful to recognize and understand the differing dimensions of grief. Figure 11.4 shows the types of grief discussed in this section.

Figure 11.4. Grief takes many forms. This diagram's two overlapping circles illustrate how "normal" grief lasts the expected amount of time based on one's culture and relationship to the person who died. Other dimensions of grief fall outside this "normal" range when they differ in duration (time) or relation (culture).

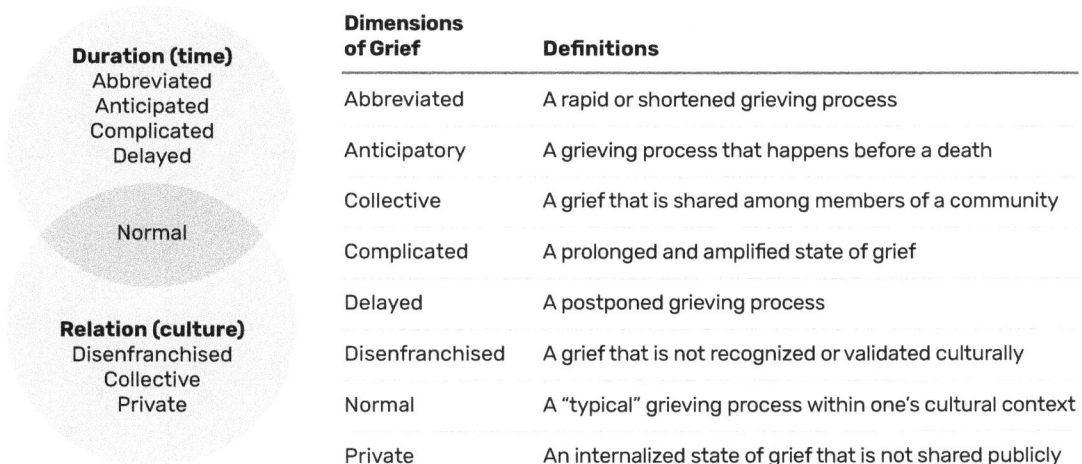

Dimensions of Grief	Definitions
Abbreviated	A rapid or shortened grieving process
Anticipatory	A grieving process that happens before a death
Collective	A grief that is shared among members of a community
Complicated	A prolonged and amplified state of grief
Delayed	A postponed grieving process
Disenfranchised	A grief that is not recognized or validated culturally
Normal	A "typical" grieving process within one's cultural context
Private	An internalized state of grief that is not shared publicly

Duration (time)
Abbreviated
Anticipated
Complicated
Delayed

Normal

Relation (culture)
Disenfranchised
Collective
Private

Normal and Complicated Grief

Normal grief, sometimes referred to as uncomplicated grief, suggests that a person is processing their thoughts, behaviors, and feelings in a way that is typical within their cultural context (Shear, 2012). Within U.S. dominant culture, symptoms of normal grief often include:

- » crying and sadness
- » feelings of anger, loneliness, and emptiness
- » sleep problems, a lack of energy, and changes in appetite
- » feeling apathetic about life in general
- » difficulty concentrating or completing tasks
- » social withdrawal
- » questioning spiritual beliefs, career choices, or life goals

While there is no set timetable for grief, these responses generally subside over time. People who experience normal grief will gradually learn to cope and adjust to the loss and establish a "new normal" in the ensuing months (Cleveland Clinic, 2023).

With normal grief, people experience a variety of emotional and psychological responses, but over time, these lessen as they work through the grieving process. However, **complicated grief**, sometimes referred to as **prolonged grief**, follows a different trajectory. During the first few months after a loss, the characteristics of complicated grief are often the same as those associated with normal grief. But for someone experiencing complicated grief, these responses do not fade over time; they continue, often for years, interfering with a person's ability to feel or function normally. The responses can also become more severe and intense rather than subsiding over time.

People experiencing complicated grief may be stuck in an amplified state of mourning. The yearning for the person who has died persists and can grow even stronger. The severity and persistence can be incapacitating and interfere with a person's ability to maintain relationships and engage in daily activities. Ongoing grief responses can leave a person unable to cope and inhibit the healing process. Processing complicated grief often requires assistance and support from trained mental health care or counseling professionals.

Complicated grief is often characterized by a deep sense of longing and inability to cope with the reality of the loss. Individuals with complicated grief may struggle to find meaning in life after the death of a loved one, and their pain can feel overwhelming and unmanageable. Common symptoms of complicated grief include:

- » intense, recurring sorrow, pain, and emptiness
- » preoccupation with thoughts of your loved one's death
- » excessive avoidance of reminders of your loved one
- » persistent anger or rage over the death
- » feeling that life holds no meaning or purpose

If these symptoms persist and affect one's ability to function in daily life, seeking professional support may help the grieving person process the loss and find ways to cope (Shear et al., 2005).

Time-Based Grief

In addition to complicated grief, which involves a prolonged state of grief, other forms of grief can be impacted by time. Some people may experience **delayed grief**, which occurs when the grieving process is deferred. Instead of experiencing the thoughts and emotions that accompany grief immediately after a death, a person feels them days, weeks, or even months later. They may experience the initial emotional and psychological reactions to a death, but the actual work of grieving is postponed. In some cases, the immediate shock of the loss pauses the body's ability to work through these emotions. In other situations, the need to manage practical matters, such as making funeral arrangements, tending to legal and financial affairs, and meeting daily obligations, takes primacy. These pressing priorities consume time and energy, preventing the individual from grieving until they've handled these responsibilities.

Sometimes, the grieving process may begin before a physical death. For example, receiving a terminal illness diagnosis can prompt the onset of grief reactions. **Anticipatory grief** refers to mourning responses experienced before death. The responses mirror those associated with post-loss grief, but working through these feelings and thoughts can also be more challenging when faced with the uncertainties surrounding the end of life. The unpredictability of the disease trajectory, treatment outcome, and the stress of responsibilities and demands placed on the caregiver can be additional stressors in navigating grief.

Abbreviated grief describes when a person moves through the grieving process more quickly than is typical for other people. Though it may not seem possible to others that someone can fully work through grief in a short amount of time, it can happen. Grieving for a short time is not necessarily problematic. It does not mean the person no longer cares about their loved one, nor does it suggest they failed to process their grief adequately. Abbreviated grief is common when there is no pre-existing close relationship with the deceased person, such as a distant relative, a fellow employee, or a community leader. Even with close relationships, abbreviated grief can occur. Those who experience anticipatory grief may grieve a loss more quickly because they have already done much of the emotional and psychological work involved in the grieving process.

Private and Collective Grief

Depending on the nature of the loss, grief may have private or communal components. **Private grief** can involve the internal processing of emotions and may be expressed only in private settings, reflecting the individual's way of coping with loss. When grief is not acknowledged, culturally validated, or may not be publicly mourned, it is sometimes referred to as hidden grief or **disenfranchised grief** (Doka, 1989).

As previously discussed, social and cultural norms define appropriate and expected grieving practices. Each society's norms determine what is considered legitimate feelings or displays of grief, including under what circumstances grief is "normal." These norms depend on the individual's relationship with the person who died and the circumstances of the death. For example, in U.S. dominant culture, a person might experience disenfranchised grief when an ex-spouse or partner dies, with the death of someone they don't know directly, or with a miscarriage. When a person experiences a loss that doesn't fit within society's norms, the related grief may not be acknowledged or validated by society.

The lack of social recognition of a death-related loss can lead to difficulties in processing and expressing grief. When a person experiences disenfranchised grief, others may not see the need to provide sympathy and social support. As a result, their grief reaction may be socially minimized or misunderstood. An overall lack of support makes it particularly hard to process and work through the grieving process and can prolong the emotional pain of loss.

In place of more traditional sources of social support, people processing disenfranchised grief often find it helpful to make connections to others who have shared similar losses and create their own grief rituals or practices. Online and social media options connect people with resources such as helplines, live chats, and 24/7 support groups. Memorial websites and social media pages dedicated to deaths associated with disenfranchised grief can be a safe place to share and receive support in a community of people who have had similar losses. Communities often have memorials that can be helpful for people who are experiencing disenfranchised grief, such as candlelight vigils and remembrance walks for Pregnancy and Infant Loss Remembrance Day (October 15), which is observed in the U.S., U.K., Canada, and Australia.

Sometimes, people grieve for a person who died who was not directly connected to them. As social beings, we feel connected to others and can empathize and share in their loss, even though we may not know the deceased individual (Wagoner et al., 2019). **Collective grief** refers to the shared experience of loss when it affects a group of people, such as a community, a nation, or a global population. Broadly experienced grief is particularly apparent after major events that result in widespread tragedy or mass casualties, such as natural disasters, the COVID-19 pandemic, famines, or other high-profile events.

Collective grief can be amplified when the deaths involve violence, as in the case of mass shootings, terrorist attacks, or war. Grief can also be widely shared when a significant public figure dies. For example, the deaths of Diana, Princess of Wales, professional athlete Kobe Bryant, and internationally known performer Michael Jackson led to a global outpouring of grief responses. As an expression of their grief, people left flowers and personal messages, held vigils, and created makeshift memorials in public spaces to honor their memories. Entire communities can also experience collective grief, especially after the death of a prominent leader or in response to a shared tragedy, such as a natural disaster, a school shooting, or a community-wide accident.

The intensity of grief can be affected by whether someone knew, interacted with, or felt close to the person who died. These feelings of connection can be affected by being near places associated with the person, such as their home, school, workplace, or the location where they died. Collective grief responses are also shaped by public perceptions of the widespread social loss associated with a death. For example, the death of a public figure can lead to concerns about political stability (Queen Elizabeth II) or represent a significant loss in terms of their creative contributions (Robin Williams, comedian and performer) or athletic talent (Bill Walton, professional basketball player and sports announcer).

Observing others openly mourn a loss has benefits. Although witnessing others' sadness can make us sad ourselves, we can find comfort in processing these events as a community. Communal grief allows us to examine and express our feelings about the loss. Expressions of collective grief can also be experienced in virtual communities. Websites and social media offer a place to connect with others anytime, from anywhere, without geographical limitations. In these virtual communities, people who may not have local support options or who feel uncomfortable in group settings can share their emotional pain and feelings of loss with others.

Grief and Relationships

Grief is a deeply personal experience, yet it is shaped by various social, cultural, and individual factors that influence how we feel and behave when mourning. Specific factors, such as the nature of the relationship with the person who died, the cause of death, and the stage of life we are in when the loss occurs, play a significant role in how we process grief.

For example, the cause of death can shape the grief experience in different ways. A sudden or traumatic death, like an accident or violent incident, may lead to shock, confusion, and prolonged grief, as the loss feels unexpected and harder to process. In contrast, a death after a long illness might be accompanied by feelings of relief, exhaustion, or guilt, especially if the grieving person was a caregiver.

The stage of life also affects mourning. For a child who loses a parent, the loss may be experienced as a profound disruption of stability and security. Adults, on the other hand, might process the death of a parent with complex emotions, including an awareness of their mortality or their role as the new "head" of the family. Losing a peer during adolescence or early adulthood may provoke feelings of injustice or fear, while the loss of a spouse later in life often leads to profound loneliness and questions about identity.

Like societal norms, cultural norms define how grief is expressed and the rituals surrounding death. In some cultures, mourning is highly communal, involving public ceremonies, shared meals, and weeks or months of formal rituals. In others, grief might be more private, with the expectation that individuals will cope in quieter, more solitary ways. These cultural expectations can influence how comfortable people feel expressing their emotions or seeking support from others.

Lastly, social structures and personal relationships influence the mourning process by shaping who is expected to grieve and how. A close relationship with the deceased often leads to more visible and intense mourning, but as we've seen earlier in the chapter, even distant or conflicted relationships can generate complex emotions. For example, someone estranged from a family member might struggle with unresolved guilt or regret after their death, while societal cues might tell them that they have no "right" to grieve openly. These social and cultural factors create a framework that helps individuals understand their grief in context, guiding them toward the support systems available and helping them navigate the social meanings attached to death and mourning.

Special Circumstances: Stigmatized Deaths

Factors associated with the cause of death can exacerbate feelings of loss, sadness, and loneliness. For example, in the case of suicide, where death is sudden, unexpected, and often violent, the circumstances can amplify grief and complicate the grieving process. A loss due to suicide can trigger a host of intense and confusing emotions, such as guilt, rejection, and even anger. Survivors may punish themselves by asking "what if?" after a death by suicide. They may overestimate their ability to change the outcome and condemn themselves or others for failing to intervene.

At the same time, suicide can erect barriers to the very social support systems people need. Public uneasiness in addressing suicide death can limit survivors' access to social support and grief resources. A **social stigma** is any attribute or behavior that singles out a person or group for different treatment. Suicide is considered a stigmatized death because the social discomfort can isolate survivors from family, friends, and community. Many religions and cultures condemn suicide as a sin or personal failure, which adds to the social stigma. Because family members may disagree about how to discuss the death publicly, survivors may be reluctant to acknowledge or disclose the circumstances of such a death. The stigma around suicide makes it difficult for family and friends who do want to speak openly to feel comfortable doing so. The decision to keep the suicide a secret or avoid discussing the topic can increase isolation and decrease social support systems (Tal Young et al., 2012).

Special Circumstances: Age, Social Roles, and Relationships

Mourning behaviors and the grieving experience are affected by a person's ability to understand and process the meaning and implications of death. People continue to develop cognitively and psychologically across the life course. From infancy through late adulthood, our ability to understand ourselves, others, and our social environment expands and becomes more complex. Therefore, reactions to life events such as death are influenced by a person's developmental stage. The most significant and rapid development occurs during infancy, childhood, and adolescence. During these stages, children's and teens' responses to death may share some similarities with adults, but their specific thoughts, beliefs, and behaviors may differ depending on their ages (Osterweis et al., 1984).

An understanding off developmental age-based grieving responses can help you support children and their families as they mourn a death. First and foremost, be mindful that children will process grief and express mourning behaviors differently than adults, and they may experience intermittent grief reactions for years. Although there may be similarities to adult reactions, such as sadness and loneliness, most responses will be influenced by the child's developmental age. For example, children ages 3–5 may have difficulty understanding the permanence of death. They may only fully come to terms with the finality of death several months after the event, while children ages 6–8 can immediately begin to process the loss (Christ, 2000; Dougy Center, n.d.).

Young children often express their emotions and feelings through art or play. They may reenact the funeral and family members' responses to the death, or they might pretend to interact with the person who died. They can appear emotively flat when they talk about the person who has died and may bluntly tell visitors, "My grandma died." This detachment allows them to watch the reactions of others to discern how they should respond. Children may repeatedly ask questions about the death, seeking reassurance that nothing has changed and reaffirming the permanency of the loss.

While tweens and teens better understand the permanence of death, specific information about a death can be more distressing. It can act to reaffirm the reality and raise questions about the implications of death and the effect it will have on their lives. Information and discussions about the death of a loved one can generate anxiety around the meaning of life, prompt feelings of guilt, and trigger "what if" questions about what they could or should have done while the person was alive. During grief and loss, teens often seek comfort and support from their friends and pursue stronger relationships with their peers (Christ, 2000; Dougy Center, n.d.).

Across the life course, periods of bereavement are more commonly experienced during adulthood. Experiencing the death of a loved one during adulthood can significantly alter a person's social status and social identity. The shifts in social status may lead to changes not only in self-perception but also in the ways a person is perceived by others, and the changes may continue for some time. For example, a middle-aged widow or widower may find their social life significantly curtailed because people tend to socialize in couples. An elderly person may find that most of their friends and relatives have died, resulting in fewer social connections. Making new friends may be difficult. Thus, social isolation and feelings of loneliness are common, often long after the bereavement period (Osterweis et al., 1984).

Losses occur with increasing frequency as we and those around us age. During this mid-life stage, people's social networks tend to become larger. As a person ages, so do many of their friends and peers, which also increases the likelihood of deaths among their friends. As a result, the experience of adults has often, by default, become the basis for much of what we generally understand about the grieving process. But later in adulthood, commonly experienced grief responses can become more challenging. For adults over the age of seventy, grief-related stress combined with any current health issues can pose a higher risk of health complications. Many seniors are more likely to experience isolation and loneliness and are therefore more likely to experience grief alone and suffer without an adequate social support network. But at the same time, older adults demonstrate high levels of resilience, generally taking the same amount of time to process grief following bereavement as other adults (Ryan & Coughlan, 2011).

A survivor's grief reactions are also influenced by the nature of their relationship with the person who died. The grief associated with the death of a spouse, for example, differs from the grief experienced with the death of a child, a grandparent, or a close friend. Relationship factors, such as emotional closeness, social role, and feelings toward the person while alive, can influence grief responses. When a survivor depended on the person who died for emotional, social, or financial support, guidance, companionship, or care, the loss takes on additional meanings. The grief experience can also be impacted when the bereaved had a complicated relationship or unresolved issues with the person who died.

The death of a loved one can affect a survivor's social status and sense of social identity, which then becomes an additional grief task. This loss or change in social position and self-identity is often based on the relationship of the survivor to the deceased person. In some situations, society acknowledges this change by introducing language or social identifiers to represent the new status. For example, when a person dies, their spouse is socially recognized as a widow or widower, or when a young child's parents die, they become an orphan. Adapting to these new social statuses and their associated roles becomes part of the grieving process and adjustment to the loss of a loved one. These social identifiers announce the change so others can respond accordingly and help during the grieving process. Yet, there are times when grief work associated with a relationship-based status and role change can be more difficult. When we don't have words to describe and identify the status changes, the bereaved and their support networks may struggle with the shift into a new social position.

Box 11.2: How to Cope when a Friend or Loved One Dies by Suicide

The loss of a loved one is difficult under any circumstances; however, the grief can be magnified when the death is by suicide. A suicide death can trigger intense and confusing emotions. Survivors can feel isolated and abandoned because others may not know what to say or how to help and avoid the subject entirely. Here are some strategies that can help survivors begin to process their grief.

> » **Accept the full range of emotions.** You might expect to feel grief and despair, but other common feelings include shock, denial, guilt, shame, anger, confusion, anxiety, loneliness, and even, in some cases, relief. Those feelings are normal and can vary throughout the healing process.
> » **Don't worry about what you "should" feel or do.** There's no standard timeline for grieving and no single right way to cope. Focus on what you need and accept that others' paths might be different from yours.
> » **Care for yourself.** Do your best to get enough sleep and eat regular, healthy meals. Taking care of your physical self can improve your mood and give you the strength to cope.
> » **Draw on existing support systems.** Accept help from those who have been supports in the past, including your family, your friends, or members of your faith-based community.
> » **Talk to someone.** Many loss survivors suffer in silence, so sharing your feelings can help. (American Psychological Association, n.d.)

Additional information and resources:

> » **American Foundation for Suicide Prevention (AFSP)** offers support for loss survivors, including a wide array of resources such as support groups, a Survivor Outreach Program, and guides for coping with suicide loss. Website: https://afsp.org/ive-lost-someone/
> » **Suicide Awareness Voices of Education (SAVE)** offers resources for grieving friends and families, including articles, guides, and a list of support groups across the country. Website: https://www.save.org

Box 11.3: Talking to Children and Teens About Death by Suicide

Parents, teachers, school administrators, and other adults in a child's life often feel unprepared to help a young person cope with a death by suicide. These strategies can help you foster open dialogue and offer support.

» **Deal with your own feelings first.** Pause to reflect on and manage your own emotions so you can speak calmly to the child or children in your life.

» **Be honest.** Don't dwell on details of the act itself, but don't hide the truth. Use age-appropriate language to discuss the death with children.

» **Validate feelings.** Help children name their emotions: "It sounds like you're angry," or "I hear you blaming yourself, but this is not your fault." Acknowledge and normalize the child's feelings. Share your own feelings, too, explaining that while each person's feelings are different, it's okay to experience a range of emotions.

» **Avoid rumors.** Don't gossip or speculate about the reasons for the suicide. Instead, when talking to a child or teen, emphasize that the person who died was struggling and thinking differently from most people.

» **Tailor your support.** People grieve at different paces and in different ways. Some might need privacy as they work through their feelings. Respect their privacy but check in regularly to let them know they don't have to grieve alone. Others might want someone to talk to more often. Still, others prefer to process their feelings through art or music. Ask the child how they'd like you to help. Let them know it's okay to just be together.

» **Don't ask for an explanation.** Survivors often feel as though they're being grilled: Was there a note? Did you suspect anything? The survivor may be searching for answers, but your role for the foreseeable future is simply to be supportive and listen to what they have to say about the person, the death, and their feelings. (American Psychological Association, n.d.; Harvard Health, 2019)

A person's sense of social identity is complex, and the loss of a loved one can raise questions: Who am I? How do I fit in? How do I interact with others now? For example, when Aubrey's life partner of seventeen years died, she described her frustration over repeatedly having to explain her situation: "People seemed to minimize the loss I was struggling with because we weren't husband and wife. If we would have been 'married' people would have automatically seen me as a widow and acknowledged what I was feeling and experiencing. It was just one more thing I had to deal with and figure out how I fit in." A similar struggle around the loss of social position came up when Tanya was talking to friends shortly after her teenage daughter died in a car crash. She abruptly stopped talking, looked at her friends, and then asked, "Ella was my only child. Am I still a mom?" Without language to describe the challenges of life without her daughter and their relationship, Tanya struggled to share the depth of her grief with others.

The specific nature of family relationships impacts the grieving process when a family member dies. These relationships involve varying levels of interconnectedness, interdependency, common experiences, and a shared sense of identity as a social unit. The death of a close family member is frequently described as one of the most profound and devastating losses a person will experience. However, survivors experience loss differently depending on their relationship with the person who died. For example, a spouse or life partner's death represents the loss of the marital bond and partnership they shared. They are co-managers of the household and family unit, companions, and sexual partners, and death severs that relationship. Grief often includes the survivor suddenly having to take on all the family responsibilities and household tasks, which may also involve a loss of income.

The death of a child goes against the expected order of life. People generally assume that death comes later in life and that children will outlive their parents. Therefore, when a child dies at a young age or before their parents, the grieving process can be more challenging and often requires professional assistance in processing that grief. Children represent generational continuity and hope for the future, and the death of a child can jar this understanding.

The parent-child bond is a profound and intense connection. Parents of children who have died often describe feeling as if a part of them also died. Grieving the death of a child can also be more enduring. Parents and family members usually grieve throughout their lives. They witness their child's siblings and friends celebrate life benchmarks (graduation, marriage, children) and grieve what death has denied for their deceased child. The grief experience of each family member generally reflects the nature of their status position to the deceased person. For example, siblings grieve their lost relationship with the person who died, adjusting to the hole left in the family unit; grandparents mourn the death of their grandchild while trying to support their children (the parents) in their sorrow (Christ et al., 2003).

The age of a child who dies can also affect the grieving process. The death of an infant or young child can be especially difficult, including miscarriages, perinatal deaths (deaths immediately before or shortly after birth), stillborn infants, and sudden infant death syndrome (SIDS).

The birth of a child is a joyous occasion and a time for celebration. Families and loved ones anticipate welcoming a new member to the family. Even before the child is born, the parents, family members, and friends envision what life will be like with this child. When a death occurs at the beginning of the life span, these hopes and dreams for the child are also grieved. When the death of a child occurs during the first few years of life, the familial bonds established thus far in life have strengthened that connection, adding to the grief and loss (Christ et al., 2003; Canadian Paediatric Society, 2001).

Special Circumstances: Grieving the Death of a Pet

For many Americans, the notion of family includes at least one pet. In 2023, 63% of American households included a pet, and nearly all pet owners (97%) consider them family. Pets have become such an integral part of people's lives that half of all pet owners say their pets are as much a part of their family as their human relatives. Although pets can include a wide variety of animals, 49% of pets are dogs, 23% are cats, and nearly a quarter of pet owners have both dogs and cats (Brown, 2023).

Figure 11.5. This statue in Edinburgh, Scotland, memorializes Greyfriars Bobby, who faithfully guarded his owner's grave for fourteen years until he died.

If pets are a part of your family, you may have experienced some of the benefits associated with pet ownership. Pets can enrich life by keeping you more active and socially engaged. They can help reduce stress and anxiety, provide companionship, unconditional love, and affection, and be a source of joy and happiness (Brooks et al., 2018; *Health benefits of pets*, 2024). However, pets generally have a shorter life span than humans, which means that pet owners are likely to experience the loss of a family pet several times.

One example of the emotional bond between humans and pets is the statue of Greyfriars Bobby in Edinburgh, Scotland (figure 11.5). This statue commemorates the loyal dog who, after the death of his owner, spent fourteen years guarding his owner's grave. Bobby's story highlights the profound connections that can exist between people and animals. It also speaks to how such bonds are remembered and memorialized, reflecting the significance of pet loss as a deeply human experience.

When a pet dies, grief often includes the same emotions and responses that occur with other types of deaths. It commonly includes sorrow, sadness, loneliness, confusion, anger, and depression. These grief responses are impacted by the closeness and intensity of the relationship you had with your pet. Grief is often more difficult if the owner has to euthanize their pet. Support systems can help us navigate the grieving process. Despite the prevalence of household pets, pet owners commonly report they experience disenfranchised grief after a pet's death (Adams, 2021). Although they may receive support for their loss initially, pet owners often feel a lack of support for the depth of their grief and feel rushed to get through the grieving process. Box 11.4 describes one person's experience after the death of a pet and provides resources.

Box 11.4: Grieving the Loss of a Pet

As you read the following vignette, consider these questions:

- » How do the bonds we form with pets differ from those we form with humans, and how might these differences shape our grieving process when a pet dies?
- » In what ways can the loss of a pet challenge societal expectations of grief, and what does this reveal about how we view animal companionship in relation to human relationships?
- » How can the mourning of a pet's death provide insights into broader themes of attachment, loss, and the role of animals in our emotional well-being?

* * *

Pippin came into my life as a puppy and was part of my life for fourteen years. He was a sweet, happy, goofy, intuitive dog. He was there for me through the roughest times in my life. He was there with love and emotional support when my husband wanted a divorce. He was there with love, emotional, and physical support as I battled cancer. He got me moving when I needed to walk. When Pippin was diagnosed with heart issues, I did everything to make his last years happy. He never let his heart slow him down until the day he collapsed in the kitchen. It was heartbreaking to euthanize him. After he passed, I heard from many people whose lives Pippin had touched. Many people understood my grief, but I'm sure many others did not. I will always have a dog in my life. Dogs provide unconditional and unending love without judgment.

Joyce, 2024

* * *

The following organizations offer resources to assist people grieving the loss of a pet:
- » The Association for Pet Loss and Bereavement, https//www.aplb.org
- » The Humane Society of the United States, https://www.humanesociety.org

---

Memorializing and Honoring

Throughout recorded history, people have created memorials and erected monuments to honor those who have died. Influenced by culture and religion, and shaped by the historical period, memorials preserve the memory of the deceased person and commemorate their life. Memorials provide an opportunity to acknowledge the significance of a life, no matter how short or long. This manner of honoring and paying respect allows us to celebrate life, share the deceased person's story, and recognize their impact on others. Memorializing the loss helps people remember, brings the bereaved together, presents the opportunity to share stories, and provides comfort and closure.

A memorial, whether personal or public, offers a place to grieve. Memorials, such as traditional grave markers, represent an enduring memory of a loved one and function as a gathering place for family and friends. They provide a place for survivors to reflect and focus on the memories of the deceased individual. Headstones and grave markers give people a designated space to work through and resolve any unfinished emotional issues with the deceased person. These tangible symbols of a life may also help the bereaved person feel supported and validated in their grief. Visits to a memorial site can provide people with a feeling of ongoing connection to the deceased person, which can ease their loneliness as they navigate the loss.

Remembering and honoring someone who has died can be connected to significant locations, symbolic items, or experiences and activities. While many people continue to visit the grave site or the place where their loved one's ashes were scattered, memorials and remembrances are not limited to a grave marker, columbarium niche, or final resting place. Families may choose to dedicate a bench in a park or formal public garden that the deceased person loved and visited. Others may plant a tree, shrub, or flowers, or create a memorial garden as a remembrance. Gathering to celebrate their birthday or participating in special events they found important can also be a meaningful way to honor a loved one. People often create a shrine or altar in their homes where they set out photos of their loved ones, personal memorabilia, religious items, or candles.

A person may opt to keep the cremains or have their loved one's ashes made into jewelry, a glass suncatcher, or statuary. Some companies will even convert cremains into memorial diamonds that can be worn. Keeping personal items of the deceased person, such as a piece of jewelry, an article of clothing, or an item they regularly used, can help maintain a feeling of connection. For example, two years after their dad's death, my daughter still drives her dad's truck, and my son uses his dad's woodworking tools; each item embodies years of shared memories.

Public Monuments

Public monuments are physical representations of our collective desire to honor those who have died. They are a means to reflect on the past and examine the present. Permanent memorials such as the Vietnam Veterans' Memorial, Martin Luther King, Jr. Memorial, and the Sandy Hook Memorial are established to honor the memories of those who influenced history, who sacrificed their lives for others, or whose tragic deaths impacted the lives of countless individuals, communities, and the nation at large (figure 11.6). These monuments are often strategically placed at or near specific sites where the deaths or events occurred. The construction of a large public memorial can take years, sometimes decades, to complete. It involves a long process to gain consensus on the design and secure a location and funding.

The functions of public memorials can be complex. They can provide solace and support the grieving process, but at the same time, they can cause distress. This can be especially true when the deaths resulted

Figure 11.6. Known as the "Stone of Hope," this granite memorial honors Martin Luther King, Jr. and his contributions to civil rights.

from a violent, traumatic event. A memorial site that is open to a whole community, with varied experiences and connections to the loss of life, can remind people of a tragedy but also resurface painful details and past experiences. Memorials provide a place for a community to grieve for their dead, but the design should strive to support visitors' need to "revisit rather than relive" the loss of life (as cited in Yuan, 2018).

Spontaneous Memorials

Public memorials can also emerge through impromptu collaboration. **Spontaneous memorials**, also known as spontaneous shrines or temporary memorials, are created after a person's untimely death or a tragic event where numerous deaths occurred. These temporary memorials appear within hours and continue to grow for days, weeks, or even months. The rapid public response to acknowledge and publicize untimely and violent deaths often starts with someone leaving some flowers near the site of the deaths. Others follow by bringing candles, pictures, mementos, and personal messages, adding to the public display of their grief for the lives lost and support for the survivors (figure 11.7).

Temporary shrines provide a gathering place that encourages people to reflect on a tragic incident. In the immediate aftermath of immense or untimely loss of life, when emotions are new and raw, spontaneous memorials become safe places where the stunned and grieving can find comfort and work through their individual and collective grief. Placing a memento at a memorial, along with countless others, is a comforting act that can give people a sense of purpose and help them feel less powerless. This act can mark a shift from being frozen in a state of numbness to feeling like they can begin to move forward.

Mass casualty events, whether they are human-made tragedies or natural disasters, often prompt communal expressions of grief. When people feel out of control, a deep-seated human desire

Figure 11.7. After Queen Elizabeth II's death on September 8, 2022, spontaneous memorials appeared across the United Kingdom with flowers, messages, and tributes.

emerges to bear witness to the tragedy. Feeling the need to do something and not knowing what, people leave symbolic items to acknowledge those who died. Large-scale tragic events also attract high-profile media attention, and details spread rapidly, reinforcing the sense of a shared national tragedy. As news spreads, the impact of these deaths extends beyond the immediate community. People may travel long distances to visit the memorial site and honor those who died.

In addition to traditional memorial items such as flowers, candles, photos, and personal messages, people frequently choose symbolic memorabilia that reflect the lives of the people who died. The structure, site, and items left at spontaneous memorials are often linked to the circumstances of the deaths. For example, within hours of the mass shooting at a 2017 country music festival in Las Vegas, Nevada, where sixty people died, a spontaneous memorial started to take shape. Among the traditional items, mourners left cowboy hats and boots, blue bandanas, spurs, and other symbols of country western culture (Winston, 2017).

After the 2013 death of nineteen members of the highly trained Granite Mountain Hotshot firefighting team, a spontaneous memorial was erected outside a nearby fire station in Prescott, Arizona. The deaths were memorialized with a temporary shrine consisting of nineteen shovels propped up against a fence in honor of the fallen firefighters. This site became a gathering place where friends, family, and community members could mourn the firefighters who died battling the fast-moving Yarnell Hill wildland fire. To express their grief and honor their service, visitors left purple balloons (a color traditionally representing fallen firefighters), shirts, caps, and gear with insignias representing fire departments from across the nation as well as from other countries (Gaynor, 2013).

Although not a mass casualty event, the sudden death of a high-profile individual who touches the lives of the public can elicit a very similar response. People often feel connected to public figures such as politicians, community leaders, entertainers, or athletes. We know details about their day-to-day lives and professional work, and follow them through media coverage, making it feel as if we know them personally. When Princess Diana died in 1997, memorials sprang up at the site of the car crash, Kensington Palace, the Princess' home, and at locations around the world. There were thousands of visitors to these spontaneous memorials who were moved to do something to express their sorrow and shared sense of grief (Eyre, 1999). Box 11.5 compares the different ways permanent and spontaneous memorials support communal grief.

Box 11.5: Permanent Versus Spontaneous Memorials

Both permanent and spontaneous memorials serve as forms of public grieving, allowing people to express their sorrow collectively in response to loss. However, they differ in their timing, audience, and lasting impact.

Spontaneous memorials are usually created in the immediate aftermath of a death or tragedy. These impromptu tributes—such as flowers, candles, photos, and handwritten notes—often appear at the site of the event. They provide an instant and emotional outlet for grief, drawing people who are nearby or directly affected by the loss. A well-known example of this is the spontaneous memorials that arose after the death of Princess Diana in 1997, when thousands of people left flowers, cards, and personal items outside Kensington Palace.

In some cases, spontaneous memorials evolve into permanent memorials. For example, after the 9/11 attacks, spontaneous displays of remembrance popped up across the United States at locations such as firehouses and Ground Zero. Over time, these temporary tributes were replaced with permanent structures, including the 9/11 Memorial & Museum in New York City.

Permanent memorials, by contrast, are more deliberate and long-lasting. These structures, statues, or plaques are often commissioned after time has passed, designed to provide a lasting tribute that can be visited for years to come. The Vietnam Veterans Memorial in Washington, DC, is a prominent example of a permanent memorial, serving as a long-term site of reflection and remembrance for those who died during the Vietnam War.

In essence, spontaneous memorials capture the raw, immediate response to loss, while permanent memorials offer a space for ongoing reflection and remembrance over time.

Roadside and Urban Corner Memorials

In the United States and many other countries around the world, spontaneous roadside memorials are created to honor roadway deaths. Typically, these impromptu shrines are placed alongside highways and streets to mark where the person died or the location that led to their death. Most commemorate those who died in vehicle crashes, but others may represent deaths of pedestrians, bicyclists, or victims of other violent, traumatic roadside incidents.

Roadside memorials are usually created by family and friends of the deceased person, but they can be created by community members as well. These memorials vary in form, size, and content. Some roadside memorials are anonymous with modest crosses, while others are more elaborate with flowers, candles, memorial signs, personal mementos, or other symbolic items. They may exist for a few weeks or may be maintained, refreshed, or added to for many months or even years.

While roadside expressions of grief and remembrance are common, they are also controversial. According to many, roadside memorials are more than just a statement of loss. They assert that memorials remind and warn others of the potential roadway dangers and encourage safer behaviors. Opponents of these spontaneous memorials argue that they distract drivers' attention, decreasing road safety. A recent study found that roadside memorials do capture drivers' visual attention, but the focus is relatively brief. The presence of memorials "did not affect perceived risk and did not produce a clear systematic effect on preferred travel speed" (Beanland & Wynne, 2019).

People often turn to roadside and urban corner memorials to honor and remember loved ones who have died, particularly in violent or untimely circumstances. These public displays, where family and friends leave flowers, trinkets, cards, balloons, or even artwork, become places of collective mourning and personal reflection. Whether due to a tragic accident, such as a driver striking two young girls playing in a leaf pile, or other devastating events like fires, murders, or armed attacks, these memorials allow people to express their grief tangibly while they continue to navigate their lives. In creating these spaces, individuals acknowledge the deep emotional impact of the loss and ensure that the memory of their loved ones lives on.

Legality

Roadside memorials are common across the country, but their legality exists in a complicated gray area. In many jurisdictions, such memorials are explicitly banned, yet enforcement is inconsistent. Local governments often refrain from removing or regulating these displays because of their emotional significance to the grieving families. Additionally, roadside memorials can serve as a sobering reminder to other motorists, possibly encouraging safer driving in high-risk areas.

In some states, such as Alabama, Arizona, and New York, laws prohibit all forms of roadside memorials. Despite this, it is not unusual for communities to exercise discretion, allowing the tributes to remain temporarily, especially in the immediate aftermath of a tragedy. However, when memorials obstruct public spaces or pose a safety hazard, enforcement may become stricter.

Other states strike a balance by allowing roadside memorials with specific restrictions. For example, regulations may limit the size, placement, or duration of these displays. Some states only permit memorials for a limited time—usually three to six months—after which they must be removed. This approach aims to respect the grieving process while maintaining public safety and order along roadways.

Cyber Memorial

In addition to physical roadside memorials, the internet offers a virtual space for creating spontaneous shrines, allowing people to commemorate loved ones in ways that transcend geographical boundaries. Cyber shrines, often created through dedicated web pages or social media platforms, serve as digital memorials where friends and family members can share memories, post photographs, and honor the lives of those who have died. These virtual spaces often include photographs of the material shrines, photo montages, and other associated images, helping to preserve the memory of these physical tributes long after they have been removed or faded from the roadside.

One of the key features of cyber shrines is their accessibility. Unlike physical memorials, which are often limited by location and time, these virtual shrines allow individuals from all over the world to participate in the mourning process. Websites dedicated to these memorials usually provide features like virtual candles, where visitors can light a symbolic flame in memory of the deceased, or virtual condolence books, where people can leave messages of support and remembrance. These digital tools create an interactive environment, inviting a wider community to grieve together, share stories, and reflect on the impact of a life lost.

The rise of cyber shrines also speaks to the evolving ways in which people process grief in an increasingly digital age. As online spaces become more integrated into everyday life, they offer an additional layer of remembrance that complements traditional, physical memorials. For some, these virtual spaces provide a sense of permanence that physical shrines cannot, ensuring that the memory of their loved one remains accessible and active long after the roadside flowers or candles have disappeared. Box 11.6 explores other technological advances and their impact on the grieving process.

Box 11.6: Griefbots, Deathbots, and AI Ghosts

The technology exists to create a chatbot version of your loved one who has died, and some companies offer this service. These specialized chatbots, referred to as griefbots, deathbots, or AI (artificial intelligence) ghosts, simulate conversations with humans in real time. This same technology is used in home and phone devices such as Alexa or Siri and by businesses and organizations for routine tasks and customer interaction.

A griefbot is created by feeding it the deceased person's data, such as their social media posts, online messages, videos, photos, and emails. The program identifies patterns in the person's communications, preferences, interactions, and interests to generate a digital likeness. This griefbot can also be paired with a visual representation (an avatar) of the loved one to make it more lifelike.

Reliance on computer technology, internet resources, and social media has already become a part of the grieving process. Social media accounts often remain active after a person has died and can be turned into a memorial page where friends and family can share memories. Photo apps regularly display pop-up reminders of loved ones who have died. People can scroll through old messages and conversations (Stokes, 2021). Griefbots take this experience a step further by adding an interactive component that imitates how the loved one would have responded in a conversation.

The availability and commercialization of griefbots have prompted discussions about their impact on the grieving process (Krueger & Osler, 2023). Griefbots can provide companionship and fill the abrupt loss of shared time spent with the person who died. They can offer the opportunity to get answers to questions someone never had a chance to ask. Griefbots can be a virtual resource when coping with the emotions and changes in life after a death.

However, griefbots may also pose challenges during the grieving process. Grieving may be deferred, disrupted, or stalled when someone interacts with a griefbot. Having the ability to interact with the likeness of the person who died can limit one's emotional and psychological adjustment to the reality of the loss and adaptation to life without them. The bereaved person can also become dependent on the griefbot to fulfill the roles of the deceased. In response to these technological changes, funerary preplanning resources have begun encouraging people to leave written guidance about their preferences concerning their social media accounts and the use of their digital information.

* * *

Questions to consider:
> » Why might a person choose to engage with a griefbot while others would not?
> » If you could interact with a digital version of a loved one who has died, would you seize the opportunity, or do you find the idea off-putting?
> » What might be some ethical considerations when using the data and communications of a deceased loved one?

Conclusion

This chapter has explored the complexities of loss and the differences between grief, bereavement, and mourning. As you learned, grief refers to the emotional response to loss, an internal experience that can vary greatly from person to person. Bereavement is the state of having lost someone, a condition that encompasses the entire process of adapting to life without the deceased. Mourning, on the other hand, involves the outward expressions of grief, which are often shaped by cultural and social norms.

Various frameworks attempt to explain how individuals navigate the grief process, ranging from linear models like the stages of grief to more fluid approaches that acknowledge the unpredictability and individuality of each person's journey. Some theories emphasize the importance of integrating loss into one's life over time, while others focus on how people oscillate between grief and the need to continue with daily life.

Grief itself can take many forms. From anticipatory grief, which occurs before a loss happens, to complicated grief, which can feel never-ending, these types reflect the diverse ways that people experience and express loss. The nature of the death—whether sudden, violent, or accidental—plays a significant role in shaping how grief unfolds. In cases of unexpected loss, shock and trauma can intensify the grieving process, making it more difficult to cope.

Memorials, both personal and public, offer a means of remembering and honoring those who have passed. Whether through physical shrines, such as roadside or urban corner memorials, or digital tributes like cyber shrines, these expressions of remembrance provide comfort and help preserve the memory of loved ones. They also allow communities to share in the mourning process, transforming grief from a solitary experience into a collective act of remembrance.

As this book has shown, grieving is a complex, yet necessary and vital process after the loss of a loved one. Death triggers emotional and psychological reactions that need to be attended to and processed. These responses are affected by personal attributes, social structures, and cultural traditions and beliefs. Some grief feelings and responses may be commonly experienced, yet grief is also uniquely individual. Grief has no standard timetable or uniform trajectory. At first, it may be intense and then gradually decrease over time, or it may linger for long periods. It can come and go or unexpectedly pop up. As the opening vignette describes, those who are in supportive roles need to be there when they are needed, for as long as needed.

The grief experience is also affected by the type of relationship one has with the person who died.

A death leaves a hole in one's life; one's connection to and interactions with that person influence our response to that loss. For example, the death of a companion, a life partner, child, friend, coworker, political leader, or celebrity each represents a different type of loss and, therefore, a different grief experience. Their death can represent lost companionship, unfulfilled hopes and dreams, or uncertainty about the future. The type of loss and its meaning to the bereaved shape the grief experience, the kind of support they may need, and how they choose to memorialize their loved one.

Death is an unavoidable part of the human experience. No matter who you are, where you are in life, or the circumstances surrounding the end of life, death is never easy. It brings challenges, stress, sadness, and pain. The dying process and bereavement are times of adjustment as we learn to live without the person who has passed. Sometimes, we have the chance to prepare for the loss as death approaches. Other times, death comes unexpectedly, catching us off-guard and setting in place a different grief experience.

Expanding our understanding of the many facets of death, dying, and bereavement helps us prepare for the inevitable end of life. And there is comfort in knowing we are not alone. Becoming more familiar with death-related terminology and concepts expands our understanding of the death experience and increases our ability to understand what we and those around us are feeling and experiencing. It allows us to be more comfortable in talking about death and communicating our grief. We can also become more effective in listening and responding to others who need our support.

For professionals who work in death-related occupations or those who plan on entering these fields of work, expanding your understanding of death beyond the scope of your job can augment your training and expertise. Personal, social, and cultural factors shape the experience of dying and influence every aspect of death and grief. Social institutions, such as health care and governmental systems, impact the options and the processes available for those involved in caregiving, as well as the choices the dying person and their loved ones face.

What happens during the death experience before you become involved affects your work, and your work affects what happens next after you fulfill your duties. Developing a deeper and broader understanding of institutional factors, as well as social and cultural preferences, affects how you approach your work and how you support the dying person and their family.

Summary

» Social expectations shape how people behave in the bereavement role.
» Circumstances and the survivor's relationship influence the intensity, duration, and expression of grief.
» Mourning is the public acknowledgment of death and its impact on survivors.
» Grief models, like those of Kübler-Ross and Worden, illustrate common responses to loss and stages of grief.
» Grief is not a linear process and includes various types, such as normal, anticipatory, delayed, complicated, collective, and disenfranchised grief.

» The qualities of the relationship between the survivor and the deceased person, such as interconnectedness, expectations, and responsibilities, impact the grieving process.

» Memorials offer survivors a space to reflect on the deceased's life and their relationship with them.

Review Questions

1. What are the key differences between grief, bereavement, and mourning?
2. How do various frameworks explain the ways people move through the grieving process?
3. What types of grief exist, and how do they influence the experience and expression of loss?
4. In what ways do sudden, violent, or accidental deaths impact the experience of grief?
5. How are personal and public memorials used to honor and remember those who have died?

Key Terms

Review these key terms from the chapter. You can find their definitions in the glossary at the end of the book.

» abbreviated grief

» anticipatory grief

» bereavement

» collective grief

» complicated grief

» delayed grief

» disenfranchised grief

» grief

» memorials

» mourning

» normal grief

» private grief

» public monuments

» spontaneous memorials

» social stigma

» stages of grief model

Acknowledgments

This book has been the result of the collective efforts of numerous individuals. From the initial concept to the final publication, many talented people have played a crucial role. I owe a tremendous debt of gratitude to the entire Chemeketa Press team for making this book a reality. Their unwavering dedication, expertise, and guidance were instrumental in bringing my vision to life. The team walked me through the process, provided feedback and suggestions, and took care of every detail along the way.

A special thank you to my editors, Stephanie Lenox and Abbey Gaterud, whose patience, support, and encouragement were invaluable throughout this process. I also deeply appreciate the assistance of Chemeketa's research librarians, Kathleen Veldhuisen, Theresa Yancey, and Michele Burke. Their time and expertise in navigating databases and finding essential references were instrumental in the creation of this book.

Thank you to my peer reviewers, Carlos Lopez and Sharon Benjamin, whose insightful and constructive feedback significantly enhanced the quality of this work. I also extend my gratitude to the students who provided extensive feedback on earlier drafts of this book. Their perspectives and suggestions refined and improved the content, ensuring its relevance and accessibility.

To the many professionals whose work routinely involves death and dying who were willing to share their expertise and insights, I offer my profound gratitude for your time and openness. Your contributions provided valuable perspectives that enriched the depth and authenticity of this book. The collective understanding of death, dying, and bereavement you bring to your work is so impactful and has greatly influenced the content of this book. I am also deeply grateful to all those who shared their personal stories about death and dying. Your willingness to openly recount such intimate and personal experiences has provided a depth of understanding about how academic content plays out in real people's lives.

A heartfelt thank you to my friends and family who have been with me every step of the way as I wrote this book. Their unwavering support and encouragement have been a constant source of strength. They have been my sounding board, offering feedback and suggestions that have helped shape the content of this book. Their patience and understanding have allowed me to navigate the challenges of writing, and their belief in me has kept me motivated and inspired. Special thanks to Stacy and Karen, whose steadfast support has been especially impactful as they walked with me throughout this process. And to my children, Sgt. Peter Antoine, Dr. Sarah-Cate Antoine, EMS Telecommunications Operations Supervisor Rosa Antoine, and Sgt. Torin Liden, who have always been my strength and my pride and whose professional paths have been a tremendous source of inspiration throughout this journey.

Glossary

Abbreviated grief: a foreshortened grieving process that moves more quickly than is typical. (Chapter 11)

Active dying, active dying phase: the final stage of the death experience; generally, within a few days or hours of death. (Chapter 4, 7)

Active listening: the act of being attentive to the speaker, asking questions, and paraphrasing to ensure you understand what is being said. (Chapter 4)

Aesthetics: the appreciation of beauty, artistic values, and pleasing appearance. (Chapter 3)

Affordable Care Act (ACA): a comprehensive health care reform law and its amendments that address health insurance coverage, health care costs, and preventive care. (Chapter 8)

Agents of socialization: social institutions, social groups, and significant individuals that shape our beliefs and behaviors and help society function. (Chapter 2)

Amalgamation: the process of blending two different cultures to create a distinctively new culture. (Chapter 4)

Anticipatory grief: mourning responses that can be experienced before the impending death. (Chapter 11)

Aquamation: also referred to as water cremation, a process to dispose of the body that uses alkaline hydrolysis to break down the body's soft tissues. (Chapter 10)

Assimilation: the process of members of a subculture adopting aspects of a dominant culture. (Chapter 4)

Attended death: death that occurs in a health care setting or where there is an existing health care provider-patient relationship. (Chapter 10, 11)

Awareness contexts: the different levels of knowledge and acceptance of a medical situation, particularly in the terminal stages. (Chapter 7)

Bereavement: the period of sorrow and distress after the loss of a significant other. (Chapter 11)

Biological pathology: the study of the origin, nature, and trajectory of disease. (Chapter 5)

Body disposition: the method used for handling the remains of a deceased person. (Chapter 10)

Brain death: permanent and irreversible loss of brain functions, including brainstem reflexes. (Chapter 1)

Bureaucracy: an organization guided by rational thought and characterized by authority, a hierarchical chain of command, a clear division of labor, and explicit rules and procedures. (Chapter 8)

Celebration of life: a ceremony dedicated to honoring the positive aspects of a person's life. (Chapter 10)

Chronic disease: a condition lasting more than one year that requires ongoing medical attention and can lead to the death of a patient. (Chapter 5)

Clinical death: the customary method of determining death that centers on the cessation of basic vital signs of life, the absence of breathing, and a heartbeat. (Chapter 1)

Collective grief: the shared experience of loss when it affects a group of people, such as a community, a nation, or a global population. (Chapter 11)

Columbarium (plural: columbaria): a building, room, or freestanding wall designed to hold urns containing human cremains. (Chapter 10)

Comfort care: *see Palliative care.*

Complicated grief: sometimes referred to as prolonged grief; the experience of intense, persistent grief responses whereby the grieving process is slowed or halted by complications. (Chapter 11)

Confirmation bias: the tendency to interpret new evidence as a confirmation of one's existing beliefs or search for information that supports or confirms one's prior beliefs. (Chapter 5)

Coroner: a public official, not usually trained in medicine, who certifies the cause of death and may investigate deaths in unusual or suspicious circumstances. (Chapter 10)

Cremation: the thermal process of reducing human remains that also includes the subsequent mechanical pulverization of any remaining bone fragments into small particles. (Chapter 10)

Crowdsource (medical): an emerging trend that uses social media platforms to obtain medical information, diagnoses, and medical advice. (Chapter 5)

Cultural framework: the underlying structure or system that organizes and shapes one's beliefs, norms, values, and practices. (Chapter 4)

Cultural humility: the recognition that people's personal and cultural backgrounds impact the understanding of what should be done and how things should be done. (Chapter 4)

Cultural lag: when material culture changes faster than nonmaterial culture, resulting in a struggle to process the meaning and implications of the changes. (Chapter 6)

Culturally competent health care organization: an organization that, according to the American Hospital Association, "acknowledges the importance of culture, incorporates the assessment of cross-cultural relations, recognizes the potential impact of cultural differences, expands cultural knowledge, and adapts services to meet culturally unique needs." (Chapter 6)

Culture: a complex system of shared norms, language, symbols, beliefs, values, and specific rituals and practices. (Chapter 4)

Curative care: the traditional approach of Western medical facilities aimed at addressing illness or disease through treatment to promote recovery. (Chapter 8)

Death certificate: official government statement that includes the cause, date, and place of death as well as personal identifying and demographic information. (Chapter 10)

Death trajectories: Common patterns found at the end of life; end-of-life projection plotted on x-y graphs that consider the length of time to death, course of the dying process, and likely causes of death. (Chapter 7)

Death-accepting perspective: a way of thinking that accepts or affirms the realities of death. (Chapter 2)

Death-denying perspective: a way of thinking that attempts to avoid or mask the realities of death. (Chapter 2)

Death-positive movement: a movement that includes social activities such as death cafes that promote the awareness and acceptance of death through open discussion. (Chapter 2)

Decedent: a person who has passed away, typically used in legal contexts concerning estates, inheritance, or judicial affairs. (Chapter 10)

Delayed grief: the experience of a deferred grief process. (Chapter 11)

Diagnosis: the determination and technical description of the nature and circumstances of disease, injury, or congenital defect. (Chapter 5)

Direct burial: entombment that takes place quickly, generally without many of the typical funeral rites. (Chapter 10)

Disease trajectory: the likely progression of the disease over time, the manifestation of symptoms, needed treatment regimens, and the overall impact of the disease. (Chapter 5)

Disenfranchised grief: sometimes referred to as hidden grief; an experience of grief that is not socially acknowledged, culturally validated, or publicly mourned. (Chapter 11)

Dominant culture: the culture that possesses sufficient economic, political, and social power to establish its norms, values, and beliefs as the standard, which is reinforced by social structure and social institutions. (Chapter 3)

Embalming: the process of preserving a body from decay, usually involving the arterial injection of chemicals. (Chapter 10)

Final disposition: *see Body disposition.*

Funeral concierge: a professional who assists families with personalized planning and logistical coordination of funeral and memorial services. (Chapter 10)

Funeral director: a professional who manages funeral arrangements, coordinates services, and provides support to grieving families. (Chapter 10)

Funeral home: a business that provides services related to the care, preparation, and arrangements for a person's burial or cremation. It often includes facilities for memorial services, visitations, and the handling of legal documentation. (Chapter 10)

Funerary practices: practices related to the commemoration of the dead and the final disposition of the body. (Chapter 4)

Gender paradox of suicide: the discrepancy whereby women are more likely to attempt suicide, but men are much more likely to die by suicide. (Chapter 9)

Good death: a death that is free from avoidable distress, pain, and suffering and aligns with patients' and their families' wishes. (Chapter 7)

Green burial: an eco-friendly burial method where the body is interred in a biodegradable container without embalming or the use of nonbiodegradable materials. (Chapter 10)

Grief: the personal reaction to a loss. (Chapter 11)

Health literacy: the degree to which individuals can find, understand, and use information and services to inform health-related decisions and actions for themselves and others. (Chapter 5)

Home health agencies: organizations that provide medical services to patients in their homes. (Chapter 7)

Homicide: the intentional or unintentional killing of one person by another, often analyzed in sociology for its social, cultural, and structural causes and impacts. (Chapter 9)

Hospice: specialized, end-of-life health care focused on quality of life, comfort care, and medical, psychological, and social needs; treats the person and the symptoms of disease and illness rather than the disease itself. (Chapter 7)

Integrated delivery network (IDN): loosely connected provider groups, provider networks, and independent practices. (Chapter 8)

Interment: the process of placing a body or cremains in a final location, such as a cemetery or columbarium. (Chapter 4)

Lawn-style cemetery: a burial ground characterized by a formal arrangement of graves, trees, and shrubs to create a lawn-like setting. (Chapter 10)

Legal death: irreversible circulatory and respiratory cessation and whole-brain death, including brain stem reflexes. (Chapter 1)

Life events: significant occurrences or milestones, such as marriage, childbirth, or loss, that influence an individual's social roles and relationships. (Chapter 1)

Mass casualty incident: an event causing a large number of injuries or deaths, overwhelming local resources, and requiring coordinated emergency response. (Chapter 9)

Master status: a social position that supersedes all the other social statuses a person may hold. In a sociological context, master status refers to the primary status position of an individual that shapes their interactions and relationships with others in a particular context. (Chapter 7)

Medicaid: a federal health care program that covers medical costs for people who qualify based on their limited income and available resources. (Chapter 8)

Medical examiner: a public official, usually a physician, who investigates death in unusual or suspicious circumstances. (Chapter 10)

Medicare: a national health insurance program for older and disabled individuals. (Chapter 8)

Memorial park: a designated area, often landscaped and maintained, where deceased individuals are memorialized through plaques, markers, or dedicated spaces. (Chapter 10)

Memorial service: an end-of-life gathering held without the remains present or that takes place after the final disposition of the body. (Chapter 10)

Memorials: events or monuments designed to preserve the memory of the deceased person and commemorate their life. (Chapter 11)

Microculture: subgroups within a subculture. (Chapter 4)

Mortality rates: statistical measurements that represent the frequency of deaths in a given population over a specified period. (Chapter 10)

Mortician: a professional responsible for preparing bodies for burial or cremation and arranging funerals. (Chapter 10)

Mortuary cosmetologist: a specialist who applies cosmetic and restorative techniques to prepare deceased individuals for viewing. (Chapter 10)

Mourning: the expression of grief. (Chapter 11)

Multicultural society: a society that includes a diverse array of ethnic and cultural groups. (Chapter 3)

Natural organic reduction (NOR): also referred to as human composting, a process that involves recreating the conditions found in the natural world that facilitate the body's decomposition. (Chapter 10)

Non-transplant anatomical donation organizations (NADO): organizations that recover anatomical specimens used for scientific research and medical education. Specimens are not used for human transplants. (Chapter 10)

Normal grief: sometimes referred to as uncomplicated grief; an expression of grief that suggests that a person is processing their thoughts, behaviors, and feelings in a way that is typical within their cultural context. (Chapter 11)

Nursing care facilities: residential facilities that provide personal and medical care for people who don't need to be in the hospital but can't be cared for at home. (Chapter 7)

Open-disclosure model: a frank discussion between the health care provider and the patient concerning the medical facts, available options, and the expected outcomes of the situation. (Chapter 6)

Open market: an economic system where goods and services are traded freely, with prices determined by supply and demand rather than centralized control. (Chapter 8)

Palliative care: also known as comfort care; the provision of practical social and emotional support in addition to needed medical care at the end of life; this specialized medical care focuses on the relief of pain and symptoms based on what matters most to the patient. (Chapters 7, 8)

Patient-centered care: a health care approach that prioritizes the needs, preferences, and values of patients in planning and delivering care. (Chapter 6)

Placebo effect: the psychological phenomenon in which changes in physical or mental health are attributed to a treatment or medication, regardless of whether the change or the correlation to the treatment is real. (Chapter 6)

Potter's field: a dedicated space for the burial of indigent, unclaimed, or unknown persons. (Chapter 10)

Precision medicine: customized health care and treatment decisions tailored to an individual based on factors such as genetics, environment, and lifestyle instead of a one-drug or one-treatment-fits-all approach. (Chapter 6)

Private grief: the personal and individual experience of mourning, distinct from public or communal expressions of loss. (Chapter 11)

Profane: the everyday concerns of the individual; the opposite of sacred. (Chapter 4)

Public monuments: structures or sculptures created to commemorate individuals, events, or cultural values, often serving as focal points for collective memory and public mourning. (Chapter 11)

Quality-of-life perspective: the belief that quality of life is based on a personal standard of health, comfort, happiness, and purpose. (Chapter 7)

Register of death: an official record maintained by governmental or authorized entities that documents the occurrence of deaths. (Chapter 10)

Religion: a social institution or community that shares beliefs and practices about a power greater than themselves. (Chapter 4)

Religious framework: a system organized around finding meaning, purpose, and a sense of connection to a higher presence. (Chapter 4)

Right-to-die legislation: laws that allow terminally ill patients who meet legally specified criteria to end their life by taking doctor-prescribed medication; also referred to as death with dignity, aid-in-dying, or medical aid in dying. (Chapter 7)

Rites of passage: an action or event that marks a change in a person's social status and their social role expectations. (Chapter 4)

Rural cemetery: park-like spaces removed from an urban environment to allow mourners to spend time in nature while visiting the graves of loved ones. (Chapter 10)

Sacred: elements that are associated with a higher power, worthy of devotion and reverence, and are set apart from routine daily activities; the opposite of the profane. (Chapter 4)

Sanctity-of-life perspective: the belief that all life is sacred and has intrinsic meaning. (Chapter 7)

Secondary traumatic stress (STS): emotional distress experienced by individuals indirectly exposed to the trauma of others, often through caregiving or professional roles. (Chapter 9)

Shared decision-making model: an emphasis on traditional family-centered choices about health care. (Chapter 6)

Social conflict approach: a sociological theory that examines how issues surrounding power and competition for resources impact social order, social structure, and social processes. (Chapter 1)

Social construction of reality: the process whereby people create a shared reality through their observations, actions, and social interaction that is then experienced as the objective reality. (Chapter 2)

Social death: the loss of social identity, loss of social connectedness, and loss associated with the disintegration of the body. (Chapter 1)

Social institution: an organized system with a recognized purpose to meet a societal need, such as the institutions for education, religion, government, family, mass media, medicine, science, and the military. (Chapter 2)

Social location: a sociological concept that examines how variables such as age, race, gender, marital status, education, or social class affect how people see, understand, and experience the world. (Chapter 1)

Social status: a person's social position or ranking in relation to other people within society. (Chapter 1)

Social stigma: a social attribute or behavior that marks a person or group for differing social treatment. (Chapter 5, 11)

Socialization: the process by which people learn the characteristics, beliefs, and behaviors of the groups to which they belong. (Chapter 2)

Society: a group of people who are involved with each other through persistent interactions, or a large social grouping sharing the same geographical or social territory. (Chapter 2)

Socioeconomic status (SES): a more total measure of social class or social standing in society. Often measured by an index of income, wealth, occupation, and social prestige. (Chapter 5)

Sociohistorical context: how historical events and social practices influence each other. (Chapter 2)

Spontaneous memorials: informal, temporary tributes created at sites of loss or tragedy to honor and remember those affected. (Chapter 11)

Stages of grief model: a framework introduced by Elisabeth Kübler-Ross that marked a sociocultural shift in the understanding of the psychological and emotional experiences surrounding death and dying; also referred to as the DABDA model for the five commonly experienced stages involved in the acceptance of end-of-life: denial, anger, bargaining, depression, and acceptance. (Chapter 11)

Structural-functional approach: a sociological theory that focuses on the structure of society and how it is organized and designed to meet the needs of society with specific attention to social institutions. (Chapter 1)

Subculture: a distinct group within a dominant culture that maintains its own separate beliefs and practices. (Chapter 3)

Sudden traumatic death: sudden unexpected death caused by a violent action or situation; causes intense and overwhelming emotional responses. (Chapter 9)

Suicidal ideation: thinking about, considering, or planning suicide. (Chapter 9)

Suicide: death caused by self-directed injurious behavior with the intent to die as a result of the behavior. (Chapter 9)

Suicide cluster: an excessive number of suicides or suicide attempts, more than would be normally expected, that occur in close time or geographic proximity. (Chapter 9)

Suicide contagion: the phenomenon where exposure to suicide or suicidal behavior within a community increases the risk of others contemplating or attempting suicide. (Chapter 9)

Symbolic interaction approach: a sociological theory that focuses on the study of how people communicate and interact; emphasizes the role of socially shared symbols, language, and social constructs and how they shape patterns of socially expected interaction. (Chapter 1)

Technical imperative: the belief that new technological advancements are inevitable and necessary and must be accepted and used for the overall good of society. (Chapter 6)

Thanatology: the scientific study of death, dying, and bereavement. (Chapter 1)

Traditional burial: a funeral practice in which the body is prepared, placed in a casket, and present at the funeral service, followed by burial or entombment. (Chapter 10)

Trauma: a deeply distressing or disturbing experience, often with lasting psychological, emotional, or physical impacts. (Chapter 9)

Trauma-informed care (TIC): an approach to health care and services that acknowledges the prevalence of trauma, seeks to avoid re-traumatization, and prioritizes safety, empowerment, and healing for individuals. (Chapter 9)

Treatment adherence: the extent to which a patient consistently follows a prescribed medical or therapeutic regimen to achieve desired health outcomes. (Chapter 6)

Treatment plan: a care plan to meet the patient's health needs and track progression toward treatment goals. (Chapter 6)

Tricare: government-sponsored health insurance program that covers nearly 10 million current and former members of the military and their dependents. (Chapter 8)

Unattended death: death that occurs outside an existing health care provider-patient relationship or where the deceased may not be found for days, weeks, or longer. (Chapter 10)

Undertaker: the historically used term for the role of mortician, which is the preferred, current job title in the United States. (Chapter 10)

Underinsured: the state of being insured but not having enough coverage to meet the full cost of a claim. (Chapter 8)

Veterans Health Administration (VHA): the largest integrated health care system in the United States providing benefits to Armed Services veterans, including Reserve Units and the National Guard, who have met service minimums. (Chapter 8)

Western medicine: sometimes referred to as allopathic medicine, a system of evidence-based medicine that uses scientifically proven treatments to address specific emergent diseases and ailments. (Chapter 1)

Whole body donation: the agreement to give one's entire body to science after death for research and education. (Chapter 10)

References

Chapter 1

American Medical Association. (1968, August 5). A definition of irreversible coma: Report of the Ad Hoc Committee of the Harvard Medical School to examine the definition of brain death. *JAMA, 205*(6), 337–340. https://doi.org/10.1001/jama.1968.03140320031009

Ansell, C. (1997). A personal memoir of Herman Feifel. In S. Strack (Ed.), *Death and the quest for meaning: Essays in honor of Herman Feifel*. Aronson.

Association for Death Education and Counseling. (n.d.). Mission and vision. https://www.adec.org/page/Mission_Statement

Baan, A., Allo, M. D. G., & Patak, A. A. (2022). The cultural attitudes of a funeral ritual discourse in the indigenous Torajan, Indonesia. *Heliyon, 8*(2), e08925. https://pubmed.ncbi.nlm.nih.gov/35198784/

Bliatout, B. T. (1993). Hmong death customs: Traditional and acculturated. In D. P. Irish, K. F. Lundquist, & V. J. Nelson (Eds.), *Ethnic variations in dying, death, and grief: Diversity in universality* (pp. 79–100). Taylor & Francis. https://doi.org/10.4324/9781315798547

Bondeson, Jan. (2002). *Buried alive: The terrifying history of our most primal fear*. Norton.

Cage, F. (2020, April 30). *When medical resources are limited, who should get care first?* Reuters. https://www.reuters.com/graphics/HEALTH-CORONAVIRUS/ETHICS/oakpezqllvr/

Corr, C. A. (1992). A task-based approach to coping with dying. *Omega, 24*(2), 81–94. https://doi.org/10.2190/CNNF-CX1P-BFXU-GGN4

Corr, C. A. & Corr, D. M. (2003). Death education. In C. Bryant (Ed.), *Handbook of death and dying* (Vol. 1, pp. 293–301). Sage.

DeSpelder, L. A. & Strickland, A. L. (2007). Culture, socialization, and death education. In D. Balk (Ed.), *Handbook of thanatology* (pp. 303–314). Routledge.

Emanual, E. J., Persad, G., Upshur, R., Thome, B., Parker, M., Glickman, A., Zhang, C., Boyle, C., Smith, M., & Phillips, J. P. (2020, March 23). Fair allocation of scarce medical resources in the time of COVID-19. *The New England Journal of Medicine, 382*(21), 2049–2055. https://doi.org/10.1056/NEJMsb2005114

Fine, R. L. (2005, October). From Quinlan to Schiavo: Medical, ethical, and legal issues in severe brain injury. *Baylor University Medical Center Proceedings, 18*(4), 303–310. https://doi.org/10.1080/08998280.2005.11928086

Georgiou, A. (2024, March 27). Archaeologists discover 6,000-year-old burial mounds at future Intel site. *Newsweek*. https://www.newsweek.com/archaeologists-discover-6000-year-old-burial-mounds-future-intel-site-1880523

Hajar, R. (2012, October). The air of history (part II) medicine in the Middle Ages. *Heart Views, 13*(4), 158–162. https://doi.org/10.4103/1995-705X.105744

Hook, C. C., & Mueller, P. S. (2005). The Terri Schiavo saga: The making of a tragedy and lessons learned [Special issue]. *Mayo Clinic Proceedings, 80*(11), 1449–1460. https://doi.org/10.4065/80.11.1449

Kastenbaum, R. J. (1993). Reconstructing death in postmodern society. *Omega, 27*(1), 75–89. https://doi.org/10.2190/P4XJ-EGNE-E157-G3

Kemp, A. R. (2014). *Death, dying, and bereavement in a changing world*. Pearson.

Králová, J. (2015). What is social death? *Journal of the Academy of Social Sciences, 10*(3), 235–248. https://doi.org/10.1080/21582041.2015.1114407

Nair-Collins, M. (2024, July). The Uniform Determination of Death Act is not changing. Will physicians continue to misdiagnose brain death? *The American Journal of Bioethics*, 1–12. https://doi.org/10.1080/15265161.2024.2371129

Narayanan, V. (2021). Treatise of thanatology [Letter to the editor]. *Indian Journal of Palliative Care, 27*(4), 580–582. https://doi.org/10.25259/IJPC_106_21

Noppe, I. C. (2007). Historical and contemporary perspectives on death education. In D. Balk (Ed.), *Handbook of thanatology* (pp. 329–335). Routledge.

Morey, A. I. & Kitano, M. K. (1997). *Multicultural course transformation in higher education*. Allyn & Bacon.

Schroeder, H., Margaryan, A., Szmyt, M., Theulot, B., Włodarczak, P., Rasmussen, S., Gopalakrishnan, S., Szczepanek, A., Konopka, T., Jensen, T. Z. T., Witkowska, B., Wilk, S., Przybyła, M. M., Pospieszny, Ł., Sjögren, K.-G., Belka, Z., Olsen, J., Kristiansen, K., Willerslev, E., … Allentoft, M. E. (2019, May 28). Unraveling ancestry, kinship, and violence in a Late Neolithic mass grave. *Proceedings of the National Academy of Sciences of the United States of America, 116*(22), 10705–10710. https://pmc.ncbi.nlm.nih.gov/articles/PMC6561172/

Strack, S. (2003). Feifel, Herman. In R. J. Kastenbaum (Ed.), *Macmillan encyclopedia of death and dying* (Vol. 1, pp. 286–288). Macmillan.

Toller, P. W. (2008). Bereaved parents' negotiation of identity following the death of a child. *Communications Studies, 59*(4), 306–321. https://doi.org/10.1080/10510970802467379

Wass, H. (2003). Death education. In R. J. Kastenbaum (Ed.), *Macmillan encyclopedia of death and dying* (Vol. 1, pp. 211–218). Macmillan.

Whitbourne, S. K. (1987). Personality development in adulthood and old age: Relationships among identity style, health, and well-being. In K. W. Schaie (Ed.), *Annual Review of Gerontology and Geriatrics*, Vol. 7, pp. (189–216). Springer Publishing Company. https://psycnet.apa.org/record/1988-97081-008

Chapter 2

American Academy of Child and Adolescent Psychiatry. (2020). *Screen time and children*. Facts for Family Guide. https://www.aacap.org/AACAP/Families_and_Youth/Facts_for_Families/FFF-Guide/Children-And-Watching-TV-054.aspx

Adler, B. (Ed.). (2007). *Letters from Vietnam*. Penguin Random House.

Anstett, É. (2022). Never-ending funerals. Annual burials and reburials of victims of mass violence in present-day Bosnia and Herzegovina. *Death Studies, 47*(6), 666–678. https://doi.org/10.1080/07481187.2022.2131046

Bassett, J. F., & Bussard, M. L. (2021). Examining the complex relation among religion, morality, and death anxiety: Religion can be a source of comfort and concern regarding fears of death. *Omega, 82*(3), 467–487. https://doi.org/10.1177/0030222818819343

Berger P. & Luckmann T. (1966). *The social construction of reality: A treatise in the sociology of knowledge*. Doubleday.

Bertman, S. L. (2003). Visual arts. In R. J. Kastenbaum (Ed.), *Macmillan encyclopedia of death and dying* (Vol. 2, pp. 913–917). Macmillan.

Brooks, M. (2023, October). How much screen time is too much? *Psychology Today*. https://www.psychologytoday.com/us/blog/tech-happy-life/201812/how-much-screen-time-is-too-much

Centers for Disease Control and Prevention. (2020, May 15). QuickStats: Percentage of deaths, by place of death—National vital statistics system, United States, 2000–2018. *Morbidity and Mortality Weekly Report, 69*(611), http://dx.doi.org/10.15585/mmwr.mm6919a4

Chan, S., & Williams, D. (2021, April 29). *A deadly California wildfire was set to cover up a murder, authorities say*. CNN. https://www.cnn.com/2021/04/29/us/california-wildfire-murder-trnd/index.html

Crawford, N. C. (2013). *Accountability for killing: Moral responsibility for collateral damage in America's post-9/11 wars*. Oxford University Press. https://doi.org/10.1093/acprof:oso/9780199981724.003.0001

Duncan, A. (2023, December 29). Memento mori and vanitas. *The Art Story*. https://www.theartstory.org/definition/memento-mori-vanitas/

Eshbaugh, E., & Henninger, W. (2013, March 1). Potential mediators of the relationship between gender and death anxiety. *Individual Differences Research, 11*(1), 22–30.

Flintoff, C. (2012, June 25). *In Alaskan cemetery, native and orthodox rites mix*. NPR. https://www.npr.org/2012/06/25/155431017/in-alaskan-cemetery-native-and-orthodox-rites-mix

Hartig, H., & Doherty, C. (2021, September 2). *Two decades later, the enduring legacy of 9/11.* Pew Research Center. https://www.pewresearch.org/politics/2021/09/02/two-decades-later-the-enduring-legacy-of-9-11/

Kastenbaum, R. J. (2012). *Death, society, and human experience* (11th ed.). Pearson.

Leming, M. R. (1980). Religion and death: A test of Homans' thesis. *Omega, 10*(4), 347–64.

Leming, M. R. & Dickinson, G. E. (2020). *Understanding dying, death, and bereavement* (9th ed.). Cengage.

Meier, A. (2017, October 16). Luxurious, terrifying visions of death in Renaissance memento mori. *Hyperallergic.* https://hyperallergic.com/396888/luxurious-terrifying-visions-of-death-in-renaissance-memento-mori/

National Hospice and Palliative Care Organization. (2020, August 17). *NHPCO releases new facts and figures report on hospice care in America* [Press release]. Retrieved from https://www.nhpco.org/hospice-facts-figures/

Natural disaster risks in Houston. (n.d.). *Understanding Houston.* https://www.understandinghouston.org/topic/disasters/disaster-risks#resources

Nesbitt, R. (2024, May 23). *Burlingame student's artwork to be displayed at US capitol.* KRON4. https://www.kron4.com/news/bay-area/burlingame-students-artwork-to-be-displayed-at-us-capitol/

Orrell, B., Cox, D. A., & Wall, J. (2022, October 25). *The social workplace: Social capital, human dignity, and work in America* [Survey report]. Survey Center on American Life. https://www.americansurveycenter.org/research/the-social-workplace-social-capital-human-dignity-and-work-in-america/

Pajari, I. (2015). Soldier's death and the logic of sacrifice. *COLLeGIUM: Studies across Disciplines in the Humanities and Social Sciences, 19,* 179–201. http://hdl.handle.net/10138/158351

Pentaris, P., & Tripathi, K. (2022, May 16). Palliative professionals' views on the importance of religion, belief, and spiritual identities toward the end of life. *International Journal of Environmental Research and Public Health, 19*(10), 6031. https://pmc.ncbi.nlm.nih.gov/articles/PMC9141656/

Rakha, N. (2009). *The crying tree.* Random House.

Schonfeld, D. J., & Kappelman, M. (1992, March 4). Teaching the toughest lesson—about death. *Education Week.* https://www.edweek.org/education/opinion-teaching-the-toughest-lesson-about-death/1992/03

Solano County Office of Emergency Services. (n.d.) *LNU Lightning Complex Fires.* https://www.solanocounty.com/depts/oes/lnu_lightning_complex_fire/default.asp

Stanford Medicine Children's Health. (n.d.) *A child's concept of death.* https://www.stanfordchildrens.org/en/topic/default?id=a-childs-concept-of-death-90-P03044

Statista Research Department. (2024, August 12). *United States: How afraid are you of death?* Statista. https://www.statista.com/statistics/959347/fear-of-death-in-the-us/

Substance Abuse and Mental Health Administration. (2017). *Tips for survivors: Coping with grief after a disaster or traumatic event.* U.S. Department of Health & Human Services. https://store.samhsa.gov/sites/default/files/d7/priv/sma17-5035.pdf

Sumiala, J., & Hakola, O. (2013). Introduction: Media and death [Special issue]. *Thanatos, 2*(2). https://journal.fi/thanatos/article/view/131943/80607

Thomas, W. I., & Thomas, D. S. (1928). *The child in America: Behavior problems and programs.* Knopf.

Weaver, J. D. (2013). Disasters. In R. J. Kastenbaum (Ed.), *Macmillan encyclopedia of death and dying.* (Vol. 1, pp. 231–240). Macmillan.

Weiskittle, R. E. & Gramling, S. E. (2018). The therapeutic effectiveness of using visual art modalities with the bereaved: A systematic review. *Psychology Research and Behavior Management, 11,* 9–24. https://doi.org/10.2147/PRBM.S131993

West Virginia Office of Miners' Health, Safety, and Training. (2010). *West Virginia Upper Big Ranch Mine Disaster investigative report summary.* https://minesafety.wv.gov/PDFs/Performance/EXECUTIVE%20SUMMARY.pdf

Whitman, Walt. (2021) *Leaves of grass.* Project Gutenberg. (Original work published 1855) https://www.gutenberg.org/cache/epub/1322/pg1322-images.html#link2H_4_0185

Chapter 3

AJMC Staff. (2021, January). *A timeline of COVID-19 developments 2020*. American Journal of Managed Care. https://www.ajmc.com/view/a-timeline-of-covid19-developments-in-2020

Ayodeji, O. (2013, December). Christians' perception of the concepts of death and judgment: A multimodal discourse analytical study of selected editions of *Christian Women Mirror* magazine. *International Journal of English and Literature, 4*(10), 508–511. https://academicjournals.org/article/article1383744854_Ayodeji.pdf

Boisi Center for Religion & American Public Life. (n.d.). *An introduction to Christian theology* [Papers on religion in the United States]. Boston College. https://www.bc.edu/content/dam/files/centers/boisi/pdf/bc_papers/BCP-Christianity.pdf

Boone, R. (2021, September 7). *Idaho hospitals begin rationing health care amid COVID surge*. Associated Press. https://apnews.com/article/business-health-public-health-coronavirus-pandemic-idaho-db21f9a14254996144e78aafb1518259

Brean, D. R. (2019, September 19). *Memory and mourning: Death in the gilded age*. The Frick Pittsburgh. https://www.thefrickpittsburgh.org/Story-Memory-and-Mourning-Death-in-the-Gilded-Age

Bushman, B. J., & Anderson, C. A. (2009). Comfortably numb: Desensitizing effects of violent media on helping others. *Psychological Science, 20*(3), 273–277. https://doi.org/10.1111/j.1467-9280.2009.02287.x

Celiberti, S. (2021, October 6). *Mid-late Victorian mourning dress*. Lancaster History. https://www.lancasterhistory.org/victorian-mourning-dress/

Centers for Disease Control and Prevention. (2018, March 21). *History of the 1918 flu pandemic*. U.S. Department of Health and Human Services, National Center for Immunization and Respiratory Diseases. https://www.cdc.gov/flu/pandemic-resources/1918-commemoration/1918-pandemic-history.htm

Centers for Disease Control and Prevention. (n.d.-a). *CDC Museum COVID-19 timeline*. U.S. Department of Health and Human Services. Retrieved October 7, 2022, from https://www.cdc.gov/museum/timeline/covid19.html

Centers for Disease Control and Prevention. (n.d.-b). *Leading causes of death, 1900–1998*. U.S. Department of Health and Human Services, National Center for Health Statistics. Retrieved October 7, 2022, from https://www.cdc.gov/nchs/data/dvs/lead1900_98.pdf

Concannon, D. (2020, September 25). *Are we becoming desensitized to mass death?* Alliant International University. https://www.alliant.edu/blog/are-we-becoming-desensitized-mass-death

Ducharme, J. (2018, January 24). Here's why you can shut out the shock of mass shootings. *Time*. https://time.com/5116457/kentucky-marshall-county-shooting-desensitization/

Eisenhower Foundation. (2020). *Cold war kids: Duck and cover*. https://www.eisenhowerfoundation.net/sites/default/files/2020-05/Duck%20and%20Cover%20lesson.pdf

Elflein, J. (2024, May 22). *COVID-19 deaths worldwide as of May 2, 2023, by country and territory*. Statista. https://www.statista.com/statistics/1093256/novel-coronavirus-2019ncov-deaths-worldwide-by-country/

Kearl, M. C. (2003). War. In R. J. Kastenbaum (Ed.), *Macmillan encyclopedia of death and dying*. (Vol. 2, pp. 924–927). Macmillan.

Kratz, J. (2018, January 25). *The first television war*. National Archives. https://prologue.blogs.archives.gov/2018/01/25/vietnam-the-first-television-war/

Library of Congress. (n.d.). *Television*. https://guides.loc.gov/american-women-moving-image/television

Mergen, B. (1999, October). ¿American? Studies: A dialogue across the Americas. *American Studies International, 37*(3), 5–17.

Mrug, S., Madan, A., Cook, E. W., & Wright, R. A. (2015, May). Emotional and physiological desensitization to real-life and movie violence. *Journal of Youth and Adolescence, 44*(4), 1092–1108. https://doi.org/10.1007/s10964-014-0202-z

National Cancer Institute. (2020, September 25). *Cancer statistics*. U.S. Department of Health and Human Services, National Institutes of Health. https://www.cancer.gov/about-cancer/understanding/statistics

National Park Service. (2011). *The custom of mourning during the Victorian era*. U.S. Department of the Interior. https://www.nps.gov/jofl/learn/historyculture/upload/MourningArticle2011.rtf

O'Neill, A. (2024, August 9). *United States: Life expectancy 1860–2020*. Statista. https://www.statista.com/statistics/1040079/life-expectancy-united-states-all-time

Pew Research Center. (2022, September). *Modeling the future of religion in America*. https://www.pewresearch.org/religion/2022/09/13/how-u-s-religious-composition-has-changed-in-recent-decades/

Rappaport, H. (2003). *Queen Victoria: A biographical companion*. Bloomsbury.

Reynolds, K. D., & Matthew, H. C. G. (2007). *Queen Victoria*. Oxford University.

Roberts, J. D. & Tehrani, S. O. (2020). Environments, behaviors, and inequalities: Reflecting on the impact of the influenza and coronavirus pandemics in the United States. *International Journal of Environmental Research and Public Health, 17*(12), 4484. https://doi.org/10.3390/ijerph17124484

Samuel, L. R. (2013). *Death American style: A cultural history of dying in America*. Rowman & Littlefield.

San Filippo, D. (2006, January). Historical perspectives on attitudes concerning death and dying. *Faculty Publication, 29*. https://digitalcommons.nl.edu/faculty_publications/29

Siegel, R. L., Giaquinto, A. N., & Jemal, A. (2024, January/February). Cancer statistics, 2024. *CA: A Cancer Journal for Clinicians, 74*(1), 12–49. https://doi.org/10.3322/caac.21820

Scot, A. (2022, June 27). A brief note on dominant culture and subculture. *Global Journal of Sociology and Anthropology, 11*(2), https://www.internationalscholarsjournals.com/articles/a-brief-note-on-dominant-culture-and-subculture-88619.html

Stevens, H. R., Oh, Y. J., & Taylor, L. D. (2021, July 16). Desensitization to fear-inducing COVID-19 health news on Twitter: Observational study. *Journal of Medical Internet Research, 1*(1). https://doi.org/10.2196/26876

Taylor, Lou. (1983). *Mourning dress: A costume and social history*. G. Allen and Unwin.

Thornton, R. (1990). *American Indian holocaust and survival: A population history since 1492*. Civilization of the American Indian Series. University of Oklahoma Press.

Warraich, H. (2018). *How modern medicine changed the way people die*. Wharton University of Pennsylvania Public Policy. https://knowledge.wharton.upenn.edu/article/modern-death/

Watkins, K. (2015). *It came across the Plains: The 1918 influenza pandemic in rural Nebraska* [Doctoral dissertation, University of Nebraska Medical Center]. DigitalCommons@UNMC. https://digitalcommons.unmc.edu/etd/42

U.S. Census Bureau. (2010). *Urban and rural populations in the United States*. Our World in Data. https://ourworldindata.org/grapher/urban-and-rural-populations-in-the-united-states

U.S. Census Bureau. (2017). *National population projections, 2015–2060, and National Center for Health Statistics Life Tables, 1960–2014* [Data set]. https://www.census.gov/data/tables/2017/demo/popproj/2017-summary-tables.html

U.S. Department of Veterans Affairs. (n.d.). *America's wars* [Fact sheet]. Office of Public and Intergovernmental Affairs. Retrieved October 7, 2022, from https://www.va.gov/opa/publications/factsheets/fs_americas_wars.pdf

U.S. Federal Civil Defense Administration. (1953). *Home shelters for family protection in atomic attack: Technical manual*. U.S. Government Printing Office. https://catalog.hathitrust.org/Record/102471767/Home

Vinovskis, M. A. (1976). Angels' heads and weeping willows: Death in early America. *Proceedings of the American Antiquarian Society, 86*(2) pp. 273–302. https://web.archive.org/web/20160906042954id_/http://www.americanantiquarian.org/proceedings/44524984.pdf

Chapter 4

American Society of Clinical Oncology. (2018, April). *Understanding grief within a cultural context*. Cancer.Net. https://web.archive.org/web/20230928211446/https://www.cancer.net/coping-with-cancer/managing-emotions/grief-and-loss/understanding-grief-within-cultural-context

Asad, K. W. & Nawait, M. S. (2018, May 16). Grief and bereavement practices among Igbo people of southeastern Nigeria: Implications for counseling. *Interdisciplinary Journal of Education, 1*(1), 110–121.

Beyers, J. (2017). Religion and culture: Revisiting a close relative. *HTS Theological Studies, 73*(1), a3864. https://doi.org/10.4102/hts.v73i1.3864

Brooten, D., Youngblut, J. M., Charles, D., Roche, R., Hidalgo, I., & Malkawi, F. (2016). Death rituals reported by White, Black, and Hispanic parents following the ICU death of an infant or child. *Journal of Pediatric Nursing, 31*(2), 132–140. https://doi.org/10.1016/j.pedn.2015.10.017

Cervank, U. (2017, September 26). *Traditional Romani mourning and funeral customs.* Ujaranza's Blog. https://ujaranzacervanak.wordpress.com/2017/09/26/traditional-romani-mourning-and-funeral-customs/

Chandratre, S., & Soman, A. (2021, August). End of life care practices for Hindu patients during COVID-19. *Journal of Palliative Care, 37*(1), 3–7. https://doi.org/10.1177/08258597211036243

Directorate General of Democracy and Human Dignity. (2023). *Religions and beliefs: Roma and travelers.* Council of Europe. https://rm.coe.int/factsheets-on-romani-culture-1-9-religion-and-beliefs/1680aac36d

Donovan, R., & Williams, A. M. (2015, January). Care-giving as a Canadian-Vietnamese tradition: "It's like eating, you just do it." *Health & Social Care in the Community, 23*(1), 79–87. https://doi.org/10.1111/hsc.12126

Durkheim, É. (1947). *The elementary forms of religious life* (J. Swain, Trans.) Free Press. (Original work published 1915)

Ekore, R. I., & Lanre-Abass, B. (2016). African cultural concept of death and the idea of advance care Directives. *Indian Journal of Palliative Care, 22*(4), 369–372. https://doi.org/10.4103/0973-1075.191741

Esposito, M. L., & Kahn-John, M. (2020, October 1). How should allopathic physicians respond to Native American patients hesitant about allopathic medicine? *AMA Journal of Ethics, 22*(10), E837–844. https://doi.org/10.1001/amajethics.2020.837

Gallup. (2024, March 29). *How religious are Americans?* https://news.gallup.com/poll/358364/religious-americans.aspx

Griffin, J. K. (2017, April 23). *Home-goings: A Black American funeral tradition.* Anthropological Perspectives on Death. https://web.archive.org/web/20240623034515/https://scholarblogs.emory.edu/gravematters/2017/04/23/home-goings-a-black-american-funeral-tradition/

Hui, D., Nooruddin, Z., Didwaniya, N., Dev, R., De La Cruz, M., Kim, S. H., Kwon, J. H., Hutchins, R., Liem, C., & Bruera, E. (2014, January). Concepts and definitions for "actively dying," "end of life," "terminally ill," "terminal care," and "transition of care": A systematic review. *Journal of Pain and Symptom Management, 47*(1), 77–89. https://pmc.ncbi.nlm.nih.gov/articles/PMC3870193/

Irwin, L. (2022, August 23). *Santeria.* Cuba on the Horizon. https://web.archive.org/web/20231209223329/https://cubaonthehorizon.cofc.edu/santeria/

Kaufert, J. M., & Putsch, R. W. (1997). Communication through interpreters in healthcare: Ethical dilemmas arising from differences in class, culture, language, and power. *The Journal of Clinical Ethics, 8*(1), 71–87. https://doi.org/10.1086/JCE199708111

Matsumura, S., Bito, S., Liu, H., Kahn, K., Fukuhara, S., Kagawa-Singer, M. & Wenger, N. (2002). Acculturation of attitudes toward end-of-life care. *Journal of General Internal Medicine, 17*(7), 531–539. https://pmc.ncbi.nlm.nih.gov/articles/PMC1495074/

Morris, R. A. (1991). *Old Russian ways: Cultural variation among three Russian groups in Oregon.* AMS Press. http://wigowsky.com/fob/RMbook.htm

Old Believers - religion and expressive culture. (n.d.). Countries and Their Cultures. Retrieved November 7, 2024, from https://www.everyculture.com/North-America/Old-Believers-Religion-and-Expressive-Culture.html#ixzz80IlELTlH

Pew Research Center. (December 12, 2022). *Key findings from the Global Religious Futures Project.* https://www.pewresearch.org/religion/2022/12/21/key-findings-from-the-global-religious-futures-project/

Romani customs and traditions: Death rituals and customs. (1997). The patrin web journal. https://oocities.org/~patrin/death.htm

Staudt, C. (2013, December). Whole-person, whole-community care at the end of life. *Virtual Mentor, 13*(12), 1069–1080. https://doi.org/10.1001/virtualmentor.2013.15.12.msoc1-1312

United States Conference of Catholic Bishops. (n.d.). *Anointing of the sick.* https://www.usccb.org/prayer-and-worship/sacraments-and-sacramentals/anointing-of-the-sick

United States Holocaust Memorial Museum. (2021, March 19). *Roma (gypsies) in pre-war Europe.* https://encyclopedia.ushmm.org/content/en/article/roma-gypsies-in-prewar-europe

Chapter 5

Baider, L. (2012, April). Cultural diversity: Family path through terminal illness. *Annals of Oncology, 23*(3), iii62–iii65. https://doi.org/10.1093/annonc/mds090

Doka, K. J. (1993). *Living with life-threatening illness: A guide for patients, their families, and caregivers.* Jossey-Bass/Wiley.

Drew, J., Cashman, S. B., Savageau, J. A., & Stenger, J. (2006). The visiting specialist model of rural healthcare delivery: A survey in Massachusetts. *Journal of Rural Health, 22*(4), 294–299. https://www.umassmed.edu/contentassets/6721bf81617f46c0a4757b66f821359b/a-little-known-aspect-of-health-care-delivery-in-rural-areas-the-visiting-specialist.pdf

Fehring, R. J., Miller, J. F., & Shaw, C. (1997, May). Spiritual well-being, religiosity, hope, depression, and other mood states in elderly people coping with cancer. *Oncology Nursing Forum, 24*(4), 663–671. PMID: 9159782.

Fontenot, J., Brigance, C., Lucas, R., & Stoneburner, A. (2024, May 8). Navigating geographical disparities: Access to obstetric hospitals in maternity care deserts and across the United States. *Pregnancy and Childbirth, 24*(1), 350. https://doi.org/10.1186/s12884-024-06535-7

Fox, S. & Duggan, M. (2013, January 15). *Health online 2013.* Pew Research Center, Pew Internet Project. https://www.pewinternet.org/wp-content/uploads/sites/9/media/Files/Reports/PIP_HealthOnline.pdf

Gass, M. A. (2021, November 24). *Risks and benefits of self-diagnosis using the internet.* Salem State University Digital Repository. https://digitalrepository.salemstate.edu/handle/20.500.13013/897

Gonsalves, G., & Staley, P. (2014, December 18). Pandemic, paranoia, and public health—the AIDS epidemic's lessons for Ebola. *New England Journal of Medicine, 371*(25), 2348–2349. https://doi.org/10.1056/NEJMp1413425

Groce, N. E., & Zola, I. E. (1993). Multiculturalism, chronic illness, and disability. *Pediatrics, 91*(5), 1048–1055. https://doi.org/10.1542/peds.91.5.1048

Guk, K., Han, G., Lim, J., Jeong, K., Kang, T., Lim, E. K., & Jung, J., (2019, June). Evolution of wearable devices with real time disease monitoring for personalized healthcare. *Nanomaterial, 9*(6), 813. https://doi.org/10.3390/nano9060813

Hagger, M. S., Koch, S., Chatzisarantis, N. L. D., & Orbell, S. (2017). The common sense model of self-regulation: Meta-analysis and test of a process model. *Psychological Bulletin, 143*(11), 1117–1154. https://doi.org/10.1037/bul0000118

Hung, P., Casey, M. M., Kozhimannil, K. B., Karaca, P., & Moscovice, I. S. (2018, February 16). Rural-urban differences in access to hospital obstetric and neonatal care: how far is the closest one? *Journal of Perinatology, 38.* 645–652. https://doi.org/10.1038/s41372-018-0063-5

Juckett, G. (2005). Cross-cultural medicine. *American Family Physician, 72*(11), 2267–2274.

Keisler-Starkey, K. & Bunch, L. (2021, September). *Health insurance coverage in the United States: 2020* (Report No. P60-274). U.S. Census Bureau Current Population Reports, U.S. Government Publishing Office. https://www.census.gov/content/dam/Census/library/publications/2021/demo/p60-274.pdf

Keselman, A., Arnott Smith, C., Murcko, A. C., & Kaufman, D. R. (2019, February). Evaluating the quality of health information in a changing digital ecosystem. *Journal of Medical Internet Research, 21*(2). https://doi.org/10.2196/11129

Kim, G. J., & Goldstein, L. (2017, November 9). The effects of religion and spirituality on coping efficacy for death and dying: Clear practitioner-patient communication offers patients who are dying the best chance of achieving a "good death." *Practical Pain Management, 17*(7). https://www.medcentral.com/pain/chronic/ehlers-danlos-syndrome-emerging-challenge-pain-management

Radionova, N., Ög, E., Wetzel, A.-J., Rieger, M. A., & Preiser, C. (2023, May 29). Impacts of symptom checkers for laypersons' self-diagnosis on physicians in primary care: Scoping review. *Journal of Medical Internet Research, 25.* e39219 https://doi.org/10.2196/39219

Rural Health Information Hub. (2022, November 11). *Healthcare access in rural communities.* https://www.ruralhealthinfo.org/topics/healthcare-access

Rural Health Information Hub. (n.d.). *Rural data explorer.* Retrieved February 3, 2023, from https://www.ruralhealthinfo.org/data-explorer?id=200

Tarakeshwar, N., Vanderwerker, L., Paulk, E., Pearce, M. J., Kasl, S. V., & Prigerson, H. G. (2006). Religious coping is associated with the quality of life of patients with advanced cancer. *Journal of Palliative Medicine, 9*(3), 646–57. https://doi.org/10.1089/jpm.2006.9.646

Valizadeh, L., Zamanzadeh, V., Negarandeh, R., Zamani, F., Hamidia, A., & Zabihi, A. (2016, March 1). Psychological reactions among patients with chronic hepatitis B: A qualitative study. *Journal of Caring Sciences, 5*(1), 57–66. https://doi.org/10.15171/jcs.2016.006

Van Wilder, L., Pype, P., Mertens, F., Rammant, E, Clays, E., Devleesschauwer, B., Boeckxstaen, P., & De Smedt, D. (2021, November 18). Living with a chronic disease: Insights from patients with a low socioeconomic status. *BMC Family Practice, 22*, 233–243. https://doi.org/10.1186/s12875-021-01578-7

Young, W. C., Nadarajah, S. R., Skeath, P. R., & Berger, A. M. (2015). Spirituality in the context of life-threatening illness and life-transforming change. *Palliative and Supportive Care, 13*(3), 656–660. https://doi.org/10.1017/S1478951514000340

Chapter 6

American Cancer Society. (n.d.). *Survival rates for breast cancer.* https://www.cancer.org/cancer/types/breast-cancer/understanding-a-breast-cancer-diagnosis/breast-cancer-survival-rates.html

American Hospital Association. (2013, June). *Becoming a culturally competent health care organization.* Health Research & Educational Trust. https://www.aha.org/system/files/hpoe/Reports-HPOE/becoming-culturally-competent-health-care-organization.PDF

Anderson, R. T. (1984). An orthopedic ethnography in rural Nepal. *Medical Anthropology, 8*(1), 46–59. https://doi.org/10.1080/01459740.1984.9965888

Atreja, A., Bellam, N., & Levy, S. R. (2005). Strategies to enhance patient adherence: Making it simple. *Medscape General Medicine, 7*(1), 4. https://pmc.ncbi.nlm.nih.gov/articles/PMC1681370/

Beavis, A., Krakow, M. Levison, K, & Rositch, A. F. (2018, November). Reasons for lack of HPV vaccine initiation in NIS-teen over time: Shifting the focus from gender and sexuality to necessity and safety. *Journal of Adolescent Health, 63*(5), 652–656. https://doi.org/10.1016/j.jadohealth.2018.06.024

Candib, L. M. (2002). Truth telling and advanced planning at end of life: Problems with autonomy in a multicultural world. *Family, Systems, and Health, 20*(3), 213–228. https://doi.org/10.1037/h0089471

Chakrabarti, S. (2014). What's in a name? Compliance, adherence and concordance in chronic psychiatric disorders. *World Journal of Psychiatry, 4*(2). https://doi.org/10.5498/wjp.v4.i2.30

Doka, K. J. (1993). *Living with life-threatening illness: A guide for patients, their families, and caregivers.* Jossey-Bass/Wiley.

Eibs, T., Koscalova, A., Nair, M., Grohma, P., Kohler, G., Bakhit, R. G., Thurashvili, M., Lasry, E., Bauer, S. W., & Jimenez, C. (2020, September 1). Qualitative study of antibiotic prescription patterns and associated drivers in Sudan, Guinea-Bissau, Central African Republic and Democratic Republic of Congo. *BMJ Open, 10.* https://pubmed.ncbi.nlm.nih.gov/32973055/

Fang, X., Sauter, D. A., & van Kleef, G. A. (2020). Unmasking smiles: the influence of culture and intensity on interpretations of smiling expressions. *Journal of Cultural Cognitive Science, 4*(3), 293–308. https://doi.org/10.1007/s41809-019-00053-1

Galanti, G. (2014). *Caring for patients from different cultures: Case studies from American hospitals* (5th ed.). University of Pennsylvania Press.

Health Literacy Council. (2022). *Everyday words for public communication.* Centers for Disease Control and Prevention. https://www.cdc.gov/ccindex/everydaywords/index.html

Hofmann, B. (2002). Is there a technological imperative in health care? *International Journal of Technology Assessment in Health Care, 18*(3), 675–689. https://doi.org/10.1017/S0266462302000491

Johnson, E., van Zijl, K., & Kuyler, A. (2023, October 13). Pain communication in children with autism spectrum: A scoping review. *Pediatric & Neonatal Pain, 5*(4), 127–141. https://doi.org/10.1002/pne2.12115

LeBlanc, T. W., & Tulsky, J. (2020). Discussing goals of care. *UpToDate*. Retrieved October 17, 2024, from https://www.uptodate.com/contents/discussing-goals-of-care

Matsumura, S., Bito, S., Liu, H., Kahn, K., Fukuhara, S., Kagawa-Singer, M. & Wenger, N. (2002). Acculturation of attitudes toward end-of-life care. *Journal of General Internal Medicine, 17*(7), 531–539. https://pmc.ncbi.nlm.nih.gov/articles/PMC1495074/

Mayo Clinic. (2021, November 16). *When cancer returns: How to cope with cancer recurrence*. https://www.mayoclinic.org/diseases-conditions/cancer/in-depth/cancer/art-20044575

Mayo Clinic. (n.d.). *Cancer treatment*. Retrieved October 21, 2022, from https://www.mayoclinic.org/tests-procedures/cancer-treatment/about/pac-20393344

Murdan, S., Wei, L., van Reit-Nales, D. A., Gurmu, A. E., Usifoh, S. F., Tăerel, A., Yıldız-Peköz, A., Krajnović, D., Azzopardi, L. M., Brock, T., Fernandes, A. I., Souza dos Santos, A. L., Anto, B. P., Vallet, T., Lee, E. E., Jeong, K., Akel, M., Tam, E., Volmer, D., ... Furnham, A. (2023, November 26). Association between culture and the preference for, and perceptions of, 11 routes of medicine administration: A survey in 21 countries and regions. *Exploratory Research in Clinical and Social Pharmacy, 12*, 100378. https://doi.org/10.1016/j.rcsop.2023.100378

National Cancer Institute. (2020, September 25). *Cancer statistics*. National Institutes of Health. https://www.cancer.gov/about-cancer/understanding/statistics

National Cancer Institute. (n.d.). Cancer. In *NCI dictionary of cancer terms*. Retrieved October 21, 2022, from https://www.cancer.gov/publications/dictionaries/cancer-terms/def/cancer

National Center for Health Marketing. (2007, October 3). Plain language thesaurus for health communications. Centers for Disease Control and Prevention. https://stacks.cdc.gov/view/cdc/11500

Nilchaikovit, T., Hill, J. M. & Holland, J. C. (1993). The effects of culture on illness behavior and care: Asian and American differences. *General Hospital Psychiatry, 15*(1), 41–50. https://doi.org/10.1016/0163-8343(93)90090-B

Ottawa Hospital Research Institute. (2015). *Ottawa personal decision guide*. https://decisionaid.ohri.ca/docs/das/OPDG.pdf

Ottawa Hospital Research Institute. (2021, October 12). *Patient decision aids: Ottawa decision support framework*. https://decisionaid.ohri.ca/odsf.html

PDQ Supportive and Palliative Care Editorial Board. (2014). PDQ planning the transition to end-of-life care in advanced cancer [Patient version]. *National Cancer Institute*, PMID: 26389514. https://www.cancer.gov/about-cancer/advanced-cancer/planning/end-of-life-pdq.

Rogger, R., Bello, C., Romero, C. S., Urman, R. D., Luedi, M. M., & Filipovic, M. G. (2023, July 5). Cultural framing and the impact on acute pain and pain services. *Current Pain and Headache Reports, 27*, 429–436. https://doi.org/10.1007/s11916-023-01125-2

Plain Language Action and Information Network. (n.d.). *What is plain language?* U.S. General Services Administration, https://www.plainlanguage.gov/about/definitions/

Sagi, D., Spitzer-Shohat, S., Schuster, M., Daudi, L., & Rudolf, M. C. J. (2021, July 28). Teaching plain language to medical students: Improving communication with disadvantaged patients. *BMC Medical Education, 21*(407), https://doi.org/10.1186/s12909-021-02842-1

Searight, H. R., & Gafford, J. (2005, February). Cultural diversity at the end of life: Issues and guidelines for family physicians. *American Family Physician, 71*(3), 515–522. https://www.aafp.org/afp/2005/0201/p515.html

Siegel, R. L., Giaquinto, A. N., & Jemal, A. (2024, January/February). Cancer statistics, 2024. *CA: A Cancer Journal for Clinicians, 74*(1), 12–49. https://doi.org/10.3322/caac.21820

Singh, H., Haghayegh, A. T., Shah, R., Cheung, L., Wijekoon, S., Reel, K., & Sangrar, R. (2023, July 12). A qualitative exploration of allied health providers' perspectives on cultural humility in palliative and end-of-life care. *BMC Palliative Care, 22*(92). https://doi.org/10.1186/s12904-023-01214-4

Taylor, C. J., Ordóñez-Mena, J. M., Roalfe, A. K., Lay-Flurrie, S., Jones, N. R., Marshall, T., & Hobbs, F. D. R. (2019, February 13). Trends in survival after a diagnosis of heart failure in the United Kingdom 2000-2017: Population based cohort study. *BMJ*. https://doi.org/10.1136/bmj.l223

Tonorezos, E., Devasia, T., Mariotto, A. B., Mollica, M. A., Gallicchio, L., Green, P., Doose, M., Brick, R., Streck, B., Reed, C., & de Moor, J. S. (2024, July 13). Prevalence of cancer survivors in the United States. *JNCI: Journal of the National Cancer Institute*, https://doi.org/10.1093/jnci/djae135

Von Korff, M. & Tiemens, B. (2000, February). Individualized stepped care of chronic illness. *Western Journal of Medicine, 172*(2) 133–137. https://pmc.ncbi.nlm.nih.gov/articles/PMC1070776/

Wang, H., Zhao, F., Wang, X., & Chen, X. (2018, November). To tell or not: The Chinese doctors' dilemma on disclosure of a cancer diagnosis to the patient. *Iranian Journal of Public Health, 47*(11), 1773–1774. https://pmc.ncbi.nlm.nih.gov/articles/PMC6294856/

Wang, Y., Zhang, X., Huang, Y., & Ma, X. (2024, January 16). Palliative care for cancer patients in Asia: Challenges and countermeasures. *Oncology Reviews, 17*(11866). https://pmc.ncbi.nlm.nih.gov/articles/PMC10824851/

White, J. L., Grabowski, M. K., Rositch, A. F., Gravitt, P. E., Quinn, T. C., Tobian, A. A., & Patel, E. U. (2023, August 31). Trends in adolescent human papillomavirus vaccination and parental hesitancy in the United States. *Journal of Infectious Diseases, 228*(5), 615-626. https://doi.org/10.1093/infdis/jiad055

Chapter 7

Ballentine, J. M. (2018). *The five trajectories: Supporting patients during serious illness.* CSU Shiley Institute for Palliative Care. California State University. https://dl.icdst.org/pdfs/files3/e05db244c15801597e435c8fc4fd4039.pdf

Buchholz, K. (2022, August 31). *Where assisted suicide is legal.* Statista Daily Data. https://www.statista.com/chart/28133/assisted-dying-world-map/

Bureau of Indian Affairs. (n.d.). *Expanding broadband access.* Retrieved November 7, 2024, from https://www.bia.gov/service/infrastructure/expanding-broadband-access

Cardenas, V., Fennell, G., & Enguidanos, S. (2023, May). Hispanics and hospice: A systematic literature review. *The American Journal of Hospice & Palliative Care, 40*(5): 552–573. https://doi.org/10.1177/10499091221116068

Carteret, M. (2010, November 3). *Cultural aspects of death and dying.* Dimensions of Culture. https://www.dimensionsofculture.com/2010/11/cultural-aspects-of-death-and-dying/

Centers for Medicare and Medicaid Services. (n.d.). *Swing bed providers.* Retrieved November 2024, from https://www.cms.gov/medicare/payment/prospective-payment-systems/skilled-nursing-facility-snf/swing-bed-providers

Choundry, M., Latif, A., & Warburton, K.G. (2018, February). An overview of the spiritual importance of end-of-life care among the five major faiths of the United Kingdom. *Clinical Medicine, 18*(1), 23–31. https://doi.org/10.7861/clinmedicine.18-1-23

Dingley, C., Ruckdeschel, A., Kotula, K., & Lekhak, N. (2021, October 26). Implementation and outcomes of complementary therapies in hospice care: An integrative review. *Palliative Care and Social Practice, 15.* https://journals.sagepub.com/doi/10.1177/26323524211051753

Dugdale, L. S., Lerner, B. H., & Callahan, D. (2019, December 20). Pros and cons of physician aid in dying. *Yale Journal of Biology and Medicine, 92*(4): 747–750. https://pmc.ncbi.nlm.nih.gov/articles/PMC6913818/

Dumanovsky, T., Augustin, R., Rogers, M., Lettang, K., Meier, D. E., & Morrison, R. S. (2016, January). The growth of palliative care in U.S. hospitals: A status report. *Journal of Palliative Medicine, 19*(1), 8–15. https://www.ncbi.nlm.nih.gov/pmc/articles/PMC4692111/

Funk, C., & Lopez, M. H. (2022, June 14). *Hispanic Americans' trust in and engagement with science.* Pew Research Center. https://www.pewresearch.org/wp-content/uploads/sites/20/2022/06/PS_2022.06.14_hispanic-americans-science_REPORT.pdf

Glaser, B. G. & Strauss, A. L. (1965). *Awareness of dying.* Aldine Transaction.

Hospice Alliance. (n.d.). *Complementary therapies.* Retrieved September 30, 2022, from https://www.hospicealliance.org/services/complementary-therapies/

Johnson, K. S., Kuchibhatla, M., & Tulsky, J. A. (2008, September 2). What explains racial differences in the use of advance directives and attitudes toward hospice care? *Journal of the American Geriatrics Society, 56*(10), 1953–1958. https://doi.org/10.1111/j.1532-5415.2008.01919.x

Kreling, B. (n.d.). *Latino families and hospice*. American Hospice Foundation. Retrieved November 7, 2024, from https://americanhospice.org/learning-about-hospice/latino-families-and-hospice/

Kreling, B., Selsky, C., Perret-Gentil, M., Huerta, E. E., & Mandelblatt, J. S. (2010, June). "The worst thing about hospice is that they talk about death": Contrasting hospice decisions and experience among immigrant Central and South American Latinos with US-born White, non-Latino cancer caregivers. *Palliative Medicine, 24*(4), 427–434. https://doi.org/10.1177/0269216310366605

Lee, M. C., Hinderer, K. A., & Kehl, K. A. (2014). A systematic review of advance directives and advance care planning in Chinese people from Eastern and Western cultures. *Journal of Hospice & Palliative Nursing, 16*(2), 75–85. https://doi.org/10.1097/njh.0000000000000024

LoPresti, M. A., Dement, F., & Gold, H. T. (2014). End-of-life care for people with cancer from ethnic minority groups. *American Journal of Hospice and Palliative Medicine, 33*(3), 291–305. https://doi.org/10.1177/1049909114565658

Lunney, J. R., Lynn, J., and Hogan, C. (2002). Profiles of older Medicare decedents. *Journal of American Geriatrics Society, 50*(6), 1109. https://doi.org/10.1046/j.1532-5415.2002.50268.x

Lynn, J. (2004). *Sick to death and not going to take it anymore! Reforming health care for the last years of life*. University of California Press.

Massachusetts Medical Society. (2017, January). *What is patient-centered care?* NEJM Catalyst. https://catalyst.nejm.org/doi/full/10.1056/CAT.17.0559

Mayo Clinic. (2021, March 2). *Hospice care: Comforting the terminally ill*. Mayo Foundation for Medical Education and Research. https://www.mayoclinic.org/healthy-lifestyle/end-of-life/in-depth/hospice-care/art-20048050

Meier, E. A., Gallegos, J. V., Montross-Thomas, L. P., Depp, C. A., Irwin, S. A., & Jeste, D. V. (2016). Defining a good death (successful dying): Literature review and a call for research and public dialogue. *American Journal of Geriatric Psychiatry, 24*(4), 261–271. https://doi.org/10.1016/j.jagp.2016.01.135

Michas, F. (2022, October 10). *Distribution of nursing homes in the United States from 2003 to 2022, by ownership type*. Statista. https://www.statista.com/statistics/716813/distribution-of-nursing-homes-in-us-by-ownership-type

Mintz, S. (2024, August 26). *A culture of denial: How Americans confront and process death*. Inside Higher Ed. https://www.insidehighered.com/opinion/blogs/higher-ed-gamma/2024/08/26/how-americans-confront-and-process-death

National Center for Health Statistics. (2017). *Health, United States, 2017: Figure 30* (Place of death, by age: United States, 2006, 2011, 2016). Centers for Disease Control and Prevention. https://www.cdc.gov/nchs/data/hus/2017/fig30.pdf

Oregon Health Authority. (n.d.-a). *Oregon's death with dignity act*. State of Oregon. Retrieved January 30, 2023, from https://www.oregon.gov/oha/ph/providerpartnerresources/evaluationresearch/deathwithdignityact

Oregon Health Authority. (n.d.-b). *Oregon's death with dignity act: FAQs*. State of Oregon. https://www.oregon.gov/oha/ph/providerpartnerresources/evaluationresearch/deathwithdignityact/pages/faqs.aspx

Ornstein, K. A., Roth, D. L., Huang, J., Levitan, E. B., Rhodes, J. D., Fabius, C. D., Safford, M. M., & Sheehan, O. C. (2020, August 3). Evaluation of racial disparities in hospice use and end-of-life treatment intensity in the regards cohort. *JAMA Network Open, 3*(8), Article e2014639. https://doi.org/10.1001/jamanetworkopen.2020.14639

Parker, J. (2021, September 28). *Obstacles persist for rural patients to access hospice*. Hospice News. https://hospicenews.com/2021/09/28/obstacles-persist-for-rural-patients-to-access-hospice/

Peña, J., Alvarez Figueroa, M., Rios-Vargas, M., & Marks, R. (2023, May 25). *One in every four children in the United States were of Hispanic origin in 2020*. United States Census Bureau. https://www.census.gov/library/stories/2023/05/hispanic-population-younger-but-aging-faster.html

Pew Research Center. (2024). Home internet access—broadband and smartphone only service by selected characteristics: 2016 To 2021 [by sex, race, age, education, income, and urbanicity, selected years] ProQuest Statistical Abstract of the U.S. 2024 Online Edition. Retrieved from https://statabs-proquest-com.chemeketa.idm.oclc.org/sa/docview.html?table-no=1181&acc-no=C7095-1.24&year=2024&z=D19CD958ECF1A183704272A59F1CE9BDC7F29E79

Rural Health Information Hub. (n.d.-a). *Rural home health services*. Retrieved November 7, 2024, from https://www.ruralhealthinfo.org/topics/home-health

Rural Health Information Hub. (n.d.-b). *Rural long-term care facilities.* Retrieved November 7, 2024, from https://www.ruralhealthinfo.org/topics/long-term-care

Rural Health Information Hub. (2021, July 28). *Rural hospice and palliative care.* https://www.ruralhealthinfo .org/topics/hospice-and-palliative-care

Rural Policy Research Institute. (2022, July). *Nursing homes in rural America.* University of Iowa College of Public Health. https://rupri.public-health.uiowa.edu/publications/other/Nursing%20Home%20Chartbook.pdf

Spilsbury, K., & Rosenwax, L. (2017, December 8). Community-based specialist palliative care is associated with reduced hospital costs for people with non-cancer conditions during the last year of life. *BMC Palliative Care, 16*(68). https://doi.org/10.1186/s12904-017-0256-2

Steindal, S., Goncalves Nes, A. A., Godskesen, T. E., Dihle, A., Lind, S., Winger, A., & Klarare, A. (2020). Patients' experiences of telehealth in palliative home care: Scoping review. *Journal of Medical Internet Research, 22*(5), Article e16218. https://doi.org/10.2196/16218

Temel, J. S., Greer, J. A., Muzikanski, A., Gallegher, E. R., Admane, S., Jackson, V. A., Dahlin, C. M., Blinderman, C. D., Jacobsen, J., Pirl, W. F., Billings, A., & Lynch, T. J. (2010, August 19). Early palliative care for patients with metastatic non–small-cell lung cancer. *New England Journal of Medicine, 363*(8). https://doi.org/10.1056/NEJMoa1000678

U.S. Department of Health and Human Services. (2021, October). *Health insurance coverage and access to care among Latinos: Recent trends and key challenges* (Issue Brief No. HP-2021-2). Office of the Assistant Secretary for Planning and Evaluation. https://aspe.hhs.gov/sites/default/files /documents/68c78e2fb15209dd191cf9b0b1380fb8/ASPE_Latino_Health_Coverage_IB.pdf

Vogels, E. A. (2021, August 19). *Some digital divides persist between rural, urban, and suburban America.* Pew Research Center. https://www.pewresearch.org/short-reads/2021/08/19/some-digital-divides-persist -between-rural-urban-and-suburban-america/

Wachterman, M. W. & Sommers. B. D. (2021, February 2). Dying poor in the US—Disparities in end-of-life care. *JAMA, 325*(5), 423–424. https://doi.org/10.1001/jama.2020.26162

Weng, K., Shearer, J., & Grangaard Johnson, L. (2022). Developing successful palliative care teams in rural communities: A facilitated process. *Journal of Palliative Care, 25*(5), 734–741. https://doi.org/10.1089 /jpm.2021.0287

Wheeler, S. B., Reeder-Hayes, K. E., & Carey, L. A. (2013, August 12). Disparities in breast cancer treatment and outcomes: Biological, social, and health system determinants and opportunities for research. *The Oncologist, 18*(9), 986–993. https://doi.org/10.1634/theoncologist.2013-0243

WWAMI Rural Health Research Center. (n.d.) *Palliative care in the rural U.S.* Retrieved October 21, 2022, from https://familymedicine.uw.edu/rhrc/studies/palliative-care-in-the-rural-u-s/

WWAMI Rural Research. (2021, March). *Post-acute care trajectories for rural Medicare beneficiaries: Planned versus actual hospital discharges to skilled nursing facilities and home health agencies* [Policy Brief]. University of Washington. https://familymedicine.uw.edu/rhrc/wp-content/uploads/sites/4/2021/03/RHRC _PBMAR2012_MROZ.pdf

Chapter 8

Al-Qadi, M. M. (2021, January). Workplace violence in nursing: A concept analysis. *Journal of Occupational Health, 63*(1), e12226. https://doi.org/10.1002/1348-9585.12226

American Medical Association. (2023, October). *AMA president sounds alarm on national physician shortage.* https://www.ama-assn.org/press-center/press-releases/ama-president-sounds-alarm-national-physician -shortage

American Association of Colleges of Nursing. (2022, October). *Nursing shortage* [Fact sheet]. https://www .aacnnursing.org/Portals/42/News/Factsheets/Nursing-Shortage-Factsheet.pdf

Arapakis, K., French, E., Jones, J., & McCauley, J. (2022, November). How should we fund end-of-life care in the US? *The Lancet Regional Health – Americas, 15*(100359) https://doi.org/10.1016/j.lana.2022.100359

Berlin, G., Bilazarian, A., Chang, J. & Hammer, S. (2023, May 26). *Reimagining the nursing workload: Finding time to close the workforce gap.* McKinsey & Company. https://www.mckinsey.com/industries/healthcare/our-insights/reimagining-the-nursing-workload-finding-time-to-close-the-workforce-gap#/

Blau, M. (2017, July 15). *"Are you saying I'm dying?" Training doctors to speak frankly about death.* PBS. https://www.pbs.org/newshour/health/saying-im-dying-training-doctors-speak-frankly-death

Boyle, P. (2021, September 7). *Hospital innovate amid dire nursing shortages.* AAMC. https://www.aamc.org/news/hospitals-innovate-amid-dire-nursing-shortages

Carroll, A. E. (2015, June 1). To be sued less, doctors should consider talking to patients more. *The New York Times.* https://www.nytimes.com/2015/06/02/upshot/to-be-sued-less-doctors-should-talk-to-patients-more.html

Centers for Disease Control and Prevention. (2020, May 15). *QuickStats: Percentage of deaths, by place of death - National vital statistics system, United States, 2000–2018.* https://www.cdc.gov/mmwr/volumes/69/wr/mm6919a4.htm

Centers for Medicare and Medicaid Services. (2015, November). *Nursing home toolkit: Nursing homes—a guide for Medicaid beneficiaries' families and helpers.* Department of Health and Human Services. https://www.cms.gov/Medicare-Medicaid-Coordination/Fraud-Prevention/Medicaid-Integrity-Education/Downloads/nursinghome-beneficiary-booklet.pdf

Cha, A. E., & Cohen, R. A. (2022, February 11). *Demographic Variation in Health Insurance Coverage: United States, 2020.* (National Health Statistics Reports, Number 169). Centers for Disease Control and Prevention. https://www.cdc.gov/nchs/data/nhsr/nhsr169.pdf

Chen, P. (2013, May 6). *Bedside manner: Conversations with patients about death* [Interview]. NPR. https://www.npr.org/2013/05/06/181636287/bedside-manner-conversations-with-patients-about-death

Collins, S. R., Haynes, L. A., & Masitha, R. (2022, September 29). *The state of U.S. health insurance in 2022* [Issue briefs]. Commonwealth Fund Biennial Health Insurance Survey. https://www.commonwealthfund.org/publications/issue-briefs/2022/sep/state-us-health-insurance-2022-biennial-survey

Cubanski, J., & Freed, M. (2022, November 17). *The typical Medicare beneficiary has close to 70 different Medicare Advantage and Medicare part D stand-alone plan options for 2023.* KFF. https://www.kff.org/medicare/slide/the-typical-medicare-beneficiary-has-close-to-70-different-medicare-advantage-and-medicare-part-d-stand-alone-plan-options-for-2023/

De Lew, N., Greenberg, G., & Kinchen, K. (1992). A layman's guide to the U.S. health care system. *Health Care Financing Review, 14*(1), 151–169. https://pmc.ncbi.nlm.nih.gov/articles/PMC4193322/

Drossman, D. A., Chang, L., Deutsch, J. K., Ford, A. C., Halpert, A., Kroenke, K., Nurko, S., Ruddy, J., Snyder, J., & Sperber, A. (2021, November 28). A review of the evidence and recommendations on communication skills and the patient–provider relationship: A Rome Foundation working team report. *Gastroenterology, 161*(5), 1670–1688.e7. https://doi.org/10.1053/j.gastro.2021.07.037

Farmer, B. (2019, January 19). *Morphine, and a side of grief counseling: Nursing students learn how to handle death.* NPR. https://www.npr.org/2019/01/19/686830475/morphine-and-a-side-of-grief-counseling-nurses-learn-how-to-handle-death

Frakt, A. (2019, May 1). *The rural hospital problem.* JAMA Archive. https://jamanetwork.com/channels/health-forum/fullarticle/2759647

French, E. B., McCauley, J., Aragon, M., Bakx, P., Chalkley, M., Chen, S. H., Christensen, B. J., Chuang, H., Cote-Sergent, A., De Nardi, M, Fan, E., Echevin, D., Geoffard, P.Y, Gastaldi-Menager, C., Gortz, M. Ibuka, Y, Kallestrup-Lamb, M., Karlsson, … & Kelly, E. (2017, July). End-of-life medical spending in last twelve months of life is lower than previously reported. *Health Affairs, 36*(7). https://doi.org/10.1377/hlthaff.2017.0174.

Grundy, A., McLain, K., & Zelibor, Y. (2024, February 29). *Medical Expenditure Panel Survey.* U.S. Census Bureau, U.S. Department of Commerce. https://www.census.gov/library/stories/2024/02/health-care-costs.html

Hamel, L., Wu, B., & Brodie, M. (2017, April). *Views and experiences with end-of-life medical care in the U.S.* The Henry J. Kaiser Family Foundation. https://www.kff.org/report-section/views-and-experiences-with-end-of-life-medical-care-in-the-us-findings/

Humphrey, K. E., Sundberg, M. Milliren, C. E., Graham, D. A., Landrigan, C. P. (2022, March). Frequency and nature of communication and handoff failures in medical malpractice claims. *Journal of Patient Safety, 18*(2), 130–137. https://doi.org/10.1097/PTS.0000000000000937

Kane, C. K. (2021). *Policy research perspectives: Recent changes in physician practice arrangements.* American Medical Association. https://www.ama-assn.org/system/files/2021-05/2020-prp-physician-practice-arrangements.pdf

Kaufman, S. R. (2005). *And a time to die: How American hospitals shape the end of life.* University of Chicago Press.

Keisler-Starkey, K., Bunch, L. N., & Lundstrom, R. A. (2023, September). *Health insurance coverage in the United States: 2022.* U.S. Census Bureau. https://www.census.gov/content/dam/Census/library/publications/2023/demo/p60-281.pdf

Kruser, J. M., Aaby, D. A., Stevenson, D. G., Pun, B. T., Balas, M. C., Barnes-Daly, M. A., Harmon, L., & Ely, E. W. (2019, December 11). Variability in end-of-life care delivery in intensive care units in the United States. *JAMA Network Open, 2*(12), Article e1917344. https://doi.org/10.1001/jamanetworkopen.2019.17344

Military Benefit Association. (n.d.). *Tricare health insurance explained.* Retrieved February 21, 2023, from https://www.militarybenefit.org/membership-benefits/get-educated/tricare-health-insurance/

Muir, K. J., Porat-Dahlerbruch, J., Nikpour, J., Leep-Lazar, K., & Lasater, K. B. (2024, April 1). Top factors in nurses ending health care employment between 2018 and 2021. *JAMA Network Open, 7*(4), e244121. https://doi.org/10.1001/jamanetworkopen.2024.4121

National Association of Insurance Commissioners. (2022). *U.S. health insurance industry analysis report 2022.* https://content.naic.org/sites/default/files/inline-files/health-2022-mid-year-industry-report.pdf

National Center for Health Workforce Analysis. (2022, November). *Nurse workforce projections, 2020-2035.* Human Resources and Services Administration. https://bhw.hrsa.gov/sites/default/files/bureau-health-workforce/Nursing-Workforce-Projections-Factsheet.pdf

National Nurse-Led Care Consortium. (2021, June). *The evolving role of nurse practitioners in health care centers and considerations for provider satisfaction.* https://nurseledcare.phmc.org/images/pdf/NCA/2021/Evolving_Role_of_NPs_FINAL.pdf

Orlowski, J. M. (2022) as cited in Robeznieks, A. (2022, April 13). *Doctor shortages are here-and they'll get worse if we don't act fast.* American Medical Association. https://www.ama-assn.org/practice-management/sustainability/doctor-shortages-are-here-and-they-ll-get-worse-if-we-don-t-act

Papanicolas, I., Woskie, L. R., & Jha, A. K. (2018, March 13). Health care spending in the United States and other high-income countries. *JAMA, 319*(10), 1024–1039. https://doi.org/10.1001/jama.2018.1150

Smith, A. K., McCarthy, E., Weber, E., Stijacic-Cenzer, I., Boscardin, J., Fisher, J., & Covinsky, K. (2012, June). Half of older Americans seen in emergency department in last month of life; most admitted to hospital, and many die there. *Health Affairs, 31*(6), 1277–1285. https://doi.org/10.1377/hlthaff.2011.0922

Tate, S. M. (2022). *Nurses leaving the profession in the first two years* [Doctoral dissertation, University of Arizona]. University Libraries, University of Arizona. http://hdl.handle.net/10150/663238

Tyler, H. (2017). *Nursing education on caring for the dying* (Publication No.3329). [Doctoral dissertation, Waldon University]. Waldon University Dissertations and Doctoral Studies Collection. https://scholarworks.waldenu.edu/dissertations/3329/

U.S. Department of Health and Human Services. (n.d.). *Affordable care act* (ACA). Retrieved February 21, 2023, from https://www.healthcare.gov/glossary/affordable-care-act/

U.S. Department of Veterans Affairs. (n.d.). *Health care for spouses, dependents, and family caregivers.* Retrieved February 21, 2023, from https://www.va.gov/health-care/family-caregiver-benefits/

U.S. Government Accountability Office (GAO). (2019, April 30). *Veterans Health Administration: Past performance system recommendations have not been implemented* [Report to congressional requesters]. https://www.gao.gov/products/gao-19-350

Welch, W. P., Xu, L., DeLew, N., & Sommer, D. B. (2023, August). *Ownership of hospitals: An analysis of newly-released federal data and a method for assessing common owners* (Data brief HP-2023-14). Department of Health and Human Services. https://aspe.hhs.gov/sites/default/files/documents/582de65f285646af741e14f82b6df1f6/hospital-ownership-data-brief.pdf

Williams, D. W., Quinlan, C. M., & Reid, A. E. (2022, June 16). A "good death" for all: The need to teach racially sensitive end-of-life care. *Journal of General Internal Medicine, 37*, 2306–2307. https://doi .org/10.1007/s11606-022-07489-2

Yang, Jenny. (2024, July 4). *Top 10 largest healthcare systems in the United States as of 2024, by number of hospitals.* Statista. https://www.statista.com/statistics/245010/top-us-for-profit-hospital-operators-based-on -number-of-hospitals/

Chapter 9

Abrams, Z. (2023, October 27). Stress of mass shootings causing cascade of collective traumas. *Monitor on Psychology, 53*(6). https://www.apa.org/monitor/2022/09/news-mass-shootings-collective-traumas

American Psychological Association. (n.d.) *Trauma.* https://www.apa.org/topics/trauma

Balt, E., Mérelle, S., Robinson, J., Popma, A., Creemers, D., Brand, I. van den, Bergen, D. van, Rasing, S., Mulder, W., & Gilissen, R. (2023, April 7). Social media use of adolescents who died by suicide: Lessons from a psychological autopsy study. *Child and Adolescent Psychiatry and Mental Health, 17*(48). https://doi .org/10.1186/s13034-023-00597-9

Bastomski, S. & Duane, M. (2018, July). *Research brief: Homicide co-victimization.* Office for Victims of Crime. https://ovc.ojp.gov/library/publications/research-brief-homicide-co-victimization

Callanan, V. J., & Davis, M. S. (2012). Gender differences in suicide methods. *Social Psychiatry Psychiatric Epidemiology, 47*(6), 857–69. https://doi.org/10.1007/s00127-011-0393-5

Calvo, S., Carrasco, J. P., Conde-Pumpido, C., Esteve, J., & Aguilar, E. J. (2024, June 5). Does suicide contagion (Werther effect) take place in response to social media? A systematic review. *Spanish Journal of Psychiatry and Mental Health.* https://doi.org/10.1016/j.sjpmh.2024.05.003

Carr, J. (2020, February 3). *National study confirms nurses at higher risk of suicide than general population* [Press release]. UC San Diego Health. https://health.ucsd.edu/news/press-releases/2020-02-03-national-study -confirms-nurses-at-higher-risk-of-suicide/

Casant, J., & Helbich, M. (2022, February 25). Inequalities of suicide mortality across urban and rural areas: A literature review. *International Journal of Environmental Research and Public Health, 19*(5), 2669. https://doi .org/10.3390/ijerph19052669

Center for Victim Research. (2018). *Homicide co-victimization* [Research brief]. https://justiceresearch .dspacedirect.org/server/api/core/bitstreams/e1eefebb-2719-4b5f-bcce-7f24e1a68e6b/content

Centers for Disease Control and Prevention. (n.d.). *WISQARS leading causes of death visualization tool.* Centers for Disease Control and Prevention. https://wisqars.cdc.gov/lcd/

Centers for Disease Control and Prevention. (2018, March 19). *Emergency responders: Tips for taking care of yourself.* Centers for Disease Control and Prevention. https://emergency.cdc.gov/coping/responders.asp

Centers for Disease Control and Prevention. (2022a, March 2). *Stats of the States - Homicide Mortality.* https:// www.cdc.gov/nchs/pressroom/sosmap/homicide_mortality/homicide.htm

Centers for Disease Control and Prevention. (2022b, May 4). *Bicycle Safety.* https://www.cdc.gov /transportationsafety/bicycle/index.html#print

Centers for Disease Control and Prevention. (2022c, August 31). *About Workplace Violence.* https://www.cdc.gov /niosh/violence/about/

Centers for Disease Control and Prevention. (2022d, November 2). *Risk and protective factors.* https://www.cdc .gov/suicide/factors/index.html

Centers for Disease Control and Prevention. (2023a). *Disparities in suicide.* https://www.cdc.gov/suicide/disparities/

Centers for Disease Control and Prevention. (2023b, February 3). *Reducing workplace violence in gasoline stations and convenience stores.* https://www.cdc.gov/niosh/docs/wp-solutions/2023-121/default.html

Centers for Disease Control and Prevention. (2023c, October 3). *Pedestrian safety.* https://www.cdc.gov /transportationsafety/pedestrian_safety/index.html

Centers for Disease Control and Prevention. (2024a). *Facts about suicide.* https://www.cdc.gov/suicide/facts /index.html

Centers for Disease Control and Prevention. (2024b, April 25). *Risk and protective factors for suicide*. Centers for Disease Control and Prevention. https://www.cdc.gov/suicide/risk-factors/index.html

Centers for Disease Control and Prevention. (2024c, July 18). *Suicide data and statistics*. Centers for Disease Control and Prevention. https://www.cdc.gov/suicide/facts/data.html

Centre for Addiction and Mental Health. (n.d.). *Is there a cost to protecting, caring for and saving others? Beware of compassion fatigue*. https://www.camh.ca/en/camh-news-and-stories/is-there-a-cost-to-protecting-caring-for-and-saving-others-beware-of-compassion-fatigue

Cerel, J., Brown, M., Maple, M., Singleton, M., van de Venne, J., Moore, M., Flaherty, C. (2018, March 7). How many people are exposed to suicide? Not six. *Suicide and Life-Threatening Behavior 49*, 529–534. https://doi.org/10.1111/sltb.12450

Chinni, D. (2021, October 22). *Unpacking the geography of America's youth suicide epidemic*. American Communities Project. https://www.americancommunities.org/chapter/unpacking-the-geography-of-americas-youth-suicide-epidemic/

Cohen, S. (2022, March 15). *Suicide rate highest among teens and young adults*. UCLA Health System. https://www.uclahealth.org/news/suicide-rate-highest-among-teens-and-young-adults.

Colman, I. (2018, July 30). Responsible reporting to prevent suicide contagion. *Canadian Medical Association Journal, 190*(30), E898–E899. https://doi.org/10.1503/cmaj.180900

Comstock, C., & Platania, J. (2017, March). The role of media-induced secondary traumatic stress on perceptions of distress. *American International Journal of Social Science, 16*(1), https://docs.rwu.edu/cgi/viewcontent.cgi?article=1252&context=fcas_fp

Crosby, A. E., Han, B., Ortega, L. A., Parks, S. E, & Gfroerer, J. (2011, October 21). Suicidal thoughts and behaviors among adults aged ≥18 years: United States, 2008-2009. *MMWR Surveillance Summaries, 60*(SS13), 1–22. https://www.cdc.gov/mmwr/preview/mmwrhtml/ss6013a1.htm

Currier, J. M., Holland, J. M., & Neimeyer, R. A. (2007, February 23). Sense-making, grief, and the experience of violent loss: Toward a mediational model. *Death Studies, 30*(5), 403–428. https://doi.org/10.1080/07481180600614351

Davis, M. A., Cher, B., Friese, C. R., & Bynum, J., (2021, April 14). Association of US nurse and physician occupation with risk of suicide. *JAMA Psychiatry, 78*(6), 1–8. https://www.ncbi.nlm.nih.gov/pmc/articles/PMC8047773/

DeAngelis, T. (2022, November 1). Veterans are at higher risk for suicide. Psychologists are helping them tackle their unique struggles. *Monitor on Psychology, 53*(8), 56. https://www.apa.org/monitor/2022/11/preventing-veteran-suicide

Doucette, M. L., Bulzacchelli, M. T., Frattaroli, S., & Crifasi, C. K. (2019, March 18). Workplace homicides committed by firearm: Recent trends and narrative text analysis - injury epidemiology. *Injury Epidemiology, 6*(5). https://doi.org/10.1186/s40621-019-0184-0

Dutheil, F., Aubert, C., Pereira, B., Dambrun, M., Moustafa, F., Mermillod, M., Baker, J. S., Trousselard, M., Lesage, F.-X., & Navel, V. (2019, December 12). Suicide among physicians and health-care workers: A systematic review and meta-analysis. *PLOS ONE, 14*(12). https://doi.org/10.1371/journal.pone.0226361

Dyvik, E. H. (2023). *G7: Murder Rate by country*. Statista. https://www.statista.com/statistics/1374211/g7-country-homicide-rate/

Dyrbye, L.N., West, C.P., Satele, D., Boone, S., Tan, L., Sloan, J., Shanafelt, T.D. (2014, March). Burnout among US medical students, residents, and early career physicians relative to the general US population. *Academic Medicine, 89*(3), 443–445. https://pubmed.ncbi.nlm.nih.gov/24448053/

Enochs, E. (2024, June 20). *Yes, the way we talk about suicide matters*. PS. https://www.popsugar.com/health/suicide-language-49367360

FBI. (2019). *Crime clock*. https://ucr.fbi.gov/crime-in-the-u.s/2019/crime-in-the-u.s.-2019/topic-pages/crime-clock

FBI. (2020, July 20). *Crime in the U.S. 2019*. https://ucr.fbi.gov/crime-in-the-u.s/2019/crime-in-the-u.s.-2019

Gould, M.S. (1990). Suicide clusters and media exposure. In S. J. Blumenthal & D. J. Kupfer (Eds.), *Suicide over the life cycle: Risk factors, assessment, and treatment of suicidal patients* (pp. 517–532). American Psychiatric Association.

Gould, M. S. (2001). Suicide and the media. In H. Hendin & J. J. Mann (Eds.), *The clinical science of suicide prevention* (pp. 200–224). New York Academy of Sciences.

Gould, M. S., & Lake, A. M. (2013). The contagion of suicidal behavior. In *Contagion of violence: Workshop summary* (pp. 68–73). Institute of Medicine and National Research Council. The National Academies Press. https://doi.org/10.17226/13489

Governors Highway Safety Association. (2023). *Pedestrian traffic fatalities by state: 2022 Preliminary data.* https://www.ghsa.org/resources/Pedestrians23

Gramlich, J. (2023, April 6). *Gun deaths among U.S. children and teens rose 50% in two years.* Pew Research Center. https://www.pewresearch.org/short-reads/2023/04/06/gun-deaths-among-us-kids-rose-50-percent-in-two-years/

Haas, A. P., & Lane, A. (2015, March). Collecting sexual orientation and gender identity data in suicide and other violent deaths: A step towards identifying and addressing LGBT mortality disparities. *LGBT Health, 2*(1), 84–87. https://doi.org/10.1089/lgbt.2014.0083

Hoffner, C. A., & Cohen, E. L. (2017, October 19). Mental health-related outcomes of Robin Williams' death: The role of parasocial relations and media exposure in stigma, help-seeking, and outreach. *Health Communications, 33*(12), 1573–1582. https://doi.org/10.1080/10410236.2017.1384348

James, S. E., Herman, J. L., Rankin, S., Keisling, M., Mottet, L., & Anafi, M. (2016). *The report of the 2015 U.S. transgender survey.* National Center for Transgender Equality. https://transequality.org/sites/default/files/docs/usts/USTS-Full-Report-Dec17.pdf

Kalmoe, M. C., Chapman, M. B., Gold, J. A., & Giedinghagen, A. M. (2019). Physician suicide: A call to action. *Missouri Medicine, 116*(3): 211–216. https://www.ncbi.nlm.nih.gov/pmc/articles/PMC6690303/

KFF. (2024, February 22). *Recent increases in firearm deaths of children and adolescents have been driven by gun assaults, black youths are disproportionally affected* [Press release]. https://www.kff.org/mental-health/press-release/recent-increases-in-firearm-deaths-of-children-and-adolescents-have-been-driven-by-gun-assaults-black-youths-are-disproportionally-affected/

Korhonen, V. (2024, July). *Homicide in the United States.* Statista. https://www.statista.com/topics/12305/homicide-in-the-united-states/

Laboe, C. W., Jain, A., Bodicherla, K., & Pathak, M. (2021, November 6). Physician suicide in the era of the COVID-19 pandemic. *Cureus, 13*(11), e19313. http://doi.org/10.7759/cureus.19313

Lamba, N., Khokhlova, O., Bhatia, A., & McHugh, C. (2023, September 22). Mental Health Hygiene during a health crisis: Exploring factors associated with media-induced secondary trauma in relation to the COVID-19 pandemic. *Health Psychology Open, 10*(2). https://doi.org/10.1177/20551029231199578

LeardMann, C. A., Powell, T. M., Smith, T. C., Bell, M. R., Smith, B., Boyko, E. J., Hooper, T. I., Gackstetter, G. D., Ghamsary, M., & Hoge, C. W. (2013, August 7). Risk factors associated with suicide in current and former US military personnel. *JAMA, 310*(5), 496–506. http://doi.org/10.1001/jama.2013.65164

Lundorff, M., Holmgren, H., Zachariae, R., Farver-Vestergaard, I., & O'Connor, M. (2017, April 1). Prevalence of prolonged grief disorder in adult bereavement: A systematic review and meta-analysis. *Journal of Affective Disorders, 212*, 138–149. https://doi.org/10.1016/j.jad.2017.01.030

McElroy, A. (2023, April 3). *Data spotlight: Men in nursing: Five-year trends show no growth.* American Association of Colleges of Nursing. https://www.aacnnursing.org/news-data/all-news/data-spotlight-men-in-nursing-five-year-trends-show-no-growth

McGough, M., Amin, K., Panchal, N., & Fox, C. (2023, July 18). *Child and teen firearm mortality in the U.S. and peer countries.* KFF. https://www.kff.org/mental-health/issue-brief/child-and-teen-firearm-mortality-in-the-u-s-and-peer-countries/

Michel, K., Frey, C., Schlaepfer, T., & Valach, L. (1995, January 1). Suicide reporting in the Swiss print media. *The European Journal of Public Health, 5*(3), 199–203. https://doi.org/10.1093/eurpub/5.3.199

National Center for Statistics and Analysis. (2023, October). *Summary of motor vehicle traffic crashes: 2021 data* (Traffic Safety Facts. Report No. DOT HS 813 515). National Highway Traffic Safety Administration. https://crashstats.nhtsa.dot.gov/Api/Public/ViewPublication/813515

National Highway Traffic Safety Administration. (n.d.). *Seat belts*. https://www.nhtsa.gov/vehicle-safety/seat-belts

North Carolina Department of Health and Human Services. (n.d.). *Hurricane Helene storm related fatalities*. Retrieved October 1, 2024, from https://www.ncdhhs.gov/assistance/hurricane-helene-recovery-resources /hurricane-helene-storm-related-fatalities

Nijborg, L. C., Kunst, M. J., Westerhof, G. J., de Keijser, J., & Lenferink, L. I. (2024, January 29). Grief and delivering a statement in court: A longitudinal mixed-method study among homicidally bereaved people. *European Journal of Psychotraumatology, 15*(1), 2297541. https://doi.org/10.1080/20008066.2023.2297541

Ramchand, R., Schuler, M. S., Schoenbaum, M., Colpe, L., & Ayer, L. (2021, November 8). Suicidality among sexual minority adults: Gender, age, and race/ethnicity differences. *American Journal of Preventative Medicine, 62*(2), 193–202. https://doi.org/10.1016/j.amepre.2021.07.012

Ryan, C., Huebner, D., Diaz, R.M., Sanchez, J., (2009). Family rejection as a predictor of negative health outcomes in white and Latino lesbian, gay, and bisexual young adults. *Pediatrics, 123*(1), 346–52. http://doi .org/10.1542/peds.2007-3524

Substance Abuse and Mental Health Services Administration. (2014). SAMHSA's concept of trauma and guidance for a trauma-informed approach. HHS Publication No. (SMA) 14-4884. https://store.samhsa .gov/sites/default/files/sma14-4884.pdf

The Trevor Project. (2023, September 22). *Acceptance from adults is associated with lower rates of suicide attempts among LGBTQ Young People*. https://www.thetrevorproject.org/research-briefs/acceptance-from-adults-is -associated-with-lower-rates-of-suicide-attempts-among-lgbtq-young-people-sep-2023/

The Trevor Project. (2022). *2022 national survey on LGBTQ youth mental health*. https://www.thetrevorproject .org/survey-2022/#suicide-by-race

Thompson, R. R., Jones, N. M., Holman, E. A., & Cohen Silver, R. (2019, April). Media exposure to mass violence events can fuel a cycle of distress. *Science Advances, 5*(4). http://doi.org/10.1126/sciadv.aav3502

Tiesman, H. M., Elkins, K. L., Brown, M., Marsh, S., & Carson, L. M. (2021a). *Suicides among first responders: A call to action*. Centers for Disease Control and Prevention. https://blogs.cdc.gov/niosh-science -blog/2021/04/06/suicides-first-responders/

Tiesman, H., Weissman, D., Stone, D., Quinlan, K., & Chosewood, L. C. (2021b). *Suicide prevention for healthcare workers*. Centers for Disease Control and Prevention. https://blogs.cdc.gov/niosh-science -blog/2021/09/17/suicide-prevention-hcw/

Tobin-Tyler, E. (2023, May 25). Intimate partner violence, firearm injuries and homicides: A Health Justice approach to two intersecting public health crises. *Journal of Law, Medicine & Ethics, 51*(1), 64–76. http:// doi.org/10.1017/jme.2023.41

Torok, T. J., Tauxe R. V., Wise R. P., Livengood, J. R., & Sokolow, R. (1997, August 6). Large community outbreak of salmonellosis caused by intentional contamination of restaurant salad bars. *Journal of the American Medical Association, 278*(5), 389–395. https://www.ojp.gov/ncjrs/virtual-library/abstracts/large -community-outbreak-salmonellosis-caused-intentional

United Nations Office on Drugs and Crime. (2015, March). *International classification of crime for statistical purposes*, version 1.0. https://www.unodc.org/documents/data-and-analysis/statistics/crime/ICCS/ICCS _English_2016_web.pdf

U.S. Department of Defense. (2023, September 28). *DOD announces new actions to prevent suicide in the military* [Press release]. https://www.defense.gov/News/Releases/Release/Article/3541077/dod-announces-new -actions-to-prevent-suicide-in-the-military/

U.S. Department of Health and Human Services. (n.d.). *Suicide prevention*. National Institute of Mental Health. https://www.nimh.nih.gov/health/topics/suicide-prevention

U.S. Department of Justice. (2010, February 19). *Justice Department and FBI announce formal conclusion of investigation into 2001 anthrax attacks* [Press release]. https://www.justice.gov/opa/pr/justice-department -and-fbi-announce-formal-conclusion-investigation-2001-anthrax-attacks

U.S. Department of Veterans Affairs. (2022). *2022 national veteran suicide prevention annual report*. Office of Mental Health and Suicide Prevention. http://mentalhealth.va.gov/docs/data-sheets/2022/2022-National -Veteran-Suicide-Prevention-Annual-Report-FINAL-508.pdf

Wallace M., Gillispie-Bell V., and Cruz K., (2022). Homicide during pregnancy and the postpartum period in the United States, 2018–2019. *Obstetrics and Gynecology, 138*(5), 762–769. http://doi.org/10.1097/AOG.0000000000004567

Walling, M. A. (2021). Suicide contagion. *Current Trauma Reports, 7*(4), 103–114. http://doi.org/10.1007/s40719-021-00219-9

Youth.gov. (n.d.) *Federal Data.* https://youth.gov/youth-topics/violence-prevention/federal-data

Chapter 10

Bauer, A. (2021, March 22). *Can you legally bury someone in your backyard? (& how).* US Urns Online. https://www.usurnsonline.com/burial/home-burials/

Bohne, R. (2024, June 10). *Funeral homes: Share by ownership U.S. 2023.* Statista. https://www.statista.com/statistics/736768/funeral-homes-share-by-ownership-us/

Boring, P. (2014, April 25). *Death of the death care industry and eternal life online.* Forbes. https://www.forbes.com/sites/perianneboring/2014/04/25/the-death-of-the-death-care-industry-and-eternal-life-online/?sh=7c3949371c1a

Center for Health Statistics. (2018). *Matters of record.* Oregon Health Authority. https://www.oregon.gov/oha/PH/BIRTHDEATHCERTIFICATES/REGISTERVITALRECORDS/Documents/OHA%209753C%20Death%20Cert.%20NL%20Final.pdf

Crawford, C. (2017, November 21). *Ethical issues in today's funeral industry.* Chron. https://smallbusiness.chron.com/ethical-issues-todays-funeral-industry-62750.html

Cremation Association of North America. (n.d.-a). *Alkaline hydrolysis.* https://www.cremationassociation.org/alkalinehydrolysis.html

Cremation Association of North America. (n.d.-b). *Cremation process.* https://www.cremationassociation.org/page/CremationProcess

Cremation Society of America. (2019, May 28). *What do I do with cremated remains?* https://www.cremationsocietyofamerica.com/what-do-i-do-with-cremated-remains/

Dembosky, A. (2024, March 22). *The ultimate green burial? Human composting lets you replenish the earth after death.* NPR. https://www.npr.org/sections/health-shots/2024/03/22/1240080757/the-ultimate-green-burial-human-composting-lets-you-replenish-the-earth-after-de

Federal Trade Commission. (2015). *Complying with the funeral rule.* https://www.ftc.gov/system/files/documents/plain-language/565a-complying-with-funeral-rule_2018.pdf

Fierro, M. (2003). Comparing medical examiner and coroner systems. In *Medicolegal death investigation system: Workshop summary* (pp. 23–28). Institute of Medicine and National Research Council. National Academies Press. https://www.ncbi.nlm.nih.gov/books/NBK221913/

Flintoff, C. (2012, June 25). *In Alaskan cemetery, native and orthodox rites mix.* NPR. https://www.npr.org/2012/06/25/155431017/in-alaskan-cemetery-native-and-orthodox-rites-mix

Franklin County Coroner's Office. (n.d.). *Deaths reportable to the coroner.* https://coroner.franklincountyohio.gov/CRNR-website/media/CRNR-documents/deaths-reportable-to-the-coroner.pdf

Green Burial Council. (n.d.). *Green burial defined.* https://www.greenburialcouncil.org/greenburialdefined.html

Green Burial Council. (2022, July 25). *Your guide to a backyard burial.* https://www.greenburialcouncil.org/blog/your-guide-to-a-backyard-burial

Hawryluk, M. (2022, September 23). *Death is anything but a dying business as private equity cashes in on the $23 billion funeral home industry.* Fortune, Kaiser Health News. https://fortune.com/2022/09/22/death-care-funeral-home-industry-private-equity/

Hennigan, W. J. (2020, November 19). *Inside New York City's mass graveyard on Hart Island.* Time. https://time.com/5913151/hart-island-covid/

How qualified is your coroner? (n.d.). Frontline, PBS. https://www.pbs.org/wgbh/pages/frontline/post-mortem/things-to-know/how-qualified-is-your-coroner.html

Kelmar, P., (2022, August 6). *Death certificates breathe life into setting public health priorities*. U.S. PIRG Education Fund. https://pirg.org/edfund/articles/death-certificates-breathe-life-into-setting-public-health-priorities/

Kewley, F. (2021, August 20). *A guide to the interment of ashes*. Farewill. https://farewill.com/articles/a-guide-to-the-interment-of-ashes

Klein, Christopher. (2022, February 8). *Abraham Lincoln's funeral train: How America mourned for three weeks*. History. https://www.history.com/news/abraham-lincoln-funeral-train

Laderman, G. M. (2003). *Death and dying: Funeral industry*. Encyclopedia of Death and Dying. http://www.deathreference.com/En-Gh/Funeral-Industry.html#ixzz7v2AP78Jw

Lucas, M. (2021, October 27). *Everything you ever wanted to know about a U.S. national cemetery*. Military Connection. https://militaryconnection.com/blog/everything-you-ever-wanted-to-know-about-a-u-s-national-cemetery/

MacLean, V. M., & Williams, J. E. (2003). The history of the American cemetery. In C. D. Bryant (Ed.), *Handbook of death and dying* (Vol. 2, pp. 743–756). Sage Reference.

Marsden-Ille, S. (2023, March 9). *What is the 2023 cremation rate in the US? How is this affecting prices?* Cremation. https://www.us-funerals.com/2023-us-cremation-rate/#.ZCIownbMJPY

Miller Temple, K., (2018, October 30). *Death certificates: A closer look at detail*. The Rural Monitor: Rural Health Information Hub. https://www.ruralhealthinfo.org/rural-monitor/death-certificate-detail

Montoya, O. (2023, May 11). *Black Cemetery near Columbus makes national list of "endangered" places*. Georgia Public Broadcasting. https://www.gpb.org/news/2023/05/10/black-cemetery-near-columbus-makes-national-list-of-endangered-places

National Center for Health Statistics. (2009). The U.S. vital statistics system: A national perspective. In *Vital statistics: Summary of a workshop* (Appendix B, pp. 87–109). National Research Council (US) Committee on National Statistics, National Academies Press. https://www.ncbi.nlm.nih.gov/books/NBK219884/

National Park Service. (n.d.). *History of national cemeteries*. U.S. Department of the Interior. https://www.nps.gov/articles/000/national-cemeteries-history.html

New York allows rare glimpse of its potter's field cemetery. (2016, June 27). Reuters. https://www.reuters.com/article/us-new-york-potters/new-york-allows-rare-glimpse-of-its-potters-field-cemetery-idUSKCN0ZD2T7

Nordin, K. D. (n.d.). *Native American religions*. Encyclopedia of Death and Dying. http://www.deathreference.com/Me-Nu/Native-American-Religion.html

National Funeral Directors Association. (2023, September 1). *U.S. cremation rate expected to top 80% by 2045* [Press release]. https://nfda.org/news/media-center/nfda-news-releases/id/7717/us-cremation-rate-expected-to-top-80-by-2045

Office of Public and Intergovernmental Affairs. (n.d.) *Celebrate America's freedoms: The National Cemetery Administration* [brochure]. U.S. Department of Veterans Affairs. https://www.va.gov/opa/publications/celebrate/nca.pdf

Passy, J. (2017, June 25). *Costco and Amazon even have deals on caskets*. MarketWatch. https://www.marketwatch.com/story/even-if-you-buy-a-cheap-casket-at-costco-or-amazon-it-could-cost-you-in-the-end-2017-06-19

Potter, E. W. and Boland, B. M. (1992). *Guidelines for evaluating and registering cemeteries and burial places* (National Register Bulletin 41). U.S. Department of the Interior, National Park Service, Interagency Resources Division, National Register of Historic Places. https://www.nps.gov/subjects/nationalregister/upload/NRB41-Complete.pdf

Reimers, E. (2003). Cemeteries and cemetery reform. In R. J. Kastenbaum (Ed.), *Macmillan Encyclopedia of Death and Dying* (Vol. 1, pp. 115–118). Macmillan.

Schalkham, G. (2006, April 3). *Even in death, segregation is part of our history*. Joint Base Langley-Eustis, U.S. Department of Defense. https://www.jble.af.mil/News/Commentaries/Display/Article/260425/even-in-death-segregation-is-part-of-our-history/

Sherman, D. (2020, April 20). *Grave matters: Segregation and racism in U.S. cemeteries*. The Order of the Good Death. https://www.orderofthegooddeath.com/article/grave-matters-segregation-and-racism-in-u-s-cemeteries/

Shiffman, J., & Grow, B. (2017, October 24). *Body donations: Frequently asked questions*. Reuters. https://www.reuters.com/article/usa-bodies-qanda/body-donations-frequently-asked-questions-idUKL2N1MV1FY

What happens to those who die poor or unclaimed in NYC. (2019, June 15) *The Economist, 431*(9147), 36. https://www.economist.com/united-states/2019/06/15/what-happens-to-those-who-die-poor-or-unclaimed-in-nyc

Young, S. (2022, December 30). *Who decides cause of death? It may be a business owner -- or an 18-year-old.* CNN. https://www.cnn.com/2022/12/30/health/coroners-cause-of-death-khn-partner/index.html

Chapter 11

Adams, J. N. (2021). *Pet death as disenfranchised loss: Examining post traumatic growth and attachment in college students* [Doctoral dissertation, University of Colorado]. https://hdl.handle.net/10217/232602

American Psychological Association. (n.d.). *Coping after suicide loss.* American Psychological Association. https://www.apa.org/topics/suicide/coping-after

Beanland, V., & Wynne, R. A. (2019, August 14). Effects of roadside memorials on drivers' risk perception and eye movements. *Cognitive Researcher: Principles and Implications, 4*(1), PMC6694370. https://doi.org/10.1186/s41235-019-0184-1

Brown, A. (2023, July 7). *About half of U.S. pet owners say their pets are as much a part of their family as a human member.* Pew Research Center. https://www.pewresearch.org/short-reads/2023/07/07/about-half-us-of-pet-owners-say-their-pets-are-as-much-a-part-of-their-family-as-a-human-member/

Brooks, H. L., Rushton, K., Lovell, K., Bee, P., Walker, L., Grant, L., & Rogers, A. (2018, February 5). The power of support from companion animals for people living with mental health problems: A systematic review and narrative synthesis of the evidence. *BMC Psychiatry, 18*(31). https://doi.org/10.1186/s12888-018-1613-2

Canadian Paediatric Society. (2001, September). Guidelines for health care professionals supporting families experiencing a perinatal loss. *Paediatrics & Child Health, 6*(7), 469–477. https://pmc.ncbi.nlm.nih.gov/articles/PMC2807762/

Corless, I. B., Limbo, R., Szylit Bousso, R., Wrenn, R. L., Head, D., Lickiss, N., & Wass, H. (2014, January 1). Languages of grief: A model for understanding the expressions of the bereaved. *Health Psychology and Behavioral Medicine, 2*(1), 132–143. https://doi.org/10.1080/21642850.2013.879041

Christ, G. H., Bonnano, G., Malkinson, R., & Rubin, S. (2003). Bereavement experiences after the death of a child. In M. J. Field & R. E. Behrman (Eds.), *When children die: Improving palliative and end-of-life care for children and their families* (pp. 553–579). National Academies Press. https://www.ncbi.nlm.nih.gov/books/NBK220798/

Cleveland Clinic. (2023, February 22). *What is grief?* https://my.clevelandclinic.org/health/diseases/24787-grief

Doka, K. J. (1989). *Disenfranchised grief: Recognizing hidden sorrow.* Lexington Books.

Dougy Center. (n.d.). *Developmental responses to grief.* https://www.dougy.org/assets/uploads/Developmental-Responses-to-Grief-ages-2-18.pdf

Eyre, A. (1999). In remembrance: Post-disaster rituals and symbols. *Australian Journal of Emergency Management, 14*(3), 23–29. https://knowledge.aidr.org.au/media/3836/ajem-14-03-07.pdf

Gaynor, T. (2013, July 3). *Arizona town reeling over loss of firefighters in blaze.* Reuters. https://jp.reuters.com/article/usa-fires-arizona-hometown/arizona-town-reeling-over-loss-of-firefighters-in-blaze-idINDEE96203A20130703

Harvard Health. (2019, May 29). *Left behind after suicide.* https://www.health.harvard.edu/mind-and-mood/left-behind-after-suicide

Health benefits of pets: How your furry friend improves your mental and physical health. (2024, April 11). University of California-Davis Health. https://health.ucdavis.edu/blog/cultivating-health/health-benefits-of-pets-how-your-furry-friend-improves-your-mental-and-physical-health/2024/04

Khosravi, M. (2021). Worden's task-based approach for supporting people bereaved by COVID-19. *Current Psychology, 40*(11), 5735–5736. https://doi.org/10.1007/s12144-020-01292-0

Krueger, J., & Osler, L. (2023, November 15). *Communing with the dead online: Chatbots, grief, and continuing bonds.* University of Exeter ORE. https://philarchive.org/rec/KRUCWT

Mughal, S., Azhar, Y., Mahon, M. M., & Siddiqui, W. J. (2022, May 22). Grief reaction and prolonged grief disorder. In *StatPearls.* National Center for Biotechnology Information. https://www.ncbi.nlm.nih.gov/books/NBK507832/

Osterweis, M., Solomon, F., & Green, M. (Eds.). (1984). *Bereavement: Reactions, consequences, and care*. National Academies Press. https://doi.org/10.17226/8

Oyebode, J. R., & Owens, R. G. (2013). Bereavement and the role of religious and cultural factors. *Bereavement Care, 23*(2), 60–64. https://doi.org/10.1080/02682621.2013.812828

Ross Rothweiler, B., & Ross, K. (2019, November 20). Fifty years later: Reflections on the work of Elisabeth Kübler-Ross, M.D. *American Journal of Bioethics, 19*(12), 3–4. https://doi.org/10.1080/15265161.2019.1674551

Ryan, P. & Coughlan, B. J. (Eds.) (2011). Older adults' experience of loss, bereavement and grief. In P. Ryan & B. J. Coughlan (Eds.). *Ageing and older adult mental health: Issues and implications for practice* (pp. 109–126). Routledge/Taylor & Francis Group.

Shear, K., Frank, E., Houck, P. R., & Reynolds, C. F. (2005, June 1). Treatment of complicated grief: A randomized controlled trial. *JAMA, 293*(21), 2601–2608. https://doi.org/10.1001/jama.293.21.2601

Shear, M. K. (2012, June). Grief and mourning gone awry: Pathway and course of complicated grief. *Dialogues in Clinical Neuroscience, 14*(20), 119–128. https://doi.org/10.31887/DCNS.2012.14.2/mshear

Stokes, P. (2021). *Digital souls: A philosophy of online death*. Bloomsbury.

Tal Young, I., Iglewicz, A., Glorioso, D., Lanouette, N., Seay, K., Ilapakurti, M., & Zisook, S. (2012). Suicide bereavement and complicated grief. *Dialogues in Clinical Neuroscience, 14*(2), 177–186. https://doi.org/10.31887/DCNS.2012.14.2/iyoung

Testoni, I., Alexander Wieser, M., Kapelis, D., Pompele, S., Bonaventura, M., & Crupi, R. (2020, May 11). Lack of truth-telling in palliative care and its effects among nurses and nursing students. *Behavioral Sciences, 10*(50), 88. https://doi.org/10.3390/bs10050088

Tyrrell, P., Harberger, S., Schoo, C., & Siddiqui, W. (2023, February 26). Kübler-Ross stages of dying and subsequent models of grief. In *StatPearls*. National Center for Biotechnology Information. https://www.ncbi.nlm.nih.gov/books/NBK507832/

Wagoner, B., Bresco, I., & Awad, S. H. (2019). *Remembering as a cultural process*. Springer.

Winston, K. (2017, October 10). In Las Vegas as before, spontaneous shrines bring healing after horror. *National Catholic Reporter*. https://www.ncronline.org/news/las-vegas-spontaneous-shrines-bring-healing-after-horror

Worden, J. W. (2018). *Grief counseling and grief therapy: A handbook for the mental health practitioner* (5th ed.). Springer.

Yuan, K. (2018, May 25). When do memorials help? *The Atlantic*. https://www.theatlantic.com/membership/archive/2018/05/when-do-memorials-help/561329/

Image Credits

Index

The letter f following a page number indicates a figure. Tables, charts, and other illustrations are labeled as figures.